£15-99
2/36

HINDU NATIONALISM AND INDIAN POLITICS

This book presents a comprehensive and perceptive study of the Bharatiya Jana Sangh through the first two decades of its history from 1951. The Bharatiya Jana Sangh was the most robust of the first generation of Hindu nationalist parties in modern Indian politics and Bruce Graham examines why the party failed to establish itself as the party of the numerically dominant Hindu community.

The author explains the relatively limited appeal of the Bharatiya Jana Sangh in terms of the restrictive scope of its founding doctrines; the limitations of its leadership and organization; its failure to build up a secure base of social and economic interests; and its difficulty in finding issues which would create support for its particular brand of Hindu nationalism. Bruce Graham ends with a major survey of the party's electoral fortunes at national, state and local levels.

Hindu nationalism and Indian politics will become essential reading for specialists in South Asian Studies and modern Indian history, political scientists and specialists in comparative politics.

HINDU NATIONALISM
AND INDIAN POLITICS
The Origins and Development of the
Bharatiya Jana Sangh

B. D. GRAHAM
University of Sussex

The right of the
University of Cambridge
to print and sell
all manner of books
was granted by
Henry VIII in 1534.
The University has printed
and published continuously
since 1584.

CAMBRIDGE UNIVERSITY PRESS

CAMBRIDGE

NEW YORK   PORT CHESTER

MELBOURNE   SYDNEY

Published by the Press Syndicate of the University of Cambridge
The Pitt Building, Trumpington Street, Cambridge CB2 IRP
40 West 20th Street, New York, NY 10011, USA
10 Stamford Road, Oakleigh, Melbourne 3166, Australia

© Cambridge University Press 1990

First published 1990

Printed and bound in Great Britain by
Redwood Press Limited, Melksham, Wiltshire

British Library cataloguing in publication data

Graham, B. D.
Hindu nationalism and Indian politics: the origins and development
of the Bharatiya Jana Sangh – (Cambridge South Asian Studies; 47)
1. India. Politics. Role of Muslims, history
I. Title
322'.1'0954

Library of Congress cataloguing in publication data

Graham, Bruce Desmond, 1931–
Hindu nationalism and Indian politics: the origins and
development of the Bharatiya Jana Sangh / B. D. Graham.
p.   cm.
Includes bibliographical references.
ISBN 0 521 38348 X
1. Bharatiya Jana Sangh – History.   I. Title.
JQ298   B5G73   1990
324.254'083'09–dc20   89-38036 CIP

ISBN   0 521 38348 X

TM

CONTENTS

ILLUSTRATIONS

Maps

Figure

TABLES

Dr Shyama Prasad Mookerjee addressing the Buddhist Conference at Sanchi, in the state of Bhopal, November 1952.
Courtesy: *The Times of India*, Reference Department.

PREFACE

My interest in the Jana Sangh dates back to 1962 when, as a Research Fellow in the Department of Political Science at the Institute of Advanced Studies of the Australian National University, I began to gather material on the party's early years. An increasing preoccupation with the origins of Hindu nationalism and puzzlement at the Jana Sangh's inability to attract a mass following led eventually to the writing of this book.

I am indebted to many people and institutions for assistance with my research: to the Australian National University for two periods of fieldwork in India and to Professor R. S. Parker, then head of the Department of Political Science, who encouraged me to pursue the project; to the University of Sussex and to my colleagues in its School of African and Asian Studies for their support; to the Nuffield Foundation, which made possible a further visit to India in 1984; and to friends who have read drafts and made suggestions regarding points of interpretation and lines of enquiry.

In particular I wish to thank Professor D. A. Low, Professor P. D. Reeves, Professor J. H. Broomfield, Dr Hellmut Pappe, Professor W. H. Morris-Jones, Mr John Rosselli and Dr Urmila Phadnis for their criticism and help. I am under a special obligation to Professor F. G. Bailey, for his constant interest in my work; to Dr Subrata Mitra, for the care with which he read and criticized the penultimate draft of the manuscript; and to Professor Ravinder Kumar, not only for the assistance which he gave me as Director of the Nehru Memorial Museum and Library, but also because his friendship and the warm hospitality of his parents, the late Sri and Srimati Pran Nath Pandit, greatly enriched my early research periods in Delhi.

In India many politicians and journalists spared the time to talk to me and I wish to express my gratitude to them for the help and guidance which they gave me when I was gathering my material. My thanks are also due to the following libraries and their staff: in England, to the Library of the University of Sussex, the British Library, the India Office

Library, and the Library of the Institute of Development Studies; in Canberra, to the Australian National Library and the Library of the Australian National University; and in Delhi, to the Nehru Memorial Library, the National Archives, and the Library of the Indian School of International Studies at Sapru House.

I am also indebted to Mr Richard Fisher, Dr Gill Thomas, Dr Margaret Deith and their colleagues of the Publishing Division of Cambridge University Press for the care which they took in preparing the manuscript for publication.

Chapter 2 of this book includes material which was also used in my articles, 'Syama Prasad Mookerjee and the communalist alternative', in D. A. Low (ed.), *Soundings in Modern South Asian History* (London: Weidenfeld and Nicolson, 1968), and 'The Congress and Hindu nationalism', in Low (ed.), *The Indian National Congress: Centenary Hindsights* (Delhi: Oxford University Press, 1988).

University of Sussex   B.D.G.
June 1989

ABBREVIATIONS

AIBEA	All-India Bank Employees' Association
AIBEF	All-India Bank Employees' Federation
AICC	All-India Congress Committee
AITUC	All-India Trade Union Congress
BJP	Bharatiya Janata Party
BJS	Bharatiya Jana Sangh
BMS	Bharatiya Mazdoor Sangh
CPI	Communist Party of India
CPI (M)	Communist Party of India (Marxist)
DAV	Dayananda Anglo-Vedic
DMK	Dravida Munnetra Kazhagam
FASII	Federation of Associations of Small Industries of India
HMS	Hindu Mahasabha
HRS	Hindi Raksha Samiti
IAS	Indian Administrative Service
INC	Indian National Congress
INTUC	Indian National Trade Union Congress
IPS	Indian Police Service
KMPP	Kisan Mazdoor Praja Party
LS	Lok Sabha
MLA	Member of the Legislative Assembly
MP	Member of Parliament
NDF	National Democratic Front
NOBW	National Organisation of Bank Workers
PCC	Provincial or Pradesh Congress Committee
PD	Parliamentary Debates
PEPSU	Patiala and East Punjab States Union
PSP	Praja Socialist Party
RRP	Ram Rajya Parishad
RS	Rajya Sabha
RSS	Rashtriya Swayamsevak Sangh
SBSS	Sarvadeshik Bhasha Swatantrya Samiti

Abbreviations

SGMS	Sarvadaliya Goraksha Maha-Abhiyan Samiti
SGPC	Shiromani Gurudwara Prabandhak Committee
SP	Socialist Party
SSP	Samyukta Socialist Party
UP	United Provinces (to 26 January 1950) and thereafter Uttar Pradesh
UPSC	Union Public Service Commission

1

The challenge of Hindu nationalism

For many Indians, the achievement of independence on 15 August 1947 was the culmination of a long struggle, the moment when, in Jawaharlal Nehru's words, 'the soul of a nation, long suppressed, finds utterance'.[1] People looked forward to the creation of a new political order, one in which the problems and conflicts associated with the British Raj would vanish like the morning mist. Instead, the new nation found itself exposed to a high degree of stress and instability. At a time when it should have been able to direct its energies wholeheartedly towards policies of social and economic reform, the bitter legacy of the communal rioting which had accompanied partition threatened to undermine it. The tension between Hindus and Muslims throughout the northern provinces was matched by the strained relations between India and Pakistan at the international level. In India the main hope for peace and secularism appeared to be the ruling party, the Indian National Congress, but even within its ranks there were those who insisted on India's having a moral obligation to safeguard the well-being of Pakistan's non-Muslim minorities. When the All-India Congress Committee (AICC) met in November 1947 for the first time after independence, its retiring President, J.B. Kripalani, well known for his firm commitment to secularism, likened the positions of the two countries to those of Britain and Germany on the eve of the Second World War:

The issue at stake is the very existence of our State. It is time we realised that the politics of the Muslim League and the principles which govern its policy in Pakistan are the very negation of all that the Congress has stood for and on which we seek to build our own State in India. We believe in a secular, democratic state and, whatever the provocation and whatever measures we may be obliged to adopt to safeguard its security, we cannot think in terms of a communal state. The League, on the other hand, with its creed of Islamic exclusiveness, its cult of communal hatred and its practice of terrorism and treachery is an exact replica of the German Nazis. The more we appease its

[1] Michael Brecher, *Nehru: A Political Biography* (London, 1959), pp. 355–6.

1

appetite the more it will devour till, like the Nazis in Europe, it will become a menace to the peace of Asia. If we do not take a firm stand to-day and prepare against this menace, we shall like Chamberlain's England, rue our folly.

While Kripalani made it clear that he did not favour war against Pakistan, he went on to say:

I do believe that the only way to avoid the ghastly tragedy of a war between India and Pakistan is to make India strong. There are many sanctions, economic and other, short of war, which we can use to help Pakistan see that friendly and amicable relations with India are to the mutual advantage of both the countries.[2]

For contemporary observers, the closing months of 1947 were a time of great disillusionment and distress, when the essential conditions of order were being undermined. Writing at the end of 1948, the General Secretaries of the AICC reviewed the situation which had obtained after independence in the following terms:

India had numerous and intricate problems to solve and the freedom it attained on August 15 provided an opportunity to solve them. The major obstacle to the proper and effective solution of these problems was communal disharmony and the demand for the partition of the country to which it finally led. The Congress having agreed under pressure of circumstances to this partition it was hoped that the country would be rid of communal disharmony and the Indian Government would set itself seriously to tackle our social and economic problems. This hope however was not realised. Partition came by mutual agreement but the course of events which led to it had filled people's minds and hearts with such distrust and suspicion of one another that communal harmony could not be the immediate outcome of an agreement, under the compulsion of events, at the top. The communal infection had spread to the common man, penetrating his mind so that he became a temporary pervert. Cruelty for him turned into glory and treachery, arson, loot, murder, dishonouring of women, and killing of children became a moral imperative. This situation was exceedingly painful and distressing to Gandhiji and he pitted his whole vast moral might against it. The elemental passions of men were in action and Government and public organisations were very often helpless against their fury.[3]

The judgement underlying this passage is a severe one. The General Secretaries were saying, in effect, that the intensity of communal feeling had weakened the resilience of the new state and had reduced the capacity of its political institutions to maintain law and order; in their

---

[2] Indian National Congress, *Congress Bulletin* (Allahabad), 31 December 1947, p. 5.
[3] Indian National Congress, *Report of the General Secretaries Nov. 1946–Dec. 1948* (New Delhi, n.d.), pp. 22–3.

eyes, only a moral crusade like that which Gandhi was waging at the time offered any hope for peace.

Yet the seemingly impossible was achieved. Within a decade of these events India had set her feet firmly on the path away from communalism. The Constituent Assembly had provided for a secular state in the Constitution of 1950; the integrity of the legal system had been preserved; and the Congress Party under Nehru's leadership had remained a pluralistic and non-communal organization, while maintaining its ascendancy in representative politics and setting the norms for political competition in the process. This outcome is difficult to explain, and historians and political scientists are left with a puzzle. How did India remain a secular state while many of its neighbours, such as Pakistan, Ceylon and Malaya, were unable to maintain a clear boundary between religion and politics? Why did the Indian National Congress, having confirmed its commitment to secularism, not find itself displaced by a political movement identified openly with the values of Hinduism? According to the 1941 Census, Hindus numbered 239 million, 75 per cent, in a total population of 319 million in the territories which came to India after partition, so that theoretically, a party assured of Hindu support could have taken control of the country as a whole and also of the great majority of its constituent units. Moreover, the 43 million Muslims who had remained in India constituted a potential source of opposition to any political movement aiming at Hindu domination, and a pattern of action and reaction between two such forces could easily have produced a party system reflecting communal divisions.

The central puzzle resolves itself into two questions: firstly, what factors inhibited the development of political groups which were trying to develop a broad Hindu nationalist constituency, and, secondly, what prevented them from replacing Congress in the affections of the Hindu majority? One way of exploring these questions is by following the fortunes of the Bharatiya Jana Sangh (Indian People's Party), which was formed in 1951 and soon became the most aggressive and determined of the Hindu nationalist parties which were attempting to win power by constitutional means. To outline briefly the main stages in its development: its first units were established in the north, where it attracted increasing support in the states of Uttar Pradesh, post-1956 Madhya Pradesh, Rajasthan and the Punjab and in the union territory of Delhi. It won significant shares of the popular vote in the northern states in the general elections of 1957 but could not sustain its rate of growth in the following decade. It achieved its best results in the 1967 election, after which Jana Sangh groups in the northern legislatures had sufficient weight to play a leading role in the short-lived coalition governments which were then formed. In the elections of the early 1970s, however, the party lost valuable ground and subsequently joined with other non-Congress groups to offer a combined opposition to Mrs Gandhi's central government, only to find itself suppressed along with them during the emergency regime of 1975–77. When the emergency was lifted in January 1977, it joined with its allies to form the Janata Party, and the Jana Sangh as such was formally dissolved in April of that year. The Janata Party held power at the centre and in several states during the late 1970s, but when, in 1980, severely weakened by defections, it was soundly defeated by Mrs Gandhi's Congress Party, many of the former Jana Sanghis finally resumed an independent existence. In April 1980 they helped to establish the Bharatiya Janata Party (BJP), which has so far failed to reach the levels of support attained by its predecessor in the 1960s.

The Jana Sangh's attempt, in the 1950s and 1960s, to supplant Congress as the major party in the states of northern India was the first real test of the claim that Hindu nationalism was the natural philosophy of the Hindi-speaking heartland and therefore the key to political power in this region. The attempt failed and the reasons for that failure reveal much about the essential responsiveness of the Hindu majority to appeals to its sense of community. Much more was at stake here than the fortunes of a party and in investigating the Jana Sangh's inability to win over large numbers of Hindus who were supporting the secular Congress we can discover a great deal about the nature of Indian party politics in the Nehru era, and about the social and traditional bases of Hindu nationalism itself.

With these objectives in view, this study will consider the activities of the Jana Sangh between its formation in 1951 and its participation in the general elections of 1967. Having discussed the party's origins, we shall examine how its leadership and its organization developed in the 1950s and 1960s. We shall then consider, firstly, its efforts to present itself as a rallying point for Hindu nationalism and, secondly, its parallel attempt to establish a social base for itself by concerted appeals to a distinctive range of interest groups. Finally we shall look at the extent to which such bids for support produced tangible gains for the party in the representative politics of the period. While we may at times be tempted to regard it as just one of the minor parties struggling to survive in the competitive atmosphere of post-independence politics, that impression is misleading. What made the Jana Sangh different and more dangerous was that it brought into the political arena its burning vision of an India which, having returned to its roots, would be transformed into an organic Hindu nation.

2

The immediate origins of the Jana Sangh

In a large measure, the shape of India's party system after independence depended upon the changes which were taking place in the Indian National Congress, that huge and widely spread political association which had headed the nationalist movement during the days of the British Raj. Given its aim of achieving the greatest possible degree of unity amongst the Indian people, the Congress had grown accustomed to absorbing, and to some extent reconciling, a wide range of political ideas. In 1947 it contained within its ranks representatives of three important intellectual groups with quite definite but divergent views of what form the new polity should take. Of these, the first wished to see India as a liberal-democratic state with a constitution that was both secular and parliamentary in character; the second hoped for the formation of a socialist state in which collectivist principles governed social and economic organization; and the third was working to realize a state which embodied Hindu traditions and values. Each of these three groups exerted considerable influence within Congress and yet none was fully enclosed within it, for each one was generating its own distinctive pressure groups outside Congress boundaries. In the normal course of events, the tension between such bodies of opinion might have produced a multi-party system of some kind in the new state, but in India such an outcome was unlikely in view of the firm hold which Congress had established over its political life. While it was possible that one or more of these groups might be able to establish an electoral base of its own and develop independently of the ruling party, in the short term at least Congress looked likely to retain its dominance of the party system. Much depended upon how far it was prepared to go in accommodating the different groupings within its structure and incorporating their ideas in its own policies.

Any group which wished to advance its cause had, therefore, to decide whether it could do so better by working within the Congress to gain a decisive influence over the latter's policies, or by forming a separate party, with the risk thus incurred of finding itself isolated and powerless.

Those who favoured the idea of a Hindu-oriented state – and it is on them that we must now focus – were attracted by both these courses. But before we can discuss how they dealt with the choice of means, we must take account of a basic division within their camp. There were significant differences of temperament between those Hindus who were essentially backward-looking, whom we may conveniently call Hindu traditionalists, and those who, though revivalist, were forward-looking, whom we may call Hindu nationalists. Whereas the Hindu traditionalists were conservative in their approach, enlisting time-honoured values to justify the continuation of a hierarchical social order, the Hindu nationalists wanted to remould Hindu society on corporatist lines and to fashion the state accordingly. In organized politics these elements were concentrated mainly in three bodies: first of all, there was a large and influential group of Hindu traditionalists within the Congress; secondly, a mixture of Hindu traditionalists and Hindu nationalists within the Hindu Mahasabha (Hindu Congress); and, finally, a contingent of militant Hindu nationalists within the Rashtriya Swayamsevak Sangh (RSS or National Volunteer Organization).

Inside the Congress, the Hindu traditionalists looked for leadership more to the Home Minister, Vallabhbhai Patel, than to the Prime Minister, Jawaharlal Nehru. They held strong views about partition, which they either accepted with extreme reluctance or treated as something which could or should be undone. They considered that Indian society should draw increasingly on ancient Hindu traditions and rely less on western ideas, and they supported proposals to make Hindi the national language. Coming mainly from northern India, they saw themselves as the vanguard of a rising Hindi-speaking middle class which they believed would displace the older, more westernized and generally English-speaking middle class which had grown up under the British.

Many members of the Hindu Mahasabha held similar views, but this organization also contained groups which favoured a Hindu nationalist approach to the moulding of Hindu (and, by implication, Indian) society and were overtly hostile to Pakistan rather than simply critical of the act of partition. The origins of the Mahasabha are usually traced back to the formation of various provincial Hindu Sabhas in the years before the First World War, but it was not until the 1920s and 1930s that it began to change from a voluntary association into a body which had many of the characteristics of a political party. Under the leadership of Vinayak Damodar Savarkar, who became its President in 1937, it took a direct interest in elections and in party politics generally, and presented itself as a credible rival to the Congress and the Muslim League. However, it

failed to make any significant headway in the post-war years and entered
the independence period as a relatively decentralized body, based mainly
on its major provincial Hindu Sabhas and strongly identified with
upper-caste and socially conservative views.[1]

The RSS had developed on quite different lines. Founded at Nagpur in
1925, it had become the most successful of a class of associations which
specialized in recruiting young men and adolescents into informal militia
bands (known as *shakhas*) within a centralized framework presided over
by full-time workers and teachers. Under its first leader, Dr Keshav
Baliram Hedgewar, the RSS spread beyond its points of origin in
Maharashtra to northern India, and when Hedgewar died in 1940 his
successor, Madhav Sadashiv Golwalkar, a Maharashtrian Brahman
who had been a teacher at the Benares Hindu University, concentrated
on developing the organization's philosophy and doctrine. The ordinary
RSS volunteers, or *swayamsevaks*, were encouraged to think of themselves as a brotherhood dedicated to the improvement of Hindu society
and to the eventual creation of a *Hindu rashtra*, or Hindu nation. They
were especially active in the Punjab and in northern India during the
period of high communal tension preceding and accompanying partition, and were an object of admiration in some quarters and of fear in
others during the first few months of independence. Yet for all its
activism, the RSS remained something of an unknown quantity;
although it was outspoken in its attachment to Hindu nationalism, it
avoided stating its views on specific social and economic issues and thus
remained politically mobile, capable of shifting quite rapidly to unexpected positions within the party system, including those in the vicinity
of the Congress Party.[2]

In late 1947, therefore, there were three groups which were well placed
to attract support on Hindu traditionalist or Hindu nationalist grounds
but it was difficult to predict which of the three would be the most

---

[1] On the origins of the Hindu Mahasabha, see Indra Prakash, *A Review of the History
and Work of the Hindu Mahasabha and the Hindu Sanghatan Movement* (New Delhi,
1938), pp. 1-31; Richard Gordon, 'The Hindu Mahasabha and the Indian National
Congress, 1915 to 1926', *Modern Asian Studies*, IX, 2 (1975), pp.145–71; Jürgen Lütt,
'Indian nationalism and Hindu identity: the beginnings of the Hindu Sabha movement',
Paper read to the 7th International Conference of the Association of Historians of Asia,
Bangkok, August 22–26, 1977, pp. 2–9; B.B. Misra, *The Indian Political Parties: An
Historical Analysis of Political Behaviour up to 1947* (Delhi, 1976), pp. 161–5; Mushirul
Hasan, *Nationalism and Communal Politics in India 1916–1928* (Columbia, Mo., 1979),
pp. 254–6.

[2] For a detailed account of the origins and early organization of the RSS see Walter
Andersen, 'The Rashtriya Swayamsevak Sangh – I: Early concerns', *Economic and
Political Weekly* (Bombay), VII, 11 (11 March 1972), pp. 589–97. See also Walter K.
Andersen and Shridhar D. Damle, *The Brotherhood in Saffron: The Rashtriya
Swayamsevak Sangh and Hindu Revivalism* (Boulder and London, 1987), pp. 26–50.

successful or how relations between them would alter under changing circumstances. Much depended on whether there were any further outbreaks of communal violence and, if there were, whether they could be quickly brought under control. Even without any further actual violence, the government had to deal with the legacy of the earlier disturbances: the anxieties of Hindus and Sikhs who had left the regions allocated to West Pakistan and who were now in urgent need of shelter and work and reassurance. It was difficult to predict what impact they would have in their new localities, and whether their powerfully felt grievances would be translated into a convinced irredentism. A similar danger existed in the east: there was still a substantial Hindu minority in East Pakistan, and any crisis there could send further streams of refugees pouring into Assam and West Bengal, to swell the demand for the return to India of its lost territories. From 1946 onwards there had been communal rioting in a number of places and there was always the possibility that fresh disturbances could break out in the Muslim minority areas of the United Provinces and Bihar. All these factors inevitably coloured popular attitudes towards Pakistan, which was seen not so much as a sovereign state but as a collection of seceding provinces, answerable to India for the treatment of its non-Muslim minorities. Any sudden deterioration in relations between the two countries was bound to create support for the slogan of *Akhand Bharat!* (Undivided India!). Even the business of constitution-making was a likely source of tension, when matters bearing upon religious and communal rights, such as that of Muslims to preserve their own areas of customary law affecting marriage and the family, were being considered.

From the standpoint of 1947 it was easy to imagine that a crisis in any one of these contexts might swing the political agenda away from social and economic issues towards communal issues, thereby increasing the amount of energy flowing towards those groups representing nationalist and Hindu traditionalist ideas. Such a change in the political balance would almost certainly have been to the advantage of the Hindu traditionalists, who might have succeeded in dominating the Congress Party, perhaps attracting into it the Hindu Mahasabha and even the RSS. On the other hand it was also possible that, were Congress to remain firmly committed to secularism despite a worsening of communal relations, Hindu support might have been drawn away from it towards the Mahasabha. Finally, it was conceivable that the RSS might have ventured into party politics in its own right. None of these developments could be ruled out in the period immediately after partition. Now we must turn to the actual train of events and see what outcome they produced.

The reaction against Hindu nationalism, 1948–49

As far as Hindu traditionalists were concerned, the key to Indian politics in the closing months of 1947 lay in the relationship between Nehru and Patel, the Prime Minister and the Home Minister respectively in the central Council of Ministers. Although at first they worked closely together to maintain order and restore sanity after the savage communal rioting which had occurred in the Punjab, it was Nehru who had to bear the main burden. He was committed to the idea of building a secular state, providing a place for minorities and accepting Pakistan as an established fact, whereas Patel, while upholding the principles of the rule of law and the fair treatment of all communities, was prepared to question the sincerity of Pakistan and to challenge Indian Muslims to prove their loyalty to their country. It was Nehru who was fighting against the current. The war in Jammu and Kashmir soon became a symbol of all that was assumed to be wrong in relations between India and Pakistan: Indian troops had been sent to the state to repel tribal invaders, who were generally believed to have the support of Pakistan, and the crisis strengthened the view that relations between the two Dominions could never be settled by peaceful discussions. Although Nehru had the backing of Gandhi and, within the Cabinet, of ministers such as Maulana Abul Kalam Azad and Rafi Ahmad Kidwai, there was a considerable weight of opinion against him. On the other hand, Patel's position was potentially strong: not only did he enjoy a good measure of support within the Cabinet but he also had the loyalty of a number of leaders within the Congress organization. Moreover, through Dr Shyama Prasad Mookerjee, a former president of the Hindu Mahasabha and the Minister for Industries and Supplies, he had an important potential link with the moderate elements of the Mahasabha.

Rather than challenge Nehru's secularist ideas directly, the Hindu traditionalists tried to make the positive case that the policies of the Indian government should reflect to a large degree the sentiments of the country's Hindu majority, especially when it was a matter of dealing with Pakistan, given the latter's treatment of her non-Muslim minorities. Were Congress to accept this position, the argument ran, it would be possible for supporters and members of the Hindu Mahasabha to transfer their allegiance to the ruling party, leaving the Mahasabha either to dissolve itself or to confine its activities to cultural work,[3] and

---

[3] An overlap with the Mahasabha was out of the question, because since 1934 the Congress constitution had precluded members of any of its elected committees from being a member 'of any similar committee of a communal organisation the object or programme of which involves political activities which are, in the opinion of the Working Committee, anti-national and in conflict with those of the Congress' (Article V (c)). The Mahasabha had been placed in this category.

for members of the RSS also to find their way into Congress ranks. Patel gave a clear indication that he was thinking in such terms in a speech which he made at a public meeting at Lucknow on 6 January 1948, when he said that

if Pakistan is itching for conflict and war, it should come out in the open instead of resorting to back-door tactics in Kashmir.

Referring to a conference of nationalist Muslims in Lucknow, he claimed that they had not said a word about what Pakistan was doing in Kashmir and warned that

It should not surprise Muslims if doubts were entertained about their loyalty. They could not ride on two horses. Those who were disloyal could not remain in India for the atmosphere would become too hot for them.[4]

However, he also cautioned members of the RSS and the Hindu Mahasabha not to offend those Muslims who had remained in India.[5] Referring specially to the RSS, he warned that

they should leave the knife and *dunda* [stick] and proceed more cautiously. Congressmen in office should deal with the RSS in a different manner and not depend on their authority and ordinances. They were after all not working for selfish motives and they had their faults and it was Congressmen's duty to win them over and not to suppress them. The RSS on their part should let the four crores of Muslims to remain in peace in India and not divert the Government's attention.

He recommended that the Mahasabha should wind up its organization and merge with the Congress:

The Mahasabha should not think that they alone have the monopoly of speaking for Hindu culture and religion.[6]

His speech was, in fact, that of a Congressman who was prepared to envisage members of the Mahasabha and the RSS being admitted to the Congress fold and of a Hindu who felt justified in specifying standards of conduct not only for India's Muslim minority but also for Pakistan.

Although at the time that Patel was making his Lucknow speech the rioting had ceased in Delhi, relations between the communities remained tense and, on 12 January 1948, Gandhi announced that in an effort to bring about friendship between Hindus, Sikhs and Muslims he would undertake a fast. This he did until the 18th, when he received assurances

---

[4] From a report by a special correspondent in *Hindustan Times* (Delhi), 7 January 1948, pp. 1 and 8. Cf. the report in *National Herald* (Lucknow), 7 January 1948, p. 1.
[5] *National Herald*, 7 January 1948, p. 1.
[6] *Hindustan Times*, 7 January 1948, pp. 1 and 8.

from community leaders that fighting would end. Then, on 30 January, the unthinkable happened – he was assassinated by Nathuram Vinayak Godse, a young Maharashtrian. Godse, who belonged to an extreme group in the Mahasabha, had been a member of a small volunteer organization, the Hindu Rashtra Dal, and, in the early 1930s, of the RSS. After the assassination, the Hindu Mahasabha and the RSS were both treated by the Government of India as constituting a threat to law and order: Golwalkar, as head of the RSS, and V.G. Deshpande, the General Secretary of the Mahasabha, were arrested and the government declared that no organization preaching violence or communal hatred would be tolerated.[7] On 4 February, the Home Ministry released a communiqué announcing that the RSS was an unlawful association,[8] and the subsequent arrest of a number of its leaders and members reduced its activity to a minimum.

These decisions met with general approval. As far as liberal Congressmen were concerned, the case for banning the RSS was as much a political as a legal one, for they saw this organization as the precursor of an Indian form of fascism. The *National Herald* of Lucknow expressed this fear in the following terms:

The case of the R.S.S. is one of the mysteries of modern India but a mystery which ought not to be tolerated. It seems to embody Hinduism in a Nazi form and whatever its professional appearance there was something secret behind its physical parades and that secret is becoming something sinister. Such a policy and organization with physical training and drill was nothing but the screen for a private army. If some progressive-minded people did not come out openly to condemn it all these days, it was with the idea of not feeding it with publicity. But such caution seems to have been misplaced and, whatever may be the strength of the organization or the innocence of some of its members, it has to go immediately.[9]

The comparison with the para-military form taken by the German Nazi Party in the 1920s implied that the RSS should be curbed before it undermined Indian democracy in the same way that the Nazi Party had destroyed the Weimar Republic.

Later investigation revealed that Godse had acted as part of a conspiracy,[10] in which it was known that the RSS had not been involved.

---

[7] *Statesman* (Calcutta), 3 February 1948, pp. 1 and 10.
[8] Press Information Bureau Release, 4 February 1948, in S.L. Poplai (ed.), *India 1947–50, Volume One, Internal Affairs* (Bombay, 1959), pp. 555–6.
[9] Editorial, 'Our immediate duty', *National Herald*, 4 February 1948, p. 4.
[10] On the backgrounds of the conspirators, see Ministry of Home Affairs, Government of India, *Report of Commission of Inquiry into Conspiracy to Murder Mahatma Gandhi* (New Delhi, 1970), Part I, pp. 55–7 and 77–83.

Nevertheless, at the time Patel, as Home Minister, had acted in accordance with the accepted view that the activities of both the RSS and the Mahasabha had made them a danger to public security.[11] The intense public feeling aroused by Gandhi's death had moved the balance of advantage within the Congress Party towards the liberals, who were strengthened by a profound moral reaction against the social and political views of the Hindu nationalist groups. Patel's Lucknow speech belonged to another age; the idea of opening the Congress to members of the RSS and the Mahasabha was no longer tenable, and Nehru could now take the offensive: 'The communalism of the Muslim League and the Hindu Mahasabha', he said in Delhi on 2 February, 'has done much mischief and created much distress in India, and we cannot tolerate any more the anti-national activities of any group'.[12] In fact, there was already considerable pressure on the authorities to take further measures against the Mahasabha: according to N.V. Gadgil, a Congress leader from Maharashtra who was then Minister for Works, Mines and Power, the conference of provincial Governors which met on 2 and 3 February had reached a consensus,

that those individuals and institutions which had a hand in the assassination of Gandhiji should be dealt with sternly. This was discussed in the Cabinet also after the Conference. Shyama Prasad [Mookerjee] was unable to give any opinion. The previous day I had suggested to him to issue a statement stating that Communal parties had no place in a democracy. He did issue such a statement a day or two later. In the Cabinet discussion I took the view that any action against the Hindu Mahasabha at the time would be subject to the charge of political animus and suggested that action should be taken only in the case of individuals and institutions against whom we had irrefutable proof. Vallabhbhai [Patel] supported my view.[13]

Thus the Hindu Mahasabha was not banned, but it found itself in a shadowy area between what was morally acceptable in political life and what was not.

Mookerjee was a crucial mediator between the government and the Mahasabha at this stage. Having served as its Working President, he had become full President of the Mahasabha following Savarkar's resign-

---

[11] See letter from Patel to Nehru, 27 February 1948, from New Delhi, in Durga Das (ed.), *Sardar Patel's Correspondence 1945–50*, VI (Ahmedabad, 1973), pp. 56–8; letter from Patel to Shyama Prasad Mookerjee, 18 July 1948, from New Delhi, in *ibid.*, pp. 323–4; letter from Patel to Nehru, 28 March 1950, from New Delhi, in *ibid.*, X (Ahmedabad, 1974) p. 18.

[12] *Statesman* (Calcutta), 3 February 1948, p. 1.

[13] N.V. Gadgil, *Government from Inside* (Meerut, 1968), p. 148. Cf. another account by Gadgil in an article published in the Marathi weekly, *Lok Satta*, 7 June 1964, given in translation in *Organiser* (New Delhi), 27 July 1964, pp. 5–6.

ation from that post at the end of 1944, but when India became independent he took the view that the organization should no longer be restricted to Hindus alone.[14] The public hostility directed towards the Mahasabha after Gandhi's assassination made it easier for him to press home his arguments, and on 6 February he declared that

in my considered judgement the Hindu Mahasabha has today two alternatives before it. The first is that it can break away from its political activities and confine its attention to social, cultural and religious matters alone, it being open to its members to join such political parties as the, may choose. The other alternative is for the Hindu Mahasabha to abandon its communal composition, to reorient its policy and throw its doors open to any citizen, irrespective of religion, who may be willing to accept its economic and political programme.[15]

At first his views appeared to carry weight and the Mahasabha's Working Committee, at a meeting on 14–15 February, adopted resolutions which expressed shame that Gandhi's assassin had been connected with the organization, declared support for the government 'in its efforts to suppress terrorism or subversive activities in any shape or form', and announced its decision

to suspend its political activities and to concentrate on real Sangathan work, the relief and rehabilitation of refugees and the solution of our diverse social, cultural and religious problems for the creation of a powerful and well-organized Hindu society in Independent India.[16]

However, on 8 August the Working Committee rescinded this decision and plumped for Mookerjee's second alternative, the resumption of political activities with an open membership. When a subcommittee began to draw up a resolution along these lines for submission to a meeting of the organization's All-India Council there were, according to Mookerjee, 'sharp differences of opinion'. Finally a Working Committee meeting at Delhi on 6–7 November decided in favour of the resumption of political activities, with membership being confined to Hindus. Mookerjee resigned from the Working Committee on 23 November in protest against this decision, which was nevertheless confirmed by a meeting of the All-India Committee on 26 December.[17]

[14] Mookerjee, press statement, 23 November 1948, *Statesman* (Calcutta), 24 November 1948, p. 7.
[15] Mookerjee, statement of 6 February 1948, *ibid.*, 7 February 1948, pp. 1 and 7.
[16] Texts cited in Poplai (ed.), *India 1947–50*, I, pp. 550–2.
[17] *Statesman* (Calcutta), 9 November 1948, p. 4; 24 November 1948, p. 7 (Mookerjee's statement of 23 November); 27 December 1948, p. 5; 28 December 1948, p. 10; *Times of India* (Bombay), 8 August 1948, p. 3; 9 August 1948, p. 7; 27 December 1948, pp. 1 and 7. See also Motilal A. Jhangiani, *Jana Sangh and Swatantra: A Profile of the Rightist Parties in India* (Bombay, 1967), pp. 12–13; Craig Baxter, *The Jana Sangh: A Biography of an Indian Political Party* (Philadelphia, 1969), pp. 24–7.

Explaining his position at the time of his resignation, Mookerjee pointed out that Hindus were sufficiently numerous to defend their interests without having to form exclusive associations:

In the India of today, more than 85% of her people are Hindus and if they are unable to protect their own economic and political interests or India's inherent rights through the working of a fully Democratic constitution, no separate political party, which would confine its membership to the Hindu fold alone, could ever save Hindus or their country.

On the other hand, if the majority community itself retains its political exclusiveness it would inevitably encourage the growth of communal political organizations representing the interests of various minority groups within the country itself, leading to highly prejudicial results.[18]

It was clear that the old guard within the Mahasabha had simply treated the Working Committee's earlier undertaking to suspend its political activities as a tactical retreat and that, with the danger of suppression averted, they saw no reason why the organization should not revert to its original form. Mookerjee himself had been placed in a difficult position and there were now voices calling for him either to break with the Mahasabha altogether or to resign from the Government of India.[19]

Meanwhile, the RSS too was under pressure to modify its organizational aims. After a period of six months' imprisonment, Golwalkar was set at liberty on 6 August 1948 and then wrote to Nehru and Patel to complain about the official ban on the RSS. Since Nehru considered that the question of whether to continue the ban or not was a matter for the Home Ministry, Patel, as Home Minister, saw Golwalkar in Delhi at the end of October. He proposed that the RSS should produce a written constitution and that this document should contain a declaration of loyalty to the Constitution of India and the national flag, provision for a democratic organization, and undertakings to confine its activities to 'cultural' work and to avoid violence and secrecy. These terms were not accepted by the RSS leaders, and the provincial governments, with the concurrence of the central government, therefore continued the ban.[20] Then, on 13 November, Golwalkar cancelled an earlier directive which

---

[18] Mookerjee, press statement, 23 November 1948, *Statesman* (Calcutta), 24 November 1948, p. 7.

[19] See letter to the editor from P.R. Lele, Bombay, 29 December 1948, in *Times of India* (Bombay), 31 December 1948, p. 6. See also 'Candidus', 'Indian political notes', *ibid.*, 30 December 1948, p. 6.

[20] See Home Ministry press note, 14 November 1948, *Statesman* (Calcutta), 14 November 1948, p. 1. See also Home Ministry communiqué of 12 July 1949, in Poplai (ed.), *India 1947–50*, I, pp.557–8; and documents given in *Justice on Trial: A Collection of the Historic Letters between Sri Guruji and the Government (1948–49)* (Fifth edition, Bangalore, 1969), published by the RSS, Karnataka.

he had issued to disband the RSS and called on his followers 'to resume our work in the normal manner'.[21] He was arrested on the following day and sent back to gaol in Nagpur. On 9 December the RSS began demonstrations against the ban and thousands of its members were arrested in the weeks which followed. Golwalkar announced an end to the agitation on 14 January 1949 and various mediators then tried to clear the ground for further negotiations. Finally, agreement was reached with the central government about a written constitution and the ban on the organization was lifted on 12 July 1949.[22] The constitution stated that the aim of the RSS was 'to weld together the diverse groups within the Hindu Samaj' and that it adhered 'to peaceful and legitimate means for the realization of its ideals'. Regarding methods, it specified that

The Sangh as such, has no politics and is devoted to purely cultural work. The individual *Swayamsevaks,* however, may join any political party, except such parties as believe in or resort to violent and secret methods to achieve their ends; persons owing allegiance to such parties or believing in such methods shall have no place in the Sangh.[23]

The actual organization of the RSS at about this time has been described in detail by an American observer, J.A. Curran. He suggests that Golwalkar's authority as Sar Sanghchalak (chief leader) was considerable, but that he formulated strategy and policy in consultation with a group of lieutenants (including the General Secretary, Prabhakar Balwant Dani) who made up the core of his National Executive Committee (Kendriya Karyakari Mandal). The task of ensuring that provincial and subordinate units carried out central directives was entrusted to a corps of provincial organizers (*pracharaks*), who were the most able of the Sangh's full-time workers and had taken vows of continence and austerity. Under each provincial *pracharak* were subordinate organizers, forming lines of authority and control down to the

[21] Statement issued by Golwalkar in New Delhi on 13 November 1948 (text given in Appendix XII of *Justice on Trial,* pp. 87–91).

[22] Home Ministry communiqué of 12 July 1949, in Poplai (ed.), *India 1947–50,* I, pp. 557–8. For general accounts of the ban see J.A. Curran, *Militant Hinduism in Indian Politics: A Study of the R.S.S.* (New York, 1951), pp. 18–22; Andersen, 'The Rashtriya Swayamsevak Sangh – III: Participation in politics', *Economic and Political Weekly,* VII, 13 (25 March 1972), pp. 673–7; Andersen and Damle, *Brotherhood in Saffron,* pp. 50–5.

[23] The text of this preamble and the first five articles of this constitution are given in Poplai (ed.), *India 1947–50,* I, pp. 554–5, from which the above quotations are taken. For a translation from Hindi of the full set of rules, see D.R. Goyal, *Rashtriya Swayamsevak Sangh* (New Delhi, 1979), pp. 206–17 (Appendix V). For discussion of the detailed provisions, see Baxter, *The Jana Sangh,* pp. 45–8, and the *Statesman* (Calcutta), 6 September 1949, p. 7.

leaders of the local branches (*shakhas*). The members of a *shakha* would meet each day to take part in physical exercises and games, and about once a week for a *bauddhik* (intellectual) session consisting of a talk on the aims of the RSS, followed by questions and answers. The individual *swayamsevak* found himself part of a highly prescribed regimen, wore a distinctive uniform (white shirt, khaki shorts, black cap, leather belt, socks and shoes), was constantly reminded of the need for discipline and, through the questions and promptings of the *mukhya shikshak* (chief instructor) of his *shakha*, was taught the attitudes he was expected to adopt. Parallel to the hierarchy of organizers was a less powerful hierarchy of public RSS leaders known as *sanghchalaks*; apart from Golwalkar, the Sar Sanghchalak, they were usually established professional or business men, Hindus of orthodox views, able to devote only part of their time to *Sangh Karya* (work for the Sangh). Along with the provincial *pracharaks* and elected provincial delegates they were entitled to attend meetings of a broad-based council, the Akhil Bharatiya Pratinidhi Sabha (All-India Delegates Committee), but the most important central body was undoubtedly the Kendriya Karyakari Mandal.[24] The training of RSS cadres was carried out in special officer-training camps, of which there were fourteen in 1950, able to handle an annual intake of 10,000 men in courses of four to six weeks in length, with one for advanced cadres at a camp near Nagpur.[25]

Curran suggested that the RSS derived most of its funds from donations which the *swayamsevaks* made each year at a special ceremony when offerings, known as *dakshina* (the term for the gift which a student gives to his teacher at the end of his education under the orthodox Hindu system), were made before the Sangh's triangular saffron-coloured flag, the *Bhagwa-Dhwaja,* and ranged from thousands

---

[24] This description is based upon Curran, *Militant Hinduism*, pp. 43–59, with additional material from: Richard D. Lambert, 'Hindu communal groups in Indian politics', in Richard L. Park and Irene Tinker (eds.), *Leadership and Political Institutions in India* (Princeton, N.J., 1959), pp. 215–18; 'Shyamnandan', *R.S.S.: The National Urge* (Patna, n.d.), esp. pp. 49–55; Ram Lall Dhooria, *I was a Swayamsevak: An Inside View of the R.S.S.*) (New Delhi: Sampradayikta Virodhi Committee, n.d.); 'An insider', *R.S.S.: How it Functions* (New Delhi: Sampradayikta Virodhi Committee, n.d.); *Spotlight on R.S.S.* (Bradford: Friends of India Society, 1976); Govind Sahai, *A Critical Analysis of Rashtriya Swayamsevak Sangh* (Delhi, n.d.) (this pamphlet was first published in December 1948 and was revised in 1956). For recent studies of the RSS, see Nana Deshmukh, *RSS: Victim of Slander: A Multi-dimensional Study of RSS, Jana Sangh, Janata Party and the Present Political Crisis* (New Delhi, 1979); Goyal, *Rashtriya Swayamsewak Sangh*; K. R. Malkani, *The RSS Story* (New Delhi, 1980); Balraj Madhok, *R.S.S. and Politics* (New Delhi, 1986); Andersen and Damle, *Brotherhood in Saffron*.

[25] Curran, *Militant Hinduism*, pp. 49–50.

of rupees to a few pice.[26] It had been the hope of the founder, Dr Hedgewar, that the RSS could be financed by contributions from its own members but it probably depended to some extent on moderately wealthy backers of the kind who supported the *Organiser*, an English-language journal sympathetic to the RSS. This was financed by Bharat Prakashan (Delhi) Limited (a private limited company registered on 3 June 1946, with an authorized capital of Rs 2,000,000 divided into 100,000 ordinary shares of Rs 20 each), whose managing director, Lala Hansraj Gupta, RSS Sanghchalak for Delhi, also headed a number of firms engaged in light engineering, chemicals, banking and insurance, and electrical goods, while the other directors included a landlord and banker, an advocate, a Delhi merchant, and an engineer.[27] Here is one indication of the kind of support which Hindu nationalists could obtain in the towns of northern India from groups on the margins of middle-class society which were resentful of the social and economic privileges of the established English-speaking and westernized élites.

After the lifting of the ban, Golwalkar went on a lengthy speaking-tour of India, during which one of his main concerns must have been to estimate the damage suffered by his organization as a result of the government's sanctions. At this stage the membership of the RSS had fallen from its 1947 level of between 400,000 and 500,000 members to about 100,000, but by the first quarter of 1951 the level had risen again to a little above 600,000.[28] This rapid recovery indicates that the basic network of local workers and leaders had remained intact throughout the ban, and that the organization had been able to build up ordinary membership once official pressure had lessened. As a reporter in the United Provinces noted during Golwalkar's tour:

How hordes of disciplined volunteers sprang up in every town to greet him caused surprise to many. Apparently, the RSS has suffered no reverse by the internment of its leaders.

He also observed that the Sangh

seems to draw for its strength in this province upon young men, though it is known to possess among its admirers a large number of big landlords and industrialists.[29]

---

26 See *ibid.*, pp. 61–2; *Organiser*, 30 August 1949, pp. 11–12.
27 The prospectus of the company was published in the *Organiser*, 18 December 1947, p. 16. For other business positions held by Hansraj Gupta see Times of India, *The Indian and Pakistan Year Book and Who's Who 1951* (Bombay, n.d.), p.758. See also *Organiser*, 16 April 1967, p. 9.
28 See Curran, *Militant Hinduism*, p. 43.
29 *Statesman* (Calcutta), 6 September 1949, p. 7.

In fact the RSS had a special appeal for the lower-middle-class youth of the towns; like the Arya Samaj, it offered them membership of a generalized Hindu community and an escape from the narrow identification of caste and occupational groupings. In the words of one RSS slogan: 'Every shakha was an ashram where Hindus were nationalised and nationalists Hinduised'.[30]

The search for a Hindu nationalist outlet, 1949–51

The balance between the Hindu-oriented groups and their opponents had been changed significantly by the events which were set in train by Gandhi's assassination. Until January 1948 Nehru and the liberal wing within Congress were on the defensive whereas Patel, judging from the content of his Lucknow speech, was assuming that the Hindu traditionalist wing of the party would be strengthened to the point where some connection with the Mahasabha and the RSS would be possible. However, after Gandhi's death the Mahasabha was virtually obliged to give an undertaking that it would leave party politics altogether; the RSS found itself the object of a comprehensive political ban and, for the first time in its history, was forced to accept a written constitution; and Nehru and the liberals were thus given a valuable breathing space, within which the war in Kashmir was brought to an end (though the dispute about the state continued), the major task of rehabilitating the refugees was set in motion, and memories of the partition riots faded to some extent.

By the autumn of 1949 the balance was shifting once more in the opposite direction. Public hostility towards the Mahasabha, the RSS and other Hindu nationalist groups was beginning to dissipate; the trial of those accused of complicity in Gandhi's assassination had ended; the removal of the ban on the RSS had been accepted without an outcry; and the Hindu Mahasabha was resuming its political activities without hindrance. At the same time, issues concerning the rights of Hindus were being raised in a number of debates, including those set in motion by the Constitution Bill, which passed its third reading in the Constituent Assembly on 26 November 1949. The bill set out a constitution which firmly upheld the values of social and religious pluralism. Its section on fundamental rights proclaimed the principles of equality before the law, of freedom of speech, assembly and movement and of freedom of religion; and it stood for the cultural and educational rights of minorities, thereby clearing the way for the introduction of far-reaching social reforms. This much the Hindu traditionalists were prepared to

[30] 'The story of the Sangh', *Organiser*, 30 August 1949, p. 12.

accept, but a number of them took issue with those clauses of the bill which dealt with the official language of the union and they pressed the claims of Hindi in the Devanagari script with considerable determination.[31] In the end, they were forced to accept the compromise (eventually embodied in Article 343 of the Constitution) that English should continue to be used for all the official purposes of the Union for fifteen years. However, their reluctance to take measured account of the rights of minorities, whether regional or cultural, was symbolic of their desire for a more organic, more Hindu-oriented national community than the assembly had envisaged.

Fierce controversy also surrounded the Hindu Code Bill, which was intended to provide for a unified system of law governing Hindu marriage and inheritance and also to extend the rights of Hindu women by enforcing monogamy, recognizing the principle of inheritance through a daughter, and giving a woman complete rather than limited control of her property. Many orthodox Hindus were opposed to the measure and its passage through the Constituent Assembly (Legislative) was continually delayed.[32] At a more general level, the whole Hindu lobby was afraid that the central government would use the powerful regulating institutions which it had inherited from the British Raj to intervene in areas of custom which had previously lain outside the domain of public law.

This was the prospect which convinced Hindu nationalist groups that they needed to strengthen their influence in party politics. Some saw the Mahasabha as the most obvious body to support, others toyed with the idea of forming a new party, and yet others returned to the notion that the Congress could still be converted to their outlook. The RSS, for all the bitterness engendered by the 1948–49 ban, was still inclined to consider the third possibility and to strengthen its connections with the Hindu traditionalists within the ruling party. The links between the two organizations were more extensive than many suspected at the time: in the months following independence, RSS workers in the United Provinces had been advised, when working in small towns and villages, to try to convince local Congress leaders that not only was the RSS not opposed to the Congress but that senior Congressmen were sympathetic to its aims;[33] and, in 1949, a newspaper report from the United Provinces commented on 'the sympathy the RSS derives from the rank and file of

---

[31] On the consideration of the language issue by the assembly, see Granville Austin, *The Indian Constitution: Cornerstone of a Nation* (Bombay, 1972), pp. 265–307.

[32] See D.E. Smith, *India as a Secular State* (Princeton, 1963), pp. 279–80; Times of India, *The Indian and Pakistan Year Book and Who's Who 1951*, pp. 567–8.

[33] According to a captured RSS document, *Statesman* (Calcutta), 6 February 1948, p. 5.

the Congress and also from a section of its leaders'.[34] Under the new RSS constitution, its *swayamsevaks* were free to join any political party (except those which believed in or resorted to 'violent and secret methods to achieve their ends') and there appeared to be no serious obstacle to their applying for Congress membership. The question of their eligibility was first raised by the Bihar Provincial Congress Committee, and the Congress Working Committee ruled on 5 October 1949 that members of the RSS could enrol themselves as members of the Congress in terms of that organization's constitution. However, it also stipulated that 'volunteers of any other organisation cannot be enrolled as Congress Volunteers', that is, that *swayamsevaks* could not join the Congress Seva Dal.[35]

There can be no doubt that this was a considered decision because, when it came under attack, the Congress President, Dr Pattabhi Sitaramayya, stated at Kanpur on 10 October that the RSS was not 'the enemy of the Congress', nor was it a communal political organization like the Muslim League or the Hindu Mahasabha: 'It may be and is a communal body but it has repudiated all connexion with politics'.[36] Other Congressmen disagreed with this view and on 17 November the Working Committee effectively reversed the earlier decision. Pointing out that all primary members of Congress were subject to rules of discipline and that 'the members of R.S.S. are no exception to these rules even if they choose to become primary members', it cited the directive that no Congressman should organize or join any volunteer *dal* other than the Congress Seva Dal, which was tantamount to saying that an RSS *swayamsevak* could not be even a primary member of the Congress so long as he remained attached to the RSS.[37] This whole controversy was conducted in terms which were often ambiguous and obscurely legalistic, but the outcome was clear: the Working Committee, having earlier decided that double membership (of both the Congress and the RSS) was permissible, had changed its mind and resolved that it should be avoided.

Why was the policy reversed? Nehru's own role must be considered: he had been absent from the meeting on 5 October (he was on the point of leaving India for a trip abroad) but had returned in time to attend the crucial meeting on 17 November and may well have persuaded the committee to adopt a different view. Another explanation is offered by Curran, who claims that a pro-RSS group of Congressmen had

[34] *Ibid.*, 6 September 1949, p. 7.
[35] *Congress Bulletin*, September–October 1949, p. 15.
[36] *Statesman* (Calcutta), 11 October 1949, p. 3.
[37] *Congress Bulletin*, November–December 1949, pp. 2–3.

persuaded Vallabhbhai Patel to try to attract RSS members to Congress ranks. According to Curran, the decision of 5 October was part of a scheme, which Nehru had accepted, to discover whether many *swayamsevaks* would apply for Congress primary membership and whether there would be many complaints from Congressmen about the initiative. In the end, there were few recruits and many complaints.[38] The *Organiser*, which favoured the RSS, carried an editorial praising the decision of 5 October[39] and later one of its special correspondents linked the reversal to Nehru's return to India, claiming that the alleged differences between Nehru and the Congress Working Committee indicated the existence of 'deep fissures' within Congress:

> behind this personal government looms large the ominous shadow of the *chhota* Communists viz. Socialists, the Communists and the Jamiat-ul-Ulema. All these forces – weak in themselves but powerful in their negative mischievous manoeuvres, know that a *rapprochement* between Sangh and Congress would mean a new lease of life to the Congress, and with that a fresh postponement in their share of power. They want to fish in the disturbed waters of the Congress politics. Any consolidation of the Congress organisation and a strengthening of the forces of nationalism and Bharatiya culture is gall and worm-wood to them. And hence their combined *jehad* against any such development.[40]

The division between the Hindu traditionalists and the liberal secularists within the Congress was widened by their divergent reactions to the outbreaks of communal violence which occurred in East Bengal and West Bengal during the winter of 1949–50. In India as a whole, there was a widespread belief that the disturbances had begun in East Bengal, sparked off by the discriminatory policies of the Pakistani authorities, and as a result there was strong public pressure for the government to deal firmly with Pakistan. Within the Cabinet, Nehru, who hoped for a negotiated settlement, proposed that he and Liaquat Ali Khan, the Prime Minister of Pakistan, should tour the two Bengals, an idea which Liaquat Ali refused to consider, while Patel, who favoured an exchange of populations, called for a hard line to be taken with Pakistan. Nehru himself was obliged to consider war as a possible course of action,[41] but

---

[38]　Curran, *Militant Hinduism*, pp. 65–7. See also Andersen, 'The Rashtriya Swayamsevak Sangh – III', p. 678.

[39]　'A wise decision', *Organiser*, 11 October 1949, p. 3.

[40]　'Deep fissures in Congress', *ibid.*, 30 November 1949, pp. 1 and 15.

[41]　See Sarvepalli Gopal, *Jawaharlal Nehru: A Biography, Volume Two: 1947–1956* (London, 1979), pp. 82–7, and exchanges of letters between Nehru and Patel between 20 February and 29 March 1950 in Das (ed.), *Sardar Patel's Correspondence 1945–50*, X, pp. 1–23. See also Michael Brecher, *Nehru: A Political Biography* (London, 1959), p. 428; Balraj Madhok, *Dr. Syma Prasad Mookerjee: A Biography* (New Delhi, n.d.), pp. 41–2; K.L. Panjabi, *The Indomitable Sardar: A Political Biography of Sardar Vallabhbhai Patel* (Bombay, 1962), pp. 190–1; Gadgil, *Government from Inside*, p. 84.

on 17 March 1950, after several visits to Calcutta and West Bengal, he made clear to the Indian Parliament that he was against an exchange of populations. Instead he suggested that he and Liaquat Ali Khan should make a joint statement assuring the minorities in both countries of protection and fair treatment.[42]

The crisis had again revived the question of whether India should remain a secular state or whether it should represent the outlook of its Hindu majority. As applied to the Bengal crisis, the crucial test was whether the government would treat the rioting as a problem whose solution required the co-operation of both countries or whether it would act on the simple premise that Pakistan was condoning the persecution of her Hindu minorities. On 26 March, Nehru wrote to Patel proposing that either the Congress Working Committee or the All-India Congress Committee (AICC) should meet to settle a clear line of policy. Reminding Patel of Gandhi's wish that they two should work together in the government, Nehru virtually implied that they were no longer doing so. Having identified the conflict between communalism and secularism as his main concern and having defended the idea that India should be a secular state, Nehru referred to the insecurity of Indian Muslims and of minorities in general, and suggested that 'the fact that you and I pull in different directions, and in any event the belief that we do so, is exceedingly harmful'.[43] In his reply, Patel denied that there had been differences 'as regards the secular ideals to which we all subscribe and for which we all stand', but he went on to say that

our secular ideals impose a responsibility on our Muslim citizens in India – a responsibility to remove the doubts and misgivings entertained by a large section of the people about their loyalty founded largely on their past association with the demand for Pakistan and the unfortunate activities of some of them. It is in this light that to my mind some tangible steps to deal with the present situation become urgent and that is why I have been insisting on a well-considered, firm and determined line of approach.[44]

That there were serious disagreements within the Cabinet became more obvious after Liaquat Ali had accepted Nehru's invitation to visit Delhi. When the general principle of an agreement between the two countries was discussed, Shyama Prasad Mookerjee is reported to have expressed a lack of confidence in Pakistan's good faith and to have demanded the insertion of a penal clause to provide for sanctions against

[42] *P.D.*, Part 2, III, 17 March 1950, pp. 1700–8, especially pp. 1705–6.
[43] Letter from Nehru to Patel, 26 March 1950, in Das (ed.), *Sardar Patel's Correspondence 1945–50*, X, p. 13.
[44] Letter from Patel to Nehru, 28 March 1950, in *ibid.*, p. 19.

whichever country failed to honour the agreement, a demand which would almost certainly have wrecked the impending negotiations. Nehru and others rejected this strongly,[45] and the two leaders began their talks on 2 April. Four days later, on the 6th, Mookerjee submitted his resignation as a minister to Nehru. He had done so, he said, as a result of

the policy pursued regarding Indo-Pakistan relationship, specially relating to Bengal. The agreement which, I suppose, will be finalised today does not touch the basic problem and is not likely to offer any solution. I can under no circumstances be a party to it. Apart from the fact that it will bring little solace to the sufferers, it has certain features which are bound to give rise to fresh communal and political problems in India, the consequences of which we cannot foresee today. In my humble opinion the policy you are following will fail. Time alone can prove this.[46]

In spite of Mookerjee's protests, Nehru and Liaquat Ali signed the agreement (which became known as the Delhi Pact) on 8 April, thus affirming the intention of their respective governments to uphold the rights of their minorities, to facilitate the movement of migrants, and to restore communal harmony in the two Bengals.[47] Appeals from both Nehru and Patel that, in the national interest, Mookerjee should not press his resignation, failed to persuade him to alter his decision, and on the 19th, the day that a presidential communiqué announced his departure (and that of K.C. Neogy, another Bengali, and the Minister for Commerce) from the Cabinet,[48] Mookerjee justified his stand before Parliament. He spoke of the need to protect the Hindus of East Pakistan, of his doubt that this could be done by a limited agreement such as the

---

[45] See references by Mookerjee, *P.D.*, Part 2, IV, 19 April 1950, p. 3017, and *ibid.*, XIV, 10 August 1951, c. 365; and reports in *Pioneer* (Lucknow), 6 April 1950, p. 1 (special correspondent); 9 April 1950, p. 1. See also Gadgil, *Government from Inside*, pp. 88 and 142, and his article in *Lok Satta*, 7 June 1964, translated on *Organiser*, 27 July 1964, pp. 5–6. In this article and in his book (pp. 86–7) Gadgil also describes other Cabinet clashes relating to the Delhi Pact.

[46] Letter from Mookerjee to Nehru, 6 April 1950, from New Delhi, in Das (ed.), *Sardar Patel's Correspondence 1945–50*, X, p. 130. For the events surrounding Mookerjee's resignation and his subsequent career, see B.D. Graham, 'Syama Prasad Mookerjee and the communalist alternative', in D. A. Low (ed.), *Soundings in Modern South Asian History* (London, 1968), pp. 330–74.

[47] For the text of the agreement see *P.D.*, Part 2, IV, 10 April 1950, pp. 2678–80. See also a later statement by Nehru (*ibid.*, Part 1, IV, 1 August 1950, cc. 7–11); Gopal, *Jawaharlal Nehru: A Biography*, II, pp. 87–8; and Chaudhuri Muhammad Ali, *The Emergence of Pakistan* (New York and London, 1967), pp. 273–4. A supplementary agreement was announced on 16 August 1950 (see *Statesman* (Delhi), 17 August 1950, pp. 1 and 5).

[48] See letter from Rajendra Prasad to Nehru, 14 April 1950, in Das (ed.), *Sardar Patel's Correspondence 1945–50*, p. 133; *Statesman* (Calcutta), 16 April 1950, p. 1; 20 April 1950, pp. 1 and 7; see also Gopal, *Jawaharlal Nehru: A Biography*, II, pp. 88–9.

Delhi Pact, and claimed that the riots 'formed part of deliberate and cold planning to exterminate minorities from East Bengal'.[49] Then, having returned to Calcutta, he began to attack the Delhi Pact and what he saw as the Government of India's weakness in its dealings with Pakistan. Although the rioting in the east had abated, Mookerjee continued to advocate the need for a firm stand against Pakistan; in August he told Parliament that the Delhi Pact had failed and that, with respect to the Hindus in Pakistani territory, the Government of India had three courses open to it – to declare that Pakistan's failure to protect her Hindu citizens had destroyed the basis of partition and that India would now assume the responsibility for protecting them; to demand one-third of the territory of East Pakistan for the resettlement of Hindu refugees; or to oblige Pakistan to agree to an exchange of populations in the eastern part of the subcontinent. Speaking of the first proposal, he said, 'I know the danger of it. I know what it means. It means war. This is a method which was contemplated by Mahatma Gandhi himself in extreme circumstances'.[50] Back in Calcutta again he told a meeting that 'The present policy of appeasement of Pakistan must cease. Whether we start with a definite plan of economic sanctions or we intensify military action is a matter of procedure and strategy'.[51]

Mookerjee's general views on how the government should deal with Pakistan had much in common with those of the Congress Party's Hindu traditionalists, who showed their dislike of Nehru's secular policies by supporting the candidature of Purushottamdas Tandon for the national presidency of the party. A veteran Congressman from Uttar Pradesh, Tandon had worked hard in the cause of Hindi, had expressed strong opposition to partition, and had contested the previous Congress presidential election of 1948 from a Hindu traditionalist position. When presiding over the All-India Refugee Conference at Delhi on 29–30 July 1950, he had claimed that the main difficulty for the Hindus in East Bengal was that Pakistan was being administered as an Islamic state.[52] Once his intention to stand had become known, Nehru wrote to him expressing reservations about his candidature; alluding to the need to 'fight against communalism', he claimed that

you have become to large numbers of people in India some kind of a symbol of this communal and revivalist outlook and the question rises in my mind: Is the Congress going that way also? If so, where do I come into the picture, whether it

[49] *P.D.*, Part 2, IV, 19 April 1950, pp. 3017–22.
[50] *Ibid.*, V, 7 August 1950, cc. 425–61.
[51] *Times of India* (Delhi), 4 September 1950, p. 1.
[52] *Statesman* (Delhi), 30 July 1950, pp. 1 and 6.

is the Congress or whether it is the Government run by the Congress? Thus this larger question becomes related to my own activities.[53]

Nehru also wrote to Patel to tell him why he could not support Tandon, and was not persuaded by the argument that he should refer the policy questions to the Congress plenary session which was to be held at Nasik on 20–21 September 1950, about three weeks after the results of the presidential election would be known. He eventually informed Patel that he would not serve on the Working Committee under Tandon, whatever the Nasik session might decide:

That decision was taken for two major reasons: that Tandon had pursued during the past two years and was still pursuing a policy which, to my thinking, was utterly wrong and harmful and his election would undoubtedly give an impetus to this policy, and I must dissociate myself completely from it. Secondly, because the election was becoming more and more a [clash] between varying policies and Tandon became a kind of symbol of one and was as such being supported widely by Hindu Mahasabha and RSS elements.[54]

The second candidate in the contest for the Congress presidency was J. B. Kripalani, who was identified with Nehru's position, and, once the Prime Minister's objections to Tandon became public knowledge, ordinary Congressmen came to regard the election as an indirect trial of strength between Nehru and Patel. In the event, Tandon narrowly defeated Kripalani in the ballot and, although the subsequent Nasik session of the Congress adopted resolutions in accord with Nehru's views, especially on communal questions and on relations with Pakistan, Nehru refused to become a member of Tandon's Working Committee. He eventually joined that body with extreme reluctance, and then became increasingly involved in the party's organizational affairs. The Hindu traditionalists were at first heartened by Tandon's success but Patel's death on 15 December 1950 left them virtually leaderless and thereafter, throughout the spring and summer of 1951, Nehru and his allies gradually regained the initiative. In the end, Tandon was forced to resign as Congress President and Nehru himself was elected to the post at an AICC meeting on 8 September 1951.[55]

Though the long struggle which ended with the defeat of Tandon can be seen now as marking the downward curve in the power of the Hindu

---

[53] Letter from Nehru to Tandon, 8 August 1950, in Das (ed.), *Sardar Patel's Correspondence 1945–50*, X, p. 198.
[54] Letter from Nehru to Patel, 27/28 August 1950, in *ibid.*, p. 221.
[55] The fullest account of this complicated conflict is given in Stanley A. Kochanek, *The Congress Party of India: The Dynamics of One-Party Democracy* (Princeton, 1968), pp. 27–53.

traditionalists within Congress, this outcome could not have been predicted with any confidence until well into 1951; in mid-1950, Hindu nationalist politicians, for whom the conflict was of the utmost importance, were in two minds about what course of action they should follow: whether to remain in close touch with the Hindu traditionalists within the Congress and hope that the organization would move in their direction under the influence of Patel and Tandon, or whether to consider independent action on the assumption that Congress would move away from them towards a liberal and secularist position under Nehru's leadership. Mookerjee's own movements should be judged against this background of uncertainty; as we shall see, he began to explore the possibility of forming a new Hindu nationalist party in the summer of 1950 but made no public move to establish one until late in the spring of 1951, by which time it was clear that the tide in the Congress was flowing towards Nehru and his supporters.

It must have been shortly after his resignation from the Cabinet in April 1950 that Mookerjee raised the idea of a new party with Golwalkar, the RSS leader. In the course of their discussions the latter claimed to have told him

that the RSS could not be drawn into politics, that it could not play second fiddle to any political or other party since no organisation devoted to the wholesale regeneration of the real i.e. cultural, life of the Nation could ever function successfully if is [sic] was tried to be used as a hand-maid of political parties.

For his part, Mookerjee told Golwalkar that 'the new political party also could not be made subservient to any other organisation'. There were other areas of conflict too: Mookerjee had stated at a press conference that the Hindu Mahasabha was communal 'inasmuch as it believed in Hindu Rashtra', and Golwalkar pointed out to him that 'we of the RSS had equal, if not more, emphatic belief in the Bharatiya Rashtra being Hindu Rashtra, and as such the RSS would be for him equally deserving to be kept at arm's length'. However, after Mookerjee 'acknowledged that he had made an inadvertent remark and expressed full agreement on the Hindu Rashtra ideal', Golwalkar agreed to assist him and chose some of his colleagues, 'staunch and tried workers', to help in establishing a new party.[56] The arrangement was, in effect, an

---

[56] 'A tribute to Dr. Shyamaprasad: how Jana Sangh was born', *Organiser*, 25 June 1956, pp. 5–7, reproduced in K. R. Malkani (ed.), *Organiser Silver Jubilee Souvenir 1973* (New Delhi, 1973), pp. 183–5, quotations from pp. 184–5. See also Deshmukh, *R.S.S.: Victim of Slander*, p. 83. On differences within the RSS about its general approach to party politics and on its early contacts with Mookerjee, see Andersen and Damle, *Brotherhood in Saffron*, pp. 123–5, and also Myron Weiner, *Party Politics in India: The Development of a Multi-Party System* (Princeton, N.J., 1957), pp. 181–7; Baxter, *The Jana Sangh*, pp. 54–62.

agreement that several RSS organizers, or *pracharaks*, were to be seconded to Mookerjee as the first administrators and managers of the proposed party.

Soon after this, Mookerjee appears to have conferred with Dr N.B. Khare, then President of the Hindu Mahasabha, and to have asked for his support. According to Khare, several other Mahasabha figures, including Mahant Digvijai Nath, V.G. Deshpande and Ashutosh Lahiri, were present at the meeting, which took place in Delhi on either 31 July or 1 August 1950; he claimed that Mookerjee had asked him

to wind up the Hindoo Mahasabha and join his *new party which he was going to establish under his own leadership with the help of Mr. M.S. Golwalkar of the Rashtriya Swayam Sewak Sangh.* I was very much surprised at the suggestion of Dr Mukherjee and I said to him, 'Your new party is just in the air yet. Its programme also is not yet chalked out. How can I wind up an organised old party and join your new party under these conditions? It will be highly improper to do so.'[57]

This seems to have been Mookerjee's only approach to the Mahasabha and he probably realized that neither it nor the newly established Ram Rajya Parishad could offer a secure foundation for a broadly based movement. The Mahasabha had still not shaken off its reputation for exclusiveness and both it and the Ram Rajya Parishad were regarded as parties for high-caste Hindus and as pillars of religious orthodoxy.

However, Mookerjee continued to explore the idea of a new party. In the late autumn of 1950, he was discussing it with three men who were influential in the Delhi and Punjab areas, Lala Yodhraj, the Chairman of the Punjab National Bank, Balraj Madhok, a teacher in Camp College, which served mainly the refugee communities in New Delhi, and Mauli Chandra Sharma, an experienced Delhi politician; they used to meet in the house of Lala Yodhraj and got as far as considering the draft of a party manifesto.[58] A larger group, including Madhok and Sharma, gathered in New Delhi on 16 January 1951 to consider the possibility of forming a party based on the states of the Punjab, the Patiala and East Punjab States Union (PEPSU), Himachal Pradesh, and Delhi. According to the account given by Madhok, Mookerjee raised the question of forming an all-India party as well, and a subcommittee was appointed to

---

[57] N. B. Khare, *My Political Memoirs or Autobiography* (Nagpur, n.d.), p. 427. For a less specific reference to Mookerjee's contacts with Mahasabha leaders at this time, see Nitya Narayan Banerjee, 'Some memories of Dr. Mookerji', *Organiser*, 10 July 1966, p. 12.

[58] From interview with Balraj Madhok, New Delhi, 12 May 1984. See also Madhok, *Stormy Decade (Indian Politics) 1970–1980* (Delhi, Second edition, 1982), p. 195; Madhok, *R.S.S. and Politics*, p. 50 (in this source, Madhok includes Bhai Mahavir amongst those who took part in discussions about the draft manifesto).

prepare a draft manifesto and a constitution. Provisionally, the title Bharatiya Jana Sangh (Indian People's Party) was proposed, for although Mookerjee felt that the new party should stand for Hindu Rashtra as the basis for Indian unity, he was willing to use the adjectives 'Bharatiya' and 'Indian' as well as 'Hindu' until the latter description was generally accepted.[59]

Then, plans were complicated by a dispute amongst the RSS leaders at Nagpur as to whether they should endorse Golwalkar's undertaking to supply young organizers for a new party. Finally Mookerjee, impatient at the delay, decided to go ahead on his own.[60] In a speech on 8 April 1951 he spoke of the need for a 'new All-Bharat political party'[61] and he established a West Bengal 'People's Party' at a conference on 28 April.[62] This showed the RSS that he was prepared to form a party in any case,[63] and it was presumably shortly after this conference that it finally agreed to assist him. A major party unit representing the whole of the 'greater Punjab' was established at a conference at Jullundur on 27 May 1951, with Lala Balraj Bhalla as President and Balraj Madhok as General Secretary.[64] Probably in response to the representations of this unit, the Election Commission of India announced on 7 September that an All-India Bharatiya Jana Sangh had been allocated the *dipak* (lamp) symbol as a national party for the forthcoming general election.[65] Two days later, at a meeting in Delhi, attended by Mookerjee and by the presidents and secretaries of the 'greater Punjab' unit and of the newly formed units in Uttar Pradesh and Madhya Bharat, it was decided to hold a convention at Delhi in October to establish the national party.[66] A number of additional units were formed in northern, eastern and western India in the weeks which followed, and finally, on 21 October 1951, representatives from the various units and other interested groups met in convention at Delhi, where the Bharatiya Jana Sangh was founded. Mookerjee was appointed its President, a provisional Working Committee was chosen, and a manifesto approved.[67] The party was now a reality.

[59]　Madhok, *Mookerjee*, pp. 55–7. See also *Times of India* (Delhi), 15 March 1951, p. 3.
[60]　From interview with Balraj Madhok, New Delhi, 12 May 1984.
[61]　*Organiser*, 16 April 1951, p. 1.
[62]　*Ibid.*, 7 May 1951, pp. 8–9 and 14. See also *Times of India* (Delhi), 29 April 1951, p. 1.
[63]　From interview with Balraj Madhok, New Delhi, 15 May 1984. See also Madhok, *Stormy Decade*, p. 195; *R.S.S. and Politics*, pp. 50–1.
[64]　See *Organiser*, 21 May 1951, pp. 1, 4 and 14; 4 June 1951, pp. 1, 14 and 8–9; *The Tribune* (Ambala), 28 May 1951, p. 3; *Times of India* (Delhi), 29 May 1951, p. 4; reference by Mookerjee in *P.D.*, Part 2, XII, 1 June 1951, cc. 9853–4; Madhok, *Mookerjee*, pp. 57–8.
[65]　Election Commission of India, *Report on the First General Elections in India 1951–52*, I, *General* (New Delhi, 1955), p. 84.
[66]　*Times of India* (Delhi), 11 September 1951, p. 5; *Organiser*, 17 September 1951, p. 1; Madhok, *Mookerjee*, p. 59.

The members of the provisional Working Committee were as follows:

President: Shyama Prasad Mookerjee
General Secretaries: Bhai Mahavir and Mauli Chandra Sharma (both
of Delhi)

Members:

Lala Balraj Bhalla (President, Punjab unit)
Balraj Madhok (General Secretary, Punjab unit)
Mahashaya Krishna (Delhi)
Rang Bihari Lal (President, Delhi unit)
Rao Krishna Pal Singh (President, Uttar Pradesh unit)
Deendayal Upadhyaya (General Secretary, Uttar Pradesh unit)
Dada Dave (Madhya Bharat)
Bapu Saheb Sohni (President, Berar unit)
Vimal Chandra Banerji (Jabalpur – President, Mahakoshal unit)
Raj Kishore Shukla (Vindhya Pradesh)
Chiranjiva Lal Mishra (President, Rajasthan unit)
Ghisu Lal (Ajmer)
Shivkumar Dwivedi (President, Bihar unit)
Manmatha Nath Das (West Bengal)
P.H. Krishna Rao (Bangalore – Vice-President, Karnataka unit)

This list indicates several interesting features of the party's early
leadership structure. Even at this stage, its northern bias was clear: the
majority of the members came from a solid block of territory cotermi-
nous with the Hindi-speaking belt, with an eastwards extension through
Bihar to West Bengal, and the remainder of the country was represented
by officers of only two units – Berar, in the south-west of Madhya
Pradesh, and Karnataka in Mysore. There were no members at all
from the Part A states of Bombay, Madras, Assam and Orissa or from
the Part B states of Hyderabad, Saurashtra and Travancore-Cochin.
There were several RSS recruits in this team (Mahavir, Madhok,
Upadhyaya and Sohni) and, according to Madhok, Mahavir had been
nominated as one of the two general secretaries as a result of a tacit
understanding between Mookerjee and the leaders of the RSS.[68]

[67] *Organiser*, 29 October 1951. A detailed account of the stages in the formation of the Jana
Sangh is given in Baxter, *The Jana Sangh*, pp. 66–78.
[68] The list of the provisional Working Committee is from *Times of India* (Delhi), 22
October 1951, p. 5. See also Madhok, *R.S.S. and Politics*, p. 52, for references to the first
Working Committee (whose members included Umashankar Mulshankar Trivedi,
Yashodhar Mehta, Lala Balraj Bhalla, Guru Dutt Vaidya, Mahashaya Krishna and
Madhok) and to the understanding which led to the appointment of Mahavir as one of
the general secretaries.

The party's first manifesto gave important indications as to where the party was trying to place itself in relation to other groups. As far as economic and social issues were concerned, it was adopting a liberal rather than a conservative approach, envisaging reforms where they would enhance the independence and freedom of producers but assuming a restricted role for the state in the regulation of economic life. It declared itself for economic and administrative decentralization and accepted that the provision of food, clothing and shelter was the most pressing economic problem before the country. Acknowledging the importance of increasing production in food, cotton and jute, the manifesto advocated various measures to bring this about, including the provision of better storage facilities and better seeds, the consolidation of holdings, and improvements in irrigation facilities. It also declared that the party would abolish the jagirdari and zamindari systems of land tenure, compensating the former owners and distributing land to the tillers, and promised to improve conditions in the villages, to popularize cottage industries, and to prevent cow-slaughter. In the field of industry, the manifesto declared that those industries especially concerned with essential defence needs should be publicly owned, but that private enterprise should be encouraged as far as other large industries were concerned. At the same time it promised that steps would be taken 'to put a check on profiteering and concentration of economic power in the hands of the big few through cartels and combines'. It also stated that the party would strive to make the country self-sufficient in consumer goods through the widespread development of small-scale and cottage industries, to which end it proposed various measures, including the speedy development of hydroelectric energy, the establishment of rural polytechnics, and the provision of marketing facilities for cottage industries.

The parts of the programme which referred to issues of concern to Hindu nationalists were relatively moderate in emphasis. When promising special aid 'to the backward sections of the people', the manifesto stated the party's belief in the equal rights of all Indian citizens 'irrespective of caste, creed or community', while declaring that it would not recognize minorities and majorities based on religion; it qualified its advocacy of Hindi as the all-India language by offering 'full encouragement' to other Indian languages; and it adopted a relatively mild stand on the Hindu Code Bill, proposing only that the kinds of changes envisaged by the measure should not be made in the absence of popular and electoral approval. However, it recommended firm policies in dealing with Pakistan, declaring that, so long as that country remained a separate entity, the Jana Sangh would stand 'for a strict policy of reciprocity and not one of appeasement, as hitherto pursued to the detriment of Bharat's national interest and honour'. In the same vein, it declared that Kashmir was an integral part of India, that the Kashmir dispute should be withdrawn from the United Nations, and that there should be no further question of a plebiscite in that state.[69]

There can be no doubt that Mookerjee considered that the Jana Sangh's major task was to take a definite position on issues affecting India's relations with Pakistan. In a newspaper article published in December 1951 just before the first general elections, he summed up the party's domestic policies and went on to state that

Apart from all these, there is one fundamental feature of our party's programme which differentiates it from others. This relates to the post-partition problems affecting the peace and welfare of the country at large. The Jana Sangh feels that the partition of India was the biggest tragedy that could fall on the country.

He affirmed that

The Jana Sangh believes that the future welfare of the people of India and Pakistan demands a reunited India, and it will work towards this end, keeping this as its goal and aim.

Declaring that India should take full responsibility, if necessary, for the protection of the minorities in Pakistan, he repeated the manifesto's proposals regarding Kashmir, adding that the one-third of that state under the control of Pakistan 'must be freed from her clutches at any cost'.[70]

However, another of Mookerjee's ambitions was to place the Jana Sangh at the centre of opposition to Congress within the framework of the Constitution. In the article quoted above, he claimed that the main reason for the popularity of his party

has been the fact that it has put its finger on the weak spots of the Congress administration, and its straightforward references to certain vital matters of national policy have touched the hearts of the people voicing, as they do, their suppressed feelings and anxieties. The Jana Sangh will function as a party in opposition and will put forth a constructive effort for national consolidation. This does not mean that it will hesitate to shoulder the responsibilities of administration, either singly or in coalition with others, should such an occasion arise.[71]

At the very beginning, therefore, the Jana Sangh lacked a clear policy orientation. Some of its policy statements presaged a liberal party,

---

[69] *Manifesto of All India Bharatiya Jana Sangh* [New Delhi, 1951], pp. 3–12.
[70] Shyama Prasad Mookerjee, 'The Bharatiya Jana Sangh', *Statesman* (Delhi), 21 December 1951, p. 4.
[71] *Ibid.*

willing to work within the parliamentary framework, while others appeared to foreshadow a militant Hindu nationalist organization, motivated by hostility towards Pakistan and towards the Muslim minority in India. Which of these conflicting identities would be strengthened in the short run would depend on how the party would react to the politics of the new parliament and to further developments in the communal situation within the country and in India's relations with Pakistan.

The Jana Sangh and the Kashmir agitation of 1952–53

Both during the Bengal crisis of 1950 and in the subsequent Congress presidential election Nehru had been dismayed to encounter what he took to be the pervasive influence of 'communalism', a term which he used to cover not only the activities of the Hindu nationalists but also of Hindu traditionalists such as Purushottamdas Tandon. Having succeeded Tandon as Congress President in September 1951, he immediately issued the following warning to the presidents of Pradesh Congress Committees (PCCS):

Recent events have shown that some members of the Congress have functioned almost as if they were members of the Hindu Mahasabha or some like communal organisation. Indeed, some people have actually resigned from the Congress and gone over to the Jana Sangh. This itself is significant because a real Congressman should be as far removed from the communal organisations as anything can be. Our chief opponents in our work and in the elections are the communal organisations.[72]

In a circular letter of 19 September published in the *Congress Bulletin* he declared that

there is almost nothing in common between the Congress approach and the communal approach. Therefore, Congress candidates must be chosen with particular care so that they might represent fully the non-communal character and approach of the Congress. Persons who have been connected with communal organisations should therefore be suspects from this point of view. This is important as there has been a certain infiltration, in the past, of communal elements in the Congress.[73]

Nehru was effectively attempting to redraw the intellectual boundaries of the Congress, even if this meant surrendering territory to opposition parties which were willing to extend a welcome to Hindu

---

[72] Nehru, letter to PCC presidents, 19 September 1951, in *Congress Bulletin*, September 1951, p. 173.
[73] Nehru, circular letter, 19 September 1951, in *ibid.*, p. 176.

traditionalists. Being less exclusive and more modern in its outlook than the Mahasabha, the Jana Sangh could well have attracted people of this persuasion to its ranks in the early 1950s but it lacked both the organizational resilience and the certainty of purpose needed to exploit this opportunity. Although it had all the trappings of a complete party (a president, general secretaries, a working committee, and an array of state units), it was at this early stage little more than a tenuous network of leadership connections. These radiated out from Mookerjee and his lieutenants through an inexperienced and untried hierarchy of young RSS organizers towards thousands of new members and would-be election candidates who were trying to secure endorsements (or 'obtain tickets', to use the popular phrase) for the impending poll. To a large extent, the party's success in the election would depend on how effectively this network could be made to function, and that in turn depended very much on its organizational strategy, which had still to be settled.

The political outlook of Mookerjee and his principal lieutenant, Mauli Chandra Sharma, had been formed during the 1920s and 1930s, when the basic conventions of Indian party politics had developed within the institutions provided by the Government of India Acts of 1919 and 1935 and within the agitational campaigns launched by the Congress Party. They therefore tended to conceive of parties as organizations which combined elements of a centralized and disciplined hierarchy with elements of internal democracy; as a result, they acted as though the Jana Sangh had a high command, or leadership core, which could control the key central institutions of the party (working committee, election committee and parliamentary board) while permitting some scope for the development of central plenary bodies like the AICC and the customary sessions of delegates for the discussion of broad policy issues. Their inclination towards a 'Congress' style of party organization was consistent with a preference for building up strength through constitutional channels and with a strategy of conforming to the general policies of the ruling party, while maintaining sufficient distance from it to gain the support of the Hindu traditionalists, who were no longer welcome in Nehru's Congress. At the head of such a party Mookerjee would have been in a good position to attract other political groups to his side in the new parliament and to become the official Leader of the Opposition in the lower house, the Lok Sabha; he would then have been well placed to lead a broad alliance of non-Congress groups to victory in the second general elections, due in either 1956 or 1957.

However, the Jana Sangh, unlike, for example, the early Socialist

Party, did not consist in the main of people who had broken away from Congress and who were therefore disposed to recreate the institutional framework of their former party. Most of the Jana Sangh's junior leaders were encountering representative politics for the first time and their political experience, if any, had been gained through the RSS or the Arya Samaj. They saw the Congress as both effete and ineffective, and, though they were immensely loyal to Mookerjee, they regarded him not so much as a parliamentary leader as a man of decision and action, able to challenge the Prime Minister almost in a personal sense, as he had done at the time of his resignation from the Cabinet in April 1950. Where organization was concerned, they were accustomed not to that of the Congress model but to that of the RSS, with its emphasis on maintaining a disciplined hierarchy of professional workers, on the principle of authoritative leadership and on the fixity of doctrinal goals. Moreover, in terms of strategy they were quite prepared to envisage the use of agitational campaigns against the government as a means of realizing demands and rallying public opinion.

The early Jana Sangh thus contained two divergent tendencies: it was torn between those forces which were drawing it towards a constitutional role and those which were pulling it towards agitational politics. The influence of the constitutional forces was weakened by the results of the 1951–52 general elections, which the Congress won with large majorities; only three Jana Sangh members, including Mookerjee, were returned to the Lok Sabha and a mere handful of the party's candidates gained places in the Legislative Assemblies at the state level. In the central parliament, Mookerjee tried to retrieve the situation by forming an alliance with groups to the right of Congress. By the first meeting of the new parliament in May 1952 he had managed to construct a small United Nationalist Party, drawn mainly from the Jana Sangh, Hindu Mahasabha, Akali Dal, Ganatantra Parishad and Jharkhand groupings,[74] and further negotiations led to the merger of this body with an Independent Democratic Party to form a National Democratic Party, consisting of 32 members in the Lok Sabha and 10 in the Rajya Sabha.[75]

[74] *Statesman* (Delhi), 17 May 1952, p. 5.
[75] *Ibid.,* 28 May 1952, p. 5. A list of the party's members, with their affiliations and constituencies, is given in Table II of Baxter, *The Jana Sangh,* p. 110. The 32 Lok Sabha members listed are taken from a report in the *Organiser,* 30 June 1952, p. 1. See also the section on this party in Hari Sharan Chhabra (ed.), *Opposition in the Parliament: A Unique, Authentic and Comprehensive Biographical Dictionary of M.P.'s on Opposition Benches* (Delhi, 1952), pp. 41–78, which includes the party's draft programme (pp. 43–4) and an index of 30 Lok Sabha members (p. 42). This index omits three names included in the *Organiser's* list (N.D. Govindaswami Kachiroyar, N. Sathinathan and Shivamurthi Swami) and adds that of M.D. Ramaswami, who was returned in a by-election from a Madras constituency.

However, the Speaker of the Lok Sabha refused to recognize either this or any other of the non-Congress groups as the official Opposition Party in the house, ruling that such a party should have at least fifty members and possess certain other specific attributes.[76]

With his parliamentary role thus restricted, Mookerjee began to search outside Parliament for areas in which the government could be challenged, and he turned to the Kashmir dispute. This encompassed many of the issues about which he and many other Jana Sangh leaders felt most intensely – the reluctance (as they saw it) of the Government of India to deal firmly with Pakistan, its apparent indulgence towards local Muslim politicians, and its supposed indifference to the sufferings of Hindu minorities.

By the summer of 1952, the international dispute over the status of Kashmir had already reached a stalemate. Pakistan was still refusing to acknowledge the validity of the state's accession to the Dominion of India; the cease-fire line which had come into effect on 1 January 1949 still separated the armies of India and Pakistan; and the United Nations Security Council was still no further ahead in its efforts to persuade the two countries to demilitarize the territory so that a plebiscite could be held to decide its future. In reality, Kashmir had been divided into two successor states, one, called Azad Kashmir, under the control of Pakistan and the other, known as Jammu and Kashmir, under the control of India and defined as a Part B state under its Constitution. The Jana Sangh had early taken the position that Kashmir was an integral part of India, that the reference of the dispute to the United Nations should be withdrawn, and that the proposal for a plebiscite should be abandoned[77] but its main concern was to exert pressure on the Government of India to change its policies towards the Government of Jammu and Kashmir.

Article 370 of the Indian Constitution provided that Article 238, which applied to Part B states in general, should not apply to the state of Jammu and Kashmir and that the power of the Indian Parliament to make laws for the state should be limited to matters specified in orders of the President of India, in consultation with the state government regarding the areas of policy covered by the Instrument of Accession (foreign affairs, defence and communications) and with its concurrence in other matters. This left the state government with virtual control over

---

[76] *Statesman* (Delhi), 5 June 1952, p. 8. On the ruling, see W.H. Morris-Jones, *Parliament in India* (London, 1957), p. 155.

[77] Bharatiya Jana Sangh, *Manifesto* [1951], p. 9. See also resolution of Central Working Committee, Delhi, 10 February 1952, in Bharatiya Jana Sangh, *Party Documents* (New Delhi, 1973), IV, p. 19 (hereafter referred to as *BJS Documents*).

a wide range of internal affairs and placed the Prime Minister, Sheikh Abdullah, in a powerful position. He was responsible to Maharaja Yuvraj Karan Singh, the head of state and a Hindu, but as a popular Muslim nationalist leader and as chief of the National Conference Party he enjoyed a considerable following in the Vale of Kashmir, where Muslims were a majority of the population. Elsewhere the balance of communities was different; Buddhists constituted a majority in the upland region of Ladakh and Hindus predominated in the southern districts around the city of Jammu. The main internal opposition to Sheikh Abdullah came from the Jammu area, where a party known as the Praja Parishad was active; it favoured the complete accession of Kashmir to India and expressed the resentment of the Dogra community, on which the ruling dynasty had been based, against the changes which were occurring within Jammu and Kashmir, changes such as the adoption of Urdu (identified as the tongue of the Muslim majority) as the official language and the weakening of the Maharaja's authority. The economic power of the Dogra landlords had been seriously undermined in 1951 by the Big Landed Estates Abolition Act, which had provided for the confiscation of large holdings without compensation and for the transfer of land to the tillers. The Praja Parishad was further disturbed when Sheikh Abdullah, with the approval of the Government of India, began preparations for the framing of a state constitution intended to provide a firmer legal basis for the special status of Jammu and Kashmir within the Indian Union. To this end, a Constituent Assembly had been elected at the end of 1951 and, having adopted a provisional constitution, it had begun work on a definitive document.[78]

The Jana Sangh did not have its own party units in Jammu and Kashmir but it was in sympathy with the Praja Parishad and with its vigorous leader, Prem Nath Dogra, a Brahman, formerly a civil servant in the princely state, who had at one stage headed the RSS groups in Jammu city. On 8 February 1952 he and some other demonstrators had been arrested after a clash with the police and Mookerjee had raised the matter in Parliament.[79] A few months later the Jana Sangh's Central Working Committee, referring to the agreement of the Constituent Assembly of Jammu and Kashmir to approve a state flag and to replace

---

[78] On the Kashmir issue, see Sisir Gupta, *Kashmir: A Study in India–Pakistan Relations* (Bombay, 1966); Alastair Lamb, *Crisis in Kashmir: 1947 to 1966* (London, 1966); P. N. K. Bamzai, *A History of Kashmir* (Delhi, 1962); Michael Brecher, *The Struggle for Kashmir* (New York, 1953); Josef Korbel, *Danger in Kashmir* (Princeton, N. J., 1954); Balraj Madhok, *Kashmir: Centre of New Alignments* (New Delhi, n.d.); 'Kashmir', issue No. 58 of *Seminar* (New Delhi, June 1964).

[79] *P.D.*, Part 2, I, 12 February 1952, cc. 300–3. See also resolution of Central Working Committee, Delhi, 10 February 1952, *BJS Documents*, IV, pp. 19–20.

the hereditary ruler by an elected head of state, claimed that such decisions were 'in clear violation of India's sovereignty and the spirit of India's Constitution'. Noting that 'Jammu and Ladakh have through their representatives clearly expressed their determination to have full accession with India irrespective of the wishes of the people of Kashmir Valley', it requested the Government of India to give the people of the two former regions an opportunity 'to express their wishes regarding integration with India independently of the Constituent Assembly of the State'. [80] Mookerjee took up the issue in Parliament and on 26 June he again pressed the Union government to persuade the Government of Jammu and Kashmir to accept full integration under the Indian Constitution, alluding also to the possibility that Jammu and Ladakh could be offered the chance of separate integration with India.[81]

Mookerjee was on secure ground at this time because the Government of India's apparent tolerance of Sheikh Abdullah's claim to internal autonomy was widely resented, but in July 1952 representatives of the Government of India and of the Government of Jammu and Kashmir held talks in Delhi and reached agreement on many of the matters in dispute. In particular, the Government of Jammu and Kashmir accepted that the Supreme Court should have an original jurisdiction in disputes between the central and state governments, jurisdiction regarding fundamental rights within the state, and appellate jurisdiction in all civil and criminal cases. It had further agreed that the head of state should be recommended by the state legislature and recognized by the Indian President; that India's national flag would be supreme, although the state flag would remain in use; and that Jammu and Kashmir would be covered by the President's power to declare a state of emergency under Article 352 of the Constitution, subject to the concurrence of the state government in the case of such a declaration being caused by 'internal disturbance'.[82] Most groups were prepared to accept this settlement (known as the Delhi Agreement) as an important step towards full integration, but the Praja Parishad remained intransigent and there was strong sympathy within the Jana Sangh for its refusal to compromise. Mookerjee must have been aware of the danger of his party's being drawn by its ally into a confrontation with the authorities and, visiting the state in August, he counselled caution. According to one account,

---

[80] Resolution of the Central Working Committee, Delhi, 14 June 1952, *BJS Documents*, IV, pp. 20–2, quotations from pp. 21–2.

[81] *P.D., L.S.* (First Series), Part 2, II, 26 June 1952, cc. 2570–83. The text of this speech was also published by the Central Office of the Bharatiya Jana Sangh, Delhi, as a pamphlet under the title, *Integrate Kashmir*.

[82] *P.D., L.S.* (First Series), Part 2, III, 24 July 1952, cc. 4501–21, especially 4516–21.

He found that the people of Jammu were desperately earnest about the question of accession and that their patience was reaching the breaking point. He, however, advised them not to take any hasty step and urged them to explore all constitutional and peaceful means for achieving their laudable objective. He assured them full support of Bhartiya Jana Sangh in the matter.[83]

However, the Praja Parishad was determined to press ahead with its campaign. By the end of October 1952, Prem Nath Dogra was talking in terms of launching an agitation if the Constituent Assembly of Jammu and Kashmir gave effect to its decision to elect the head of state.[84] The final crisis began in November: on the 14th the Constituent Assembly, converted into a Legislative Assembly, elected Yuvraj Karan Singh as Sadar-i-Riyasat (head of state), on the 17th he was sworn into office, and then a sequence of Parishad demonstrations began, culminating in the arrest of Prem Nath Dogra and other leaders of the party on the 26th.[85]

Unless it were to have abandoned the Praja Parishad, an action which would have exposed it to accusations of bad faith and lack of courage, the Jana Sangh had no choice but to support the agitation. On 31 December 1952 its first national session at Kanpur adopted a resolution proposing a round-table conference of representatives of the Praja Parishad, the Government of Jammu and Kashmir, and 'the recognised leaders of India', warning that otherwise there would be an all-India agitation for the complete integration of the state with India.[86] Mookerjee still wanted to explore the possibility of further negotiations, but an exchange of letters which he initiated with Sheikh Abdullah and Nehru early in the new year failed to find grounds for compromise. Nehru, who treated the campaign as Hindu communalist in inspiration, referred in one letter to the difference of outlook which separated him from the Jana Sangh leader:

I have no doubt that you wish well to India, but the fact remains that our conceptions of what is well for India appear to differ. Because of this, our past lives have moved largely in different spheres. Neither of us can wipe out or ignore that past which has produced the present. I consider the communal approach to India's problems, or to any other problems, as inherently bad, narrow and injurious to the individual, the group and the nation. You object to my using the

---

[83] Bharatiya Jana Sangh, *Kashmir Problem and Jammu Satyagraha: An Objective Study* (Delhi, n.d.), pp. 52–3.

[84] See press conference in New Delhi on 20 October and interview in Jammu on 25 October 1952 (*Statesman* (Delhi), 21 October 1952, p. 1; 26 October 1952, p. 7).

[85] *Ibid.*, 18 November 1952, p. 8; 24 November 1952, p. 1; 25 November 1952, p. 1; 27 November 1952, p. 1. See also a statement by Nehru in *P.D., L.S.* (First Series), Part 1, III, 12 December 1952, cc. 1450–7.

[86] *BJS Documents*, IV, pp. 22–4.

word communal and deny my charge. Obviously we think differently and our actions are presumably the result of our thinking.[87]

In March 1953, then, the Jana Sangh joined with the Hindu Mahasabha and the Ram Rajya Parishad in a full-scale *satyagraha*, but the public authorities in Delhi and in various centres in the Punjab had no difficulty in containing the demonstrations. Mookerjee was now vulnerable to the charge that he had allowed his party to be drawn into a potentially violent and communalist agitation against the government and that he himself had failed to keep the Kashmir problem in perspective. The first sign that his stand was causing difficulties with his own supporters in Parliament came at the end of April, when Dr A. Krishnaswami, a member of the Lok Sabha from Madras, announced that he was resigning from the National Democratic Party. Explaining his decision, he said that during the previous four months he had

repeatedly raised at party meetings questions pertaining to the Jammu Parishad agitation and Indo-Pakistan relations and have incidentally pointed out to Dr Mookerjee that his ideological bias has resulted in the neglect of all other subjects including those in which South India is interested.[88]

Mookerjee decided to visit Jammu in May 1953, possibly with the intention of regaining the initiative in this protracted dispute by transferring the debate to the courts, where his skill as an advocate could have been used to advantage. His stated reasons for making the journey were that he wanted to study the situation there for himself and to explore the possibility of a peaceful settlement,[89] but he may also have intended to make an issue of the right to free entry to the state. A permit was required for entry to Jammu from the Punjab but Mookerjee did not try to obtain one and seems to have assumed that the Punjabi authorities would prevent him from crossing the border. Had they done so, he could then have appealed to the Supreme Court against the permit system and incidentally raised the question of why the Indian Constitution should not be applied in full to Jammu and Kashmir. However, when he reached the border on the 11th it was the Kashmiri police who issued him with an order barring his entry, arrested him when he signified his intention to proceed, and interned him in a small cottage about eight miles from Srinagar. He had begun to challenge the legality of his arrest and detention before the High Court of Jammu and Kashmir when he fell ill

[87] Nehru to Mookerjee, 10 February 1953, in Bharatiya Jana Sangh, *Integrate Kashmir: Mookerjee–Nehru & Abdullah Correspondence* [New Delhi, 1953], p. 60.
[88] Statesman (Delhi), 29 April 1953, p. 7.
[89] Madhok, *Mookerjee*, pp. 251–3.

and died suddenly on 23 June.[90] His shocked supporters suspended the agitation in both Jammu and Delhi for a period of mourning and later, in response to an appeal from Nehru, they called it off altogether on 7 July.[91]

The points at issue were now obscure but one thing was made clear – the central government's ability to control Jammu and Kashmir. Just over a month later, on 8 August 1953, Sheikh Abdullah was dismissed from office by order of the Sadar-i-Riyasat and placed under arrest. The following day he was succeeded as Prime Minister of the state by Bakshi Ghulam Mohammed, who resumed the policy of integration with India. The main points of the Delhi Agreement were embodied in a proclamation of the President of India issued on 14 May 1954, and the state's Constituent Assembly eventually approved a constitution, which came into force on 26 January 1957.

In the final reckoning, the Jammu agitation had cost the Jana Sangh a great deal. By joining hands with groups such as the Jammu Praja Parishad, the Hindu Mahasabha and the Ram Rajya Parishad, it had given Nehru ample opportunity to demonstrate that it was no different from other Hindu communalist organizations, for all its pretensions to be a progressive and a modern political force. Moreover, instead of strengthening its position in constitutional politics and extending a welcome to those Hindu traditionalists whom the Congress no longer wanted, it had wasted its resources and its energies on a fruitless venture. The only positive side to the experience, from the party's point of view, was that not only its central leadership but also its cadres and workers at state and district levels had been involved in their first serious campaign and had maintained their discipline and coherence despite considerable pressure from the authorities. Those who had taken part in the *satyagraha* were to look back upon it as a time of testing which marked them off from the party's later recruits. However, the Jana Sangh was also discovering that premature agitation against a powerful state machine was a hazardous undertaking – the lesson which the RSS had learned during its own agitation of 1948–49. As Golwalkar wrote in 1954:

[90] For statements and documents relating to the arrest and internment see Umaprasad Mookerjee (ed.), *Syamaprasad Mookerjee: His Death in Detention: A Case for Enquiry* (Calcutta, 1953). See also the text of a telegram from the Chief Secretary of the Government of Jammu and Kashmir to the Deputy-Speaker of the Lok Sabha (*P.D., L.S.* (First Series), Part 2, V, 12 May 1953, cc. 6423–5).

On the proceedings before the High Court of Jammu and Kashmir see *Statesman* (Delhi), 16 June 1953, p. 7; 19 June 1953, p. 5; 20 June 1953, p. 4.

[91] *Statesman* (Calcutta), 8 July 1953, p. 1. Prem Nath Dogra claimed later to have secured various 'assurances' at this time, including unqualified application of the Indian Constitution to the state, investigation of 'police excesses' and reinstatement of employees dismissed during the Parishad agitation (*ibid.*, 31 January 1955, p. 1).

A work that is based on agitational tactics crumbles to the ground as rapidly as it is raised. There can be no control over it. Once an agitation starts there is no knowing what direction it will take.[92]

Mookerjee's death, which caused dismay throughout India, had deprived the party of its only parliamentarian of national standing and its one secure link with the powerful networks of highly placed professional and political bodies around which an anti-Congress front might have been constructed. His loss tilted the balance of power within the organization towards those who favoured RSS methods of tight discipline and executive control rather than a more open style of party operation. From now on, they were to show clearly that they were much less attached than he had been to the strategy of building up around the party a broad parliamentary front.

Conclusion

By the end of 1953 the Jana Sangh had made a number of important choices so far as orientation and strategy were concerned, but it still remained something of an enigma. Although it had adopted a formal constitution with provisions for internal democracy on the Congress pattern, it was still very reliant on the RSS for workers and moral support. In terms of policy, it was trying to present itself as the champion of the small independent producers, in both industry and agriculture, and of traders against their traditional opponents – landlords and big business, the state and the collectivist left – but it had also espoused causes, such as the advancement of Hindi, which had given it a strongly northern bias, and had adopted extreme attitudes in foreign policy, as in the case of the Kashmir dispute. For these reasons it was difficult for observers to assign it to a definite place on the political spectrum. Had it given more prominence to its economic and social policies and been less strident and dogmatic where linguistic and foreign-policy matters were concerned, it could well have become what Mookerjee had envisaged it as being, the stable core of a broad anti-Congress front with a generally liberal orientation. As it was, its extremism made it an unpredictable quantity and caused other non-Congress parties to react against it.

Could it have avoided some of its most serious mistakes and followed a course more certain to meet with electoral success? In retrospect we can see that, once Nehru had succeeded in changing the centre of gravity within Congress so that the liberal and secular aspects of its character were given more prominence, the best position for any Hindu nationalist

[92] *Organiser*, 15 August 1954, p. 6.

party to have adopted would have been one as close as possible to that once occupied by the Hindu traditionalists within Congress. Had the Jana Sangh shaped its initial strategy more carefully, moderating its Hindu nationalism and severing its connection with the RSS, it would have been well placed to exploit any strong increase in support for the Hindu traditionalist and nationalist positions, and thus to compete on equal terms with the Congress in the northern states. Had it also adopted a less strident attitude towards Pakistan, it would have been much more acceptable to Hindu traditionalists in the central and southern states, where partition had left fewer emotional scars. A party thus placed would have resembled, in some respects, the contemporary clerical parties of western Europe (such as the *Mouvement républican populaire* in France and the Christian Democrats in Italy), which represented an essentially religious constituency in moderate and material terms and had developed economic and social policies of a mildly corporatist variety. The other strain in the Jana Sangh's outlook, economic liberalism, would also have been a considerable asset, particularly as the Congress government at the centre began moving towards greater public control of the economy in the late 1950s after the adoption of the Second Five-Year Plan.

At the end of 1953, these opportunities still existed, but it was becoming increasingly unlikely that the Jana Sangh had the capacity to make the radical changes needed to exploit them. If anything, it was showing an increasing tendency to choose isolation and doctrinal purity in the slender hope that some future national crisis would bring it the support which it needed to take and hold power.

3

The doctrinal inheritance of the Jana Sangh

Before going on to consider the Jana Sangh's efforts to present itself as a vehicle of Hindu nationalism, it will be useful to take a brief look at certain strands in the Indian philosophical tradition. There are important differences of theme and emphasis between the various schools of Hindu nationalist writing, but all have their immediate origins in the intellectual ferment of the nineteenth century, when the religious and philosophical texts of Brahmanic Hinduism were the object of wide-ranging analysis and debate both in India and abroad. It is to that process that we must now turn.

Brahmanism and Hindu nationalism

Brahmanism may be briefly defined as that system of religious beliefs and practices based on the ancient texts knows as the Vedas and their associated literature. Traditionally, this literature was the preserve of the Brahman castes, transmitted for centuries by oral tradition, but in the nineteenth century it came under intensive scholarly scrutiny, first in Europe and then in India itself. As it became more accessible and, through interpretation, more comprehensible, some Indian writers and intellectuals believed that it might serve as the foundation of a reformed and broadly based faith. However, the works concerned – the four Vedas, the Mahabharata and the Upanishads – vary considerably in form and content and are not easily organized to constitute a consistent statement of belief. Although Dayananda Saraswati was able to use the Vedic texts to lay the foundations of the Arya Samaj movement in northern India, in the main religious reformers preferred to develop their moral and ethical ideas on the basis of a reasoned faith, treating the ancient Sanskrit writings more as important background material than a fundamental body of doctrine. In another context, however, the greater accessibility of this literature enabled Hindu nationalist writers to create the commanding myths of cultural survival and revival with which they justified their political theories. The basic elements of these myths were formed in the middle of the nineteenth century, when European scholars of Sanskrit, working on the texts of the four Vedas and of the Mahabharata, constructed a theory of Hindu origins which drew heavily upon idealist philosophy, seeing the development of a race as the organic expression of an essential spirit. They treated the body of ideas contained in the Vedas, and particularly the oldest of these, the Rig Veda, as primordial and believed it to have shaped and influenced the whole of the subsequent evolution of Hindu thought and institutions. Expressed as a historical myth, this theory envisaged one branch of the Aryan or Indo-European community migrating southwards from its ancient homeland towards north-western India, there to settle and develop the essential elements of Indian culture before spreading out throughout the whole of the subcontinent.[1] The main interpreter of these ideas for Indian audiences was Friedrich Max Müller, whose influential *History of Ancient Sanskrit Literature*, published in 1859, was based on this approach to the study of Hindu traditions.

Indian writers accepted the teleological reasoning behind the theory of the Vedic origins of Hindu culture and by the end of the nineteenth century were themselves presenting the main outlines of what we now recognize as Hindu nationalism.[2] The first effective synthesis of their work was a book entitled *Essentials of Hindutva*, written by the Maharashtrian nationalist, Vinayak Damodar Savarkar, and published in 1924. Referring to the idea of the initial migration, Savarkar pictured the Aryans making their home in the land of the seven rivers, the Punjab *doab*, and calling themselves 'Hindus' for the first time. He described tribes of Hindus moving from this core area to other parts of India, until Aryans and non-Aryans had come together to form a common race with a common culture. Thus established, Hindus had to face a series of religious and cultural challenges; first came Buddhism, a debilitating force which was eventually nullified by a Hindu revival; then came the period of the Muslim invaders and the Mughal empire; and finally the rallying of the Hindus by Shivaji, the Maratha chieftain who successfully resisted the emperor Aurangzeb in the seventeenth century. For

---

[1] One of the first European studies to attract attention was Rudolph Roth, *Zur Litteratur und Geschichte des Weda: Drei Abhandlungen* (Stuttgart, 1846). An extremely valuable guide to the ideas which Roth developed in his teaching is provided by a paper written in 1852 by William Dwight Whitney, an American postgraduate student who was studying under Roth at Tubingen; see Whitney, 'On the main results of the later Vedic researches in Germany', *Journal of the American Oriental Society*, III (1853), pp. 289–328.

[2] On the general themes of Hindu cultural nationalism, see Bruce T. McCully, *English Education and the Origins of Indian Nationalism* (New York, 1940: 1966 reprint), pp. 238–69 and 388–91. See also Charles H. Heimsath, *Indian Nationalism and Hindu Social Reform* (Princeton, N.J., 1964), pp. 136–42.

Savarkar, culture was inextricably linked to territory, and he claimed that membership of the Hindu nation depended upon an acceptance of India as both fatherland and holyland. He did not deny that the Indian Muslims, for example, might regard India as their fatherland but he saw them as a people who looked outside India for the sacred places of their religion and who therefore did not regard it as their holyland. In defining Hindu nationality he underlined the importance of *hindutva*, a religious, racial and cultural entity in which Hinduism as a religion formed but part of a whole. Accordingly, he stressed the need for Hindus to transcend their differences and to realize their essential unity.[3]

Initially such theories of Hindu nationalism were bounded by the regional outlooks of their various exponents. Savarkar himself worked within the Maharashtrian tradition, which highlighted the importance of Shivaji and of the later Peshwa kingdom in upholding Hindu culture; the Bengali tradition, strengthened in the first decade of the century by the Swadeshi movement and by the agitation against the partition of the province, rested heavily upon the writings of Aurobindo Ghose and of Bepin Chandra Pal; whereas the Punjabi tradition, largely shaped by the Arya Samaj, had a skilful advocate in Lala Lajpat Rai. However, in the 1920s and 1930s there was an increasing tendency for Hindu nationalists to break loose from their local settings and to address a national audience. The most uncompromising approach, in keeping with Savarkar's appeal to strengthen the organic unity of the whole community of Hindus, dwelt on the related themes of the inspired awakening and of *Hindu sangathan*, the organization of the Hindus.

At this stage, it became possible to imagine that a political organization could take these ideas and convert them into action, and of all the Hindu nationalist groupings of this period the RSS seemed most likely to do this. The first coherent exposition of its doctrine was a book published in 1939 with the title, *We; or, Our Nationhood Defined*, written by Madhav Sadashiv Golwalkar, who was to become the organization's leader in the following year. As Savarkar had done, Golwalkar argued that a nation was the product of a number of factors, including a sense of territory, racial unity, religion, culture and language, but that the factor of special importance was religion:

Our Race-spirit is a child of our Religion and so with us Culture is but a product of our all-comprehensive Religion, a part of its body and not distinguishable from it.[4]

[3] On the term, *hindutva*, see Savarkar, *Essential of Hindutva*, in *Samagra Savarkar Wangmaya: Writings of Swatantrya Veer V.D. Savarkar*, VI, *Hindu Rashtra Darshan* (Poona, 1964), p. 2, and also pp. 53–75.
[4] Golwalkar, *We; or, Our Nationhood Defined* (Nagpur, 1939), p. 22.

Although he disputed the idea that Aryans had migrated to India from some other place, Golwalkar's theory of Indian history corresponded broadly to that which Savarkar had advanced – early unity, fragment-ation, Muslim conquest and a Hindu revival cut short by the imposition of British rule. He claimed that the British had recognized the latent power of Hindu nationalism and had therefore tried to frustrate it; noting that a 'couple of shrewd Englishmen' had 'laid the first stone' of the Congress, he concluded that

The express aim of founding this body was to suppress all National outbursts, likely to dethrone the British power... And to effect it, the amazing theory was propounded that the Nation is composed of all those who, for one reason or the other happen to live at the time in the country.[5]

Golwalkar's central argument was that the servitude of the Hindus stemmed directly from the weakness of their national consciousness and he therefore considered that their main goal should be to regenerate the nation. Pursuit of this goal would inevitably involve the consolidation of Hindu society against all its enemies, the Muslims as well as the British, and the restoration of a sense of nationality. He recommended a firm policy so far as minorities were concerned:

the foreign races in Hindusthan must either adopt the Hindu culture and language, must learn to respect and hold in reverance [sic] Hindu religion, must entertain no idea but those of the glorification of the Hindu race and culture, *i.e.*, of the Hindu nation and must lose their separate existence to merge in the Hindu race, or may stay in the country, wholly subordinated to the Hindu Nation, claiming nothing, deserving no privileges, far less any preferential treatment – not even citizen's rights. There is, at least should be, no other course for them to adopt. We are an old nation; let us deal, as old nations ought to and do deal, with the foreign races, who have chosen to live in our country.[6]

The same judgement informed his attitude to the persecution of the Jews in Nazi Germany:

German race pride has now become the topic of the day. To keep up the purity of the Race and its culture, Germany shocked the world by her purging the country of the semitic Races – the Jews. Race pride at its highest has been manifested here. Germany has also shown how wellnigh impossible it is for Races and cultures, having differences going to the root, to be assimilated into one united whole, a good lesson for us in Hindusthan to learn and profit by.[7]

---

[5] *Ibid.*, p. 59
[6] *Ibid.*, pp. 47–8.
[7] *Ibid.*, p. 35.

Throughout this book, Golwalkar used two themes to convey his political message. On the one hand, he developed the idea that Hindu nationality was a natural expression of Indian culture; on the other he claimed that inspired leaders were capable of rising above the complicated patterns of ordinary politics and offering the people a vision of their true being. The themes of immanency and transcendence were employed in counterpoint, as in the following passage:

Every time our race has been down-trodden, Beings of a super-human order, veritable divinities, have been born in our land and revitalized our Nation. Every event of national regeneration has been preceded by a glorious outburst of spirituality, our indomitable race-spirit, which has always heralded a period of all-round glory.[8]

At the time Golwalkar was writing his book, the ending of British rule was still no more than a remote possibility and communal tension appeared to be increasing rapidly. After partition and the creation of Pakistan, however, his ideas had to be given a new focus to take account of the changed circumstances; in the eyes of the RSS, the conflict between Hindus and Muslims had now become one between states as well as one between communities, and Indian Muslims, regarded as being naturally in sympathy with Pakistan, were seen as a threat to the corporate solidarity of Indian society. This threat, coupled with that posed by the Communists, seemed to the RSS to require a response grounded upon values rather than programmes. Writing to Nehru at the end of 1948 to request the removal of the ban on their organization, four RSS leaders stressed the interdependence of external and internal conflicts:

Our Independence is now only one year old. All round we are beset with people whose past record and present doings in Kashmir and Hyderabad (Deccan) leave no doubt as to their hostile intentions. Within the State we have a number of disruptive forces; the constant danger of Muslims who may turn against the State at any moment and who may be even now suspected of having leanings towards the other Dominion, and the rising tide of Communism invading us from all sides getting ready response from the ignorant workers and gullible youths. The rest of the people are torn by power politics into warring groups. We do not think that the Communists can be beaten by any political or economic programme and propagandas for they can easily mislead the masses by holding out to them promises of a debasing nature. Repression will only give a fillip to the Movement. Rashtriya Swayamsevak Sangh's is the only way to meet the challenge of Communism and its is the only ideology which can harmonise and

[8] *Ibid.*, p. 66.

integrate the interests of different groups and classes and thus successfully avoid any class-war.[9]

In presenting itself as the only force capable of dealing with the problem, the RSS was making the distinguishing claim of Hindu nationalism. Unlike Hindu traditionalists, who merely claimed that the views of the Hindu majority should influence government policies, Hindu nationalists were determined to convert politics from disputes about party programmes into a great battle for the cultural heart of the nation, a battle in which those who believed in the corporate integrity of the Hindu community would be aligned against the forces of Islam on one side and the forces of communism on the other. Such a conception of political reality had more in common with religious revivalism than with party competition; it implied that the people had the capacity not only to respond to an appeal to their basic spiritual values but also to organize themselves as a huge popular rally capable of converting India into a truly Hindu state.

The Hindu nationalist inheritance of the Jana Sangh

Committed to such a view of politics, it was virtually impossible for the RSS to become a political party. Its leaders were drawn to a vision of the future in which an ideal form of Hinduism would be fully and completely expressed and the petty encumbrances of western-style parties and groupings would be swept aside. Yet the Jana Sangh, formed with its blessing, had to make its way in the existing and imperfect politics of an India under Congress rule and endowed with the structure of representative politics. If it was to be a party in the conventional sense, the Jana Sangh had to speak in terms of concrete economic and social policies and to discuss the future as if it were an intelligible extension of the present.

As we shall see, the Jana Sangh tried to effect a compromise: its party manifestos contained unmistakable allusions to the grand themes of Hindu nationalist rhetoric along with dense expositions of concrete

[9] The signatories were Hansraj Gupta (Provincial Sanghchalak, Delhi), Vasantrao Krishna Oke (Provincial Organiser, Delhi), Dharmavir (Provincial Secretary, Punjab) and Narendrajit Sinha (Provincial Sanghchalak, United Provinces). The text of the letter was published in *Organiser*, 23 October 1948, pp. 11–12 and 15, quotation from p. 15. Hyderabad, a princely state with a Muslim ruler and a predominantly Hindu population, had resisted suggestions that it should accede to India. Negotiations regarding this possibility eventually broke down and in September 1948 Indian troops launched a successful invasion of the territory, which was then placed under military rule.

economic, social and foreign policies. It was as though the party was trying to meet two incompatible expectations, one that it would carve out a social base for itself by electoral and parliamentary action within the existing regime and another that it would foster a great Hindu revival and thus entirely transform the structure of the Indian polity. The tension between these two perspectives, the one realistic and the other romantic, is most obvious in the party's early documents, when its leaders were still uncertain how to strike the balance.

The Hindu nationalist message in the party's first election manifesto, approved at its founding convention of October 1951, was contained in a lengthy introductory section, which made frequent use of Sanskrit words, such as *Bharat*, to denote India; *Bharat Varsha*, the land of India; *Bharatiya Rashtra*, the Indian nation; and *Bharatiya*, a member of the Indian nation, an Indian. These terms were probably chosen as substitutes for the less ambiguous equivalents Hindustan, *Hindu rashtra* and Hindu to sustain the Jana Sangh's claim that Indians were Bharatiyas by virtue of their common culture rather than their religion.

If we look more closely at this introductory section, we see that each paragraph was designed to emphasize a basic value within a definite sequence of propositions. The first of these was that the Indian subcontinent was one country, not two, and that partition was therefore an unnatural event:

The whole of Bharat Varsha, from Himalayas to Kanya Kumari, is and has been through the ages a living organic whole, geographically, culturally and historically. She is the mother of all Bharatiyas who all have equal rights. Its recent partition, instead of solving any problem, communal or otherwise, has given rise to many new ones. Culturally, economically, politically, as well as internationally, United India is essential. It is not a communal question at all. The party will work for it through all legitimate means.[10]

This passage led on naturally to the theme that Indians constituted a single nation, and that the full and final realization of this fact would transform not only politics in India but politics within the whole of the divided subcontinent:

Bharat is an ancient nation. Its recently obtained freedom only marks the beginning of a new chapter in her long and chequered history and is not the birth of a new nation. Bharatiya nationalism, therefore, must naturally be based on undivided allegiance to Bharat as a whole and her great and ancient culture which distinguishes her from other lands.[11]

[10] *Manifesto of All India Bharatiya Jana Sangh* [New Delhi, 1951], p. 2.
[11] *Ibid.*

The manifesto assumed that the unity of territory and nation was matched by the unity of culture, but it distinguished between the underlying singularity of form and the diversity of its expression:

Unity in diversity has been the characteristic feature of Bharatiya culture which is a synthesis of different regional, local and tribal growths, natural in such a vast country. It has never been tied to the strings of any particular dogma or creed. All the creeds that form the commonwealth of the Bharatiya Rashtra have their share in the stream of Bharatiya culture which has flown down from the Vedas in an unbroken continuity absorbing and assimilating contributions made by different peoples, creeds and cultures that came in touch with it in the course of history, in such a way as to make them indistinguishable part and parcel of the main current.

The Bharatiya culture is thus one and indivisible. Any talk of composite culture, therefore, is unrealistic, illogical and dangerous for it tends to weaken national unity and encourage fissiparous tendencies.[12]

At this point, the authors of the manifesto turned to the question of whether 'unity in diversity' implied an acceptance of the rights of minorities. They claimed that Bharatiya tradition contained the idea of a state which would ensure fair treatment for the different 'creeds and sections' of society and that a 'theocratic state' (an obvious reference to Pakistan) was not envisaged. However, in attacking the Congress doctrine of secularism they also made clear that tolerance would not be extended to those who regarded themselves as a separate community:

The Bharatiya state drawing inspiration and sustenance from this ancient culture has always been a civil institution, apart from religion, giving equal protection and extending equal patronage to all the different creeds and sections that go to form the Bharatiya society. The very idea of a theocratic state is foreign to Bharat, which has never known anything like 'Khilafat'.

Secularism, as currently interpreted in this country, however, is only a euphemism for the policy of Muslim appeasement. The so-called secular composite nationalism is neither nationalism nor secularism but only a compromise with communalism of those who demand price even for their lip-loyalty to this country.[13]

Finally, the manifesto returned to the theme of cultural regeneration. It declared that the Jana Sangh stood for

the revival of Bharatiya culture and revitalisation of true Bharatiya nationalism on its basis, with such adjustments as may be necessary to make our country truly modern, progressive and strong.[14]

[12] *Ibid.*
[13] *Ibid.*, pp. 2–3
[14] *Ibid.*, p. 3.

The party's main object was declared to be

the rebuilding of Bharat on the basis of Bharatiya 'Sanskriti' [culture] and 'Maryada' [rectitude] and as a political, social, and economic democracy granting equality of opportunity and liberty of individual so as to make her a prosperous, powerful and united nation progressive, modern and enlightened, able to withstand the aggressive designs of others and to pull her weight in the council of nations for the establishment of world peace.[15]

These introductory passages of the manifesto constantly allude to the central historical myths of Hindu nationalism and an audience familiar with the writings and speeches of Savarkar and Golwalkar would have understood the points of reference without any difficulty. Particular phrases touched on the theme of social continuity through time ('Bharat Varsha... is and has been through the ages a living organic whole'); on the essential interdependence of country, nation and culture; on the teleological explanation of spiritual purpose ('the stream of Bharatiya culture which has flown down from the Vedas in an unbroken continuity'); and on the historical conflict between Hinduism and Islam ('Secularism... is only a euphemism for the policy of Muslim appeasement'). As we shall see, the party's intellectuals expanded these themes in their writings; the Hindu nationalist content of the manifesto reflected a deeply felt commitment on the part of the Jana Sangh's founders.

The confinement of Hindu nationalism

Being a political extension of the Brahmanic tradition in Hindu religious thought, Hindu nationalism began from a restricted intellectual base and drew support mainly from upper-caste Hindus, familiar with its background and assured of its implicit acceptance of their status and their privileges. On the other hand, popular Hinduism, which rested mainly on the great devotional sects associated with the gods Vishnu and Shiva, had much stronger and broader roots in society and much greater scope for political expression. The so-called backward or middle castes were much more susceptible to the appeals of popular Hinduism than to those of Brahmanism, and were likely to be drawn to parties and leaders willing to accept the egalitarian and devotional themes of their faith. Gandhi had realized this and had been very successful in using the language and imagery of the *bhakti* movements to build up support for Congress amongst the middle and Harijan castes in the 1920s and 1930s.

Besides being limited by its intellectual origins, Hindu nationalism was also restricted in a geographical sense. Its historical mythology,

[15] *Ibid.*

based on the notion that Hinduism had begun in the north amongst the
original Aryan tribes, was gratifying to upper-caste Hindus in the
regions of old Hindustan and Maharashtra but was much less likely to
appeal to Hindu élites in the south and east. Although both the Jana
Sangh and the RSS were careful not to associate themselves too closely
with any one regional tradition of Hindu nationalism, their documents
and periodicals constantly refer to the coming of the Aryans, the wars of
the Mahabharata in the Punjab *doab*, and northern heroes such as
Shivaji, Maharana Pratap and the Rani of Jhansi. Their myths were a
synthesis of earlier regional myths, but they nevertheless expressed a
northern view of Hindu origins.

From its very inception, then, the Jana Sangh, with its selective theory
of Indian history, found its main audience amongst upper-caste Hindus.
The Congress, on the other hand, with its Gandhian heritage, could
appeal beyond the élites to the great majority of Hindus, whatever their
caste, sect or region. Right from the beginning, therefore, the Jana Sangh
was running a two-fold risk: that of being confined to a limited Hindu
constituency and that of becoming a purely northern party, committed
to the defence of Hindi, to the expression of resentment against Pakistan
and to the removal of the special status allegedly accorded to the Indian
Muslims.

4

The leadership and organization of the Jana Sangh, 1951 to 1967

The central paradox of Indian politics in the 1950s and 1960s is that the party system, although highly differentiated in terms of programmes and doctrines, was unable to organize the mass electorate into clearly defined and separated sectors of social and regional support. With some exceptions, the political parties appeared to float above society, unable to establish a durable and electorally rewarding relationship with the groups whose interests they claimed to represent. Organizational activity, punctuated by membership drives, executive meetings and large plenary sessions, gave an impression of vitality, but behind these outward forms the party structures lacked substance.

Why were so many parties unable to establish secure social bases for themselves? Part of the explanation is that the Congress Party was very successful in its attempts to inhibit the development of opposition; as the governing party, it had unmatched resources for patronage and influence, which it could use to support or undermine local factions, and during the run-up to an election it could operate like a great machine, using its wealth and prestige to ensure that its candidates were well supported and well financed in every region. It tended not to rely on zones of safe seats or on established sitting members, but to campaign everywhere, and to compensate for some inevitable losses by taking seats from opposition incumbents and Independents. The result was a quite exceptional turnover of seats, which made it very difficult for non-Congress parties to anchor themselves in particular regions or localities. The Congress method might not have proved so successful had Indian society, especially in the countryside, responded to party competition by making well-defined claims for particular economic and social benefits but there were few indications that this would happen; the Congress Raj was accepted not only as a political settlement but as the expression of a new economic and social order, exemplified in the various land reforms of the period.

Like other non-Congress parties in the 1950s, the Jana Sangh adapted itself to these circumstances as best it could and experimented with different methods of gaining some purchase in electoral and parliamentary politics. As we shall see, it tried to enter arenas where its Hindu nationalism might have given it an advantage, particularly in controversies about the rights of linguistic, regional and religious minorities; it also attempted to appeal to a number of sectional interests which might have provided it with a coherent social base; and, in elections, it did its best to match the Congress as a vote-gathering machine. Yet throughout the late 1950s and 1960s it was handicapped, firstly by the suspicion that it was closely tied to, if not dependent upon, the RSS hierarchy and its organizational headquarters at Nagpur, secondly by its reputation for being an extremist body, with intolerant views on relations between Hindus and other religious communities, and, thirdly, by the inexperience and relative obscurity of its leadership.

Could these deficiencies have been overcome? The answer must be in the affirmative: Mookerjee had shown that it was possible to make use of RSS support while retaining freedom of manoeuvre and that adherence to Hindu traditions did not exclude parallel appeals to liberal principles. A sufficiently determined leadership could have built a credible and respected party on the foundations which he had laid. A second question then arises: had the Jana Sangh followed such a course, would it have attracted sufficient support to become a major party in opposition? To frame an answer, we must judge whether Nehru did indeed take a serious political risk when he changed the orientation of his party in the course of the 1950s, first, by attempting to erect a fence between the Congress and the Hindu traditionalists, then, by moving industrial policies in the direction of greater state control and regulation and, finally, by proclaiming, at the Nagpur session of the Congress in January 1959, that the time had come to introduce co-operative joint farming as the next step in land reform. Each of these adjustments of policy represented a challenge not only to specific and privileged interest groups but also to broad layers of the people who, as Hindus, had reason to fear the ruling party's increased emphasis on secularism and pluralism, or who, as owners of small landholdings or small businesses, had reason to resist the steady extension of the power of the state within the economic order. The Jana Sangh had opposed both secularism and collectivism, but it was quite unable to pull together those interests which stood to lose from the application of the Congress Party's economic policies, partly because it lacked the skill and means to express its economic liberalism in effective language and partly because its audience suspected it of being more concerned with its cultural than with its economic objectives.

Mookerjee could well have overcome this lack of credibility. His upbringing and education had given him an innate sense of the kinds of policies which were acceptable to the middle classes, those relatively affluent, well-educated and English-speaking groups which dominated the professional, commercial and industrial life of India's modern towns and cities. These groups constituted the social and cultural élite, the true inheritors of the social values of the British Raj and the basic court of opinion in the new Republic; generally liberal in outlook, they were likely to react against any attempt by the government to increase the functions of the state at the expense of civil and political liberties. It was to them that Mookerjee was appealing when he suggested, during the campaign for the 1952 elections, that 'one-party rule' was 'tending towards malevolent dictatorship'.[1] Whereas Nehru was inclined to the view that the Congress Party alone could be trusted to uphold the regime and protect its nationalist heritage, Mookerjee stressed the need for a constitutional opposition which could offer the basis for an alternative government within the liberal and democratic tradition. However, in this respect he could not rely on the support of the young RSS workers whom he had attracted to the Jana Sangh; they lacked his affinity with the middle classes and were disposed to scorn their anglicized culture and outlook. These young *pracharaks* from the RSS were puritans, anxious to intensify the party's commitment to Hindu nationalism in the belief that this was the means of producing a new social élite which would be Hindi-speaking, austere, disciplined and traditional. This difference in perspective was also a difference about timing; Mookerjee wanted to challenge Congress rule without delay, and he apparently believed that middle-class liberalism was compatible with Hindu traditionalism, if not with Hindu nationalism, but the young men of the RSS acted as though they were a brotherhood building for some future time, in which a new élite, imbued with Hindu values, would sweep aside that which had been formed under the Raj.

The fact that there were these contrasting views about the political role of the middle classes explains differences in approach to the tasks of party-building and organization. Mookerjee was evidently trying to establish the kind of party in which lengthy and discursive plenary sessions could provide some checks on centralized and reasonably accessible executive bodies, such as the working committees of the old-style Congress; this was the type of arrangement which most politically conscious Indians found congenial and could trust. For their part, the young *pracharaks* placed most emphasis on discipline and therefore on the need for a system of overriding controls behind any ostensibly open

---

[1] *Times of India* (Delhi), 4 October 1951, p. 5.

party apparatus; they also favoured hierarchy and a strict regulation of discussion.

These approaches were ultimately irreconcilable, but during Mookerjee's lifetime there was no serious conflict, mainly because the levels of activity in the party were not sufficiently integrated to reveal serious differences of attitude or practice. Mookerjee was mainly concerned with national politics, and his handling of the party's first two all-India conferences gave people the strong impression that he wanted the organization to be open and responsive and that he was capable of shaping his young RSS lieutenants into a restricted and subordinate bureaucracy. However, in the states and districts the organization was firmly in the hands of RSS men and the strength and durability of their networks of supporters gave them an important advantage over rival groupings within the party.

This chapter will examine the succession crisis set in motion by Mookerjee's death and show how the young *pracharaks*, led by Deendayal Upadhyaya, managed to establish their ascendancy. It will then describe how the new leadership organized and controlled the party in the late 1950s and early 1960s and will conclude with a discussion of the circumstances which produced strains and tensions within the top echelons of the party in the years leading up to the fourth general elections of 1967.

The succession crisis of 1954

Let us return to the proposition that Mookerjee's death in June 1953 deprived the Jana Sangh of the one man who might have built up a solid non-Congress coalition with some prospects of power. He belonged to the top rank of Bengali society. His father, Ashutosh Mookerjee, was a judge of the Calcutta High Court from 1904 until just before his death in 1924, and served for a long period as Vice-Chancellor of Calcutta University. Born on 6 July 1901, Mookerjee was educated at the University's Presidency College, taking first an arts and then a law degree, and after his father's death went to London, where he studied at Lincoln's Inn and was called to the Bar in 1927. On his return to India, he was elected to the Bengal Legislative Council in 1929 as a Congress candidate and again in 1931 as an Independent. Although he was Vice-Chancellor of Calcutta University between 1934 and 1938, he inclined towards a career in politics; he was elected to the Bengal Legislative Assembly in 1937 and joined the Hindu Mahasabha in 1938. In December 1941 he accepted the post of Finance Minister in the provincial government formed in Bengal by Fazl-ul Huq, but resigned on 21 November 1942. He later became Working President of the All-India Hindu Mahasabha and succeeded Savarkar as full President at the end of 1944. In national politics his moderation and obvious ability soon attracted widespread support outside his own party and after independence he was appointed to the central government as Minister of Industries and Supplies. In this office he proved himself to be a very able administrator and became a prominent public figure in his own right, so that his resignation from the Cabinet in April 1950 attracted a great deal of interest and speculation.[2] Even after the formation of the Jana Sangh the national press continued to treat his public statements with considerable respect, as if he rather than the new party were the true source of its ideas and programmes. His own personal following was extensive, both in West Bengal and in northern India, and he would have had no difficulty in calling upon outside support had he been challenged within the Jana Sangh by RSS elements.

His nominal successor as leader of the Jana Sangh, Mauli Chandra Sharma, came from a very different background and faced great difficulty in asserting himself in the internal struggle for control of the party.[3] His father, Din Dayal Sharma, had been a Sanskrit scholar and a believer in the orthodox Sanatana Dharma (eternal religion) movement. He had moved from the Rohtak area of the Punjab to Delhi early in the century, and it was there that Mauli Chandra had grown up; he attended Hindu College and went on to study law, but gave that up in 1923 to concentrate on political activity. He attended the Round Table Conference in London in 1930 and 1931 as a member of the Indian States

---

[2] For details of Mookerjee's early life, see Balraj Madhok, *Dr. Syama Prasad Mookerjee: A Biography* (New Delhi, n.d.), pp. 2–8; Umaprasad Mookerjee (ed.), *Syamaprasad Mookerjee: His Death in Detention: A Case for Enquiry* (Calcutta, July 1953), pp. 78–80; Walter Andersen, 'The Rashtriya Swayamsevak Sangh – III: Participation in politics', *Economic and Political Weekly* (Bombay), VII, 13 (25 March 1972), pp. 678–9. See also letter from Mookerjee to Sir John Herbert, Governor of Bengal, 16 November 1942, in *India Unreconciled: A Documented History of Indian Political Events from the Crisis of August 1942 to February 1944* (New Delhi, second edition, 1944), pp. 100–7.

[3] For the details of this crisis see contemporary press statements (e.g. those by Mauli Chandra Sharma himself in the *Statesman* (Delhi), 4 November 1954, pp. 1 and 12; 8 November 1954, p. 1), speeches made by Sharma's sympathizers when the National Democratic Front was formed in 1956 (the preliminary conference was held in Delhi on 2–3 June and the founding conference on 2–3 September) and references to the events of 1954 made in 1973, when Balraj Madhok left the party (see in particular Manga Ram Varshney, *Jana Sangh – R.S.S. and Balraj Madhok* (Aligarh, n.d.)). See also Craig Baxter, *The Jana Sangh: A Biography of an Indian Political Party* (Philadelphia, 1969), pp. 133–6; Sisir Gupta, 'Parties between the elections', in S.L. Poplai (ed.), *National Politics and 1957 Elections in India* (Delhi, 1957), p. 37; and H.T. Davey, 'The transformation of an ideological movement into an aggregative party: a case study of the Bharatiya Jana Sangh' (unpublished D.Phil. dissertation, University of California, Los Angeles, 1969), pp. 169–75.

delegation, and later succeeded K. M. Panikkar as Secretary to the Chancellor of the Chamber of Princes.[4] After 1947 he was active in the politics of Delhi and the surrounding region, and had connections with the local RSS hierarchy, but he was relatively unknown in other parts of India. He took an active part in forming the 'greater Punjab' unit of the Jana Sangh and, as we have seen, was chosen by Mookerjee as one of the first two General Secretaries of the national party, but now that his patron was no longer there to help him he had to fall back upon his local resources. As the party's Acting President, he could certainly assume that he would have strong backing from the Jana Sangh's Delhi unit and that he could count on the loyalty of Guru Dutt Vaidya and Kunwar Lal Gupta, President and Secretary respectively of that body. In addition, he had close ties with Vasantrao Krishna Oke, the former chief organizer of the Delhi provincial branch of the RSS. However, these constituted an extremely limited set of connections compared to those which were available to his rivals in the competition for power which was about to begin.

Unless he could obtain the support of the RSS hierarchy Sharma stood little chance of being accepted as Mookerjee's successor. By the early 1950s this organization was as well established in northern India as it was in Maharashtra, and the discipline and loyalty of its cadres enabled its central headquarters in Nagpur to retain effective control over its local units. The young workers which its leadership had sent to help Mookerjee to build up the Jana Sangh now constituted not only the backbone of its administrative hierarchy but also the means by which the national leadership of the RSS could influence its internal affairs. Sharma, who was acutely aware of the differences of age and outlook which separated him from these RSS organizers, said in an interview recorded in 1974 that Mookerjee had also been aware of the exclusiveness of the RSS element in the party and of the difficulty of bringing it into full accord with the ideals of the Jana Sangh.[5] A similar claim had been made by another early leader of the party, Keshav Dev Verma, who declared in 1956 that the RSS wing had tried to keep him and Vasantrao Krishna Oke from being appointed to the Central Working Committee in December 1952, at the time of the first plenary session at Kanpur; complaining that the RSS leadership had tried to dominate the party

[4] For biographical details, see *Organiser* (Delhi), 4 June 1951, p. 8; 1 February 1954, p. 9.
[5] Oral History Transcript in Hindi of an interview with Mauli Chandra Sharma on 17 July 1974 by Hari Dev Sharma (Nehru Memorial Library, New Delhi, Accession No. 327), p. 196 (hereafter referred to as 'Sharma interview (1974)'). I should like to thank Mrs Usha Prasad of the Oral History Department of the Nehru Memorial Library for discussing the relevant section of this transcript with me.

from its birth, he said that Mookerjee had been 'well aware of this attempt on the part of the R.S.S. leaders to dominate the Jana Sangh'.[6]

The principal figure amongst the RSS organizers within the party was Deendayal Upadhyaya, who had helped to establish the Jana Sangh's unit in Uttar Pradesh and had served as its first general secretary. Born on 25 September 1916 in a village in Rajputana and orphaned by the time he was seven, he was cared for by a maternal uncle, who provided for his secondary education. In 1937 he attended the Sanatana Dharma College at Kanpur; there he joined the RSS and, having obtained his BA degree in 1939, later went to Agra to read for an MA. Subsequently he studied at Allahabad but became increasingly involved in RSS work: in 1942 he was appointed to be a full-time tahsil organizer in Lakhimpur district, north-western Oudh; in 1945 he was made joint provincial organizer for the whole of the United Provinces; and in 1947 he established a publishing concern in Lucknow, the Rashtra Dharma Prakashan, which issued the Hindi journals *Rashtra Dharma* (monthly), *Panchajanya* (weekly) and *Swadesh* (daily).[7] Other important organizers from the RSS were Sundar Singh Bhandari in Rajasthan, Kushabhau Thakre in Madhya Bharat, Jagannathrao Joshi in the Karnataka region, and Kunj Bihari Lal Rathi and Nana Deshmukh, who were with Upadhyaya in Uttar Pradesh.

Sharma found his position weak even within the party's central office. Under Mookerjee's presidency there had been two general secretaries, the first pair being Sharma and Bhai Mahavir (a young RSS organizer who was also the son of Bhai Parmananda, the Arya Samaj and Hindu Mahasabha leader of the inter-war period). After the Kanpur session of December 1952, however, Upadhyaya was brought from Uttar Pradesh to replace Mahavir, and when Sharma became Acting President following Mookerjee's death, Upadhyaya was left as the one and only General Secretary, steadily building up the authority and scope of that office. As Acting President, Sharma was not in a good position to assert himself. There was always the danger that a well-known figure outside the party might be invited to take his place, a possibility which was apparently explored in the autumn of 1953 when discussions were held about the feasibility of bringing together the Jana Sangh, the Hindu Mahasabha and the Ram Rajya Parishad to form a single party.

[6] *Times of India* (Delhi), 3 June 1956.
[7] See Sudhakar Raje (ed.), *Pt. Deendayal Upadhyaya: A Profile* (New Delhi, 1972), pp. 1–14; Upadhyaya, *Political Diary* (Bombay, 1968), pp. xi–xiv; *Organiser*, 10 December 1967, p. 3; and *The Times of India Directory and Year Book including Who's Who 1958–59* (Bombay), p. 1239. See also *Organiser*, August 1956 (special issue), p. 26; 25 February 1968, p. 3 (article by Bhaurao Deoras); 31 March 1968, p.5 (article by Sri Chand Goel).

According to one authority, many of the Jana Sangh's leaders told N.C. Chatterjee, the President of the Mahasabha, that in the event of a merger he would become the leader of a united party, and he is said to have rejected an informal proposal that he should become President of the Jana Sangh even if a merger were not achieved.[8] In December 1953, however, the negotiations for a merger were broken off after the Working Committee of the Mahasabha had objected to a statement in which Sharma had described their organization as a 'communal body'.[9]

Although he was by no means an ideal champion for the principle that the Jana Sangh should become an open party with essentially democratic methods of operation, Sharma was identified with that position whereas the RSS and its supporters within the party stood for closure, secrecy and discipline. The first confrontation between the two sides occurred behind the scenes at the time of the party's second plenary session at Bombay in January 1954, which offered Sharma his first opportunity to win the full presidency of the party and influence the crucial appointments to its Central Working Committee. His nomination was supported by the state working committees of Uttar Pradesh, Delhi, Vindhya Pradesh and West Bengal but a candidate favoured by the RSS, Umashankar Mulshankar Trivedi, the party's Treasurer, was put forward by the working committees of Rajasthan, Madhya Bharat (his home state), Madhya Pradesh and PEPSU.[10] Sharma then came under pressure to withdraw his candidature; he revealed much later that Upadhyaya had met him on a train journey and had urged him to issue a statement announcing that he was unwilling to accept the presidency. Knowing that Upadhyaya was Golwalkar's 'right hand', Sharma realized that he was out of favour with the RSS but nevertheless refused to stand down.[11] Other accounts also mention the RSS preference for Trivedi, but he himself evidently took the view that Sharma was entitled to at least one complete year as president[12] and in the end he withdrew his nomination, thus allowing Sharma to be elected unopposed. According to Keshav Dev Verma, Sharma was told when he arrived in

---

[8] Myron Weiner, *Party Politics in India: The Development of a Multi-Party System* (Princeton, 1957), p. 217.

[9] *Ibid.*, pp. 199–222. See also Walter K. Andersen and Shridhar D. Damle, *The Brotherhood in Saffron: The Rashtriya Swayamsevak Sangh and Hindu Revivalism* (Boulder and London, 1987), p. 160; resolutions of the Central General Council, Allahabad, 15 August 1953, and of the Central Working Committee, Delhi, 20 December 1953, Bharatiya Jana Sangh, *Party Documents* (New Delhi, 1973), V, pp. 112–4 (hereafter referred to as *BJS Documents*); *Statesman* (Delhi), 7 December 1953, pp. 1 and 7; and Balraj Madhok, *Political Trends in India* (Delhi, 1959), p. 99.

[10] *Organiser*, 25 January 1954, p. 1.

[11] Sharma interview (1974), pp. 220–2.

[12] Varshney, *Jana Sangh – R.S.S. and Balraj Madhok*, pp. 10–11.

Bombay for the plenary session that the RSS headquarters at Nagpur had decided in favour of another person for the presidency, but when some party leaders threatened to take the matter to the open meeting of delegates his appointment was secured.[13]

During the Bombay session, which lasted from 24 to 26 January 1954, Sharma soon found himself in conflict with the RSS element in the party over the choice of the thirty or so members of the new Central Working Committee. His intention had been to appoint between five and seven members whom he personally favoured and to take advice about the remainder, but the RSS leaders gave him a complete list of thirty names produced after consultation amongst themselves. Taken aback at the peremptory way in which this had been done, he objected to being treated merely as a mouthpiece and, specifically, to the omission of Vasantrao Krishna Oke's name from the list. He therefore proposed that the members of the Working Committee should be elected by the delegates who constituted the Central General Council, whereupon the RSS, faced with the unpredictability of such an election, gave way and acknowledged the right of the president to issue the list. Sharma added the name of Vasantrao Krishna Oke and made some other changes before announcing the composition of the new committee,[14] whose membership was as follows:[15]

President: Mauli Chandra Sharma (Delhi)
General Secretary: Deendayal Upadhyaya (Uttar Pradesh)
Treasurer: Umashankar Mulshankar Trivedi (Madhya Bharat)
Ordinary Members:
Shivkumar Dwivedi (Bihar)
Acharya Ram Dev (Punjab)
Raj Kumar Shrivastava (Uttar Pradesh)
Deva Prasad Ghosh (West Bengal)
Guru Dutt Vaidya (Delhi)
Keshari Lal Goel (Madhya Bharat)
Raj Kishore Shukla (Vindhya Pradesh)
Narayanlal Bansilal Pitti (Bombay)

---

[13] *Statesman* (Delhi), 3 June 1956, p. 4.
[14] Sharma interview (1974), pp. 222–4. Cf. the account of an interview with Sharma on 8 July 1974 in Geeta Puri, *Bharatiya Jana Sangh, Organisation and Ideology, Delhi: a Case Study* (New Delhi, 1980), p. 48, and the discussion of this episode, especially regarding the consequences of Sharma's choice of Vasantrao Krishna Oke, in Andersen and Damle, *Brotherhood in Saffron*, pp. 161–2. See also the speech by Keshav Dev Verma to the preliminary conference of the National Democratic Front (*Times of India* (Delhi), 3 June 1956), and Varshney, *Jana Sangh – R.S.S. and Balraj Madhok*, p. 11.
[15] *Organiser*, 8 February 1954, p. 2.

Sardar Chettan Singh (PEPSU)
Bapu Saheb Sohni (Madhya Pradesh)
Ram Narain Shastri (Madhya Bharat)
Bhai Mahavir (Delhi)
Vasantrao Krishna Oke (Delhi)
Nana Deshmukh (Uttar Pradesh)
Atal Bihari Vajpayee (Uttar Pradesh)
Man Singh Verma (Uttar Pradesh)
Balraj Madhok (New Delhi)
Tarakant Jha (Bihar)
Bhairon Singh Shekhawat (Rajasthan)
Sundar Singh Bhandari (Rajasthan)
Hari Prasad Pandya (Gujarat)
Hari Singh Gohil (Saurashtra)
Ramchandra Kashinath Mhalgi (Maharashtra)
Jagannathrao Joshi (Karnataka)
J.S. Ramchandramurthi (Andhra Pradesh)
Amarnath Bajaj (Delhi)

As it stood, the committee contained a significant group of young RSS recruits, built around men such as Deendayal Upadhyaya, Nana Deshmukh, Atal Bihari Vajpayee, Sundar Singh Bhandari and Jagannathrao Joshi, and, in spite of Sharma's brave stand, all the signs point to the effectiveness of the constraints placed upon him by the RSS in the choice of members.

Sharma also came under pressure from the RSS over party funds. By his account, the party was still based largely on a few towns and it was his aim to place a paid party worker in every district throughout the country. His intention was to raise between Rs 1,000,000 and Rs 1,500,000 for this purpose and to ensure that the party had its own sources of finance, but the RSS leaders, allegedly concerned to keep the Jana Sangh financially dependent on their organization, pressed him to rely on it for funds.[16]

By this stage the conflict had spread to issues of policy and these were taken up at a meeting of the party's Central General Council at Indore on 21–23 August. Sharma was unable to attend because his wife was ill, but he prepared an address which was read to the delegates in his absence. In it he warned 'that they must guard against being deflected from the two basic principles of the Jana Sangh as laid down in its constitution, namely, "secular nationalism and unflinching faith in democracy"', and he went so far as to express approval of certain aspects

---

[16] Sharma interview (1974), pp. 224–5.

of the Nehru government's domestic and foreign policies.[17] Organizational issues were also raised, and one of the secretaries of the Punjab
unit brought forward a resolution condemning the interference of the
RSS in the party's affairs, with the result that it was agreed that a further
session of the council should be held to discuss the matter in greater
detail.[18]

In his 1974 interview, Sharma recalled the fuss which his presidential
speech had caused at the Indore session and the accusation that he had
been too uncritical of the government. At a chance meeting with
Golwalkar in Delhi shortly afterwards, he had tried to clear the air, but
found Golwalkar very reserved. Aware that the RSS element within the
party was not well disposed towards him, he discussed with Eknath
Ranade, a prominent RSS leader, the possibility of resigning, but Ranade
advised him to bear with things for the remaining two or three months of
his term of office.[19] When Sharma pressed for a further session of the
Central General Council to be held on the weekend of 6–7 November
to discuss the issue of RSS interference, Upadhyaya insisted that the
matter be referred to a meeting of the Central Working Committee
which had been set for 7–8 November. He justified his action on the
grounds that the dates suggested by Sharma would conflict with those of
various provincial conferences, and that the right to convene a meeting
of the Central General Council belonged constitutionally not to the
President but to the Working Committee.[20] Sharma's response was to

[17] Statement by Sharma, *Statesman* (Delhi), 4 November 1954, p. 12. See also Sharma
interview (1974), p. 225.
[18] According to Sharma, *Statesman* (Delhi), 8 November 1954, p. 1.
[19] Sharma interview (1974), pp. 225–7.
[20] There are minor differences between the various accounts of why a second meeting of
the Central General Council was not held and why the request to call one was referred
to the Central Working Committee. In his statement of 3 November, Sharma said that
Upadhyaya had agreed to call a Central General Council meeting on 6–7 November;
that the office had been ordered to issue the notice; and that, apparently, 'after
consultation with the powers which control their decisions', Upadhyaya had refused to
call the session (*Statesman* (Delhi), 4 November 1954, p. 12). Upadhyaya's statement
acknowledged that Sharma had requested a meeting of the Central General Council,
but he justified referring the request to the Central Working Committee meeting on the
grounds already cited (*Organiser*, 8 November 1954, p. 3; see also *Statesman* (Delhi), 5
November 1954, p. 1). In an interview on 7 November, Sharma is reported to have said
that he tried to persuade the Working Committee to call a session of the Central
Council but that the committee, 'dominated by RSS elements, refused to do so despite
my repeated reminders' (*ibid.*, 8 November 1954, p. 1). However, I have found no
reference to a formal meeting of the Central Working Committee between that which
preceded the meeting of the Central General Council in August and that of 7–8
November; Sharma was probably using the term 'working committee' to refer to those
members of the committee who kept in touch with each other between formal meetings,
and thus constituted an informal executive group.

resign, not only as President but also as a member of the party, and on 3 November he issued the following statement:

Acute differences of opinion on the question of interference by the RSS in its affairs of the Jana Sangh have been growing for over a year. Many RSS workers have entered the party since its inception. They were welcomed, as RSS leaders had publically declared that it was a purely cultural body having nothing to do with politics and that its members were perfectly free to join any political party. In practice, however, it did not prove to be so[.]

The late Dr Mookerjee was often seriously perturbed by the demands of RSS leaders for a decisive role in matters like the appointment of office-bearers, nomination of candidates for elections and matters of policy. We however hoped that the rank and file of the RSS would be drawn out into the arena of democratic public life through their association with the Jana Sangh.

A vigorous and calculated drive was launched to turn the Jana Sangh into a convenient handle of the RSS. Orders were issued from their headquarters through their emissaries and the Jana Sangh was expected to carry them out. Many workers and groups all over the country resented this and the Delhi State Jana Sangh as a body refused to comply.[21]

Sharma probably hoped that his resignation, and his revelations about the influence of the RSS, would rally those in the party who favoured open and democratic practices within the organization. The crucial test came in Delhi, where, on 4 November, the President of the party's local unit, Guru Dutt Vaidya, offered to resign his office as well. He claimed that a special emissary from the RSS high command in Nagpur had tried to secure the removal of the executive of his unit and to have it replaced by another consisting of 'persons nominated by the R.S.S. authorities'.[22] However, a group of Sharma's supporters met on 5 November and decided to remain within the party for the time being, and the Jana Sangh members of the Delhi Municipal Committee gave the assurance 'that we, remaining loyal to the organisation and its ideals, will not fail to fulfil the confidence reposed in us as Jana Sangh nominees'.[23]

Sharma said after the event that he had hoped that the Central Working Committee 'would be compelled to call a session of the Pratinidhi Sabha [General Council] when I resigned, as it alone could constitutionally accept my resignation'.[24] As it was, when the committee

---

[21] Statement by Sharma in *Statesman* (Delhi), 4 November 1954, pp. 1 and 12. He had told a reporter on 1 November that he was considering resignation (*ibid.*, 2 November 1954, pp. 1 and 7).

[22] *Times of India* (Delhi), 5 November 1954, pp. 1 and 7; *Statesman* (Delhi), 5 November 1954, p. 1.

[23] *Times of India* (Delhi), 6 November 1954, p. 3.

[24] *Statesman* (Delhi), 8 November 1954, p. 1.

met on 7 November it simply accepted his resignation and appointed Bapu Saheb Sohni, a lawyer from Berar with an RSS background, to serve as Acting President.[25] Two secretaries of the Punjab unit, who complained that the committee did not have the right to accept the resignation of the President, demanded an emergency session of the General Council,[26] but without success. For its part, the Working Committee condemned what it described as Sharma's attempt 'to abuse the Jana Sangh forum to try to run down the RSS' and questioned his motives for resigning, claiming that his action was 'undemocratic and unfair to the members of this committee who have not been given the opportunity to discuss the reasons that have impelled him to resign'.[27] It went on to imply that it was Sharma himself who was the offender:

As a democratic organisation it [the Jana Sangh] refuses to suffer dictation even from its president... The Committee assures the people of Bharat that Jana Sangh has come into being under the inspiration of the real democrat and nationalist, Dr. Mookerji and will ever function as a dynamic democratic party to serve the Sovereign Democratic Republic of Bharat.[28]

The Working Committee also took steps to deal with the Delhi unit, and appointed a three-member subcommittee to prepare a report on its affairs.[29] In a show of defiance, the State General Council of the Delhi unit met on 13 and 14 November and requested its president to withdraw his resignation,[30] but it soon became clear that this was the only significant centre of resistance; although there had been reports of dissent in other northern units at the beginning of the month,[31] everything soon returned to normal. The choice of a new President was proceeding smoothly. Prem Nath Dogra, President of the Praja Parishad of Jammu and Kashmir, became a candidate for the office following the affiliation of his party with the Jana Sangh on the 7th and he was eventually elected unopposed.[32] He presided over the Jana

[25] *Organiser*, 15 November 1954, p. 3; *Statesman* (Delhi), 8 November 1954, pp. 1 and 10.

[26] *Times of India* (Delhi), 9 November 1954, p. 3.

[27] *Statesman* (Delhi), 8 November 1954, pp. 1 and 10.

[28] Cited by Jagdish Prasad Mathur, 'The Jana Sangh marches ahead', *Organiser*, 26 January 1962, p. 26. This resolution is not given in *BJS Documents*.

[29] *Times of India* (Delhi), 10 November 1954, p. 3. The subcommittee consisted of Raj Kumar Shrivastava, Raj Kishore Shukla and Atal Bihari Vajpayee.

[30] *Ibid.*, 15 November 1954, p. 9.

[31] See *ibid.*, 6 November 1954, p. 3; *Statesman* (Delhi), 2 November 1954, p. 1; 7 November 1954, p. 1. A Vice-President of the Uttar Pradesh Jana Sangh, Pandit Shiv Dayalu of Meerut, had resigned at the end of October, complaining of the interference of RSS leaders in the working of the party (*Leader* (Allahabad), 29 October 1954, p. 7).

[32] *Statesman* (Delhi), 28 November 1954, p. 9. On the nominations, see *Times of India* (Delhi), 18 November 1954, p. 3; *Statesman* (Delhi), 11 November 1954, p. 1; 19 November 1954, p. 11.

Sangh's third plenary session at Jodhpur (30 December 1954 to 1 January 1955) and chose a Central Working Committee which included 23 of the 29 retiring members,[33] an indication of how little support Sharma had enjoyed amongst the members of his executive. Finally, on 3 January 1955, the Central Working Committee accepted the report of its subcommittee and dissolved the party's Delhi unit, which then came under the control of the central organization pending the formation of new local committees.[34]

Some of those who left the Jana Sangh at this time attended the conference in June 1956 which decided to form the National Democratic Front (NDF). Sharma, who had by then joined the Congress Party and had served as a member of the Official Language Commission, nevertheless attended the meeting and told the delegates that he had left the Jana Sangh for two reasons:

> The first was that contrary to the high ideals with which the party was started, communal feeling was gradually introduced into it by the Rashtriya Swayam Sevak Sangh. Secondly, he said, like the Nazis in Germany the RSS was gradually working its way into the political arena through the Jana Sangh.[35]

At this gathering and at the subsequent founding conference of the NDF in September 1956, the RSS was accused of having interfered in the affairs of the Jana Sangh by Vasantrao Krishna Oke, Keshav Dev Verma and others.[36] Oke became President of the NDF, but the organization broke up during the 1957 election campaign, when he actually rejoined the Jana Sangh while Keshav Dev Verma and others went over to the Congress.[37]

The rhetoric of the NDF played upon the idea that the RSS had been

[33] According to the table of the memberships of the Central Working Committee given in Appendix I to Baxter, *The Jana Sangh,* pp. 317–18.

[34] *Statesman* (Delhi), 5 January 1955, p. 1; *Times of India* (Delhi), 5 January 1955, p. 3; *Organiser,* 10 January 1955, p. 4.

[35] *Statesman* (Delhi), 4 June 1956, p. 3. See also his earlier speech at Meerut on 6 March (*ibid.,* 9 March 1956, p. 9).

[36] On the conference of June 1956 see *ibid.,* 3 June 1956, p. 4; 4 June 1956, p. 3; *Times of India* (Delhi), 3 June 1956; 4 June 1956, p. 3; *Hindustan Times* (Delhi), 3 June 1956; 4 June 1956. On the September conference see *Statesman* (Delhi), 4 September 1956, p. 3; *Times of India* (Delhi), 4 September 1956, p. 3; 5 September 1956, p. 3; *Hindustan Times,* 5 September 1956, p. 3.

   Accusations of undue RSS influence on the Jana Sangh were made by another group of defectors from the Jana Sangh in 1961 (see *Link* (Delhi), 6 August 1961, p. 13).

[37] On the breaking up of the NDF see *Hindustan Times,* 4 February 1957, p. 3; 19 February 1957, p. 5; *Times of India* (Delhi), 4 February 1957, p. 7; 19 February 1957, p. 2; 24 February 1957, pp. 1 and 11. In October 1959 Vasantrao Krishna Oke was one of the general secretaries of an *ad hoc* committee set up to work for the newly formed Swatantra Party in Delhi (*Swarajya* (Madras), IV, 15 (17 October 1959), p. 4).

manipulating the Jana Sangh for its own ends, but there was more to the succession crisis of 1954 than a simple clash between pro- and anti-RSS factions. For one thing, Sharma and his supporters were in sympathy with the basic aims of the RSS and Sharma himself, as he was to make clear in his 1974 interview, greatly admired the work which the RSS claimed to be doing to strengthen the Hindu community and to promote *hindutva*. His main concern had been to avoid domination; while he appreciated what the RSS workers had done for the Jana Sangh, he felt that if the party were to grow and spread it had to be open to other influences as well.[38] The essential clash in 1954 was between the young RSS organizers, intent upon making the Jana Sangh more centralized and more disciplined, and Sharma's relatively weak group of secondary leaders, trying ineffectually to defend what remained of Mookerjee's project for an open and democratic party. Sharma's various initiatives indicated an intention to extend the executive range of the presidency, especially in the field of party finance and policy-making, to influence the composition of the core-group on the Central Working Committee, and to use the Central General Council as the main sounding board; on the other hand, the Nagpur-based RSS executive appears to have favoured a restricted role for the presidency and more powers for the principal secretaries and organizers within the Jana Sangh's hierarchy, with the Central Working Committee, the Central General Council and the annual plenary session performing a rallying and confirming function where policy matters were concerned. Allied to this disagreement about means there was a much more important disagreement about ends: Sharma, albeit less effectively, did personify the outlook which Mookerjee had represented, an outlook which assumed that the Congress could be challenged by a party which was open and accessible to middle-class politicians and which was willing to combine a controlled form of Hindu nationalism with economic and social liberalism; the RSS hierarchy, on the other hand, held the belief that the party's best chance for power lay in the distant rather than the immediate future, and that priority must be given to assembling and integrating a younger leadership which could represent an emerging middle class educated in Hindi rather than English, and traditional rather than western in its social customs and beliefs.

Under Mookerjee's leadership, the Jana Sangh had remained in touch with the main currents of liberal opinion, but henceforward it would be much more closely identified with the severe Hindu nationalism of the RSS. In the process, it would become more defensive, more provincial

[38] Sharma interview (1974), pp. 219–20.

and more responsive to the attitudes of the lower middle classes of the northern towns and cities.

The central leadership of the Jana Sangh 1955–62

Within a few months of Sharma's resignation, it became clear that the power relations within the leadership hierarchy of the Jana Sangh had settled into a new pattern. Under Upadhyaya, who quickly established himself as the figure of most consequence at the central level, the post of General Secretary became much more important than that of President, while in terms of institutions, the Central Working Committee became stronger in relation to the Central General Council and, at the informal level, the network of RSS workers was built more firmly than before into the structure of the party. As a result, the lines of communication and command now passed without a break through a chain of full-time organizing secretaries, who worked with the same self-discipline as their counterparts within the RSS itself. On the other hand, the party's state and national presidents were expected to accept limited and largely honorific roles, and Jana Sangh members of the central parliament and state legislatures were firmly controlled by the party organization.

Upadhyaya proved to be an astute and capable administrator. He took an increasing interest in the discussion of policy and party doctrine, and toured widely within India, thereby acquiring a detailed knowledge of the party's various state units. He became, in effect, the party's principal spokesman, and thus assumed a role which had earlier been exercised first by Mookerjee and later by Sharma as party President. The need for support was obvious: it would not have been possible for Upadhyaya to remain both a *de facto* head of the party and a General Secretary, and he therefore appointed two assistant secretaries to help him. Of these, Atal Bihari Vajpayee came from Uttar Pradesh and was well placed to cover the party's northern units, while Jagannathrao Joshi, from Mysore, took responsibility for the southern units. Vajpayee, who was born in Gwalior in 1926, had been educated at Victoria College, Gwalior, and at the DAV College, Kanpur, and had joined the RSS in 1941. At various times he had been editor of the journals published by Rashtra Dharma Prakashan, with which Upadhyaya had also been associated, and he had become Mookerjee's private secretary in 1953.[39]

---

[39] For biographies, see *Organiser*, August 1956 (special issue), p. 28; S.S. Bhandari (ed.), *Jana Sangh Souvenir: A Publication Brought out on the Occasion of the 15th Annual Session of Bharatiya Jana Sangh, Bombay, April 25–27, 1969*, p. 52; Government of India, Lok Sabha Secretariat, *Parliament of India: Second Lok Sabha: Who's Who 1957* (New Delhi, July 1957), pp. 495–6; 'E.K.R.' biography in *The Hindu Weekly Review* (Madras), 22 June 1964, p. 7.

Joshi had been born in 1920 in Dharwar, a district in the south of Bombay Province, and had graduated from the University of Bombay with a BA degree in 1942. After serving in the Military Accounts Department between 1942 and 1945 he became, in June 1945, a full-time worker for the RSS and, in 1951, General Secretary of the Karnataka unit of the Jana Sangh.[40]

The first clear sign that Upadhyaya had taken over the effective leadership of the party came when he stepped forward to justify to the Indian public the Jana Sangh's participation in the Goa *satyagraha* of 1955. Nehru had firmly resisted the idea of using force to remove the Portuguese authorities from their territories on the western coast of India but the Jana Sangh and other parties were more inclined to push matters to a conclusion. On 23 June 1955, the second anniversary of Mookerjee's death, Jagannathrao Joshi led a group of *satyagrahis* towards Goa but he was stopped at the border by the Portuguese police and taken prisoner.[41] Several days later Upadhyaya gave a press conference at which he demanded 'police action' against the Portuguese.[42] A Goa Vimochan Sahayak Samiti (Goa Liberation Committee), on which the Jana Sangh was represented, later decided to organize another *satyagraha* on 15 August but when the demonstrators tried to cross the border on this occasion they came under fire and a number of people were killed or wounded.[43] On 22 August in Calcutta Upadhyaya called for the pressure of public opinion to be brought to bear on the government to oblige it 'to discharge its national responsibility'[44] but the Indian police forces eventually sealed the borders of the Portuguese enclaves and on 2 October 1955 they prevented another party of volunteers, including a party under Jana Sangh and Mahasabha leaders, from entering Goa and Daman.[45]

The Goa agitation of 1955 offered the Jana Sangh a better opportunity to establish its Hindu nationalist credentials than the Kashmir agitation of 1953 had done; the issues were clear-cut and it was the Government of India rather than the opposition parties which were placed on the defensive in the public debates about the border incidents. In fact, the

---

[40] See S. Satyajit (ed.), *India Who's Who 1971: Leaders Listed by Professions* (New Delhi, 1971), p. 220; Baxter, *The Jana Sangh*, p. 184.

[41] For the decision to send the *satyagrahis*, see Central Working Committee, Delhi, 13 June 1955, *BJS Documents*, IV, pp. 39–40. Joshi was released from prison on 2 February 1957 (see *Statesman* (Delhi), 4 February 1957, p. 7).

[42] *Statesman* (Delhi), 29 June 1955, p. 1.

[43] *Ibid.* (Calcutta), 16 August 1955, pp. 1 and 7. See also Ajit Bhattacharjea, 'Can Satyagraha succeed against Fascism?', *ibid.*, 23 August 1955, p. 4.

[44] *Ibid.* (Delhi), 23 August 1955, p. 10.

[45] *Ibid.* (Calcutta), 3 October 1955, p. 7.

government was finding it hard to explain why it was now condemning a proposed course of action which it had itself justified as legitimate in earlier situations, most obviously in the 'police action' taken in Hyderabad after talks intended to bring about the state's accession to India had broken down in 1948. Moreover, the description of the volunteers who marched on the Portuguese enclaves as *'satyagrahis'* was an open attempt to identify them with those Congress activists of the British period who had maintained that moral conviction justified the breaking of laws. Whereas in the Kashmir agitation the Jana Sangh had appeared to be supporting the unreasonable claims of the Jammu Praja Parishad, in the Goa agitation the party could claim to be representing a purely patriotic interest in the recovery of misappropriated territory. From the party's point of view, the agitation served the valuable purpose of providing a unifying cause after all the internal wrangling of 1954, and it enabled Upadhyaya to show that he was capable of leading the party in a public confrontation with the authorities.

Despite their adoption of such a patriotic cause, however, Upadhyaya and his colleagues found themselves unable to reach a nationwide audience and they had therefore to accept the limitations of a party heavily biased towards the Hindi-speaking states in the preparations for the second general elections, held early in 1957. Although on this occasion the Jana Sangh returned four members to the Lok Sabha and small groups of representatives to the northern Legislative Assemblies, it again failed to establish itself as a major opposition grouping. On the other hand, its young leaders were becoming somewhat better known; among those returned to the Lok Sabha was Vajpayee, who soon established himself as a skilful debater capable of sharing with Upadhyaya the task of stating the party's policy positions. In January 1959, when the Nagpur session of the Congress adopted resolutions favouring further measures of land reform, including co-operative joint farming, Upadhyaya lost no time in claiming that the scheme, if implemented, would cause 'widespread disturbances in the political and economic structure of India',[46] and thus prepared the ground for the party's more considered denunciation of the policy later in the year. Again, when the first clashes with Chinese forces occurred on the northern border from the end of August 1959, and the central government became embroiled in an increasingly acrimonious debate about its defence and frontier policies, the Jana Sangh's central leaders hammered home the party's strong line. Upadhyaya stated at a press conference in November 1959 that 'the issue of Indo-Chinese relations'

---

[46] From a press conference in Delhi on 23 January, reported in *Organiser*, 26 January 1959, p. 3. See also a statement which he made at Lucknow on 1 February, reported in *Hindustan Times*, 4 February 1959, p. 5.

had become 'predominantly a military question' and that 'all talk about negotiations with the Chinese should cease forthwith till the aggression is vacated';[47] at the same time, Vajpayee was demanding that immediate steps should be taken to check the activities of the Communist Party of India,[48] which was being accused of having some sympathy for the Chinese cause.

By the time the Jana Sangh entered the campaign for the third general elections in 1962, its earlier isolation had been reduced to some extent; the newly formed Swatantra Party and some of the other non-Congress parties were treating it with cautious respect. Although it again concentrated on the northern states, it nevertheless succeeded in increasing its representation in the Lok Sabha and in the Legislative Assemblies. It had become a force to be reckoned with, especially in any moves to replace the Congress government at the centre by a broad centre-right coalition.

The formal and informal structure of the Jana Sangh

Thus far we have considered the structure of the early Jana Sangh mainly with reference to power relations within the party's central institutions, but to obtain a complete picture of its organizational arrangements we need to take stock of those provisions of its constitution which affected state and local, as well as national, institutions. Assuming that the party had settled down by the early 1960s following the changes set in motion by the 1954 succession crisis, we can take the constitution and rules as amended to 1963 as providing a convenient picture of the party's more mature organization. The framework at that time was as follows:[49]

Level	Plenary bodies	Executive bodies
1 Locality (gram panchayat or municipal ward)	Sthaniya Samiti (Local Committee)	Karya Samiti (Local Working Committee)
2 Development block		Mandal Samiti (Mandal Committee)

[47] *Organiser*, 16 November 1959, p. 8. He also proposed that Krishna Menon, the Minister of Defence, should be removed from office and that the CPI should be banned.

[48] *Hindustan Times*, 16 November 1959, p. 3.

[49] *Bharatiya Jana Sangh: Constitution and Rules* (Bharatiya Jana Sangh, New Delhi, n.d.), as amended by the eleventh annual session, Ahmedabad, December 1963. Cf. *Bharatiya Jana Sangh: Constitution and Rules (1960)* (Bharatiya Jana Sangh, New Delhi, n.d.), as amended by the seventh annual session, Bangalore, December 1958. Both texts are in Hindi. For an excellent survey of the 1963 constitution and rules see Motilal A. Jhangiani, *Jana Sangh and Swatantra: A Profile of the Rightist Parties in India* (Bombay, 1967), pp. 28–43.

Level	Plenary bodies	Executive bodies
3 District		Zila Samiti (District Committee)
4 State	(i) Pradeshik Pratinidhi Sabha (State General Council) (ii) Pradeshik Sammelan (State Plenary Session)	(i) Pradeshik Karya Samiti (State Working Committee) (ii) Pradeshĩk Sansadiya Adhikaran (State Parliamentary Board)
5 Regional	Anchalik Sammelan (Regional Plenary Session)	
6 National	(i) Bharatiya Pratinidhi Sabha (Central General Council) (ii) Sarvadeshik Sammelan (National Plenary Session)	Bharatiya Karya Samiti (Central Working Committee)
		Kendriya Sansadiya Adhikaran (Central Parliamentary Board)

Note: The English terms given in brackets are not always strict translations of the Hindi equivalents but they correspond to usage in Jana Sangh publications in English.

Theoretically, this structure was created from the base upwards by a process of annual organizational elections and by a parallel process of membership co-option and appointment by executive officers. Once members within each local area had elected a Working Committee, all the members of the Local Working Committees in each Mandal area elected the officers of a Mandal Committee, whose President was authorized to appoint additional members. Subsequently, all the elected members of the Mandal Committees elected the officers of the District Committee, to which further members could be appointed by the district President. Next, to provide the core membership of the State General Council, the elected members of the Mandal Committees within each district of the state chose one member for each Legislative Assembly constituency and one woman member for each district, and at their first meeting these members then elected the officers of the State Working Committee. The Council membership was augmented by the addition of various co-opted and nominated members, including Jana Sanghis who were members of the state legislature or Presidents of Zila Parishads (District Councils), or chairmen of municipalities with populations of more than 20,000, and the State President was authorized to make nominations to his State Working Committee, the size of which was limited to 31 members.

At the national level, the core membership of the Central General Council consisted of the presidents and secretaries of the District

Committees with additional representatives from districts containing more than two Lok Sabha constituencies. To this core were added the members of the Central Working Committee and the State Working Committees; representatives of front organizations nominated by the Central Working Committee; representatives of affiliated associations; all Jana Sangh members of the central parliament; and not more than 20 members to be co-opted at the first meeting of the Council. The national President of the party was chosen by a postal ballot of the core members of the Central General Council and it was his responsibility to nominate the members of the Central Working Committee, which could number no more than 31 members; from these members he then appointed two Vice-Presidents, a General Secretary, one or more secretaries and a Treasurer. The Central Working Committee was authorized to establish a Central Parliamentary Board, whose function was to direct the work of the State Parliamentary Boards appointed by the State Working Committees.

A striking feature of these arrangements was the scope which the state and national presidents were given to choose the members of their working committees and the exceptional right given to the national President to choose the officers as well as the members of the Central Working Committee. There was, as we have seen, provision for a sequence of organizational elections culminating in the choice of the core memberships of the State and Central General Councils, but the considerable numbers of co-opted and nominated members on these bodies could serve as counterweights to the elected element. The provision for the election of the national President could in theory have stimulated processes of democratic choice within the party but in fact every President was elected to office unopposed. In effect, the chain of plenary institutions in this framework was not a strong one and the main lines of control were provided through the hierarchy of working committees, where the basic decisions regarding policy and strategy were resolved.

Although the 1963 party constitution contained no articles defining the membership and purposes of the general meetings of delegates, notables and leaders which are described as 'sessions' in the language of Indian party politics, Rule 4 did specify how state, regional and national sessions were to be arranged. As far as national and regional sessions were concerned, the Central Working Committee was authorized to arrange for gatherings attended not only by regular members of the Central General Council but also by members of the State General Councils, Jana Sangh members of the central parliament and of the state legislatures and other specially appointed delegates. The first national session was held at Kanpur on 29–31 December 1952 and set the pattern for subsequent occasions. Before each such session the Central Working Committee would meet to prepare resolutions and to settle the schedule of business. The session itself would begin with the formal address of the newly elected national President, after which two or three days would be spent in discussion of policy resolutions, which were duly reported in the national press. These national sessions were festive occasions when the party was on show to the public. The general discussions were usually held in a large tent (or *pandal*) containing a raised platform on which party leaders would sit during proceedings, and there would be smaller tents and temporary buildings in the vicinity to serve as offices, canteens, exhibition centres and as venues for the sectional conferences which were sometimes held in conjunction with the main one. Shortly after the end of the session the national President would announce the membership of the incoming Central Working Committee, which met every three months or so, sometimes in Delhi and sometimes in a state capital. The Central General Council would also meet from time to time, and in the well-established state units of the party a similar cycle of meetings would take place, culminating in a plenary session at which policy resolutions would be passed and officers elected for the year ahead.

However, to understand how these processes were sustained and regulated, we need to analyse the informal power relations which lay behind the formal framework. The most important element in this power structure was the central secretariat which had developed under Upadhyaya's control. As we have seen, he at first established a pattern of two secretaries, with Vajpayee and Jagannathrao Joshi as the initial incumbents, but by March 1958 further appointments had produced a system under which individual secretaries were assigned responsibilities for particular parts of India. Within the boundaries established by the reorganization of states effected in 1956, Joshi was placed in charge of the southern zone, which comprised the Maharashtra region of Bombay state, Mysore, Kerala, Madras, Andhra Pradesh and the former French territories; Balraj Madhok was entrusted with the northern zone, consisting of the Delhi, Punjab, Himachal Pradesh and Jammu and Kashmir areas; Nana Deshmukh was given the eastern zone, including Uttar Pradesh, Bihar, West Bengal, Assam, Manipur and Tripura; and Sundar Singh Bhandari was allotted the western zone, enclosing the areas of Rajasthan, Madhya Pradesh, Orissa and the Gujarat region of Bombay state.[50]

---

[50] For an excellent account of these arrangements see Baxter, *The Jana Sangh*, pp.182–4. For a report of a meeting of the four zonal secretaries, along with Upadhyaya and Vajpayee, see *Organiser*, 17 March 1958, p. 4. See also Davey, 'A case study of the Bharatiya Jana Sangh', pp. 175–82.

All of these men shared an RSS background and each had special qualifications for his regional responsibility. We have already noted Joshi's connection with Karnataka, and this made him a natural choice for the southern region. In the same way, Madhok's knowledge of Delhi and Punjabi affairs, and his understanding of the Arya Samaj and its concerns, made him the obvious candidate for the northern post. His father had been an official employed by the princely state of Jammu and Kashmir, and Balraj was born on 25 February 1920 in Skardu, then the winter capital of Ladakh. In 1938 he joined the Dayananda Anglo-Vedic (DAV) College in Lahore and became a member of the RSS. Having obtained his MA degree in 1942, he was appointed to the staff of the Srinagar DAV College in 1944, and became its Vice-Principal in the following year. After serving as provincial organizer of the RSS in Jammu and Kashmir from 1942 to 1947, and taking part in the defence of Srinagar against the tribal invaders in 1947, he helped to form the Jammu Praja Parishad and became its general secretary. Sent away from the state in January 1948 by Sheikh Abdullah's government, he had gone to Delhi and in 1950 joined the teaching staff at Camp College, which drew students from the Punjabi refugee colonies of the capital. There he was closely involved in the formation of the Jana Sangh unit for the 'greater Punjab' region, becoming its first general secretary, and later, after the 1954 succession crisis, the President of the party's Delhi unit.[51]

Within the eastern region, the base area was the state of Uttar Pradesh, where Nana Deshmukh had been the key party figure in the mid-1950s. Born in 1917 in the Marathwada region of what was then the princely state of Hyderabad, he had been attracted to the RSS in 1933 or 1934; in 1940 he had become the RSS organizer in charge of the north-eastern part of the United Provinces and it was then that he met Upadhyaya, with whom he worked after the war in the Rashtra Dharma Prakashan in Lucknow. When Upadhyaya was made General Secretary of the Uttar Pradesh Jana Sangh in September 1951 Deshmukh was appointed organizing secretary of the unit, and in 1956 he became its general secretary.[52] In the western zone, Bhandari had an equally close association with Rajasthan; he had been born in 1921 at Udaipur, in

[51] From a biography in *Organiser*, 13 March 1966, p. 3. See also *ibid.*, August 1956 (special issue), p. 32; 27 May 1963, pp. 4 and 14; a press conference by Madhok on 12 February 1973 (*Times of India* (Delhi), 13 February 1973, pp. 1 and 10), and letter from Madhok to L.K. Advani, 7 March 1973, in Varshney, *Jana Sangh – R.S.S. and Balraj Madhok*, pp. 135–64.

[52] Interview with Nana Deshmukh, New Delhi, 14 May 1984. See also S.S. Bhandari (ed.), *Jana-Deep Souvenir: A Publication Brought out on the Occasion of the 14th Annual Session of Bharatiya Jana Sangh, Calicut, December 1967*, p. 106. Deshmukh refers to his association with Upadhyaya in his foreword to Raje (ed.), *Deendayal Upadhyaya*, p. i.

south-eastern Rajputana, and had attended Colvin High School at Sirohi and Maharana Bhupal College at Udaipur before completing his education at Kanpur, first at the Sanatana Dharma College and then at the DAV College. After a period as an advocate at the Mewar High Court and as a headmaster of a school at Udaipur, he had become an RSS organizer in 1946 and later served as secretary of the Rajasthan Jana Sangh from 1951 to 1958.[53]

The work of these regional secretaries was co-ordinated by Upadhyaya, with the aid of Vajpayee and of a central office secretary, Jagdish Prasad Mathur, who had joined the RSS in 1942 at the age of 21 and had met Upadhyaya towards the end of the war. In 1945 he had been appointed to the post of RSS organizer in the United Provinces district of Budaun, in the Rohilkhand region, before becoming an office secretary of the central headquarters of the Jana Sangh early in 1953, shortly after Upadhyaya had been made one of the two General Secretaries of the national party.[54] These men of the central secretariat, all relatively young and all from provincial backgrounds, constituted the party's first coherent high command; in each case they had been recruited as organizers at the state level and had brought to the centre their considerable knowledge of politics in the regions.

As at the centre, so within the established state units an active secretary, usually with an RSS background, provided the core of executive organization. Such men were the fixed points in the middle levels of the party hierarchy, and around them were built the networks of special officers known as 'organizing secretaries' (*sangathan mantris*). These were mainly appointed to serve at the local and district levels, but the Uttar Pradesh unit also placed them in charge of divisions, composed of groups of districts.[55] Normally, organizing secretaries were responsible to a state general secretary and through him to the appropriate zonal secretary and to the general secretary at the centre, but they were sometimes given added responsibilities.

In effect, the combination of the system of zonal secretaries at the centre with that of organizing secretaries at the state and lower levels provided the central leadership with an unobtrusive but powerful means

---

[53] Government of India, Rajya Sabha Secretariat, *Parliament of India: Rajya Sabha: Who's Who 1970* (New Delhi, 1970), pp. 35–6.

[54] Interview with Jagdish Prasad Mathur, New Delhi, 10 May 1984.

[55] For an account of the system of organizing secretaries in the UP Jana Sangh in the late 1960s see Saraswati Srivastava, 'Uttar Pradesh: politics of neglected development', in Iqbal Narain (ed.), *State Politics in India* (Meerut, 1976), pp. 356–7. In Madhya Pradesh the Jana Sangh provided for seven divisional units (see B.R. Purohit, 'Bharatiya Jana Sangh and the fourth general elections in Madhya Pradesh', *Journal of Constitutional and Parliamentary Studies*, II, 3 (July–September 1968), p. 49).

of regulating the party's activities. The system was very much modelled on the organization of the RSS, and it is not hard to see how the formal procedures of the Jana Sangh would be confined and weakened by it. Writing in 1973, Balraj Madhok was to complain that

the organising secretaries who happen to be the real power in the Jana Sangh, having been conversant only with the working system of the RSS want to run Jana Sangh on the same lines. They have nothing but, contempt for democratic forms, norms, and conventions. Dissent of any kind is anathema to them. They want to suppress all dissidents in the name of discipline. They are interested more in control than in growth of the party. That is the real problem and dilemma of Jana Sangh which will have to be resolved one day. The sooner it is resolved the better it would be for the RSS, the Jana Sangh and the country.[56]

In a separate paper he actually recommended that the institution of *sangathan mantris* should be abolished:

This is essential to develop a sense of responsibility in elected presidents and secretaries of the party and create local leadership at all levels. Whole time workers may be oppointed [sic] at different levels to extend the organisational work. But such workers should be paid by and be answerable to the respective units of the party. There are some organising secretaries who have gained wide experiences over the past years. They should seek election to the elective posts instead of functioning secretaries.[57]

Madhok expressed these views at a time when he was in conflict with the party leadership, but his judgement on how the system of organizing secretaries had worked in the party's early days is striking and revealing.

To a large extent, the control exercised by the hierarchy of secretaries was masked from the public by the screen of eminent men who were appointed to serve as presidents at the national and state levels of the party. Generally of an older generation than the secretaries, their status was similar to that of the *sanghchalaks* within the RSS, that is, they were accorded a great deal of honour and esteem but were not given much power within the organization: they were expected to tour the country making speeches to explain the party's policies but were not encouraged to play an active administrative role. Many of them had been prominent in the Hindu nationalist politics of the inter-war period through association with such bodies as the Arya Samaj, the Sanatana Dharma Sabha and the Hindu Mahasabha, and they thus helped to convey the impression that the Jana Sangh formed part of an established political

---

[56] Letter from Madhok to Lal Kishinchand Advani, 7 March 1973, in Varshney, *Jana Sangh – R.S.S. and Balraj Madhok*, pp. 158–9.
[57] From 'Some thoughts on and suggestions for revamping the Jana Sangh...', in *ibid.*, p. 129. See also his statement on 30 April 1973 (*Hindustan Times*, 1 May 1973, p. 12).

tradition and was not simply a creation of the early 1950s. The national presidents of the late 1950s and early 1960s conformed to this pattern: Prem Nath Dogra, who held the office from December 1954 to April 1956, was followed by Deva Prasad Ghosh, a distinguished academic from Bengal, who had belonged to the Hindu Mahasabha in the late 1930s, and he was succeeded in January 1960 by Pitamber Das, a High Court lawyer from Uttar Pradesh, who in turn gave way in 1961 to Avasaralu Rama Rao, an experienced lawyer from Andhra Pradesh.[58] Although all these men were respected elders who were above the fray and made no attempt to assert themselves as Mauli Chandra Sharma had done in 1954, they were of importance to the party's public reputation. In the same way, although real power lay with the party organizers and the secretariat, the Jana Sangh's Congress-type framework of large executive bodies (the central and state working committees) and their associated plenary institutions provided it with the appearance – and to some extent the promise – of open and democratic politics in the conduct of its affairs; it enabled the party to demonstrate that its delegate sessions were significant events in the formulation of its policies and that its membership was both numerous and active.

In fact, although the distinction was not clearly stated, the party's 1963 constitution provided for two categories of members, the first consisting of people aged 18 years or over who were willing to pay an annual fee of 25 *paise* and subscribe to the party's aims and the second of those who had served actively for one year on an executive or plenary body or on a front organization of the party. The first category of ordinary members was entitled to participate in the election of members of the working committees of local units but only the 'active' members were eligible for appointment to bodies above that level.

Providing that these distinctions are taken into account, the general trends in the membership and local committee strength of the party can be traced with some degree of confidence. The earliest measure is provided by figures published in February 1954, when the party was credited with more than 143,000 members and 2,000 local committees in the better organized states,[59] but it was only in the late 1950s that more

---

[58] For biographies of Deva Prasad Ghosh, see *Organiser*, 30 April 1956, pp. 8 and 14; 24 June 1963, p. 7; *The Times of India Directory and Year Book 1958–59*, p. 1162; Hari Sharan Chhabra (ed.), *Opposition in the Parliament: A Unique, Authentic and Comprehensive Biographical Dictionary of M.P.'s on Opposition Benches* (Delhi, 1952), p. 156; of Pitamber Das, see Government of India, Rajya Sabha Secretariat, *Parliament of India: Rajya Sabha: Who's Who 1970*, pp. 214–15; *Organiser*, 1 February 1960, p. 1; and of Avasaralu Rama Rao, see *ibid.*, 21 November 1960, p. 3.

[59] *Organiser*, 8 February 1954, p. 1.

systematic information became available in the General Secretary's reports. The data covering the years from 1957 to 1960 are as follows:[60]

Table 1: *Bharatiya Jana Sangh: national membership and committee totals, 1957–60*

Year	Members	Local committees	Mandal committees˜
1957	74,863	889	243
1958	209,702	1,787	455
1959	215,370	2,551	495
1960	274,907	4,313	584

Notes: (1) The figures for 1957 do not include data for the Punjab, Delhi, Andhra Pradesh and Kerala.
(2) The figures for 1958 do not include the local committees in West Bengal, Bihar, Delhi and Madhya Pradesh, and some mandal committees in Delhi, Maharashtra and Uttar Pradesh.

As noted, the 1957 figures do not include the returns from four state units, including the important ones of the Punjab and Delhi, and the actual totals for the year should perhaps be placed in the ranges of 100,000 to 150,000 members and 900 to 1,000 local committees, taking into account the Punjab and Delhi data for 1960 given in Table 2. However, even with this adjustment, the 1957 levels are relatively low and presumably reflect the falling-off of local activity which usually followed a general election campaign, just as the subsequent increases would indicate an effort to strengthen the party's base for the third general elections in 1962. The essential nucleus for local organization was the mandal committee, which under the 1958 party constitution was based on the Legislative Assembly constituency; the network of local committees was difficult to maintain, especially in periods between elections, when neither the party nor aspiring candidates had an immediate need for workers at polling-booth level. The General Secretary alluded to this problem when he reported in 1959 that

From the report of the work done it can be inferred that the mandal committees are active in most places. However local committees mostly function at the time of elections. If provisions of our constitution in respect of meetings of the different committees are strictly adhered to, the committees will automatically be

---

[60] See the General Secretary's reports for 1959 and 1960 in *ibid.*, 1 February 1960, p. 9; 2 January 1961, p. 9. See also the reports for 1957 and 1958 (*ibid.*, 14 April 1958, p. 9; 12 January 1959, p. 8). The figures for 1959 are the relatively complete ones cited in the report for 1960, and not the provisional ones given in the report for 1959, which did not include data for Karnataka and Gujarat.

activised. This is necessary both for the expansion as well as the coordination of our work.[61]

During the following year, 1960, the number of local committees jumped from 2,551 to 4,313, an increase which the General Secretary attributed 'to the fact that in areas selected for intensive work, an attempt to reach as many polling stations as possible has been made',[62] and although the figure for 1961 is not known, the fact that the party's total membership reached a peak of 597,041 at the end of the year[63] would indicate a substantial increase in its size.

The evidence regarding membership and local unit strengths at the state level is fragmentary, but there are indications that the party's coverage of territory was far from uniform. The following data[64] give some impression of the extent to which this was so.

Table 2: *Bharatiya Jana Sangh: state membership and committee totals, 1958–60*

State units	Members	Local committees	Mandal committees	Legislative Assembly constituencies[1]
Uttar Pradesh (1958)	43,107	882	91	341 (430)
Madhya Pradesh (1960)	23,000	500	49	218 (288)
Punjab (1960)	45,000	292	39	121 (154)
Maharashtra (1960)	45,000	525	64	221 (264)
Delhi (1960)	19,000	170	30	

[1]A proportion of the constituencies under the 1956 delimitation were double-member and the number of seats is given in brackets for each state.

Assuming that the Jana Sangh would have formed one rather than two mandal committees in a double-member constituency, it can be seen that it had established such units in only a small proportion of the Legislative Assembly constituencies at this point (22 per cent in Madhya Pradesh, 27 per cent in Uttar Pradesh, 29 per cent in Maharashtra, and 32 per cent in the Punjab), although by November 1963 a much higher level of 85

[61] *Ibid.*, 1 February 1960, p. 9.
[62] *Ibid.*, 2 January 1961, p. 9.
[63] *National Herald* (Lucknow), 1 February 1967, p. 4.
[64] UP figures are from the UP General Secretary's report for 1958 (*Organiser*, 16 March 1959, p. 17), and the figures for other units are from *ibid.*, 2 January 1961, pp. 7, 8, 14 and 17. There are scattered figures for the membership and committee strengths of some state units in *ibid.*, August 1956 (special issue), pp. 35–50.

mandal committees was reported for eastern Uttar Pradesh at a time when this region contained 105 Legislative Assembly constituencies.[65]

It is even more difficult to gauge the extent to which the Jana Sangh relied upon RSS workers to supply the core of its party activists. Press reports of RSS involvement in the party are numerous, but precise measures are few. Referring to the events of 1954, Mauli Chandra Sharma estimated that there were 500 to 700 workers amongst the 13,000 members of the Delhi unit of the Jana Sangh at that time[66] and this strengthens the impression that the RSS tended to supply a minority, although an extremely important one, of the party's local activists, just as RSS organizers constituted the most energetic and disciplined element within the organizational framework proper.

As noted above, membership tended to fall off after an election campaign, and we find the Central Working Committee in 1962 proposing that an effort should be made to increase the total membership from 300,000 to 500,000, which suggests that about half of the pre-election membership (597,041 at the end of 1961) had evaporated by that stage.[67] There must have been some recovery in the succeeding years, because in April 1966 the General Secretary was claiming that the total had risen from 600,000 to 1,300,000 within the space of a year. In the same report, he also pointed out that the party had achieved a significant measure of coverage, having established branches in 268 and district committees in 201 of India's 350 administrative districts.[68]

Although incomplete, the data reviewed above do indicate, first, that membership and geographical coverage would increase rapidly as the time for general elections drew near and, secondly, that the peaks of membership were on a rising line, from 600,000 in 1961 to 1,300,000 in 1966. The causes for the pre-election surge in membership are obvious; both aspiring and, eventually, nominated candidates for parliamentary and assembly constituencies bring with them their own bands of workers from their localities and encourage them both to join the party's committees and to man the array of canvassing and electioneering teams needed for the intensive activity of the campaign period. Once the

---

[65] *National Herald*, 6 November 1963, p. 7. The party intended to form mandal committees in the remaining 20 constituencies by the end of December.

[66] Sharma interview (1974), p. 226. In another interview (8 July 1974), Sharma, referring generally to this period, placed the number of RSS members at 1,200 in a total membership of 13,000 (see Puri, *Bharatiya Jana Sangh*, p. 48).

[67] *Pioneer* (Lucknow), 19 March 1962, p. 6. The membership drive was to be completed by 1 September 1962, after which mandal and state units were to be constituted, and the election of the national president completed by 1 December 1962.

[68] *Organiser*, 8 May 1966, p. 7. The membership total at the end of 1966 was given as 1,257,000 (*National Herald*, 1 February 1967, p. 4).

election is over many of the new recruits will drift away from the party but others will remain, sometimes as a token force to occupy the mandal committee in readiness for the next cycle of electoral activity. In an important sense, the Jana Sangh's heavy commitment to contesting elections had begun the process of giving its mandal committees in particular a local significance and local roots, and to that extent the party had come to resemble openly participatory parties, such as the PSP. The controlling power of the RSS remained strong, but it was conceivable by the 1960s that the party's continued exposure to periodic waves of mass membership would eventually change it into a more open and democratic organization.

Behind these patterns of membership lies the history of the party's efforts to lodge itself in as many regions as possible during the 1950s. Its base area was the north, where its units were securely established from 1951 onwards in every territory except Jammu and Kashmir; there it left the field to the Praja Parishad, which it accepted as an affiliate at the end of 1954 and finally absorbed in December 1963.[69] In western and eastern India the party's main units were formed in 1951 in Gujarat, Bihar and West Bengal and in 1952 in Maharashtra, but permanent units were not established until 1963 in Assam and Orissa. However, the extension of its organization in the southern states was hampered by its claim that Hindi should become the language for 'all the official purposes of the Union', which clashed with the strong southern preference for English. In addition, the Jana Sangh's fierce criticism of Pakistan, which attracted support in the north, aroused little enthusiasm in the south, where the partition of the subcontinent in 1947 had not created lasting bitterness. Although the Karnataka (later Mysore) unit of the party was formed in September 1951 and a unit was set up in Andhra Pradesh in December 1954, properly constituted Kerala and Tamil Nad units were not formed until 21 September and 3 October 1958 respectively.[70]

One of the party's real problems in establishing itself outside the Hindi heartland was its lack of financial resources on the scale of those available to its rivals, particularly the Congress Party. Its income was derived from such sources as donations, membership fees, purse collections, monthly payments by party members, the sale of party literature and monthly contributions from Jana Sangh Members of

---

[69] *Organiser*, 23 December 1963, pp. 13 and 14.
[70] On the formation of the Tamil Nad unit see *ibid.*, 15 September 1958, p. 3; 13 October 1958, p. 3; 24 October 1960, p. 4. The dates for the formation of the party's state units are given in Appendix D in *BJS Documents*, V, p. 180. See also Jagdish Prasad Mathur, 'The Jana Sangh marches ahead', *Organiser*, 26 January 1962, pp. 19 and 26.

Parliament and the state legislatures.[71] Writing after the 1962 election campaign, Madhok said that his party 'never expected any financial assistance from the big industrial and commercial houses' but that 'it banked on the support of the lower middle class and the small trader to meet the minimum local election expenses'.[72] Such people generally made anonymous contributions to local collections, known as 'purses', which were presented to party leaders on tour; for example, a report on fund-raising in Uttar Pradesh in 1965 mentioned total receipts of Rs 372,501[73] and purses in the Vidarbha region of Maharashtra at the time of the 1967 election campaign produced the sum of Rs 285,000.[74] Revenue from fees would have contributed a useful sum; with a minimum membership fee of 25 *paise* per annum, the record membership of 1,300,000 in 1966 should have brought the party Rs 325,000, and candidates in Uttar Pradesh were charged nomination fees of Rs 150 for a Legislative Assembly constituency and Rs 200 for a Lok Sabha constituency at this time. Such amounts sound substantial until it is remembered that the cost of the party's campaign in Uttar Pradesh alone in the 1967 elections was estimated as being Rs 5,000,000,[75] and that the party would have received far less in purses and in membership fees in other areas where it was struggling to establish itself. As Madhok had said, the party did not expect to attract money from business organizations, and the fact that funds flowing to it from such a source were far smaller than those received by the Congress or even the Swatantra Party can be gauged from records showing donations by joint stock companies to political parties in the 1960s; in the period from mid-1961 to 15 September 1964, the Jana Sangh received Rs 3,425 compared with Rs 9,813,180 received by Congress and Rs 1,565,003 received by Swatantra,[76] and in the accounting periods ending 31 December 1966 and 31

---

[71] Jhangiani, *Jana Sangh and Swatantra*, p. 39. For a comparative study of the finances of Indian political parties see A.H. and G. Somjee, 'India', *The Journal of Politics*, XXV (1963), pp. 686–702. See also A.H. Somjee, 'Party finance', in *Seminar* (New Delhi), No. 74, *Money in Politics*, October 1965, pp. 15–18.

[72] Balraj Madhok, 'Jana Sangh', in *Seminar*, No. 34, *Election Analysis*, June 1962, p. 36.

[73] Special correspondent, Lucknow, 15 June 1965 (*Organiser*, 27 June 1965, p. 1). The amounts presented were Rs 295,000 to the national president, Bachhraj Vyas; Rs 41,000 to Upadhyaya; Rs 25,000 to the state president, Ganga Ram Talwar; and Rs 11,501 to Vajpayee.

[74] *Ibid.*, 29 January 1967, p. 2.

[75] Report of an interview with Ram Prakash Gupta, the convenor of the parliamentary board of the UP Jana Sangh, 30 August 1966 (*National Herald*, 31 August 1966, p. 3).

[76] *P.D.*, *L.S.* (Third Series), XXXVIII, 17 February 1965, cc. 26–7. See also *Statesman* (Delhi), 18 February 1965, p. 1. Under Company Law a joint stock company had to record political donations on its balance sheet for submission to the Registrars of Companies.

March 1967, the Jana Sangh received a total of Rs 10,051, the Congress
Rs 1,589,764 and Swatantra Rs 463,156.[77] It is very difficult to obtain
accurate information about the sources of party funds in India and such
information as does become available often does so during internal
disputes and must therefore be treated with caution. However, from the
evidence given by Mauli Chandra Sharma in his 1974 interview, it would
seem that lack of funds was a real source of concern for the Jana Sangh
in its early years and that the RSS had a vested interest in preventing the
party from obtaining an independent means of financial support.[78] The
difficulty created by the RSS connection is brought out in a story told by
Sharma of overtures made to certain Parsi businessmen in Bombay.
While they were prepared to consider supplying the Jana Sangh with
between ten and twenty lakhs of rupees as funding for a year, they were
concerned about the influence of the RSS in its affairs and wanted to
know whether, since they were not Hindus, they would be accepted by
the party; Sharma was unable to give them an assurance that they would
be welcome when he was no longer the President.[79]

By the early 1960s, then, we see a party whose formal structure had
been warped and distorted by its informal power relations. While the
Jana Sangh's constitution and rules, as amended to 1963, still bore a
family resemblance to the Congress constitutions of the inter-war
period, its informal structure more closely resembled that of the RSS. In
other words, the outwardly democratic hierarchy of elected committees
and their associated executives was effectively controlled from within by
the tight knot of secretaries at the centre and by the supporting
framework of secretaries and organizers at the state and regional levels
of the party. This high degree of centralization and control expressed not
only a particular theory of party organization but also a distrust of the
generation of Indian politicians who were prominent in the 1950s and
who were generally English-speaking and anglicized in their outlook,
even when they were disposed to give some credence to the doctrines of

---

[77] See Annexure No. 22 in Part I of Appendix LXII, pp. 77–80, in *P.D., R.S., Sixty-Second Session* (1967), *Appendices*. This source lists the names of the contributing companies and the size of their contributions. Only three firms contributed to the Jana Sangh. The Congress and Swatantra totals (Rs 1,589,764.45 and Rs 463,156 respectively) were recalculated from the lists of individual contributions.

   The returns are those filed with the Registrars of Companies up to 31 August 1967 (see statement by Fakhruddin Ali Ahmed, Minister of Industrial Development, *P.D., R.S.,* LXII, 23 November 1967, cc. 797–8).

[78] See above, p. 000.

[79] Sharma interview (1974), p. 211–12. Cf. the account of the incident in Davey, 'A case study of the Bharatiya Jana Sangh', p. 171 (the reference is to an interview with Sharma in August 1965).

Hindu nationalism. It was as though Upadhyaya and his group had placed their trust in a new generation of public men and women who had not known the British Raj except as children and as students and who would therefore draw more readily from the inspiration of Hindu culture and Hindu traditions. Put simply, the Jana Sangh had postponed its challenge to the Congress Party until such time as the younger leadership, represented by Upadhyaya, Vajpayee and Madhok, had had time to consolidate its position and to define its intellectual objectives with confidence. By the mid-1960s this period of preparation was coming to an end and the party's new leaders were beginning to assert themselves in the wider political arenas.

Strains in the Jana Sangh leadership, 1962–67

After China's invasion of India's northern border areas in October 1962 and her unilateral implementation of a cease-fire arrangement in the following month, the Government of India again found itself under heavy fire from the opposition parties, which claimed that the country's defence and foreign policies had failed to protect vital national interests. The Jana Sangh formed part of the non-Congress alliance which developed during this crisis and it found a forceful spokesman in Dr Raghuvira, a distinguished Sanskrit scholar and former Congressman, who became President of the party in November 1962. He took a leading part in public debates until he was severely injured in a motor accident and died in a Kanpur hospital on 14 May 1963.[80] The party then recalled Deva Prasad Ghosh for a second term as President, but during his period in office, which included the death of Nehru in May 1964 and the succession of Lal Bahadur Shastri to the prime ministership, the main burden of the leadership fell upon Upadhyaya and the central secretaries.

Although among these Upadhyaya remained pre-eminent, his fellow secretaries were also, in varying degrees, gaining experience in parliamentary and public politics and could no longer be ignored when candidates for the party presidency were being considered. Vajpayee had been elected to the Lok Sabha in 1957 and, as the leader of the party's small group in the central parliament, had proved himself to be an effective speaker, especially in the field of foreign affairs; at the end of 1960 he visited the United States under an Education Exchange Programme and was thus able to observe the American presidential

---

[80] *Statesman* (Delhi), 15 May 1963, p. 1. On Raghuvira's presidency, see Davey, 'A case study of the Bharatiya Jana Sangh', pp. 189–91.

election campaign which led to the victory of John Kennedy;[81] and although he was defeated in two Lok Sabha constituencies in the 1962 general elections he was subsequently returned to the Rajya Sabha and was again chosen to lead the party's parliamentary group. Balraj Madhok had also embarked on a parliamentary career; although he failed in a bid to win the New Delhi Lok Sabha seat in the 1957 elections, he was returned for that constituency in a by-election in April 1961 and showed himself to be a resourceful and effective member of the house in the closing Lok Sabha sessions of that year. Had he not lost his seat in the 1962 elections he might well have become the leader of the party's Lok Sabha group.

By contrast, Upadhyaya had devoted himself almost exclusively to his work as General Secretary. Although his name had gone forward in the nominations for the national presidency of the party at the end of 1960, he subsequently withdrew it in favour of Rama Rao.[82] Then, in the spring of 1963, he was asked to stand as the Jana Sangh candidate in a parliamentary by-election for the Jaunpur parliamentary seat in Uttar Pradesh; he was at first very reluctant to do so but eventually bowed to pressure within the party.[83] He was defeated, but his candidature at least signified that he was now willing to move outside the strict limits of the role he had set for himself in the mid-1950s. More significant was his interest in revising the party's doctrine; in the 1950s, the nearest approach to a statement of the Jana Sangh's basic philosophy had been the preambles to its successive manifestos, but in 1964 Upadhyaya brought forward an extended text dealing with general policy matters. This was widely discussed at party meetings and finally adopted at the Central General Council meeting at Vijayawada in January 1965 as the *Principles and Policy* document,[84] its central philosophy being characterized by Upadhyaya as that of 'integral humanism'. In a significant assertion of intellectual leadership, which added considerably to Upadhyaya's status within the party, he expounded its main principles to party and public audiences.[85]

---

[81] See *Organiser*, 26 September 1960, p. 2; 14 November 1960, p. 16; Baxter, *The Jana Sangh*, p. 200.

[82] *Organiser*, 21 November 1960, p. 3.

[83] From a reminiscence by Bhaurao Deoras in Raje (ed.), *Deendayal Upadhyaya*, p. 102.

[84] See Bharatiya Jana Sangh, *Principles and Policy* [New Delhi, 1965]. For its consideration within the party, see *Organiser*, 24 August 1964, pp. 7 and 10; 14 December 1964, p. 13; 11 January 1965, pp. 2 and 15; 15 February 1965, pp. 5 and 14; *Statesman* (Delhi), 18 August 1964, p. 7; 7 November 1964, p. 4; 7 December 1964, p. 7; 26 January 1965, p. 12; 28 January 1965, p. 6.

[85] See Upadhyaya, *Integral Humanism* (New Delhi, n.d.). This brochure contains the texts of four lectures given in Poona in April 1965.

Upadhyaya's name had been mentioned as a possible successor to Deva Prasad Ghosh but in January 1965 the post of party president went to Bachhraj Vyas, who had at one stage served as RSS secretary at Nagpur and had been secretary and later President of the Maharashtra Jana Sangh unit.[86] A retiring man, he later described how Upadhyaya had backed his candidature; he claimed that at the time of the meeting of the Central General Council at Gwalior in August 1964 there had been 'common consent' that Upadhyaya should become President, and that all the 'regional committees' (presumably the state working committees) had sent in resolutions proposing Upadhyaya's name

But he was reluctant and proposed my name instead at the annual meeting of the U.P. delegates. He not only moved the proposal but with his characteristic zeal saw to it that it was accepted and carried through. So I was burdened with the responsibility of this high post...[87]

According to *Link*, a New Delhi weekly, the majority of the party's units had wanted to elect Upadhyaya as President and either Madhok or Vajpayee as General Secretary in his place. Golwalkar is then said to have intervened to insist on the choice of Vyas.[88]

As General Secretary, Upadhyaya continued to guide the party through the troubled events of 1965. In April of that year fighting broke out between India and Pakistan in the Rann of Kutch and a subsequent cease-fire agreement had no sooner come into effect than the Kashmir dispute flared up again, as armed raiders began crossing into the Vale from Azad Kashmir from about the beginning of August; by September India and Pakistan were embroiled in an open war in the Kashmir and Punjab sectors, but under heavy and concerted international pressure both countries eventually accepted the UN Security Council's call for a cease-fire, which came into effect on 23 September. This sequence of crises aroused all the old antagonisms which the Jana Sangh had harboured towards Pakistan, and the party's central bodies adopted resolutions condemning that country's actions, warning, incidentally, that

There should be no political bargaining with Indian Muslims. They must be guaranteed all constitutional rights due to them in this secular State. But all

---

[86] *Organiser*, 11 January 1965, p. 2; Baxter, *The Jana Sangh*, pp. 250–1.
[87] From a reminiscence by Vyas in Raje (ed.), *Deendayal Upadhyaya*, p. 144. The meeting referred to is presumably a session of the UP State General Council, although the actual nomination would have been made by the UP State Working Committee.
[88] *Link*, 7 March 1965, p. 13. See also Varshney, *Jana Sangh – R.S.S. and Balraj Madhok*, pp. 17–18. Vajpayee described the *Link* report as 'fantastic' (*Organiser*, 22 March 1965, p. 2.).

separatist tendencies and attitudes betraying a pro-Pak bias must be curbed and
the outlook of Indian Muslims must be nationalised.[89]

There was a distinct possibility that the Jana Sangh, responding to the
more extreme elements amongst its supporters, might now commit itself
to the demand that India should broaden the scope of the conflict and
aim at the destruction of the Pakistani state, but, even at the height of the
September fighting, it did no more than maintain that the Indian army
should occupy those parts of Kashmir which were under Pakistani
control. Upadhyaya's influence at this time was a moderating one; in his
'Political Diary', he emphasized that India's main objective must be to
destroy the Pakistani war-machine rather than undo the partition of the
subcontinent. 'Even conceding that partition is responsible for many a
problem that we are confronted with', he wrote,

we are sure that the present confrontation is not meant to annul partition. Unity
will come not by war but by a voluntary decision of the people of Pakistan. Once
they get disillusioned with their leadership, they would not like to remain
apart.[90]

Shortly after the Indo-Pakistani war had ended in a cease-fire, the
Soviet Union persuaded both countries to meet for talks at Tashkent in
January 1966. The result was the Tashkent Declaration, signed on 10
January, under which the armed personnel of both sides were to
withdraw to the positions held before 5 August 1965. However, the news
of the declaration was overshadowed by the announcement that the
Indian Prime Minister, Lal Bahadur Shastri, had died at Tashkent.
Nehru's daughter, Mrs Indira Gandhi, was chosen to take his place but
she was left with very little time to rally her government and the
Congress Party for the fourth general elections, due to take place early in
1967. Preparation for these contests was also a major concern of the Jana
Sangh, which decided to break with previous practice and to ask one of
the senior secretaries, Balraj Madhok, to be its effective national leader
in the forthcoming campaign; his election as the party's President in
succession to Bachhraj Vyas was announced on 8 March 1966.
According to Madhok's own account, he had first been approached

---

[89] Central Working Committee, Delhi, 15 August 1965, in Bharatiya Jana Sangh,
*Resolution Passed by Bharatiya Pratinidhi Sabha, August 17, 18, 1965, and Working
Committee on August 15, 1965, & September 27, 28, 1965*, pp. 9–12. This resolution is
also given *BJS Documents*, IV, pp. 77–9, but it should be noted that there are some
differences in wording between the two texts and that the text in *BJS Documents* is
attributed to the Central General Council and is dated 17 August 1965.

[90] *Organiser*, 19 September 1965, pp. 3 and 15. See also his subsequent 'Political Diary' in
ibid., 26 September 1965, p. 2.

about assuming this responsibility in mid-1965, but had then refused to allow his name to be considered:

I explained that the organizing secretaries had become accustomed to dummy Presidents and I could not be a dummy. This would lead to friction and tension. The suggestion was repeated a few months later with the plea that party needed a President during the election year who could write and speak in both Hindi and English so that the party could make a show in South India as well. I was therefore, required to accept the responsibility as a matter of duty. I agreed, but made it clear that I would have to be given a free hand if I was to show results in the general elections which were due in February 1967.[91]

As these comments show, Madhok took office with the firm intention of restoring the authority of the presidency in relation to the party secretariat, and he also asserted his right to interpret party policy. The text of a speech which he delivered at Ahmedabad on 7 August 1966 was published under the title, *What Jana Sangh Stands For*, and attracted a great deal of attention as his statement of the party's viewpoint.[92]

The shift in power to the presidency was bound to weaken the post of General Secretary and restrict Upadhyaya's freedom to act as the party's guide and spokesman. He apparently indicated at this time that he wished to be relieved of the post of General Secretary, but Madhok persuaded him to remain in office.[93] In the secretariat there were several appointments which were creating difficulties; one concerned the post of organizing secretary, which had been given to Sundar Singh Bhandari by Bachhraj Vyas during his presidency, thus placing Bhandari above the other secretaries and second in line to the General Secretary. Madhok has claimed that the RSS leadership wanted him to nominate Bhandari for the position but that Vajpayee had threatened not to join the Working Committee unless he were appointed to the post. In the end, Madhok chose Vajpayee as organizing secretary and demoted Bhandari to the rank of an ordinary secretary, alongside Jagannathrao Joshi, Nana Deshmukh and a new appointee, Yagya Datt Sharma, who had been General Secretary of the Punjab unit for several years.[94] Madhok

---

91 Balraj Madhok, *Stormy Decade (Indian Politics) 1970–1980* (New Delhi, second edition, 1982), p. 198. See also Madhok, *R.S.S. and Politics* (New Delhi, 1986), p. 59.
92 Interview with Balraj Madhok, New Delhi, 15 May 1984. See also Madhok, *Why Jana Sangh?* (Bombay, n.d.).
93 Interview with Balraj Madhok, New Delhi, 15 May 1984. In a recent publication, Madhok has pointed out that, when he was told that Upadhyaya 'would not be available to me as a general secretary', he 'overcame this hurdle after a personal request' to Golwalkar (*R.S.S. and Politics*, p. 59).
94 Madhok, *R.S.S. and Politics*, p. 59. See also Varshney, *Jana Sangh – R.S.S. and Balraj Madhok*, p. 26. For details of secretarial appointments see the lists of members of the 1965 and 1966 working committees published in *Organiser*, 8 February 1965, p. 7, and *Statesman* (Delhi), 9 May 1966, p. 7.

claimed subsequently that Bhandari had taken offence at this decision. 'Since I did not appoint you organising secretary in the wider interest of the party', he wrote to Bhandari in November 1972, 'you non-cooperated with me for the two years I was president of the Party and have continued to behave as my personal enemy since then.'[95]

Apart from dealing with such organizational problems, Madhok had to guide his party through a number of difficult political situations in the course of 1966. Perhaps the most serious was that caused by the central government's decision to divide the Punjab to form a smaller, predominantly Sikh, state of the same name and a new, predominantly Hindu, state of Haryana; the Jana Sangh had always stood out against earlier moves to subdivide the Punjab, and it set out to agitate against this proposal and finally accepted its implementation only with great reluctance. The party again became the centre of attention later in the year when it was one of the organizations blamed for the demonstration in New Delhi on 7 November against cow-slaughter, which ended in rioting. In both cases, the party was in danger of being drawn into exposed political positions by extreme elements amongst its followers but Madhok and his colleagues were able to keep it within the boundaries of constitutional politics while making its views on the issues quite clear. Madhok was thus able to build up good relations with the other non-Communist opposition parties, and with the Swatantra Party in particular, and thus placed the party in a good position from which to contest the fourth general elections, held early in 1967. From these, the Jana Sangh emerged with 35 seats in the Lok Sabha and increased numbers in the northern Legislative Assemblies, and after the poll joined a number of coalition governments at the state levels.

By 1967 the number of the party's central secretaries in the central parliament had grown significantly. Bhandari had been elected to the Rajya Sabha in April 1966 and Madhok, Vajpayee and Yagya Datt Sharma were all returned to the Lok Sabha in the 1967 elections. Madhok was thus in a position to offer the party leadership from a parliamentary base, much as Mookerjee had done in the early 1950s, thereby causing a shift in power relations which further weakened the public role of the General Secretary. The latter had either to accept this change and the inevitable loss of power which it entailed, or to strengthen his own position, and Upadhyaya's decision to bid for the presidency in succession to Madhok was in effect a reassertion of the

---

[95] Letter from Madhok to Bhandari, 22 November 1972, in Varshney, *Jana Sangh – R.S.S. and Balraj Madhok*, pp. 102–11, quotation from p. 109. See also letter from Madhok to Vajpayee, 23 September 1969, in *ibid.*, pp. 84–90, especially pp. 85–6.

authority of the organization. The differences between the two men were similar to those which had existed between Mookerjee and his RSS lieutenants in the early 1950s, but on this occasion the outcome was never in doubt. Upadhyaya was chosen to succeed Madhok as President of the Jana Sangh in December 1967 and at once took the secretariat in hand, promoting Bhandari to the post of General Secretary and appointing Vajpayee, Jagannathrao Joshi, Deshmukh and P. Parameswaran, a newcomer from Kerala, to other secretarial posts.[96] He was set to make the presidency the driving force of the organization, just as he had used the general secretaryship to co-ordinate and develop it after 1955, but this new venture was cut short when, on 11 February 1968, he was found dead, apparently murdered, near Mughal Sarai railway station. Once again, therefore, the Jana Sangh faced a crisis of leadership succession. The outcome was that Vajpayee was appointed to take Upadhyaya's place as national President and that, under his direction, the organization remained firmly in control of the party.

Conclusion

The Jana Sangh began its existence with considerable advantages: a national leader of genuine stature, the opportunity to exploit the widespread sympathy for Hindu traditionalist ideas when these were being dismissed in liberal circles as 'communalist', and a ready-made organizational cadre in the young *pracharaks* who had been seconded to the party by the RSS. Why then did the party fail to achieve the degree of electoral support which might have been predicted for it? In this chapter, we have approached this question by considering the evolution of the party's leadership and organizational framework, while acknowledging that other factors, such as the party's identification with Hindi chauvinism, must be left aside for the time being.

In an earlier chapter, we saw that Mookerjee favoured taking the party along a course which would have enabled him to appeal, first, to that field of electoral opinion which was identified with Hindu tradition-alism and had earlier been attached to the Congress Party and, secondly, to those sections of the middle classes which were likely to be alienated by the Nehru government's interest in extending the role of the state in the control of the economy. In parliamentary terms, his strategy implied building up a substantial Jana Sangh contingent in the Lok Sabha and the Rajya Sabha after the first general elections, attracting other parties to that contingent and thus constructing a broad non-Congress front,

---

[96] *Organiser*, 14 January 1968, p. 3.

with the aim of defeating the ruling party at either the second or the third general elections. Given these aims, it was a mistake for Mookerjee to have allowed himself and his party to be associated with the *satyagraha* for the closer integration of Jammu and Kashmir with India but this mistake was by no means irredeemable; had Mookerjee not died in June 1953, he would probably have experienced little difficulty in getting the party back on the path he had chosen for it in 1951.

However, the failure of Mauli Chandra Sharma to overcome the challenge presented by Upadhyaya and his supporters in the party's internal crisis of 1954 determined that the Jana Sangh would follow a course which diverged sharply from that charted by Mookerjee. Sharma, perhaps reluctantly, had been forced to defend the main lines of Mookerjee's essential project – a flexible party capable of responding to and representing those sectors of middle-class opinion which the Congress Party was tending to neglect; an open party, prepared to offer political careers to a wide variety of people and to conduct its affairs under public scrutiny; and an accommodating party, prepared to make alliances with all kinds of groups within the broad spectrum of the non-Communist opposition. On the other hand, Upadhyaya was upholding an approach to party-building which was cautious and defensive, an approach which expressed the reluctance of the RSS to accept the compromises and pragmatism of the established party system, which placed a high value on discipline and loyalty, and which relied on the ability of a young, untried but zealous leadership to make a successful bid for power at some time in the future, when the older generation of politicians had been revealed as a spent force.

Under Upadhyaya's guidance, the party developed along these lines until the mid-1960s, when its new leaders were obliged to adapt themselves to the rapid changes in national politics which followed the death of Nehru in May 1964. For the first time since independence, the opposition parties sensed the possibility of victory and began to explore the possibilities of co-operation much more systematically than in the past. The opportunity to break through the Congress Party's defences and to reach new audiences meant that the parties had to reconsider their campaign strategies, and in particular to identify election leaders who could communicate readily and effectively with the public. The Jana Sangh's response was to turn to Balraj Madhok and much of the credit for the party's relative success at the 1967 polls was given to his style of robust and direct leadership. This outcome could well have been taken as a vindication of the principle that a Hindu nationalist party does best when it trusts its constituency, and leaves controlling power with its parliamentary groups and their leaders. However, as we have seen, the

Jana Sangh actually took the opposite course, and subsequently reaffirmed the primacy of its central organizational group in the conduct of the party's affairs.

Briefly, then, the Jana Sangh under Upadhyaya, from 1955 onwards, adopted a style of party activity which maintained discipline and control at the expense of openness and adaptability and which therefore left the party badly placed to exploit the weaknesses in the Congress Party's political empire which were revealed in the early 1960s. It was the Swatantra Party and not the Jana Sangh which offered the most effective criticism of the Congress government's economic policies from the perspective of economic and political liberalism, and it was poorly organized non-partisan associations such as the Hindi Sahitya Sammelan which sustained the neglected cause of Hindu traditionalism with most credibility. The Jana Sangh's remoteness enabled it to maintain discipline, and to preserve its privileged connection with the RSS, but left it beyond the reach of those interests which were beginning to break away from the Congress Party in the second decade of independence.

5

The Jana Sangh as a Hindu nationalist rally

From its earliest days, the Jana Sangh was hampered by the confusion within its ranks over what sort of party it should aim to be: was it to assert an uncompromising and monistic view of the Indian polity and aim to become the great party of Hindu nationalism or should it represent the material interests of particular economic groups in society and thus establish a sectional base for itself in a political system which was necessarily competitive and pluralistic? These roles were incompatible and the party's attempt to combine them served only to bewilder the electorate and ultimately to inhibit the party's own development.

In this chapter, we shall concentrate on the first of these aspects, the Jana Sangh's expression of Hindu nationalism, mainly with reference to particular issues in the politics of northern India.

The Jana Sangh's theory of Hindu nationalism

Whenever the Jana Sangh's leaders justified their adherence to Hindu nationalism they referred to the organicist theories of Hindu origins and history which had been formulated during the British period. Although such references were often brief and allusive, extended accounts of the basic myths occur in the reflective writings of the party's intellectuals, amongst which those of Balraj Madhok were particularly important.[1] From a combination of these sources, it is possible to assemble the essential elements of the party's general system of beliefs.

What may be described as the 'ground of faith' so far as Hindu nationalism is concerned is the idea that, at the very beginning of Indian history, Hindus constituted an organic community, that is, a community

---

[1] Balraj Madhok set out his views on the origins and development of Indian nationalism in a series of thirteen articles, which were published in the *Organiser* between the issues of 5 July and 25 October 1954. The articles were subsequently published as *Hindu Rashtra: A Study in Indian Nationalism* (Calcutta, 1955). See also the opening chapters of Madhok, *Political Trends in India* (Delhi, 1959), pp.1–29, and *Indianisation? (What, Why and How)* (New Delhi, [1970]).

endowed with an essential spirit which would enable it to develop towards an ultimate form. This belief provides the foundation for the 'content of faith', composed of historical narratives which describe the spread of the Aryans throughout India, the weakening of the nation by Buddhism, the subsequent revival of Hinduism, its survival under Muslim rule and its frustration by the British. In essence, Hindu nationalism is a theory of Hinduism which demonstrates its characteristics not by reference to specific texts and traditions in the manner of the Sanatana Dharma Sabha, nor by reference to the interpretations of a particular philosopher or teacher in the manner of the Arya Samaj, but by the exposition of a historically derived doctrine of what Hinduism has been as a cultural force and what it could become given the right conditions. The Jana Sangh hoped to offer this notion of Hinduism as a means of transcending the limitations of sect and of achieving the ultimate ideal of Hindu Sangathan. The ethical assumptions underlying its doctrine were activist, and it therefore came into conflict with the quietist and devotional aspects of the *bhakti* tradition, especially as this was expressed in Gandhian ideas. Nevertheless, the Jana Sangh tried hard to present itself as a vehicle of universal Hinduism. From the very beginning the object of the party's leaders was to avoid sectarianism and when, at a meeting with Upadhyaya in 1953, Swami Karpatriji Maharaj of the Ram Rajya Parishad suggested that the Jana Sangh should be based on a Hindu holy book he was told by Upadhyaya that this would be impossible.[2] By avoiding textual fundamentalism, the party could remain free to define both the ground and the content of its doctrine chiefly with reference to historical tradition and only incidentally with reference to the religious books which belonged to that tradition.

However, it was difficult for the party's writers to present historical myths without emphasizing some themes at the expense of others. Thus the assumption that Hinduism had an Aryan origin necessarily entailed the further notion that it came from the north of the subcontinent. Writing in 1954, Madhok described the Aryan race of the Vedic period as occupying 'the place of mother race':

Numerous ethnic and racial groups have contributed to the making of the Indian people but life of all of them has been imperceptibly coloured and moulded in the Indian pattern by the Aryan culture and ideals, the Aryan race spirit.[3]

He pictured the Aryans spreading from north-western India to the east, calling their expanded territory *Aryavarta*, and then extending their control to the south. The whole of India then became known as Bharat

[2] From interview with Jagdish Prasad Mathur, New Delhi, 10 May 1984.
[3] Madhok, 'Indian nationalism: what makes a nation?', *Organiser*, 12 July 1954, p. 8.

Varsha and in the 'course of time the name of the entire people of India irrespective of their caste, creed or race came to be Bharatiyas after the name of the country'.[4]

These acts of naming are an essential part of the historical mythology of Hindu nationalism, and Jana Sangh writers employed the terms 'Bharat' or 'Bharat Varsh' as a way of evoking not only the Vedic and Aryan background of the Indian nation but also the idea that this nation was based on cultural as distinct from purely religious values. Within the logic of the myth, an inhabitant of Bharat is a Bharatiya because of his cultural heritage, whether he is a Muslim or a Christian or a Hindu, and it is culture which determines his capacity for national awareness, not his religious beliefs. Thus, Atal Bihari Vajpayee could argue in 1961:

The Muslims or Christians did not come from outside India. Their ancestors were Hindus. By changing religion one does not change ones nationality or culture.[5]

Another writer made a similar point with specific reference to the place of Islam in India:

In Indian thought, identity of underlying reality permits variety of surface custom or even philosophical view. But the difference or diversity or variety should not oppose the underlying reality. Difference should realise its common root in the identity. If Jana Sangh is to recognise Islam on equal terms, Islam should recognise the same identity of national being in all Bharatiyas and be loyal to it and eschew all extra-territorial loyalty to Islamic society contradicting Indian loyalty.[6]

In discussing the spread of Muslim rule in northern India, Jana Sangh writers emphasized the political rather than the religious side of the encounter and presented the period of Mughal rule in particular as one when the nation was resisting an intrusive and oppressive imperial power. In Madhok's words:

It was not a struggle between two religions or two social orders. It was a struggle between the Indian nation, the national society of India and an alien who wanted to sub-merge her.[7]

---

[4] Madhok, 'Indian nationalism: its historic roots', *ibid.*, 26 July 1954, p. 5. On the term *Bharatavarsha*, see A. L. Basham, *The Wonder that was India: A Survey of the Culture of the Indian Sub-Continent before the Coming of the Muslims* (London, 1954), pp. 488–9.
[5] *National Integration: Note Submitted by Sh. A. B. Vajpayee, Leader of the Jana Sangh Group in Parliament at the National Integration Conference held at New Delhi, on Sept. 28, 29 & 30, 1961* (Delhi, n.d.), p. 3.
[6] M. A. Venkata Rao (President of the Karnataka Jana Sangh unit), 'Jana Sangh, Islam & Humayun Kabir', *Organiser*, 1 August 1960, p. 6. He was referring to Humayun Kabir, 'Congress ideology: a statement', *India Quarterly*, XVI, 1 (January–March 1960), pp. 3–23.
[7] Madhok, 'Indian nationalism and Islam', *Organiser*, 6 September 1954, p. 7.

At the same time, the resistance to the Muslims was represented as an instinctive and culturally based response rather than a self-conscious assertion of the right to political independence. For Madhok, part of the explanation for the survival of the nation lay in the durability of local institutions.

In spite of about a thousand years of Muslim rule, when every effort was made to make this country a Muslim country, the Muslim invaders were unable to reach the villages or destroy the Indian cultural life-pattern as existed in the vast number of villages in the country because of the efficient functioning of panchayats.[8]

The period of confusion which accompanied the decline of the Mughal empire, the military campaigns of the Marathas, and the extension of British rule into northern India was invested with particular significance by Jana Sangh writers. Madhok drew a contrast between 'a process of Indianisation or Hinduisation of Islam' which was occurring during the reign of the Mughal emperor, Akbar (1555–1605), and the reaction which set in thereafter and reached a climax under the emperor Aurangzeb (1658–1707). During his reign, resistance to Muslim rule increased and 'was strongest in Maharashtra where Chhatrapati Shivaji made it a broad based national movement'. The spread of the Marathas was checked when their forces were defeated by Ahmad Shah Durrani at the third battle of Panipat in 1761, but 'he could not capitalise his victory because of the general Hindu resurgence in the country. The Marathas were soon able to assert their position at Delhi once again'. At this stage, according to Madhok, a 'sort of equilibrium between the oppressive tendencies of Islam and the protective vigour of Indian nationalism was created all over the country'. But the opportunity thus afforded to Hindu society to renew the assimilation of Indian Islam was closed off when the British arrived to initiate a new period of foreign rule.[9]

In Madhok's view, the British became aware, as the Mughals had before them, that a unified Indian nationalism was the great danger to their authority and they therefore decided to divide and rule by setting Muslims off against Hindus, and to create a safety valve in the form of the artificial Indian National Congress.[10] However, early Hindu nationalist leaders such as Bankim Chandra Chatterji, Tilak, Aurobindo Ghosh and Lala Lajpat Rai

set out to revise and revitalise that age-old Indian nationalism by a direct appeal

---

[8] Madhok in *P.D., L.S.* (Second Series), LIX, 25 November 1961, c. 1384. Cf. Madhok, *Political Trends in India*, p. 4.

[9] Madhok, 'Nationalism and Islam', *Organiser*, 13 September 1954, pp. 6 and 14.

[10] Madhok, 'Nationalism and the British', *ibid.*, 20 September 1954, p. 8. See also Madhok, 'Some consequences of 1857', *ibid.*, 13 May 1957, pp. 9–10.

to India's glorious past, her heroes and culture and history. They presented India to the Indian masses as Bharat Mata, the common mother of all true Bharatiyas whose life she had sustained through thick and thin.[11]

In spite of their efforts, the early promise of a unified nationalist movement was not fulfilled because the British fostered and encouraged the Muslim League and because Congress failed to contain Muslim separatism. Madhok criticized the Congress for agreeing to the Lucknow Pact of 1916 and therefore to the principle of separate electorates for Muslims, and for associating the non-cooperation campaign of 1920–21 with the Khilafat movement, with the result that 'Islamic consciousness, as distinct from national consciousness, and the exclusiveness and fanaticism that go with it were revived in the Muslim masses'.[12]

Congress accepted the basic communal division, which ended in the creation of Pakistan, and it thereby failed the cause of true Indian nationalism. Madhok claimed that nationalism, 'as conceived and preached' by the Congress and its allies, had

given a new lease of life to Muslim separatism and has become the biggest ally of Communism. It has still failed to draw inspiration and sustenance from the ancient roots of Indian national life which have stood the test of time. It is neither national nor secular. It is based on compromises with separatism and communalism which it seeks to employ for the political gain of the Congress. But in doing so it is cutting at the roots of Indian nationalism. It is un-Indian, un-Hindu and A-bharatiya.[13]

The basic theme underlying Madhok's account is that, although the nation had succumbed to a Muslim invasion, it nevertheless retained a strong sense of its own identity. However, the establishment of the British Raj not only prevented the nation from achieving independence but also provided an opportunity for the proponents of a separate Muslim nationalism to assert themselves politically through the agency of the Muslim League, which came into conflict with those who were trying to strengthen the national consciousness of the people as a whole. For Madhok, the closing period of British rule was marked by two quite different lines of division, that between the Raj and a desperate anti-imperialist opposition and another, more fundamental, between an essential, culturally based nationalism and an Islamic resurgence.

Such a historical perspective implied a particular view of the role of

---

[11] Madhok, 'Indian versus Muslim nationalism', *ibid.*, 27 September 1954, p. 6.

[12] *Ibid.*, p. 12. See also Madhok, *Political Trends in India*, p. 16.

[13] Madhok, 'Indian nationalism and pseudo-secularism', *Organiser*, 18 October 1954, pp. 5 and 12, final quotation from p. 12.

the state in moulding Indian society once independence had been achieved. Whereas the Congress leaders were inclined to foster a political order which was generally liberal and pluralist in form and reflected the social, regional and linguistic diversity of the country, the Jana Sangh was disposed to emphasize the need for the state to build up a sense of national unity and therefore to set limits to the expression of dissent and of social, linguistic and regional differences. Where Muslims were concerned, the party disapproved of their close identification with Urdu and their determination to preserve the *shari'at*, the rules governing social life under Islamic law. In the debates about the reorganization of states in the mid-1950s the Jana Sangh proposed the absorption of small units into larger territories within a federal framework but it also reaffirmed its faith in a unitary system under which India would have had a single cabinet and a single legislature, based on a system of about one hundred regional assemblies, or Janapadas.[14] Writing as the party's General Secretary, Upadhyaya claimed that the British had fostered provincialism to frustrate the national movement and that their successive constitutional measures were 'aimed at province-wise and state-wise fragmentation of the country'; he described the Constitution of 1950 as 'a compromise between unitary and federal tendencies'.[15]

Had it been converted into an absolute faith, this version of Hindu nationalism would have justified doctrines that the organic unity of Hindu society could be expressed only through a strong, monolithic state and that anything which might weaken that ideal, especially movements tending towards regional and linguistic nationalism, could not be tolerated. The constituent political units of such a state could be determined only by administrative criteria and should under no circumstances become the focus for cultural or religious loyalties. The Jana Sangh's intellectual inheritance inclined it in this direction and it was, as we shall see, prepared to oppose interests which it considered were weakening the unity of the national community, but there was no guarantee that the Hindu majority would identify itself with actions ostensibly taken on its behalf. There was little indication in the early 1950s that the mass of Hindus would become the solid, unified and assertive community, jealous of its dignity and rights, which had been predicted by Hindu nationalist writers. In one sense, by allowing itself to take up Hindu nationalist causes, the Jana Sangh was gambling on its

---

[14] See report of press conference by Mauli Chandra Sharma, national president of the Jana Sangh, New Delhi, 27 May 1954 (*Statesman* (Delhi), 28 May 1954, p. 7).

[15] Upadhyaya, 'Wanted – a unitary form of government', *Organiser*, 26 January 1955, pp. 27–30.

expectation that Hindus would prove strongly and aggressively jealous of their cultural and territorial rights and that they would abandon the Congress Party once its inability to defend those rights had been demonstrated.

One of the first testing points of the party's Hindu nationalist role was the Punjab, where in the 1950s its local units tried to defend the position that India, given the potential threat from Pakistan, needed to have a strong, unified state on its north-western frontier and consequently that Sikh separatism, as represented by the Akali Dal, should be firmly resisted.

The Jana Sangh and the communal conflict in the Punjab

In the Punjab the act of partition in 1947 had been accompanied by social turbulence and political instability. The sprawling and wealthy province that had existed during the British period was simply divided into two parts by a line which followed district boundaries and cut across communication networks and cultural patterns as if they were of no account. The old provincial capital, Lahore, found itself in what became the West Punjab, allocated to Pakistan, and a quadrilateral of secondary towns (Amritsar, Jullundur, Ludhiana and Ferozepore) formed the urban base for East Punjab, which belonged to India. The savage communal rioting which had accompanied partition had set in motion huge streams of terrified refugees, Sikhs and Hindus moving towards the east and Muslims towards the west. In East Punjab, the provincial government which was established by the Congress Party lacked a secure social base in what was virtually a new territory and it was soon under contrary pressures from militant Sikhism, expressed in the Akali Dal, and from Hindu nationalists working through the provincial Hindu Sabha, through the Arya Samaj (especially concerned about the advancement of the Hindi language) and through the local units of the RSS.

The politics of the Indian Punjab were increasingly dominated by a conflict between two opposed programmes about how the territorial units of the north-western region should be organized, what linguistic and educational policies should be followed there, and whether local political institutions should be rigidly separated from religious bodies. What may be described as the Hindu nationalist programme contained the following proposals: the whole of the north-west, including not only East Punjab but also the Patiala and East Punjab States Union (PEPSU), where Sikhs predominated, and the hill-country states of Himachal Pradesh and Bilaspur should be amalgamated to form a greater Punjab, or Maha-Punjab, to provide an effective frontier territory on a vital border with Pakistan; Hindi should be the language of education and should replace English and Urdu as the languages of administration and the law courts; and, although the provincial government should not be identified with the rights of any one community, it should respect existing arrangements, including the widespread provision of education through the Dayananda Anglo-Vedic (DAV) college system, which had been established by the Arya Samaj during the British period. Quite different aims were contained in the programme being advanced by the more militant elements within the Akali Dal, who wanted the Sikh-majority districts and towns of East Punjab and PEPSU separated off to constitute a Sikh state, or Punjabi Suba, where Punjabi in the Gurumukhi script would be the language of education, the administration and the law courts, and where the institutions of government would be closely associated with the religious and cultural institutions of the Sikh community.

Poised between these two extremes, the Congress Party had to work through the moderate elements in both the Hindu and the Sikh communities, in the hope that time would demonstrate the material and social benefits of co-operation and mutual tolerance within a plural society and that other types of issues, especially those connected with agrarian and industrial development, would produce ties cutting across the communal boundaries. In terms of organizations, this was also a hope that, on the Hindu side, the Arya Samaj and the RSS would accept the virtues of compromise and devote themselves mainly to cultural work and that, on the Sikh side, moderate and non-partisan groups would be in control of the Shiromani Gurudwara Prabandhak Committee (SGPC), the very wealthy body entrusted by statute with jurisdiction of the gurudwaras, the Sikh shrines and temples, and therefore the focus of a great deal of activity at the time of its periodic elections. It was not beyond the bounds of possibility that Congress might be able to work outwards from the centre of opinion, and isolate extreme elements. At the beginning, the communal feeling on both sides was directed more against the Muslim community and Pakistan than against Hindus or Sikhs. It also tended to be confined to the western districts of the state, which had absorbed the largest numbers of Sikh and Hindu refugees, leaving relatively unaffected the predominantly Hindu populations of the Haryana tract in the east and of the hill districts and states in the north, which had not suffered directly from rioting and migration.

In the course of 1948 and 1949 the Congress provincial government in East Punjab made a number of concessions to Sikh demands for special treatment. These included a provision (known as the 'Sachar formula', after Bhim Sen Sachar, a Congress Premier who held office briefly in 1949) that Punjabi in the Gurumukhi script and Hindi in the Devanagari script should be the regional languages in Punjabi- and Hindi-speaking areas respectively and that educational policies should be framed to take account of this division. In the Punjabi-speaking region, the medium of instruction to the level of matriculation was to be Punjabi, but Hindi was to be taught as a compulsory subject from the last class of the primary department, and parents and guardians were to have the right to request instruction in Hindi as a mother tongue. A converse arrangement was envisaged for the Hindi-speaking region, where Hindi was to be the medium of instruction to matriculation, Punjabi a compulsory second language, and where parents and guardians were to be accorded the right to request Punjabi as the primary medium of instruction. The position of Punjabi was further strengthened by its inclusion in the list of fourteen languages named in the Eighth Schedule of the Constitution of India, which came into force on 26 January 1950.[16] This agreement presupposed a much firmer division between Hindi- and Punjabi-speakers than was in fact the case; in the undivided Punjab, Punjabi had been spoken by members of all three communities, Hindu, Muslim and Sikh, and had not been identified with any one script, but now the Arya Samaj was leading a campaign to define it as a form of Hindi, which should therefore be written in the Devanagari script, while the Akali Dal was pressing its followers to insist upon its association with the Gurumukhi script.

Thus, the battle lines for the conflict over language, regional division, and education had already been formed by the time the Punjab unit of the Jana Sangh, with responsibility not only for the Punjab but also for PEPSU, Himachal Pradesh and Delhi, was established in May 1951. Its links with the RSS were manifest but from the outset it was also strongly influenced by the Arya Samaj, from whom many of its early leaders were drawn. In one respect the Punjab was a natural area for the Jana Sangh to cultivate because here its antipathy to Pakistan, its disapproval of partition, and its opposition to Islam could be expected to attract immediate and unqualified support. On the other hand, its attitudes

---

[16] This paragraph is based on Baldev Raj Nayar, *Minority Politics in the Punjab* (Princeton, N.J., 1966), pp. 214–21. See also Paul Wallace, 'The political party system of Punjab state, India: a study of factionalism' (Unpublished D. Phil. dissertation, University of California, Berkeley, 1966), pp. 188–200. For the text of the Sachar formula, see Government of India, Lok Sabha Secretariat, *Parliamentary Committee on the Demand for Punjabi Suba: Report* (New Delhi, 1966), pp. 79–81. For a detailed account of linguistic and communal politics in the Punjab, see Paul R. Brass, *Language, Religion and Politics in North India* (London, 1974), Part IV, pp. 275–400.

towards Sikhs and Sikhism presented it with considerable difficulty. Its intellectuals were inclined to treat the Sikhs as but one of the many sects of the extended Hindu community and to consider the doctrines of Sikhism, as expressed in the teaching of its founder, Guru Nanak (1469–1538), and preserved in the Adi Granth, as compatible with the essential tenets of Hinduism. By this reasoning, Sikhs were already Hindus and, unlike Muslims, did not need to renounce their faith and accept their ancient cultural attachments to become once more an organic part of the Hindu nation, but the Sikhs not unnaturally found such an attitude patronizing, given their sense of being a distinctive and self-sufficient religious community. At this early stage, when it was at its most intransigent, the Jana Sangh's commitment to Hindi in the Devanagari script and to a unitary state left it with little scope for compromise in its dealings with political parties and social groups which took the view that India's linguistic and cultural diversity implied a generous measure of regional autonomy within a federal structure. The political situation in the Punjab posed the problem in an acute form: if the Jana Sangh agreed that the Sikh community had special territorial rights it would be granting the case that differences of language and religion justified some degree of political separation; on the other hand, if it refused to make this concession it could find itself, at some future time, insisting that minority groups such as the Sikhs should be forcibly assimilated to the Hindi-speaking Hindu heartland for the sake of national unity.

In the event, the Punjab Jana Sangh adopted a surprisingly moderate position and positioned itself quite close to the Congress Party so far as linguistic policy was concerned. Its first programme declared 'for freedom of option to the people living in all parts of Punjab and Pepsu States in respect of the medium of instructions for their wards' both as regards the choice between Hindi and Punjabi and between the Devanagari and Gurumukhi scripts.[17] Later in the year, when the party was engaged in its first election campaign, its President, Lala Balraj Bhalla, said that although he was opposed to the demand for a Punjabi-speaking state he was in favour of adopting both Hindi and Punjabi as regional languages for the Punjab and suggested that both could be employed in offices and the lower courts, with the option of which to choose open to all.[18] In essence, this policy conceded the claims made by the Sikhs on behalf of Punjabi but it stopped short of endorsing the Sachar formula and implicitly excluded the possibility of dividing either

---

[17] *Organiser*, 4 June 1951, p. 14.
[18] *Tribune* (Ambala), 3 October 1951, p. 3. See also *Times of India* (Delhi), 6 October 1951, p. 3.

the Punjab or PEPSU into linguistically separate zones. Even so, it had provided the party with an avenue for gaining support, partly on Hindu nationalist grounds (by building on hostility towards Pakistan) and partly on social and economic grounds.

Unfortunately for the Jana Sangh, Punjabi politics in the mid-1950s were centred almost entirely on the territorial issues, where the party was quite unable to occupy the middle ground. The appointment of a Central Commission for the Reorganisation of States in December 1953 was followed by protracted and intense controversies between rival linguistic and territorial groups in several parts of India, but the conflict in the Punjab region was particularly bitter. In its submissions to the commission, the Jana Sangh proposed that the Punjab, PEPSU and Himachal Pradesh should be brought together to form a greater Punjab, thus establishing a strong, stable and 'politically reliable' state on the frontier with Pakistan.[19] The Akali Dal, on the other hand, was pressing for the creation of a separate Sikh state and built up considerable momentum for its campaign; in elections held at the end of 1954, it won a majority of the places on the SGPC and on 7 February 1955 Master Tara Singh, a prominent Akali leader, was elected as SGPC President.[20] The Akalis stepped up their programme of marches and demonstrations in the towns and cities of the region and made much more impression on the public than did their two rivals, the Maha Punjab Samiti, to which the Jana Sangh belonged, and the Maha Punjab Front. At this stage, the best outcome so far as the Jana Sangh and the Arya Samaj were concerned was that neither the Congress government in New Delhi nor the state Congress government in the Punjab would agree either to a separate Sikh state, which was unlikely, or to some division of the region into Punjabi- and Hindi-speaking sectors for administrative convenience, which seemed a possible solution to the dispute. Much depended, therefore, on whether the state government would take a hard line with the Akalis. At first it restricted itself to specific measures in particular localities, but then the Akalis decided to make a general issue of a ban on the shouting of language slogans in Amritsar, which contained the Golden Temple, the major shrine of the Sikh religion. On 10 May 1955 the Akalis began a *morcha*, a series of demonstrations directed from the gurudwaras, and Tara Singh and three companions were immediately

[19] See report of a press conference given by the Jana Sangh's national president, Mauli Chandra Sharma, New Delhi, 27 May 1954 (*Statesman* (Delhi), 28 May 1954, p. 7). On the memorandum submitted by the Punjab Jana Sangh, see *ibid.*, 2 May 1954, p. 4; and Satya M. Rai, *Partition of the Punjab: A Study of its Effects on the Politics and Administration of the Punjab (I) 1947–56* (London, 1965), pp. 236–8. On its supplementary memorandum, see *Statesman* (Delhi), 18 April 1955, p. 4.

[20] *Statesman* (Delhi), 8 February 1955, p. 10.

arrested. The demonstrations were sustained until, on 12 July, the Chief Minister, Bhim Sen Sachar, announced that the ban had been lifted to mark Nehru's return from a foreign tour.[21] The Jana Sangh's Central Working Committee, in a resolution later endorsed by its Central General Council, treated the lifting of the ban as an indication that a partition of the state was being considered and warned the people of India

that if once the Akali demand is conceded, it will encourage the process of Balkanisation of our country destroying its unity.[22]

Although the States Reorganisation Commission did recommend the formation of an enlarged Punjab, the Government of India decided that more was to be gained by formulating a scheme which made some concessions to Sikh separatism. After months of negotiation, it eventually agreed that Himachal Pradesh should be preserved as a union territory and that the new Punjab, including PEPSU, should be divided into two regions, the one Punjabi-speaking and the other Hindi-speaking. The state was to have a single Legislative Assembly, which could, however, meet as two separate regional committees; the Sachar formula and the equivalent provision in the former PEPSU areas was to be continued; and both Punjabi and Hindi were to be official languages, although, at district level and below, Punjabi was to be the language in the western region and Hindi was to be the language in the eastern region. As one of the symbols of unity, Chandigarh, the state's capital, was given a separate territory of its own.[23] The Maha Punjab Samiti and Arya Samaj launched an agitational campaign against this scheme, known as the Regional Formula, and the Punjab Jana Sangh's State General Council decided in August 1956 to resist 'by all possible means, and at all cost, the introduction of the regional formula... in full or part without getting the people's mandate through general elections'.[24] However, the new Chief Minister of the Punjab, Pratap Singh Kairon,

---

[21] *Ibid.* (Calcutta), 13 July 1955, p. 1. On the Akali agitation as a whole, see Nayar, *Minority Politics in the Punjab*, pp. 237–46.

[22] Central General Council, Calcutta, 28 August 1955, Bharatiya Jana Sangh, *Party Documents* (New Delhi, 1973), IV, pp. 102–3 (hereafter referred to as *BJS Documents*).

[23] For the text of the Formula, the details of which were tabled in the Lok Sabha by the Home Minister on 3 April 1956, see Annexure No. 26 of Appendix VI in *Lok Sabha Debates, 12th Session, 1956, Appendices*, pp. 557–8. See also the commentary in Nayar, *Minority Politics in the Punjab*, pp. 222–3, and the map of the regions in *ibid.*, p. xiv. On subsequent negotiations, see Wallace, 'The political party system of Punjab state', pp. 241–2. That part of the scheme regarding regional committees was brought into operation by a presidential order of 4 November 1957 (see Lok Sabha Secretariat, *Parliamentary Committee on the Demand for Punjabi Suba: Report*, pp. 66–78).

[24] *Statesman* (Delhi), 28 August 1956, p. 4.

took severe measures against the agitation and kept it within bounds. His position was further strengthened on 2 October 1956 when a convention of the Akali Dal advised its members and supporters to join the Congress for political activities.[25]

The new state of the Punjab came into existence on 1 November 1956 and Kairon, having been appointed its first Chief Minister, began preparing his party for the second general elections scheduled for February and March 1957. During the election campaign the Punjab Jana Sangh did its best to keep the cause of Maha Punjab alive: it issued a supplementary manifesto which attacked the Regional Formula and demanded that Hindi should be accorded a 'place of honour and prestige' in the state[26] and its General Secretary, Krishan Lal, even said that his party would support Congress candidates were the Congress High Command to implement the recommendations of the States Reorganisation Commission for the Punjab.[27] However, the Congress succeeded in winning 120 of the 154 seats in the incoming Legislative Assembly and the Jana Sangh a mere nine.

The Jana Sangh's essential dilemma remained. If it accepted the Regional Formula as a reasonable settlement, and concentrated on building up support by appeals to social and economic interests, it ran the risk of alienating the Arya Samaj, whose influence within the Hindu community was considerable and which remained deeply concerned about the weakened status of Hindi. On the other hand, if the party continued to resist the implementation of the Regional Formula, it risked not only isolating itself from moderate opinion in the state but demonstrating before the Indian public as a whole that it was unwilling to tolerate the existence of regional languages alongside Hindi. On balance, prudence and a growing awareness of the party's vulnerability would probably have inclined its national leadership to move in the direction of accepting the Regional Formula and softening the demands for Maha Punjab and a major role for Hindi, but the state party was swept into a precipitate campaign against the government before there had been adequate time for reflection.

The new campaign was inspired by the Sarvadeshik Bhasha Swatantrya Samiti (SBSS, the National Freedom of Language Committee), an agency of the International Aryan League, which was the national organization of the Arya Samaj, the operational control of which was

[25] *Ibid.*, 3 October 1956, pp. 1 and 7.
[26] Special correspondent, Amritsar, 'Punjab election scene', *Hindustan Times* (Delhi), 12 February 1957, p. 9.
[27] Press conference, Jullundur, 19 February 1957, in *Times of India* (Delhi), 20 February 1957, p. 10. See also *Hindustan Times*, 21 February 1957, p. 8.

vested in the Hindi Raksha Samiti (HRS, Hindi Protection Committee) under the leadership of Swami Atmanand Saraswati, a respected elder of the Punjab Arya Samaj. The HRS aimed to force the state government to abandon the policy of regional languages and to weaken the application of the Sachar formula in the educational system, principally by ending the requirement that Hindi and Punjabi should be taught as second languages in Punjabi- and Hindi-medium schools respectively and by giving parents the right to choose the medium of instruction in educational institutions.[28] The then President of the Punjab Jana Sangh, Acharya Ram Dev, was also a prominent figure in the Arya Samaj,[29] and the ties between the two organizations were sufficiently strong to ensure that the Jana Sangh would inevitably be drawn into the fray.

Although it was not really possible for the party's Central Working Committee to dissociate itself from the actions of its Punjab unit, it nevertheless made clear its own quite significant reservations about what was being done, when it considered the matter in Delhi on 1 June 1957. In a resolution it expressed regret that the talks between the Government of the Punjab and the HRS had broken down and claimed that, had the central government instructed the state government 'to adopt a just and non-communal policy regarding the question of language', the 'genuine doubts and fears' of the large majority of the people in the state about 'the status and future of their mother tongue' would not have arisen. It then went on to imply in effect that the Regional Formula could be made to work were such 'doubts and fears' to be allayed:

Some understanding could and should have been evolved which might have put at rest these doubts and fears and created conditions in which both Hindi and Punjabi could have been fully developed as regional languages of the Punjab both in the sphere of administration and education without doing any violence to the fundamental right of the people to get education through their mother tongue.

It still blamed the government and warned that should it persist

in its policy of appeasement of communal and separatist forces... it will lead to serious results about which no true nationalist can remain indifferent.[30]

---

[28] For the detailed demands, see Jyotirindra Das Gupta, *Language Conflict and National Development: Group Politics and National Language Policy in India* (Berkeley, 1970), p. 155.

[29] Acharya Ram Dev was president of the Punjab Jana Sangh from 1953 until about 1959. On his attitudes and positions, see Gerald A. Heeger, 'Discipline versus mobilization: party building and the Punjab Jana Sangh', *Asian Survey*, XII, 10 (October 1972), pp. 870–1.

[30] Central Working Committee, Delhi, 1 June 1957, *BJS Documents*, V, p. 25.

Such fine distinctions were forgotten in the heat of the campaign and by July Vajpayee was telling a press conference that his party had 'full sympathy with the movement launched by the Arya Samaj in the Punjab to secure for Hindi its rightful place in education and administration' and that members of the party would be allowed to take part in the movement.[31] It was identified in public with the agitation and was not given the benefit of any doubt; Nehru himself said in a letter to Swami Atmanand that nobody 'has ever considered the Jana Sangh as an organization following Gandhian methods or indeed peaceful methods' and that they 'have a different reputation and are considered a narrowly communal body'.[32] The campaign dragged on but the state government had no difficulty in keeping it under control and finally, in December 1957, the agitation was suspended.

Local incidents continued in the new year and on 8 February 1958 fighting broke out when an HRS procession was passing a Sikh shrine in Jullundur and the police had to intervene to restore order; two people were killed and twenty-eight injured but a special commission found that the use of force by the police had been 'wholly justified' and that the extent of that force 'cannot be said to have been excessive'.[33] This and other incidents were declared to have 'thoroughly laid bare the despotic character of the Punjab Government' according to a resolution adopted by the Jana Sangh's sixth national session in April[34] but it soon became clear that the party was cutting itself loose from the HRS and its activities. Speaking in May 1958, Krishan Lal, as Vice-President of the Punjab unit, said that his party was unlikely to launch any major agitation in the state for the next two years and that, without abandoning its opposition to the Regional Formula, it would concentrate on constructive work, on strengthening its organization, and on creating a public opinion in favour of its policy.[35] Accordingly, the Punjab unit refused an invitation to take part in another pro-Hindi agitation. In approving this decision and appealing to the central government 'to shed their policy of appeasement towards communal and undemocratic forces' and to give equal recognition to Punjabi and Hindi in administration and education throughout the Punjab, the

---

[31] See press conference, Gwalior, 9 July 1957, in *Statesman* (Delhi), 11 July 1957, p. 5.
[32] Letter from Nehru to Swami Atmanand, 10 August 1957, in *ibid*, 17 August 1957, pp. 1 and 7.
[33] See the report of the commissioner, Justice G. D. Khosla, in *ibid.*, 11 March 1958, pp. 1 and 12.
[34] Sixth National Session, Ambala, 5 April 1958, *BJS Documents*, IV, pp. 111–12.
[35] At Jullundur, 29 May 1958, in *Statesman* (Delhi), 30 May 1958, p. 5.

party's Central Working Committee also warned the SBSS and the HRS 'not to take any step in haste'.[36]

The hard residue of all these disputes was the doctrine that Punjabi was not a regional language like Marathi and Bengali, but a simple dialect of Hindi, and that the Sikhs were not a separate religious community, as were Muslims and Christians, but a particular sect of Hinduism. On the basis of this doctrine, the Jana Sangh refused to concede that the Punjab consisted of a pair of discrete one-language units and insisted that it should be treated as a single bilingual territory. The most persuasive advocate of these ideas was Balraj Madhok, the organizing secretary for the northern zone within the party's central secretariat, who refused to admit that the Punjab was anything other than an integral part of the Hindi heartland. He argued that the original difference between the dialects of the Ambala Division, in the eastern part of the state, and those of the Jullundur Division, in the western part, had been

completely blurred by the intermixture of millions of displaced people from West Pakistan who speak different dialects of Punjabi. As such the whole of Punjab has become in a way a unilingual Hindi speaking state like Uttar Pradesh even though it has a number of spoken languages. But since, unlike Braj and Avadhi, Punjabi has been recognised as a separate language in the Constitution, Punjab can now be better described as a bilingual state wherein both Punjabi and Hindi are spoken and understood from one end to the other.[37]

He therefore described as 'fantastic' the Akali Dal's demand that Punjabi had to be defined as Punjabi written in the Gurumukhi script; he claimed that

the real problem of Punjab is not the problem of language; it is the problem of script. If this unnecessary, illogical and irrational thing had not been accepted by the Congress Government in Punjab, all this trouble could have been avoided.[38]

However, the issues of script and language had come to stand for much broader Sikh aspirations; on arrival in the East Punjab, many of the Sikhs had found themselves in new surroundings, forced to come to terms with Hindu neighbours who were often influenced by the Arya Samaj, with its zealous advocacy of Hindi and Hindu rights. They

---

[36] Central Working Committee, Bombay, 19 July 1958, *BJS Documents*, V, pp. 31–2. See also *Statesman* (Delhi), 27 July 1958, p. 3.

[37] From a memorandum to the Das Commission, which the central government appointed to enquire into allegations of discrimination in the Punjab, reproduced in *Organiser*, 8 January 1962, p. 12. 'Braj' and 'Avadhi' refer to regional dialects of Hindi in Uttar Pradesh.

[38] *P.D., L.S.* (Second Series), LVII, 29 August 1961, cc. 5624–5, quotation from c. 5625.

therefore looked to their religious and cultural institutions to give them a sense of common purpose, with the result that their local gurudwaras and, above all, the Golden Temple at Amritsar, became their rallying points. Had the authorities been tolerant, even-handed and patient, the Sikh refugees would probably have settled down in their local communities, but the Congress administration in the East Punjab, like its counterpart in the United Provinces, was committed to the rapid substitution of Hindi in the Devanagari script for the former languages of administration, the courts and education. In the East Punjab, this meant the introduction of Hindi at the expense of English and Urdu, with which the Sikhs from the western Punjab would have been familiar, and reaction was inevitable, expressed in its most extreme form by the Akali Dal's demands for the introduction of Punjabi in the Gurumukhi script in Sikh-majority areas.

By 1951, when the Jana Sangh appeared, this pattern of reforming zeal and defensive reaction had already begun to distort the pattern of party politics in the Punjab, and the range of possible outcomes had already been narrowed. The choice of establishing a Maha Punjab now entailed, as a corollary, a continued imposition of the Hindi-only policy or, at the very least, some agreement that the Sikhs could ask for schooling in the medium of Punjabi where they formed a majority. The alternative was for the Congress and the Jana Sangh to accept that the Hindi-speaking heartland extended only a little way into the Punjab, enclosing the Ambala Division at the most, and that Punjabi should be recognized as the language of a small state made up of the Jullundur Division and the western districts of PEPSU, a state which would be identified, at least to some extent, with the cultural and religious aspirations of the Sikh community. These basic issues were posed during the rival Akali and Maha-Punjab agitations of 1955 and 1956 and the result was a grudging admission by the Congress that the state should be divided into linguistic regions. This the Jana Sangh refused to accept and, for all its talk of bilingualism, it remained committed to the notion of an undivided territory.

The Congress were the realists; they had recognized not only the degree of support mustered by the Akali Dal but also the lack of will on the part of local Hindus to battle on behalf of Hindi and the ideal of Maha Punjab. Had there really been a strong collective identification by the Hindus with the supposed Hindi heartland they would never have tolerated the series of political concessions which effectively conceded the case that the Sikhs were a separate cultural, linguistic and territorial community. On the other hand, the Jana Sanghis were being quite unrealistic; even though they had backed away from further pro-Hindi agitations after the failure of the HRS campaign of 1957, their basic approach was still anchored to the belief that the common ground between Sikhs and Hindus would lead to their reconciliation, and that the Akali Dal would eventually move to the margins of Sikh politics and wither away. They allowed themselves to be guided by doctrines about the inherent nature of the Hindu community, about the acceptability of Hindi, and about the principles of state-building which earned them neither the support of the Hindus nor the understanding of the Sikhs.

Nevertheless, the Jana Sangh's use of rhetoric in the Punjab showed an interesting reluctance to treat Sikhs and Sikhism as targets for hostility and the party's anger and frustration were directed either towards the Congress or towards the Akali Dal, as being organizations which were refusing to consider the people's feelings and anxieties, in the case of the Congress, or exploiting them, in the case of the Akali Dal. However, it had no such inhibitions about characterizing Islam and the Muslims as threats to national unity and in Uttar Pradesh, where the party claimed to find instances of Muslim separatism, its Hindu nationalist mission was expressed in direct and unambiguous terms.

The Jana Sangh and Muslim interests in Uttar Pradesh

In the 1950s there was no political party based exclusively on the Muslim community in Uttar Pradesh and the great majority of Muslims gave their allegiance to the Congress Party with its philosophy of cultural pluralism. However, while regarding themselves as Indians first and foremost, many of them also wished to retain the *shari'at*, or system of Islamic personal law, and remained strongly attached to the Urdu language and its associated literary tradition. For Hindu nationalists, such an attitude reflected the mentality which had sustained the Muslim League in the United Provinces in the final four decades of British rule and, at a further remove, was a reminder that the regions based on Delhi, Agra, Lucknow and Faizabad had formed the central points of the Mughal empire and of the Indo-Persian culture which it had generated. The Muslim League had been dissolved in this part of India in 1948 but the Jana Sangh could still pick out special targets such as the Jama'at-i-Islami (a Muslim cultural organization), the Anjuman-i-Taraqqi-i-Urdu (an association for the promotion of Urdu which had been founded in 1903 and reorganized after independence)[39] and the Aligarh Muslim University, all of which it saw as expressions of Muslim separatism.

---

[39] On the organization of this body, see Gupta, *Language Conflict and National Development*, pp. 209–13.

Having thus characterized these bodies, it saw their policy demands not as being restricted to their stated objectives but rather as part of a deep-laid scheme to rehabilitate territorial claims; hence the intensity of the controversy which built up around Muslim proposals to improve the status of Urdu. This issue was at the centre of communal disputes in Uttar Pradesh in the 1950s and 1960s. To measure its importance we need first to understand how the Muslim population was distributed throughout the state and to review the campaign for increased rights for Urdu-speakers within the state's educational and legal systems.

According to the 1951 Census, Muslims numbered 9,028,992 or 14.3 per cent of the state's total population of 63,215,742. At the district level, the highest proportions were to be found in the western and central districts of the state, and particularly in the Meerut and Rohilkhand Divisions, where Muslims constituted 22.1 and 28.5 per cent respectively of the divisional population totals. Their relatively high dependence on non-agricultural occupations was reflected in the fact that 29.9 per cent of them were located in the urban areas and that they constituted 31.3 per cent of the urban population of the state.[40] It was in the towns that sentiment for Urdu was strongest; for the Muslim middle classes Urdu, with its rich and sophisticated literature, was a language which certainly deserved a place alongside Hindi in the legal, administrative and professional institutions of the state.

Although it is often associated with the period of Mughal rule in Delhi, the origins of Urdu belong to a much earlier period. One authority places the beginning of Urdu as far back as A.D. 1027, when Mahmud of Ghazni annexed the Punjab and settled his troops in its capital, Lahore. These Persian-speaking soldiers, living amongst a people whose language was not very different from the early *khari boli* of Delhi, learnt their language and introduced Persian words into it. After Muhammad Ghori captured the Punjab in 1187, his servant Qutb-ud-din Aibak went on to take Delhi in 1193, and a considerable number of the fighting men who went with him must have spoken an early form of Urdu (the name is derived from *zaban-i-urdu*, the language of the army). It was from a mixture of this early language and *khari boli*, altered during successive invasions of Delhi by troops who spoke Persian, that Urdu is said to

---

[40] For district, divisional and state figures for Muslim and total populations, see *Census of India 1951*, Vol. II, *Uttar Pradesh*, Part II-C, *Age and Social Tables*, by Rajeshwari Prasad, I.A.S., Superintendent, Census Operations (Allahabad, 1953), Table D-II, pp. 559–75. The percentages relating to urban population are from Tables 388 and 389 in *ibid.*, Part I-A, *Report*, by Rajeshwari Prasad (Allahabad, 1953), pp. 421 and 422.

  On the Muslim population in urban areas of Uttar Pradesh between 1881 and 1961, see Brass, *Language, Religion and Politics in North India*, pp. 142–4.

have developed.[41] During the Mughal period Persian was the language of the court, the administration and the law courts, but Urdu was widely spoken in Delhi, Lucknow and the surrounding areas of northern India. During the British period, after the Governor-General in Council had decided in 1837 to authorize the use of vernacular languages instead of Persian in Bengal and the North-Western Provinces, the Sadr Diwani Adalat (the chief civil court) directed in 1839 that 'Hindustani' was to be used in all courts subordinate to it in the North-Western Provinces. Whether Hindustani in this case referred specifically to Urdu, or simply meant the language of Hindustan (that is, of Upper India), the fact remains that Urdu became the vernacular language for court purposes, while English took over from Persian as the official language for the administration and the judiciary. However, towards the end of the nineteenth century, Urdu, which is written in the Persian script, became increasingly associated with Muslim interests and the protagonists of Hindi pressed for the adoption of the Devanagari script in the courts. Consequently, in 1900 the Lieutenant-Governor of the North-Western Provinces and Oudh resolved that Devanagari as well as the Persian script could be used in the courts, and that, after one year from the date of the resolution, no one should be appointed, except 'in a purely English office', to any 'ministerial appointment' unless he knew both Hindi and Urdu.[42]

The definition of a new language policy was one of the first tasks for the United Provinces Congress ministry, headed by Govind Ballabh Pant, on the attainment of independence in 1947. The leaders of the United Provinces Congress Party were strongly committed to substituting Hindi for English as the official language of the territory, and the only matter for doubt was whether they would accept Urdu as a second, though subordinate, official language or adopt a Hindi-only policy.

---

[41] See T. Grahame Bailey, 'Urdu: the name and the language', in Bailey, *Studies in North Indian Languages* (London, 1938), pp. 1–10. This article was originally published in *The Journal of the Royal Asiatic Society*, 1930, pp. 391–400.

[42] No. 585/III–343C-68, 18 April 1900, General Administration Department, *Government Gazette, North-Western Provinces and Oudh* (Allahabad), Part VI, 21 April 1900, pp. 131–3, as corrected by No. 1027/III–343C, 26 June 1900, General [Administration] Department, *ibid.*, 30 June 1900, p. 193. See also Francis Robinson, *Separatism among Indian Muslims: The Politics of the United Provinces' Muslims, 1860–1923* (Delhi, 1975), pp. 43–4.

For a detailed discussion of the issue, see Brass, *Language, Religion and Politics in North India*, pp. 127–36, and for a systematic account of the steps which led to the adoption of Hindi in 1900, see Khalid Hasan Qadiri, 'Hasrat Mohani: a study of his life and poetry' (Unpublished D. Phil, thesis, School of Oriental and African Studies, University of London, 1971), pp. 102–5. See also Aziz Ahmad, *Studies in Islamic Culture in the Indian Environment* (Oxford, 1964), pp. 259–62; and Gupta, *Language Conflict and National Development*, pp. 101–5.

Without hesitation the Pant government took decisions which laid the foundations for a Hindi-only policy; it accepted a non-official resolution of the provincial Legislative Council recommending 'that Hindi language and Devanagari script be adopted as the State language and script of this Province' and authorized detailed provisions to that effect. On 8 October 1947 Hindi was declared to be the language of the civil and criminal courts of the United Provinces, although executive instructions provided that persons unfamiliar with the Devanagari script could present petitions or complaints to courts in the Persian script. On the same date an administrative order was issued setting out the steps to be taken to ensure the introduction of Hindi for official and administrative purposes, while permitting persons unacquainted with Hindi to use English or Urdu in correspondence with government offices.[43]

Given that English was still used extensively in administration and the courts, it was recognized that the effects of these decisions would be limited for the first few years, especially because the transitional arrangements permitted Urdu-speakers to continue using their language in dealing with public offices and the courts. However, the measures not only raised doubts about whether the government would continue to provide for the teaching of Urdu in the schools but also conveyed to Muslims the plain message that the government expected them eventually to accept Hindi and to abandon their attachment to Urdu and, with it, any claim to cultural distinctiveness. Indeed, Hindu traditionalists amongst the Congress leaders were quite prepared to make this point publicly. Purushottamdas Tandon, then Acting President of the United Provinces Provincial Congress Committee, was reported to have stated at Sultanpur in June 1948:

The Muslims must stop talking about a culture and civilisation foreign to our country and genius. They should accept Indian culture. One culture and one language will pave the way for real unity. Urdu symbolises a foreign culture. Hindi alone can be the unifying factor for all the diverse forces in the country.[44]

---

[43] See G.O. No. 4686/III-170-1947, dated Lucknow, 8 October 1947, from the Chief Secretary to Government, UP, General Administration Department, to all Heads of Departments, Commissioners of Divisions, District Officers and other Principal Heads of Offices, United Provinces, given as Appendix IV in Government of Uttar Pradesh, *Report of the Uttar Pradesh Language Committee* (*August, 1962*) (Lucknow, 1963), pp. 87–9. To this administrative order were attached copies of the notifications regarding the declaration of Hindi as the language of the civil and criminal courts in the province, and these were published subsequently, viz. No. 4586 (6)/III–170–47 and No. 4586 (7)/III–170–47, 8 October 1947, General Administration Department, *Government Gazette of the United Provinces* (Allahabad), Part I, 11 October 1947, p. 756.

[44] *National Herald* (Lucknow), 15 June 1948, p. 7.

The Congress leadership at the national level proved more tolerant in its approach to the language question and on 5 August 1949 the Congress Working Committee adopted a comprehensive resolution which recommended a number of ways in which the rights of linguistic minorities could be protected. Although it granted the need for a province or state to nominate a particular language for use in public administration and the law courts, it suggested that, in areas where a linguistic minority constituted 20 per cent of the population, public documents should be in the minority language as well as the official language, and that a person should be entitled to present petitions in his own language. It also proposed that at the primary level of schooling a child should be instructed in its mother tongue, which could be a minority language in some areas, and that even at the secondary level, under certain circumstances, a minority language might be used as the medium of instruction at the request of a sufficiently large number of children. It noted specifically that, for the purposes of the resolution, 'Urdu shall be one of the languages concerned'.[45]

The philosophy underlying this resolution, that the rights of linguistic minorities should be protected wherever possible, also informed the debates of the Constituent Assembly of India and helps to explain the relevant provisions of the Constitution of 1950. Thus, although Article 345 specified that it was for a state legislature to adopt by law 'any one or more of the languages in use in the State or Hindi as the language or languages to be used for all or any of the official purposes of that State', Article 347 provided that the President, if he were satisfied 'that a substantial proportion of the population of a State desire the use of any language spoken by them to be recognised by that State', could direct that such language should be 'officially recognised throughout that State or any part thereof for such purpose as he may specify'. Linguistic minorities could also refer to Part III of the Constitution, on Fundamental Rights, which provided that

Any section of the citizens residing in the territory of India or any part thereof having a distinct language, script or culture of its own shall have the right to conserve the same. (Article 29 (1))

and that

All minorities, whether based on religion or language, shall have the right to establish and administer educational institutions of their choice. (Article 30 (1))

The position of Urdu should also have been strengthened by its inclusion in the list of fourteen languages given in the Eighth Schedule

---

[45] *Congress Bulletin*, August 1949, pp. 7–8.

of the Constitution. Nevertheless, the Congress government in Uttar Pradesh persisted in its Hindi-only policy and used its majority in the legislature to put through the UP Official Language Act of 1951 (UP Act No. XXVI of 1951), which provided for the adoption of Hindi in the Devanagari script as the language to be used for official and other specified purposes within the state. When the measure first reached the Legislative Assembly, Nawab Jamshed Ali Khan and other Muslim leaders proposed that Hindi and Urdu should be allowed to develop side by side, but Banarsi Das, a young Congress leader, opposed this idea, arguing that Urdu was the product of conquest and that support for it showed that the theory of two nations had survived partition.[46] Having failed to sway the state government, Urdu-speakers next tried to persuade the President of India to use his authority under Article 347 to direct that Urdu should be officially recognized as a regional language in the state. A campaign to obtain signatures for the proposal was launched in November 1951 by the Anjuman-i-Taraqqi-i-Urdu, which was at that time led by Dr Zakir Husain (President) and Kazi Abdul Ghaffar (General Secretary). By July 1953 it had collected the signatures of 2.05 million adults and 2.25 million minors, and on 15 February 1954 its case was presented to the President of India by a deputation headed by Dr Husain. The memorandum which it submitted claimed that the state government had flouted the central government's directive that the medium of instruction and examination in junior basic schools should be the mother tongue of the child; instead, the state's Education Department had ordered that Hindi should be a compulsory subject in all primary schools, with the result that the teaching of Urdu had been discontinued in all municipal schools and in schools under the authority of district boards. The memorandum also demanded that Urdu should be the medium of instruction at the primary stage for children whose mother tongue was Urdu; that arrangements should be made for teaching Urdu; that adequate textbooks in Urdu should be provided, along with facilities for training teachers of Urdu; that petitions written in Urdu should be accepted by courts and offices of the state and that facilities should be provided for the disposal of those petitions; and that important government notices and laws, and government publications, should also be issued in Urdu.[47]

In the field of education, the petitioners were supported by the policy

---

[46] *Statesman* (Delhi), 20 September 1951, p. 5.
[47] See report of press conference by Dr Zakir Husain, Delhi, 16 February 1954, in *ibid.*, 17 February 1954, p. 3. See also letter from Kazi Abdul Ghaffar to the editor, 17 July 1953, in *ibid.*, 21 July 1953, p. 6; Gupta, *Language Conflict and National Development*, pp. 142–4; and Donald E. Smith, *India as a Secular State* (Princeton, N.J., 1963), pp. 424–6.

resolution which had been adopted by the Provincial Education Ministers' Conference in August 1949 and approved by the Central Advisory Board of Education and the Government of India. Regarding primary education, this resolution had specified that where the mother tongue was different from the regional or state language, and provided that it was spoken by no fewer that 40 pupils in the school or 10 pupils in a class, arrangements should be made for instruction in that mother tongue by the appointment of at least one teacher.[48] This resolution had been accepted by the state government and in principle Urdu should have been available as the medium of instruction in the state's primary schools for those whose mother tongue was Urdu. However, this formula had never been effectively implemented and at the secondary level of schooling not even the concession of the principle had been made; having taken into account the state government's language policy, the UP Board of High School and Intermediate Education decided that Hindi should be the medium of instruction and examination for high schools from 1951 onwards and for intermediate classes from 1954 onwards.[49]

The decision in favour of a Hindi-only policy meant that the Congress government in Uttar Pradesh was reasonably protected against any attack from the Jana Sangh, which had therefore to concentrate its fire upon the Anjuman-i-Taraqqi-i-Urdu and other groups campaigning on behalf of Urdu-speakers. In December 1952, the Jana Sangh's first national session declared that

The agitation being carried on in some areas of Delhi, Bihar and U.P. for recognising Urdu as the official language is, in the view of Jana Sangh, encouraged by anti-national, and separatist tendency. It is this tendency that was responsible for the partition of India on the basis of Two-nation theory. It is the duty of both the people and the administration to eradicate such tendencies which are detrimental to the unity of the Nation.

Trumping up a new language in the name of Urdu by distorting Hindi with foreign words and foreign thoughts was one of the many methods adopted by foreign rulers to weaken the unity of the nation. Spirit of nationalism has always opposed such attempts. After the attainment of Independence it is the duty of this rising nation not to encourage Urdu – a distorted form of Hindi – which is being exploited by anti-national tendencies.[50]

In April 1954 the Working Committee of the Uttar Pradesh Jana Sangh

---

[48] For the text of this resolution, see Appendix B of Government of India, Ministry of Home Affairs, *Report of the Commissioner for Linguistic Minorities (First Report)* (Delhi, 1959), p. 53.

[49] *Report of the Uttar Pradesh Language Committee*, p. 38.

[50] First National Session, Kanpur, 31 December 1952, *BJS Documents*, IV, p. 101.

stated that 'At the root of this effort of enforcing two languages and two scripts lie the harmful seeds of the two-nation theory, consequences of which are before us in the form of Pakistan'. It therefore condemned the Union Ministry of Education, which it claimed was trying to 'impose Urdu over U.P.' and said that it expected that the Uttar Pradesh government 'will keep control over these anti-national tendencies arising under cover of Urdu, and will act as fimly [sic] as before'.[51] In the following month the party's Central Working Committee made an even harsher reference to Urdu, which it claimed was

the language of no region in India, it being only a foreign and unacceptable style of Hindi with a foreign script and a foreign vocabulary imposed on India during a period of foreign domination and now being supported by some communal elements.[52]

Finally, the manifesto adopted in August 1954 declared that the Jana Sangh was not prepared to recognize English or Urdu as Indian languages and that it would take steps to remove Urdu from the list of languages given in the Eighth Schedule of the Constitution of India.[53]

In fact, however, the party's fear that concessions would be made to Urdu-speakers proved to be groundless for the Uttar Pradesh Congress made no move to recognize Urdu as a regional language, evidently for reasons very similar to those put forward by the Jana Sangh. Sampurnanand, who was Chief Minister of the Congress government in the state from December 1954 to December 1960, later wrote:

My views have remained constant all through. I do not consider Urdu a separate language but merely a style of Hindi in which words of Arabic and Persian derivation form a high percentage. I do not consider this style suitable for adoption as the official form of the national language. But I am not an enemy of it.[54]

The cause of Urdu had also been weakened by the results of the 1951 Census, which seemed to show that the proportion of Urdu-speakers in Uttar Pradesh was only 6.8 per cent although Muslims constituted 14.3 per cent of the state's total population. However, the language categories in the census were derived from answers given by the respondents themselves, and it is likely that many whose mother tongue was Urdu

---

[51] *Organiser*, 26 April 1954, p. 8.

[52] Central Working Committee, Delhi, 8 May 1954, *BJS Documents*, V, pp. 21–2.

[53] 1954 Manifesto, *ibid.*, I, p. 73.

[54] Sampurnanand, *Memories and Reflections* (Bombay, 1962), pp. 92–3. See also letter from Sampurnanand to Dr Syed Mahmud, from Naini Tal, 24 May 1958, in V.N. Datta and B.E. Cleghorn (eds.), *A Nationalist Muslim and Indian Politics: Being the Selected Correspondence of the late Dr. Syed Mahmud* (Delhi, 1974), pp. 279–83.

were included in the 10.7 per cent described as Hindustani-speakers.[55]

The prospect for Urdu seemed bleak until an amendment to the Constitution made in 1956 inserted the following Article (350 A):

It shall be the endeavour of every State and of every local authority within the State to provide adequate facilities for instruction in the mother-tongue at the primary stage of education to children belonging to linguistic minority groups; and the President may issue such directions to any State as he considers necessary or proper for securing the provision of such facilities.

The possibility of persuading the President to take action on these lines probably encouraged the Anjuman-i-Taraqqi-i-Urdu to return to the fray in February 1958, when its all-India conference met in Delhi and demanded that Urdu should be recognized as a regional language in Delhi, Uttar Pradesh, the Punjab and Bihar; that there should be instruction in Urdu in primary and secondary schools; and that the use of Urdu should be permitted in Public Service Commission examinations.[56] On 29 April 1958 a deputation of its leaders submitted a memorandum to the President[57] and on 15 May the Congress Working Committee recommended, in the course of a lengthy resolution on 'National Languages', that, 'as in the case of other national languages, the Central and State Governments should give adequate facilities for the instruction and use of the *Urdu* language as a regional language wherever it is prevalent'. It then specified ways in which the teaching of Urdu could be made available in primary and secondary schools, and recommended procedures to increase its use in law courts and in government business.[58] This was a much more detailed recommendation than earlier ones issued by the Congress leadership and it therefore gave the Jana Sangh an opportunity to criticize the ruling party for appeasing communal groups. Writing in the *Organiser*, Upadhyaya complained that

Urdu, in spite of its recognition in the Constitution, and its birth in India, has been a vehicle of Muslim separatism. It is Indian in the same sense as 'Pidgin English' is Chinese. Its script, phraseology, most of the grammar, prosody are all foreign. Its spirit is foreign. It has no grass-roots and therefore people who claim to speak Urdu have no roots in the soil. For this reason alone it had become a

---

[55] See Table 383 in *Census of India 1951*, Vol. II, *Uttar Pradesh*, Part I-A, *Report*, by Rajeshwari Prasad, I.A.S., Superintendent, Census Operations (Allahabad, 1953), p. 412. For this census, enumerators were required to record the mother tongue '*as given out by the respondents*' (*ibid.*). See also Table 4.1 in Brass, *Language, Religion and Politics in North India*, p. 190, for the proportions of Hindustani-, Hindi- and Urdu-speakers in UP, 1881–1961.

[56] *Statesman* (Delhi), 17 February 1958, p. 1.

[57] See Gupta, *Language Conflict and National Development*, p. 144.

[58] *Congress Bulletin*, May 1958, pp. 271–4.

symbol of separate Muslim Nationhood, which the Muslim League advocated. If some Muslims persist in sticking to Urdu, it is simply because they do not want to give up their old communal outlook.[59]

Soon afterwards, the Uttar Pradesh government came under direct pressure from the centre to alter its language policy. On 14 July the Union Ministry of Home Affairs issued a press note, which pointed out that, although Urdu and Hindi were 'very closely allied', Urdu was 'officially and constitutionally recognised as one of our national languages, and the various provisions that apply to these languages, apply to Urdu also'. It recommended that, in areas and regions where the Urdu language was prevalent:

(1) Facilities should be provided for instruction and examination in the Urdu language at the primary stage to all children whose mother tongue is declared by the parent or guardian to be Urdu.
(2) Arrangements should be made for the training of teachers and for providing suitable text books in Urdu.
(3) Facilities for instruction in Urdu should also be provided in the secondary stage of education.
(4) Documents in Urdu should be accepted by all courts and offices without the necessity of translation or transliteration in any other language or script, and petitions and representations in Urdu should also be accepted.
(5) Important laws, rules and regulations and notifications should be issued in the Urdu language also in areas where this language is prevalent and which may be specified for this purpose.[60]

Obviously on the defensive, the state government issued a press communiqué on 20 July expressing agreement with both the Congress Working Committee's resolution and the Home Ministry's press note and claiming that 'from the very beginning' it had accepted the first four of the five proposals listed in the latter document. Regarding the fifth provision, it pointed out that the Information Department had given the substance of important laws, rules, regulations and notifications in an Urdu journal entitled *Ittilaat* (later renamed *Naya Daur*), that it had also published from time to time Urdu books and pamphlets dealing with important pieces of legislation and other matters, and that the government's Press Information Bureau had simultaneously issued material in Hindi, Urdu and English. However, it acknowledged that 'no definite policy has so far been adopted in this connection'. Regular

---

[59] Upadhyaya, 'The politics of Urdu', *Organiser*, 26 May 1958, p. 4.
[60] This note is given in full as Annexure IV of Government of India, *Report of the Committee of Parliament on Official Language, 1958* (New Delhi, 1959), pp. 115–17, quotation from p. 116. The special provisions recommended here correspond closely to those proposed by the Congress Working Committee in its resolution of 15 May 1958 noted above.

publicity would, it said, 'be given to such matter' in *Naya Daur*, and whenever necessary the Information Department and other official agencies would 'use other methods also in those localities where a fair proportion of the population can be taken to be conversant with Urdu'. For this purpose, it selected the city of Lucknow and the six north-western districts of Saharanpur, Muzaffarnagar, Bijnor, Moradabad, Rampur and Bareilly.[61] The executive of the Uttar Pradesh Jana Sangh promptly decided to begin an agitation.[62] Claiming that a separatist movement could develop in the districts concerned and that this concession was encouraging Muslim demands in the neighbouring districts of Meerut, Bulandshahr and Budaun, the party's organizing secretary for the western part of the state urged the state government to end preferential treatment for Urdu.[63]

However, as the reports of the Commissioner for Linguistic Minorities[64] make clear, the state government did not change its language policy in any fundamental respect as a result of this brief period of pressure from Delhi. In June 1961 it appointed its own Language Committee under the chairmanship of J.B. Kripalani, to examine the provision of facilities for Urdu-speakers in the state, but the committee's report, published in August 1962, did not question the basic values of the Hindi-only policy. The results of the 1961 Census were to show that the proportion of Urdu-speakers was 10.70 per cent of the total population[65] but the provisions for teaching through the medium of Urdu remained inadequate in the early stages of education, and in high schools (from Class IX onwards) Hindi remained the sole medium of instruction and examination.[66]

---

[61] *Pioneer* (Lucknow), 21 July 1958, pp. 1 and 3. The districts of Lucknow, Meerut and Pilibhit were later added to this category on the basis of the 1961 Census data on the distribution of languages (see Ministry of Home Affairs, *Report of the Commissioner for Linguistic Minorities* (*Eighth Report*) (Delhi, 1968), p. 73).

[62] *Pioneer*, 3 August 1958, p. 3.

[63] Rama Kant Tiwari, 'A Pakistan in U.P.?', *Organiser*, 11 August 1958, p. 3.

[64] This office was established in 1957 by the President of India under Article 350 B of the Constitution of India.

[65] According to the 1961 Census, Urdu speakers numbered 7,891,714 in a total population of 73,746,401 (Appendix II to Table C-V, 'Mother-tongue', in *Census of India 1961*, Vol. XV, *Uttar Pradesh*, Part II C (ii), *Cultural and Migration Tables*, by P.P. Bhatnagar of the Indian Administrative Service, Superintendent of Census Operations, Uttar Pradesh (Delhi, 1965), p. 253). At this census, Muslims in UP numbered 10,788,089, and constituted 14.63 per cent of the population (see Table C-VII, 'Religion', in *ibid.*, p. 517).

[66] See Ministry of Home Affairs, *Report of the Commissioner for Linguistic Minorities* (*Seventh Report*) (Delhi, 1965), p. 30. See also *ibid.* (*Eighth Report*) (Delhi, 1968), p. 38, and, on the detailed provision for the teaching of Urdu-medium pupils in the state, Brass, *Language, Religion and Politics in North India*, pp. 206–10 and especially Table 4.4, 'Facilities for instruction in Urdu at the primary and secondary stages of education in Uttar Pradesh' (p. 208).

There can be no doubting the potency of the language issue in north Indian politics. Besides the very real attachment which Muslims felt for the rich literature of Urdu, they saw the protection of their language (just as in the Punjab many Sikhs saw the protection of Punjabi) as tantamount to the protection of their religious and cultural traditions. In addition, both minorities were aware that their relative positions in the middle-class professions would be weakened unless their respective languages could be established as media of instruction at every stage in the schooling system and accorded due recognition as proper means of judicial and administrative communication. In the Punjab, the Congress had not felt strong enough to resist such demands when they were made by the Akali Dal on behalf of a substantial proportion of the Sikh community but in Uttar Pradesh it was confident that it could hold the Urdu movement in check and insist upon the primacy of Hindi as the language of the state for administrative, educational and legal purposes. In the latter case, therefore, the Jana Sangh simply could not outflank the ruling party; its only real opportunity to do so came in 1958, when central pressure at last obliged the state government to permit some use of Urdu in Lucknow and in the six north-western districts, but this was a small concession, well short of the step of making Urdu the state's second official language.

The status of Urdu was an issue built into the rhetoric and mythology of politics at the state level in Uttar Pradesh, but at the level of individual districts and cities local privileges enjoyed by Muslim communities were often the focus of envy and suspicion by Hindus. One of the problems facing the Jana Sangh was what it should do about such local communal tensions; if it exploited them it ran the risk of being drawn into a pattern of rioting and violence which would severely damage its reputation for moderation and tolerance in other parts of the country, yet if it ignored them it could be accused of denying its principles where these had most application, in the day-to-day life of people in particular localities. This dilemma was posed in a particularly acute form by the communal rioting which broke out in the town of Aligarh, in western Uttar Pradesh, in October 1961.

Aligarh was also the site of the Aligarh Muslim University, which, despite the liberalizing effect of an Act of Parliament of 1951, was still regarded as a central focus of Muslim intellectual activities. It was therefore under constant attack from the Jana Sangh as a possible centre for a new generation of Muslim nationalists and in August 1961, during a debate in the Lok Sabha on the report of an inquiry committee on the university, Balraj Madhok argued that the only term of reference for the committee should have concerned 'the communal and anti-national character of the University'.[67] He went on to make the familiar accusation that

The two nation theory was born and cherished in the Aligarh University. They say they have a separate culture. When you have a separate culture, separate language, separate history, then you are a separate nation. It is this talk of a separate nation, separate culture and separate history which goes against Indian nationalism.[68]

After another member of the house had complained that it was not proper 'to condemn an entire people and a university', Madhok returned to his argument:

There may be exceptions, but I say that by and large the Aligarh University still continues to be the centre of that very mentality which resulted in the partition of this country. We are not against any individual, a particular persion [sic] or professor, but against that mentality. So long as that mentality continues, we will continue to raise our voice against this University, because we think it continues to be a plague spot in India. Until and unless this plague spot is cleared of its plague symptoms and made a national organisation, there will be danger. Let the professors be all Muslim, let the students be all Muslim, but let nationalism be taught there.[69]

The reality was much more complex than these remarks would suggest. In the first place, the faculty and students of the university represented a considerable range of views; on one side was an orthodox group, which wished to retain the Islamic character of the university, and on the other was a group associated with radical ideas. Observers often categorized the former group as 'Communalist', and alleged that it was connected to the Jama'at-i-Islami, and the latter as 'Communist', alleging that some of its members belonged to the Communist Party, but they often underestimated the influence of the diverse group of faculty who occupied the middle ground between the two extremes and who were generally secular, progressive and pro-Congress in outlook.[70] In the second place, the university's position in its local setting was by no means secure. Aligarh City had developed as a trading centre at the intersection of two overland routes, one running from east to west along

---

[67] *P.D., L.S.* (Second Series), LVI, 11 August 1961, cc. 1718–23, quotation from c. 1719.
[68] *Ibid.*, c. 1721.
[69] *Ibid.*, cc. 1722–3.
[70] On the character of the opposed groups, see Paul R. Brass, *Factional Politics in an Indian State: The Congress Party in Uttar Pradesh* (Berkeley, 1965), pp. 99–100. See also a statement by Dr K.L. Shrimali, the Union Minister of Education, in *P.D., R.S.*, XXXV, 24 August 1961, cc.1649-68, and the following letters to the editor: from Mirza Asghar Hossain, Banaras (*Hindustan Times*, 7 September 1961, p. 7), and from Mohd. Farooq, Aligarh (*ibid.*, 14 September 1961, p. 7).

the valley of the Ganges and the other from north to south through the Malwa gap to western India. It came under British control in 1803, after the war with the Marathas, and assumed its modern layout during the nineteenth century. The British established a military cantonment and a civil lines area a mile or so to the north of the old city, whose crowded streets and markets were organized around a small hillock. When the East Indian Railway reached Aligarh in 1863–64 the track was laid down between the two areas. The Muhammadan Anglo-Oriental College, the precursor of the University, was established within the former military cantonment while, within the old city, Hindu caste groups which had done well in industry and commerce encouraged the formation of degree colleges, of which by 1961 there were three – the Dharam Samaj College, the Barah Seni College and the Sri Tika Ram Kanya Mahavidyalaya – affiliated to the University of Agra. The Aligarh Muslim University thus remained somewhat isolated from the city, sustained from outside by wealthy Muslim benefactors and, after independence, by funds from the central government. It added one more factor to the delicate communal balance in the city, where Muslims constituted about one-third of the total population.[71]

The communal tensions in Aligarh gave rise to open violence in October 1961, following the spread of exaggerated rumours of what had occurred on the university campus after elections to the executive of the students' union. Some non-Muslim candidates had been returned to this body in every election since 1951 but in the campaign of September 1961 the non-Muslim groups arranged what amounted to a single list of candidates for twelve of the thirteen places, thereby producing a reaction from some of the Muslim students, who suspected a communal manoeuvre, and none of the non-Muslim candidates were elected. When the results were announced early in the morning of 2 October, a group of students celebrated the outcome by taking out effigies of the defeated candidates in a mock funeral procession, a gesture which sparked off a series of clashes in one hostel and resulted in a number of students being injured. Dramatized versions of this incident were given to the students in the local degree colleges and on the morning of the 3rd a procession of about 7,000 or 8,000 people, most of whom were students, tried to march on the university. It was dispersed by the police near the Kathpula road bridge across the railway line, but, although a major clash was avoided,

---

[71] At the time of the 1971 Census, Muslims numbered 83,456 in a total population for Aligarh City of 252,314 (from 'Town directory', in *Census of India 1971, Series 21, Uttar Pradesh, District Census Handbook, Part X-A, Town & Village Directory, District Aligarh*, by D.M. Sinha of the Indian Administrative Service, Director of Census Operations, Uttar Pradesh (Lucknow, 1973), pp. 5 and 10).

isolated acts of violence which took place during the next few days resulted in fourteen deaths. Students from Aligarh went to their homes in other districts with accounts of what had happened and soon processions and disturbances occurred in a number of towns, the worst affected being Chandausi, in Moradabad district, and Meerut City. Thirty-two people were reported to have been killed in these disturbances and about 100 injured; 2,844 people were arrested and 1,189 of them had been convicted by November.[72] What had begun as a minor incident in student politics had turned into one of the most serious outbreaks of communal violence in northern India since partition. Comparisons were made with the communal clash which had taken place in February 1961 at Jabalpur in Madhya Pradesh, when, after 17 people were reported to have been killed and many injured, disturbances occurred throughout the region.[73]

From the outset, the central leaders of the Jana Sangh claimed that the causes of the Uttar Pradesh disturbances could be found in the Aligarh Muslim University itself. At a press conference on 5 October, Balraj Madhok demanded a judicial inquiry into 'the cause of the latest incidents in the Aligarh University and the complicity of the university authorities in it'. He complained that, after partition, the central government had given the university increased aid without taking steps to change its communal character and that 'as a result it had once again become the hot-bed of pro-Pakistan and anti-national activities'.[74] Vajpayee claimed that as long as the university was 'not emancipated from the clutches of the Communalist-cum-Communist incubus, the danger of recrudescence of communal trouble in western U.P. would always persist'.[75] A special inquiry into the riots was conducted by two Jana Sangh members of the state Legislative Council, Pitambar Das (then Vice-President of the national party) and Shiva Prasad, and their report included claims that there seemed to have been a 'tacit collaboration' between Pakistani agents and Communists in creating the trouble, that riots had broken out only where processions had been attacked, and that in those towns in which there had been no

[72] A full account of these riots was given to the UP Legislative Assembly on 14 November by the UP Home Minister, Charan Singh (See *National Herald*, 15 November 1961, pp. 1 and 2). Regarding the students' union elections, see also the statement which the Vice-Chancellor made after the university's Executive Council had considered the report of a special committee of inquiry (*ibid.*, 26 November 1961, pp. 1 and 8). The total numbers of the dead and injured are from *ibid.*, 11 October 1961, p. 1.

[73] See *Statesman* (Delhi), 5 February 1961, p. 1; 6 February 1961, p. 1; 9 February 1961, p. 1; 10 February 1961 p. 1.

[74] Press conference, Hyderabad, 5 October 1961 (*National Herald*, 7 October 1961, p. 7).

[75] Press conference, Delhi, 13 October 1961 (*Times of India* (Delhi), 14 October 1961).

provocation the students had remained peaceful. They recommended a number of steps to deal with the problem and advocated a judicial inquiry into the riots.[76]

The party's Central General Council adopted a resolution in November 1961 which presented the riots in the following terms:

The conduct of Aligarh Muslim University Union-elections on communal lines, its aftermath, and subsequent aggressive acts by Muslim communalists in several towns of Western U.P. led to a spate of extremely unfortunate incidents in these areas. Even apart from violence, the communal bitterness evinced in the course of these happenings, spells danger both for democracy and nationalism.

According to the resolution, it was the duty of the government 'to be firm in dealing with threats to law and order, and of all peace loving citizens to cooperate in governmental efforts in this direction'; it recommended the holding of a judicial inquiry into the riots and demanded that 'the present communal character of the Aligarh Muslim University be abolished and it be Indianised and run like other Universities of the country'.[77]

The tone of this resolution is partly explained by the party's need to establish a version of events in which the blame could be firmly attached to Muslim communalism, for it was sensitive to charges that its local workers had also played a part in the riots. Immediately after the first outbreaks, the Home Minister in the state government, Charan Singh, himself a Hindu, had described various features of the rioting and remarked: 'All this leads one to suspect that there is a conspiracy behind these incidents – a conspiracy which is laid deep and wide'.[78] A month later, in making his report to the state Legislative Assembly, he said that, although the trouble had originated in the union elections at Aligarh Muslim University, 'it appears that thereafter an organized effort was made to spread the trouble specially by members of some parties and organizations, which do not subscribe to the concept of national integration as Government see it. It may be that this effort was not a part of their official policy, but nevertheless individual members of these bodies took a prominent part in the affair.' He claimed that some Jana Sangh workers had helped to organize a meeting of Hindu students in Aligarh City on 2 October and that in other towns Jana Sangh members had 'played an important part' in organizing meetings and hartals. Maintaining that the government was trying to place the blame for the happenings on the party and its supporters, Yadavendra Datt Dube, the

---

[76] *National Herald*, 13 November 1961, p. 3.
[77] Central General Council, Varanasi, [12] November 1961, *BJS Documents*, IV, pp. 121–2.
[78] Press conference, 10 October 1961 (*National Herald*, 11 October 1961, p. 3).

leader of the Jana Sangh's group in the Assembly, declared that the Jana Sangh could not be responsible as an organization for the action of its individual members if some had erred. He claimed that the processionists in both Aligarh and Chandausi had been demonstrating peacefully until bricks were thrown at them and that innocent people had been arrested after the riots.[79]

Two very different explanations of the riots were now at issue. The Jana Sangh's view that the basic cause was the nature of the university was again rehearsed in the Lok Sabha at the end of November 1961, when Vajpayee tabled an adjournment motion which alleged:

The failure of Government to take necessary steps to rid the Aligarh University of the virus of communal fanaticism and sectarian bigotry, a frightful manifestation whereof has been the recent chain of unfortunate incidents which spread outside the precincts of the University not only to undermine our efforts at national integration but also to endanger the law and order situation in Aligarh and other adjoining districts of Western U.P.

Madhok, in another motion, complained of the central government's failure to appoint a Visitor's Committee 'to enquire into the affairs of Aligarh University and rid it of anti-national elements'. The motions were rejected after a brief discussion in which the Minister of Education pointed out that the law and order situation was the responsibility of the state government and that the Vice-Chancellor of the university had appointed a committee to inquire into the elections to the executive of the students' union.[80] The opposite view, that the unrest had been exploited by communal organizations, was held by the state government, which actually proposed to the central government that such bodies should be banned. Explaining this request to the Rajya Sabha, the Union Minister of Home Affairs, Lal Bahadur Shastri, said that members of the state government

were greatly perturbed over incidents that took place recently at Aligarh, Meerut, Chandausi, etc. and they felt that it was necessary to take action against certain groups of people or certain organisations which were, I mean, at the back of these troubles. Of course, it is very difficult to give proof for everything that happens or that has happened, but this was one of the reasons, I think, which led them to think that some kind of action which might facilitate the Government declaring certain organisations as unlawful, should be taken.[81]

---

[79] *Ibid.*, 15 November 1961, pp. 1–2 and 4. See also Vajpayee's references to Charan Singh's charges in an election address at Lucknow, 19 November 1961 (*ibid.*, 20 November 1961, p. 2).

[80] *P.D., L.S.* (Second Series), LIX, 20 November 1961, cc. 120–9.

[81] *Ibid., R.S.*, XXXVI, 4 December 1961, cc. 884–5.

One of the main points to emerge from this material on the Aligarh riots of 1961 is that the Jana Sangh held firmly to the line that it was the fact that the university, as a Muslim institution, had special privileges which constituted the real source of trouble. The party's determination to press home the point that the university remained a potential centre for Muslim nationalism enabled it to refer indirectly to the instrumental theory of partition, which held that the Muslim League had laid the ground for Pakistan by insisting that Muslims should have special rights, such as joint electorates, reserved places in the legislatures, and the use of Urdu in administrative, educational and legal institutions. The Aligarh Muslim University was therefore presented as an affront, a kind of provocation, to true nationalists. By taking this line of argument, the Jana Sangh effectively declined to be drawn into the related argument about the social causes of the communal rioting, and about the role which its local workers were alleged to have played in the events. This in itself was significant, an indication that the party was unwilling to justify the use of violence to settle disputes between local communities, but it was clear that the problem remained. It is one thing for a party to take the position that positive discrimination in favour of a minority, to compensate for past wrongs or disadvantages, may damage the basic unity of the whole society, but quite another to arouse and focus the hostility of the majority against that minority. The claims of Muslims for special rights could be discussed in abstract terms but there always remained the danger, highlighted by the rioting in western Uttar Pradesh in 1961, that the general issues would be translated into the crude stereotypes of communal conflict and result in unrestrained violence. In its efforts to demonstrate that its opposition to what it alleged to be Muslim separatism was more consistent and thorough-going than that of the Uttar Pradesh Congress, the Jana Sangh did not hesitate to appeal to the extreme nationalism of the Hindu lower-middle-class elements in the towns and cities of the state, and thus risked being drawn into a vortex of social warfare, where violence could easily get out of control. In the case of the Aligarh riots of 1961, the violence was eventually checked and a general conflagration avoided, but the dangers of this kind of situation had been clearly demonstrated.

The Jana Sangh and the choice between Hindi and English

In all-India politics, the problems arising from the Jana Sangh's initial commitment to the ideals of integration and national unity were raised most directly by its belief that Hindi should be the language of all Indians. The party's claim that Hindi should be not only the official but also the national language of India and that it should therefore be promoted at the expense of English and the regional languages caused alarm in the non-Hindi regions, where efforts to promote Hindi were seen as part of an attempt by the north to dominate the rest of the country. According to the 1961 Census Hindi-speakers, while constituting 30.4 per cent of the total population, formed majorities only in the northern states of Uttar Pradesh (85.4 per cent), Madhya Pradesh (78.1 per cent) and the Punjab (55.6 per cent) and substantial minorities only in Bihar (44.3 per cent) and in Rajasthan (33.3 per cent). The obstacles to any India-wide expansion of Hindi were therefore formidable, because the western, eastern and southern parts of the country all contained large linguistic regions, each with its own well-established and quite distinct cultural and literary traditions.[82] Try as the champions of Hindi might to stress its kinship with those languages, such as Bengali, Marathi and Gujarati, which also belonged to the Indo-European family, the differences between them were too great to justify any plans for their future assimilation into a common linguistic bloc, and there was even more distrust of Hindi amongst the speakers of the southern languages (Tamil, Telugu, Malayalam and Kannada), which all belonged to the Dravidian family.

The Jana Sangh's early position was a relatively unqualified version of the case that the political unity of India could be maintained only by establishing Hindi as the sole channel of official communication, not only between the centre and the states but between one state and another as well. Unless Hindi became the *lingua franca* of the country as a whole, ran the argument, the way would be clear for the regional languages to dominate their respective territories, thereby laying the foundations for nationalist and secessionist movements which could ultimately destroy the integrity of the country. Hindi was far preferable to English as the official union language, it was claimed, because its indigenous origins and traditional associations would generate a national sentiment. Despite their token references to the desirability of fostering the regional languages, the party's early policy statements were based squarely on this kind of reasoning. Its 1951 manifesto stated that

The party will work for early adoption of Hindi as All India Language together with full encouragement to other Indian Languages. It believes that the adoption of Dev-Nagri script and a common technical terminology derived mainly from Sanskrit by all Indian languages will create an atmosphere of harmony, cultural unity and national solidarity in the country.[83]

[82] See Table 1, 'Number of speakers of major languages in India, 1961', and Table 2, 'Important languages in selected states', in Baldev Raj Nayar, *National Communication and Language Policy in India* (New York, 1969), pp. 26 and 64.
[83] *Manifesto of All India Bharatiya Jana Sangh* (New Delhi, 1951), p. 11.

By 1954, the party had determined its answers to the question of what languages should be taught and used in the educational system and, while agreeing that the mother tongue should be the medium of instruction in primary schools, it proposed that the state language should be used in middle and secondary schools and in universities, 'with Hindi as a compulsory subject of study'.[84] Taken together, these proposals constituted a very controversial policy – the rapid substitution of Hindi for English as the official language for Union purposes, the introduction of Hindi as a compulsory subject in schools and universities in non-Hindi-speaking regions, and the substitution of the Devanagari script for the scripts of the regional languages – and played no small part in earning for the Jana Sangh its initial reputation as a zealot in the cause of 'Hindi imperialism'.

However, like most of the early proposals regarding language policy, such statements had little practical impact on politics at the state level, mainly because the arrangements inherited from the British Raj seemed likely to be continued for the foreseeable future. It was true that Article 343 of the Constitution stipulated that Hindi in the Devanagari script should be the official language of the Union but it also provided that English should continue to be used 'for all the official purposes of the Union' for a period of fifteen years, that is, until 26 January 1965. The question of what was to be done beyond that date was considered first by an Official Language Commission, which reported in 1956, and then by a Committee of Parliament, whose report was considered by Parliament in 1959. The main outcome of the subsequent discussions was a virtual undertaking that English would remain in use as a subsidiary official language for Union purposes beyond 1965. Nehru himself told the Lok Sabha on 7 August 1959 that 'I would have it [English] as an alternate language as long as people require it and the decision for that, I would leave not to the Hindi-knowing people, but to the non-Hindi-knowing people'.[85]

At first the Jana Sangh did not dissent from this policy. Its sixth national session, held in April 1958, pointed out that Article 343 (3) of the Constitution already empowered Parliament to provide for the use of English after 1965 and offered the assurance that no 'section' of the people need entertain 'any apprehension regarding its future on the score of its familiarity or unfamiliarity with any particular language'.[86] The

[84] 1954 Manifesto, *BJS Documents*, I, p. 73. See also Central Working Committee, Delhi, 8 May 1954, *ibid.*, V, pp. 21–2.

[85] *P.D., L.S.* (Second Series), XXXII, 7 August 1959, c. 1299. See also later assurances by Nehru (*ibid.*, XXXIV, 4 September 1959, cc. 6439–48) and by G. B. Pant, Minister of Home Affairs (*ibid.*, cc. 6489–90).

[86] Sixth National Session, Ambala, 5 April 1958, *BJS Documents*, V, pp. 30–1, quotation from p. 30.

party's general aim, as expressed in its 1962 election manifesto, was simply stated as taking steps 'to introduce Hindi and the regional languages as official languages in their respective spheres, within the period prescribed in the Constitution',[87] and no reference was made to the earlier proposal for the universal adoption of the Devanagari script.

By the early 1960s it seemed likely that the continued postponement of effective measures to extend the use of Hindi would become a major concern in northern India and that the Jana Sangh would be given a further chance to exploit the issue. The Hindi-speaking middle classes of the northern provincial cities and towns could see that the older English-speaking élite still dominated the legal system, the universities, the administration and the quality press in such states as Uttar Pradesh, Madhya Pradesh and Rajasthan. The central services were still in the hands of English-speakers and, within the Union, English remained the language of communication for science, commerce, industry and the professions. Instead of inheriting the apex of the political, economic, cultural and professional structures of India by virtue of their language, Hindi speakers found themselves, a full fifteen years after independence, as only one (though admittedly the largest) of a number of regional language groups which were struggling to assert themselves within a multilingual society.

The party did its best to articulate and focus the grievances of Hindi-speakers against the continued use of English but it lacked an articulate spokesman to put its case. This gap was filled in November 1962 by the appointment of Dr Raghuvira as the party's national President. An eminent linguist and a Sanskrit scholar, his speeches combined rhetoric about the virtues of Hindi with pointed references to the entrenched position of the English-speakers in the political and professional structure of the state. He soon fastened upon the central government's intention to legislate for the continued use of English for official purposes after 1965, which he portrayed not as an understandable move to conciliate the non-Hindi states but as a deliberate attempt to maintain an indefensible privilege. In his inaugural speech to the Jana Sangh's tenth annual session in December 1962 he stated that

The Government that is being run by the Congress Party is proposing to continue English even after 1965. The colonial bureaucracy that has mono-polised government, law courts and education is jealous of its power and privileges and will not allow the coming up of the languages of the masses to take their rightful place in the administration, law courts and universities. Our

---

[87] Bharatiya Jana Sangh, *Election Manifesto 1962*, p. 9.

Anglocracy has even set up rivalries between different Indian languages. The interest of one language is considered to be inimical to that of others.[88]

In April 1963, by which time the details of the proposed bill were known, the Jana Sangh's Central Working Committee threatened that if the government used its majority in Parliament to pass the measure

the fight against the domination of English will have to be intensified and continued as long as English is not removed. The battle against English is a battle against the biggest monopoly ever established, a monopoly of all the good things of life by less than 2 per cent anglocrats, excluding all others.

It suggested that this small group of 'anglocrats' had considerable economic power.

It will be an economic fight inasmuch as today 3000 crores of rupees are spent annually by the English-media monopolists. The non-English knowing get only crumb in the form of unskilled labour at an average rate of Rs. 2 to 3 a day. Higher emoluments go to the English knowing 2 per cent or less. Fight against English will be a fight for social egalitarianism as against the high-browed supercastes of English-knowing men and women. It is they who have usurped all positions of prestige in the society, others being almost denied and debarred.[89]

The Official Languages Bill, the object of all this hostility, simply provided that after 26 January 1965 'English may continue to be used, in addition to Hindi, for all official purposes of the Union for which it had been used previously, and for transaction of business in Parliament'.[90] Representatives from the non-Hindi areas objected to the use of the word 'may' instead of 'shall' in the clause 'English may continue to be used', while pro-Hindi groups (including the Jana Sangh) complained that the measure would further delay the time when Hindi would come into its own. The bill was nevertheless approved by both houses of Parliament and received the President's assent on 10 May 1963. Dr Raghuvira's sudden death on 14 May deprived the Jana Sangh of the inspiration he had provided for its campaign, but the language dispute was already shifting towards new and equally divisive issues.

As far as non-Hindi-speakers were concerned, the provision that Hindi was the official language for Union purposes offered the Hindi lobby a permanent excuse for the progressive introduction of that

[88] Bharatiya Jana Sangh, *Presidential Address by Prof. Dr. Raghu Vira, Tenth Session, Dec. 29, 30, 31, 1962, Bhopal (M. Pradesh)*, p. 25. See also *All Indian Languages Convention, Address by Dr. Raghuvira, Sapru House, New Delhi, 11th & 12th August 1962* (Delhi, 1962).

[89] Central Working Committee, Delhi, 6 April 1963, *BJS Documents*, V, pp. 38–40, quotations from p. 39.

[90] *Statesman* (Delhi), 14 April 1963, p. 1.

language at the expense of English into various spheres of the national administration. A major indication that the central government was prepared to tolerate this process was its willingness to agree that Hindi as well as English should be a medium for the highly competitive examinations run by the Union Public Service Commission (UPSC). This chose a large proportion of the entrants to the highly paid and respected all-India services, such as the Indian Administration Service (IAS) and the Indian Police Service (IPS). Although it had been decided as early as 1960 that Hindi might at some stage be introduced as an alternative to English for UPSC examinations, the exact timing had been left unclear. Then, at a meeting between the Union Home Minister and the Chief Ministers on 12 March 1964, it was agreed that the change should be made in September 1965 provided that the UPSC could ensure a common standard for evaluating both Hindi and English examination scripts.[91] This was exactly the kind of change that non-Hindi interests had tried to avoid, because it increased the advantage of candidates from the Hindi-speaking north without offering any compensating advantages (such as the use of regional languages for the examination) for non-Hindi candidates.

In an endeavour to mark the 26 January 1965 as a day when Hindi would, in a symbolic sense, come into its own as the official language for the Union, the Union Home Ministry informed central government offices that after that date correspondence between the centre and the northern group of Hindi-speaking states should be in Hindi, although the remaining states were permitted to continue corresponding in English. Advice was given in a circular about beginning the process of adding Hindi names to the English names of offices, organizations and institutions of the central government and the Home Ministry asked all ministries to translate into Hindi such items as forms, rules and manuals.[92] Such changes were little more than gestures, but they created unease throughout the country and even caused some groups to express their hostility to Hindi through demonstrations. In Madras, the Dravida Munnetra Kazhagam (DMK), a Tamil nationalist party, asked for the 26th to be observed as a day of mourning and two of its workers committed suicide by setting fire to their clothes.[93] Student

---

[91] See parliamentary statements by Jaisukhlal Hathi (Minister of State in the Ministry of Home Affairs), *P.D., L.S.* (Third Series), XXVIII, 25 March 1964, cc. 7320–1; and *ibid.*, *R.S.*, LI, 26 February 1965, c. 1285. See also the text of the broadcast by the Prime Minister, Lal Bahadur Shastri, on 11 February 1965 (*Statesman* (Delhi), 12 February 1965, p. 7).

[92] *The Hindu Weekly Review* (Madras), 25 January 1965, p. 5.

[93] *Statesman* (Delhi), 28 January 1965, pp. 1 and 14.

demonstrations in the southern towns and cities became increasingly unrestrained, and a spiral of violence reached a climax on 10 February; in Madras state 19 people were reported to have been killed after the police had opened fire on crowds and two police sub-inspectors were burned to death by a mob.[94]

The central government had to decide whether these disturbances simply reflected a breakdown of law and order or whether they indicated widespread dissent from its language policies. According to a contemporary account, the Ministry of Home Affairs in Delhi received reports indicating that the demonstrating students 'reflected the general sentiment of the towns in the South', that the Madras government was isolated, and that Kamaraj, the Congress President, 'was being compelled to disassociate himself from the Hindi policies of the Centre'. The Minister for Home Affairs, Gulzarilal Nanda, and his advisors were reported to have dismissed these assessments and the Prime Minister, Lal Bahadur Shastri, was persuaded that a radio broadcast explaining the government's policy would deal with the problem. When the Cabinet met on the evening of 11 February to consider the text of the proposed statement, three of its members, including the influential Minister for Food and Agriculture, C. Subramaniam, argued that 'some kind of statutory guarantee' was required, but this idea was opposed by Mahavir Tyagi, an Uttar Pradesh MP and Minister for Rehabilitation. After the meeting, Subramaniam and a fellow Madrasi, O.V. Alagesan, submitted their resignations from the Council of Ministers.[95] Shastri meanwhile went ahead with his radio broadcast, assuring his listeners that Nehru's pledge that English would continue as an associate official language as long as those who did not speak Hindi wanted it would be 'honoured both in the letter and in spirit without any qualification or reservation'.[96] In the days which followed, the Cabinet came under pressure from those who agreed with Subramaniam on one side and from protagonists of Hindi on the other, and the immediate result was a significant shift in policy. A Chief Ministers' conference was arranged for 23 and 24 February and the central government was reported to be considering ways of meeting the demands of the non-Hindi states, especially by giving 'legal recognition and expression' to Nehru's assurances about the maintenance of English. As a result, Subramaniam and Alagesan withdrew their resignations.[97]

---

[94] *Ibid.*, 11 February 1965, pp. 1 and 12; *Hindu Weekly Review*, 1 February 1965, p. 3; 8 February 1965, p. 3; 15 February 1965, pp. 3 and 14.

[95] Romesh Thapar, 'Capital view: the revolt of the angry south', *The Economic Weekly* (Bombay), XVII, 8 (20 February 1965), p. 359. Cf. 'N.C.', 'New Delhi skyline', 16 February 1965, *Mainstream* (New Delhi), III, 25 (20 February 1965), p. 4.

[96] *Statesman* (Delhi), 12 February 1965, pp. 1 and 7 (text of broadcast on p. 7).

[97] *Ibid.*, 17 February 1965, pp. 1 and 7.

The Jana Sangh reacted sharply to this change of direction. Upadhyaya said on the 14th that his party would resist any move to amend the Constitution to 'appease the protagonists of English'[98] and on the following day the party's parliamentary group decided to send a letter to the Prime Minister demanding that the proposed Chief Ministers' conference be cancelled.[99] Speaking in the Lok Sabha on the 18th, U.M. Trivedi strongly defended the value of Hindi as a national language, despite hostile interruptions from DMK and other members.[100] At this stage the party's leaders were showing no sign that they were willing to see any substance in southern complaints. Upadhyaya argued that people who demanded the continuation of English for the sake of unity were

no lovers of Indian unity. It is only a clever ruse to beguile the innocent people of the country. In fact when they say so they give a veiled threat that if you do not continue the use of English, we shall secede. This veil must be cleared. National unity is an article of faith and not a matter of compromise. If there are some people who can think of disrupting unity simply because Hindi comes or English does not remain, they definitely have no faith in unity. They are either secessionists or victims of planned propaganda.[101]

However, it soon became clear that the party's units in non-Hindi states were not prepared to accept such an unyielding position. On 21 February the secretary of the West Bengal Jana Sangh told a Calcutta meeting that he and many others could not respond to Upadhyaya's appeal for an immediate acceptance of Hindi instead of English as the Union language. He said that all fourteen Indian languages should be accorded equal status and that English should remain the official language and the medium for higher education, at least for the time being.[102] Two days later the Working Committee of the Tamil Nad Jana Sangh adopted a lengthy resolution on the language question which, while conceding that Hindi fulfilled the requirements of a link language, stated that

in the present circumstances, it is not feasible to have a complete switch-over from English to Hindi immediately. Hence the Committee resolves that English may be allowed to continue for another twelve years hereof, as an associate language.

In addition, while it favoured the progressive introduction of Hindi in Madras schools, it advocated the compulsory teaching of southern

[98] *National Herald*, 15 February 1965, p. 1.
[99] *Statesman* (Delhi), 16 February 1965, p.12.
[100] *P.D., L.S.* (Third Series), XXXVIII, 18 February 1965, cc. 249–51.
[101] 'Political Diary', *Organiser*, 22 February 1965, pp. 13 and 14.
[102] *Statesman* (Delhi), 22 February 1965, p. 7.

languages in the Hindi-speaking states from the sixth standard.[103] The weight of such views within the Jana Sangh was increased when both the central executive and the All-India General Council of the RSS, which met in parallel sessions at the end of March, adopted a resolution calling for all the languages of India to be accorded equal status; for Hindi to be used as the official language at the centre and the regional languages in their particular states, providing that, for some reasonable period, those with an insufficient knowledge of Hindi should be permitted to use English; and for all the regional languages to be used for UPSC examinations, with English continuing as an additional medium for a specified period.[104]

When the Central Working Committee of the Jana Sangh met early in April it heard reports from the organizing secretaries of its southern units on the language disturbances[105] and adopted a resolution which, while demanding the immediate replacement of English by regional languages at the state level, conceded that central government employees who did not know Hindi should be permitted to use English for ten years. It also proposed that all Indian languages should be used as media for UPSC examinations but that there should be a compulsory Hindi paper for examinees whose language was not Hindi and that Hindi-speakers should sit a compulsory paper in another Indian language.[106] However, the party's leaders still took every opportunity to claim that Hindi was superior to English as a link-language; in an interview given in Madras, Upadhyaya denied that the removal of English would weaken national unity:

disintegration of a living organism invariably follows the presence in it of an element opposed to its innate nature. English is such a foreign element. Unity of India under the British has been only an artificial and negative one. Positive and constructive unity is possible only through our own languages.[107]

Meanwhile, the Congress leaders had decided that the varying strands of the government's language policies should be tied together more closely, and on 2 June their party's Working Committee adopted a series of far-reaching proposals. It recommended that all states should be obliged to apply the three-language formula, under which three languages (the mother tongue or regional language, English or a modern

---

[103] *Organiser*, 8 March 1965, p. 16. See also *Statesman* (Delhi), 25 February 1965, p. 12.
[104] *Organiser*, 5 April 1965, p. 16.
[105] *Statesman* (Delhi), 5 April 1965, p. 7.
[106] Central Working Committee, Jaipur, 3 April 1965, *BJS Documents*, V, pp. 42–4. Balraj Madhok said later that the Jana Sangh had decided not to insist on a complete change from English to Hindi for ten years in deference to the views of the party's southern units (see *Statesman* (Delhi), 20 June 1965, p. 9).
[107] *Organiser*, 26 April 1965, p. 15.

European language, and Hindi, for non-Hindi areas, or, for non-Hindi areas, another modern Indian language) were to be taught in secondary schools, and further proposed that this system should be extended to the level of universities. In a new departure, it held that UPSC examinations should be conducted not only in English and Hindi but also in other regional languages mentioned in the Eighth Schedule of the Constitution, with compulsory papers in English and Hindi or, in the case of candidates whose medium was Hindi, a paper in any other language mentioned in the Eighth Schedule. Its remaining proposals were that, as early as possible, the regional language in each state should become the medium of administration and also of instruction at the university level, that teaching standards of Hindi should be raised, and that English should continue to be taught 'as a language which has an important role'; that a phased programme for the development of Hindi should be carried out so that it could serve both as the official language of the Union and as the national link-language; and that a programme for the development of other regional languages should also be undertaken.[108] Behind this detail lay agreement on three essential points: first, that English was to continue as the official language for Union purposes for the time being; second, that the position of Indian languages other than Hindi was to be strengthened; and third, that Hindi's status as a future link-language was to be retained. However, the problems of implementation proved formidable and long delays ensued; the difficulties of further applying the three-language formula and of deciding how to conduct the UPSC examinations in all fourteen of the regional languages required careful study. A bill intended to give statutory form to Nehru's assurances to the non-Hindi language groups was presented in draft form to the Chief Ministers in June 1965 and to the Union Cabinet in August 1965, but it did not come before Parliament until the end of 1967.[109]

Given the changes in its own policy on the language question, the Jana Sangh had not been able to come out strongly against the Congress Party's proposals of 2 June 1965. When the party's Central Working Committee met in July 1965 it could only complain that the Congress resolution had given 'no indication as to how and when Hindi would become the official language of the country' and demand that there should be 'an unequivocal declaration' that Hindi was the official language of India and that 'there shall be no restrictions whatsoever on

---

[108] *Congress Bulletin*, April–June 1965, pp.145–6. See also *Statesman* (Delhi), 2 June 1965, pp. 1 and 12; 3 June 1965, p. 7
[109] See Dilip Mukerjee, 'Political commentary', *Statesman* (Delhi), 8 December 1967, p. 8. On the bill's eventual enactment as the Official Languages (Amendment) Act of 1968, see Nayar, *National Communication and Language Policy in India*, pp. 119–21.

its use in Central Government affairs'. However, it then made the important concession that those central government officials and employees who had not learnt Hindi should be permitted to use English for a period of ten years. It agreed that all Indian languages should be recognized as media for UPSC examinations and proposed their immediate use where the particular language had been accepted as the medium of instruction for university examinations in the state concerned. It opposed the idea of English being made a compulsory subject for study and proposed that it should be taught only as an 'optional Foreign Language'. Finally, it declared that the three-language formula should involve the teaching of the mother tongue, Sanskrit and Hindi (or any other modern Indian language for those whose mother tongue was Hindi).[110]

By July 1965, then, one of the Jana Sangh's early rallying cries had lost some of its force. Whereas the championship of Hindi against English had appeared to be an excellent means of securing the support of the Hindi-speaking middle class of the northern states, it had soon become clear that people in the non-Hindi-speaking states saw English as a means of competing on equal terms with the large group of Hindi-speakers for the prizes in administrative, professional and economic life. This had caused the party to modify its policy in two respects: firstly, under pressure from its active units in non-Hindi-speaking states, it had acknowledged the need for the extension of the role assigned to regional languages, and secondly, it had transferred its attack from English as a medium of official communication to English as the privileged possession of political, administrative and professional élites who, to use Dr Raghuvira's phrase, constituted an 'Anglocracy'. In short, by 1965 the Jana Sangh was having to take much greater account of the pattern of interests which had been produced by language politics and to make its policies more realistic and less abstract than they had been in the early 1950s. In doing so it had, in yet another instance, adopted a position which differed only in degree from that of the Congress and had, yet again, complicated its task of representing itself as the vehicle of Hindu nationalism.

The Jana Sangh and the partition of the Punjab in 1966

As the Jana Sangh tried harder to gain a reputation for being a responsible party, unwilling to place itself outside the law, it became increasingly wary of endorsing Hindu nationalist causes which might

---

[110] Central Working Committee, Jabalpur, 10 July 1965, in Bharatiya Jana Sangh, *Resolutions Passed by Bharatiya Karya Samiti on July, 10 & 11, 1965, Jabalpur, Madhya Pradesh* (Delhi, n.d.), pp. 3–5; see also *BJS Documents*, V, pp. 45–6.

involve it in a direct confrontation with authority. Issues which in the early 1950s had been seen as a means of arousing strong support amongst the mass of Hindus were, by the mid-1960s, being approached with circumspection. One such issue involved the territorial claims of the Sikh community. As we have noted in an earlier section, the Jana Sangh had done its best at the time of states reorganization to defend the principle of a united Punjab, and at that time the Congress leadership had also refused to countenance the idea of the partition of the state. However, the situation had altered at the end of 1965, when the central and state Congress governments showed clear signs that they were willing to give way in the face of a renewed Akali agitation for a Sikh state.

At this time the Akali Dal was divided into two factions, one headed by Master Tara Singh and the other by Sant Fateh Singh, who had been one of Tara Singh's lieutenants in the 1950s. Sant Fateh Singh's group won a convincing victory in the SGPC elections of January 1965 and one of its leaders, Sant Chanan Singh, was re-elected as SGPC President on 13 March. A few days later the general body and the Working Committee of the Sant Akali Dal authorized Sant Fateh Singh to set up a committee to negotiate with the central government on the possibility of forming a Punjabi Suba.[111] He discussed this proposal with the Prime Minister, Lal Bahadur Shastri, at meetings on 7 and 8 August, but although Shastri gave an assurance that he would do everything possible to remove 'the sense of grievances from the minds of the Sikh community' he also pointed out that the government was unable to accept the demand for a Punjabi Suba.[112]

Sant Fateh Singh then announced that if the government did not accept this demand he would undertake a fifteen-day fast, and that if he survived at the end of that period would burn himself to death.[113] The leaders of the Punjab Jana Sangh held an urgent meeting on the 23rd and the party's Working Committee decided on the 29th to form an action committee to oppose any division of the state.[114] In Upadhyaya's view, a Punjabi Suba was another name for a Sikh state: 'This Suba therefore will be a theocratic state in India. We cannot allow it.' Warning against

---

[111] *Statesman* (Delhi), 14 March 1965, p. 5; 19 March 1965, p. 9. The context of the events described in this section is analysed in detail in Brass, *Language, Religion and Politics in North India*, Part IV, pp. 275–400.

[112] According to a note presented to the Lok Sabha by the Home Minister on 23 August (see *Statesman* (Delhi), 24 August 1965, p. 7). See also a reference by the Prime Minister to these talks during a speech in the Rajya Sabha (*P.D.*, *R.S.*, LIII, 24 August 1965, cc. 1109–10).

[113] *Statesman* (Delhi), 17 August 1965, p. 1.

[114] *Organiser*, 29 August 1965, p. 16; *Statesman* (Delhi), 30 August 1965, p. 7.

concessions, he declared that the Jana Sangh 'should mobilise the nationalist forces to preserve the unity of Punjab which is essential for the unity of India'.[115] The Sant eventually agreed to postpone his fast in view of the conflict with Pakistan[116] and on 23 September the Union Home Minister, Gulzarilal Nanda, announced that the government had decided to form a cabinet committee, consisting of Mrs Gandhi, Y.B. Chavan and Mahavir Tyagi, to examine the proposal for a Punjabi Suba and that it intended to appoint a parliamentary committee to consider the matter as well.[117] The composition of the parliamentary committee was announced shortly afterwards[118] and by October the parties were engaged in a full-scale debate as to whether the Punjab should be reorganized and, if so, what form the reorganization should take.

The case for partition was presented not only by the Akali Dal and other supporters of the Punjabi Suba proposal but also by groups, such as the Haryana All-Party Action Committee, which wanted to form a Hindi-speaking state composed of the districts of eastern Punjab, and by other groups, such as the Vishal Himachal Samiti, which favoured the inclusion of the northern hill districts of the existing state in an enlarged Himachal Pradesh. Although the Punjab Congress Party had resisted demands for the partition of the state on earlier occasions, it now lacked the leadership of Kairon (who had been succeeded as Chief Minister by Ram Kishan in July 1964) and was weakened by internal disagreements.[119] Many opposition parties soon declared themselves for a Punjabi Suba and the state units of the Communist Party, the Praja Socialist Party, the Republican Party of India and the Samyukta Socialist Party joined the Sant Akali Dal in a convention which endorsed this objective on 7 November.[120] Nevertheless, the Punjab Jana Sangh refused to change its position and prepared a memorandum in which it argued forcefully against partition on the grounds that a unified Punjab was necessary, not only to provide a strong state on the border with Pakistan but to foster the economic development of the region. It reaffirmed its belief that the Punjab was bilingual, in the sense that Punjabi and Hindi were 'spoken and understood by all sections of the population', and that administration at all levels 'should be

[115] 'This Punjabi Suba business', *Organiser*, 5 September 1965, pp. 2 and 15. See also, Krishan Lal, 'Fateh Singh's fast & Tara Singh's plans', *ibid.*, 12 September 1965, p. 8.
[116] *Statesman* (Delhi), 10 September 1965, p. 1.
[117] *P.D., L.S.* (Third Series), XLVI, 23 September 1965, c. 7191.
[118] *Statesman* (Delhi), 29 September 1965, p. 5.
[119] On Congress divisions on this issue, see reports by the *Statesman's* special representative in state (*ibid.*, 16 October 1965, p. 7; 19 October 1965, pp. 1 and 12; 21 October 1965, p. 12; 23 October 1965, p. 5; 10 November 1965, p. 7).
[120] *Ibid.*, 8 November 1965, p. 7.

conducted in both the languages and both the scripts'. Claiming that a feeling of neglect lay behind the demand for a separate Haryana state or an enlarged Delhi state, it pointed out that from the beginning the Jana Sangh had favoured preferential treatment for neglected areas; it recommended the establishment of a development board for the Haryana region and its 'proper representation' on central and state cabinets. It also recommended that steps should be taken to develop the hill areas.[121]

At the heart of the Punjabi Suba dispute were the closely related linguistic and communal issues. The 1961 census had shown that the religious composition of the Punjab was 63.7 per cent Hindus, 33.3 per cent Sikhs and 3.0 per cent others in a total population of 20,306,812, with Sikhs constituting a bare majority (52.8 per cent) in the Punjabi-speaking region and Hindus a secure majority (88.1 per cent) in the Hindi-speaking region.[122] The linguistic composition had been revealed as Hindi-speakers 55.6 per cent, Punjabi-speakers 41.1 per cent and others 3.3 per cent. Although the census data showed that Punjabi-speakers constituted majorities in most of the districts in the Punjabi-speaking region, these districts also contained significant proportions of Hindi-speakers, ranging from 16.6 per cent in Bhatinda to 49.0 per cent in Gurdaspur and 52.6 per cent in Hoshiarpur, while the proportions in the important districts of Amritsar and Jullundur were 22.9 and 38.2 per cent respectively.[123] The Jana Sangh's claim that the region as a whole was bilingual rested on an assumption that many people could speak both Punjabi and Hindi but, according to the census returns, only 345,320 of the 11,297,838 Hindi-speakers had nominated Punjabi as a subsidiary language and only 400,127 of the 8,336,787 Punjabi-speakers had so nominated Hindi.[124]

---

[121] Punjab State Bharatiya Jana Sangh, *The Case of Bharatiya Jana Sangh: Memorandum (Submitted to the Parliament and Cabinet Committees to 'Find a Cooperative Solution to the Demand of Punjabi Suba,')* (Jullundur, n.d.), especially pp. 31–5. See also the report of the annual meeting of the General Council of the Punjab Jana Sangh (*Organiser*, 16 January 1966, pp. 9 and 10).

[122] See Table 1-A, 'Religious composition of Hindi-speaking and Punjabi-speaking regions in 1961', in Nayar, *Minority Politics in the Punjab*, pp. 18–19, based on *Census of India: Paper No 1 of 1963* (Delhi, 1963), pp. 30–5.

[123] See Appendix III to Table C-V, 'Mother tongue', in *Census of India 1961*, Vol. XIII, *Punjab*, Part II-C (i), *Social and Cultural Tables*, by R. L. Anand, Superintendent of Census Operations and Enumeration Commissioner, Punjab (Delhi, 1965), pp. 229–37. In this appendix small numbers of people speaking related languages have been added to the Hindi- and Punjabi-speaking categories.

[124] From Table C-VI, 'Bilingualism', in *ibid.*, pp. 264 and 269. Cf. the Jana Sangh's claim that 34.4 lakhs of the Hindi-speakers had nominated Punjabi as their subsidiary language and that 24.2 lakhs of the Punjabi-speakers had nominated Hindi as their second language (Punjab State Bharatiya Jana Sangh, *The Case of Bharatiya Jana Sangh*, Appendix C, p. 40).

The heated debates of October and November 1965 were followed by several months of confused and protracted negotiations while the Congress Party's leaders were preoccupied with the Tashkent conference and the succession crisis which followed Mr Shastri's death in January 1966. Finally, on 1 March Mrs Gandhi, who had become the new Prime Minister, told the Lok Sabha that a decision on the Punjab was imminent[125] and on 9 March the Congress Working Committee proposed the formation of a state with Punjabi as its official language and requested the central government 'to take necessary steps for the purpose'.[126]

Now that the Congress Party had changed its policy, the only organizations which stood out against the partition of the state were the Jana Sangh, the Arya Samaj and the Punjab Ekta Samiti, which had been formed in the previous autumn. A secretary of the Punjab Jana Sangh, Yagya Datt Sharma, had declared on 7 March that he would undertake a fast unto death 'to preserve the unity of the State and maintain peace and tranquillity in the face of Akali threats of violent agitation or direct action',[127] and when the Congress Working Committee's decision was announced on the 9th he began his fast in a roadside tent in the city of Amritsar. On the following days hartals were held in Hindu commercial areas in such centres as Jagadhri, Ludhiana, Jullundur, Ambala, Amritsar and Bhatinda, and soon the familiar pattern of noisy street processions, demonstrations, arrests, police firings and haphazard violence had taken shape.[128] Upadhyaya and Madhok, who separately visited the affected areas, asked the central government to declare that it was not bound by the recommendations of the Congress Working Committee and that a round-table conference of all parties would be held to discuss the issues.[129] Madhok urged the Union Home Minister to go to the Punjab and meet Yagya Datt Sharma and other leaders of opinion:

Let there be no misconception about the popularity of Shri Yagya Dutt and the cause for which he has staked his life. His death would set Punjab ablaze.

---

[125] *P.D., L.S.* (Third Series), LI, 1 March 1966, c. 3061.

[126] *Congress Bulletin*, January–March 1966, p. 23.

[127] *Organiser*, 13 March 1966, pp. 1 and 15.

[128] *Statesman* (Delhi), 13 March 1966, pp. 1 and 7. The Bar Association of India published a pamphlet entitled *Report of the Commission of Enquiry on Alleged Police Excesses in Punjab during Anti-Suba Agitation in March 1966* (New Delhi, n.d.), based on the enquiries of three of its members. The report contains detailed accounts of alleged unlawful actions by the police in Amritsar, Jullundur and Ludhiana in the period following the Congress Working Committee's decision of 9 March 1966.

[129] See Upadhyaya's statement in *Organiser*, 20 March 1966, p. 3, and his address to the Delhi State Jana Sangh conference on 12 March (*Statesman* (Delhi), 13 March 1966, p. 7).

At the same time I would appeal to the people of Punjab of all communities to maintain communal harmony at all costs. The agitation is directed against the Government and not against any community or party. Any attempt to create communal tension or riots must be resisted by every Jana Sangh worker even at the cost of his life. Shri Yagya Dutt is fasting for the unity of the Punjab and the unity of her brave people. Any attempt to destroy that unity and create a gulf between Sikhs and non-Sikhs would be the greatest dis-service and blow to that great patriot.[130]

However, the central government refused to dismiss the recommendations of the Congress Working Committee, and the Jana Sangh found itself faced with the choice of leading a violent agitation or accepting the inevitability of partition. Disturbances became more serious; there were riots in Delhi on the 14th[131] and, on the 15th, when a mob set fire to a hut in Panipat, three Congressmen were burnt to death.[132] Meanwhile, the Jana Sangh was finding it difficult to persuade its local leaders and members in the Haryana region to adhere to the policy of a united Punjab. On the 14th the Jana Sangh MP for Rohtak, Lehri Singh, announced that he had left the party[133] and on the 18th the Vice-President of the Rohtak district unit of the party also resigned, along with about 500 followers, having complained that the party's activities had encouraged violent demonstrations in the region.[134] Then, on the 19th the Union Home Minister began a series of talks with leaders of the Punjab Jana Sangh, the Arya Samaj and the Punjab Ekta Samiti and it became clear that the danger of a confrontation had passed. Instead of pressing for a reversal of policy, these organizations were now trying to influence the decisions which would flow from partition – where the boundaries of the new states would run, what language policies would apply, and what should be done about Chandigarh, the capital of the undivided state.[135]

At last the way was clear for a settlement. On the 18th the parliamentary committee had reported in favour of the reorganization of the state on a linguistic basis[136] and on the 21st the Home Minister announced that the central government, having considered the committee's recommendations, had 'decided to accept, in principle, that

---

[130] *Organiser*, 20 March 1966, pp. 1 and 16, quotation from p. 16.
[131] *Statesman* (Delhi), 15 March 1966, pp. 1 and 12.
[132] *Ibid.*, 17 March 1966, pp. 1 and 8.
[133] *Ibid.*, 15 March 1966, p. 1; *National Herald*, 15 March 1966, p. 4.
[134] *National Herald*, 20 March 1966, p. 6.
[135] *Statesman* (Delhi), 20 March 1966, p. 1; 21 March 1966, pp. 1 and 12.
[136] Lok Sabha Secretariat, *Parliamentary Committee on the Demand for Punjabi Suba: Report*, p. 27. Vajpayee, who was a member of the committee, submitted a note of dissent (*ibid.*, pp. 40–4).

the present state of Punjab be reorganised on a linguistic basis'. He acknowledged that the government had also considered representations made by various interests, including those opposed to the scheme, and had reassured them:

(i)   that the proposed reorganisation of Punjab will follow the linguistic basis, without any communal or religious factors being allowed to come into consideration;

(ii) such common links between the units resulting from the proposed reorganisation as are found feasible will be provided in consultation with the concerned interests;

(iii) the legitimate rights and interests of the minorities, linguistic and others, will naturally be fully safeguarded in the units.[137]

Madhok, who had just been elected national President of the Jana Sangh, said that his party still considered that a united Punjab was in the best interests of the country but welcomed the assurances given, particularly that concerning the preservation of common links.[138] Also on the 21st, Yagya Datt Sharma broke his fast before a large crowd in Amritsar[139] and the Arya Samaj leader, Swami Satyanand, ended his fast on the 23rd.[140]

An *Organiser* report of the negotiations which preceded the settlement suggests that once the division of the state had become a certainty the Jana Sangh's main concern had been to ensure that the two successor states would have 'common links', such as a shared capital city, a single governor and a single high court, and that this assurance had been given by the Prime Minister herself after a meeting with Vajpayee. According to this account, Vajpayee, having subsequently learned that Sant Fateh Singh was opposed to the idea of common links, had telephoned the Prime Minister's secretariat:

Shri Vajpayee insisted that Government must give renewed clarifications before the Jana Sangh High Command could finally request Yagya Dutt to end his fast. The reply came fast and firm: 'We have made a promise and we stand by it. If the Sant opposes, we'll face him. Please see that the fast ends today as promised.'[141]

In public the Jana Sangh's main task was to reconcile its Punjab unit to the fact that the fight against partition had been lost and that it had to

---

[137] *P.D., L.S.* (Third Series), LII, 21 March 1966, cc. 6896–7.
[138] *Statesman* (Delhi), 22 March 1966, p. 1.
[139] *Ibid.*
[140] *Ibid.*, 24 March 1966, p. 1. Before taking *sanyas*, Swami Satyanand had been known as Acharya Ramdev. He had been President of the Punjab Jana Sangh for several years in the 1950s (see letter from the editor, *Organiser*, 3 April 1966, p. 2).
[141] By a 'roving correspondent', *Organiser*, 27 March 1966, pp.1 and 16, quotation from p. 1.

come to terms with its former opponents. When the party's thirteenth national session met at Jullundur on 30 April 1966, Madhok used his presidential address to stress the need for future unity, and he called on the central government

to see that demarcation in Punjab is done on purely linguistic basis without allowing any political or communal consideration to come in. This is essential to prevent the extremist elements among the Akalis and the Arya-Samajists to further aggravate the already difficult situation.[142]

He suggested that the new Punjab should adopt Devanagari as an alternative script for Punjabi and that in return the 'non-Akali Hindus of Punjab should give a lead in the matter by owning Gurmukhi script unreservedly'.[143] This latter proposal was reported to have angered the Punjab Jana Sangh and to have brought into the open differences between the party and the Arya Samaj[144] but the session's general resolution on the subject simply warned against the dangers of communalism, claiming that the Jana Sangh regarded the Sikhs 'as part and parcel of the Hindu Society' and had 'full trust' in their patriotism:

We hope that they will keep themselves away from the pulls, and the leadership, which strive to sow among them seeds of separatism.[145]

The Central Working Committee dissolved the working committee which had been responsible for the party's activities in the undivided state and in its place established three *ad hoc* committees (one for the new Punjab, one for Haryana and one for Kangra); it then deputed Vajpayee, Madhok and Sundar Singh Bhandari to appoint the members of these committees and to guide their affairs.[146] An observer later noted that this decision had

gone a long way to retrieve the party's position in the State, because their interests being divergent, the Haryana Jana Sangh men were finding it difficult to carry on with their Punjab party colleagues. Political expediency demanded their separation.[147]

The partition was carried through quickly. The new states of Punjab and Haryana came into existence on 1 November 1966 and the hill areas

---

[142] Bharatiya Jana Sangh, *Presidential Address by Prof. Balraj Madhok at the Thirteenth All India Session, Jullundur (Punjab), April 30, & May 1, & 2, 1966* (n. d.), p. 9.
[143] *Ibid.*, p. 11.
[144] Staff correspondent, 'The Punjab scene', *Statesman* (Delhi), 2 August 1966, p. 7.
[145] Thirteenth National Session, Jullundur, 1 May 1966, Bharatiya Jana Sangh, *Resolutions Passed at the Thirteenth Annual Session and All India Working Committee, Jullundur, April, 30, May 1 & 2, 1966* (Delhi, n.d.), pp. 13–16, quotation from p. 16; see also *BJS Documents*, IV, pp. 124–6.
[146] Staff correspondent, *Statesman* (Delhi), 30 April 1966, p. 5.
[147] Staff correspondent, Chandigarh, *ibid.*, 5 May 1966, p. 7.

were joined to Himachal Pradesh. The central government decided to make Chandigarh a union territory so that it could serve as a capital for both the new states and also provided for a common governor, a common high court and certain other institutional ties between them. The Sant Akali Dal continued to press for the removal of such ties, and for the absorption of Chandigarh into the Punjab; Sant Fateh Singh began a fast in December 1966 to achieve these objectives but broke it on the 26th, after an agreement had been reached that the Prime Minister would decide whether Chandigarh and the Bhakra-Nangal hydro-electric and irrigation scheme should be under central or state jurisdiction, and that a committee would discuss other subjects.[148] Upadhyaya criticized the government for having made such concessions[149] but in the new Punjab the state unit of the Jana Sangh and the Akali Dal were already learning to work with each other. After the 1967 general elections, they joined with other non-Congress parties to form the United Front coalition, which took office in the Punjab under Gurnam Singh as Chief Minister on 8 March. It was later revealed that the Jana Sangh had joined the United Front on the basis of an agreement with the Sant Akali Dal that, in the new state, the existing provisions for the promotion of Hindi would remain despite the recognition of Punjabi as the state language; that private schools would continue to teach both Punjabi and Hindi; that such schools would not be discriminated against in the allocation of public grants; that Hindi should replace English as the link language; and that the United Front would fight against all separatist tendencies, including those demanding a Sikh state. For its part, the Jana Sangh agreed to abandon its claim that the Punjab was a bilingual state and that Hindus were a linguistic minority within it.[150]

When the die was cast the Jana Sangh had had no alternative other than to come to terms with the central government's decision to create a small Punjab in which Sikhs would form a large majority of the population. The party's defence of the principle of a united Punjab had always been based on the judgement that the Sikhs would eventually settle for existence within a bilingual system, insisting only upon their rights as a religious and linguistic minority and giving up all hope of obtaining a separate Punjabi Suba. In the last resort, the only way of preserving the Punjab as a single, if bilingual, state would have been the

---

[148] *National Herald*, 27 December 1966, pp. 1 and 7.

[149] *Ibid.*, 29 December 1966, p. 7. See also Krishan Lal in *Organiser*, 15 January 1967, pp. 5 and 12.

[150] J. C. Anand, 'Punjab: politics of retreating communalism', in Iqbal Narain (ed.), *State Politics in India* (Meerut, 1976), pp. 276–7. See also two reports by D. P. Kumar in *Statesman* (Delhi), 28 June 1967, p. 7; 28 September 1967, p. 9.

use of coercion, and, once the Congress Party and the Government of India had signified that they were unwilling to use such means, the Jana Sangh and its allies had either to persuade the government to change its mind or to contemplate a campaign of protest which could have led to violent confrontations with the Akali Dal and eventually with the whole Sikh community. Having excluded such a course of action, the Jana Sangh was forced once again to come to terms with local reality and modify its general policy; it did so very quickly and formed what was obviously an alliance of expediency with the Akali Dal. The ideal of Maha Punjab, for which it had sacrificed so much in the 1950s, was now a thing of the past.

The Jana Sangh and the demand for the abolition of cow-slaughter

Although the Punjab crisis of 1966 had been a difficult one for the Jana Sangh, it had accomplished its retreat in good order and had not lost touch with its most valuable non-partisan ally, the Arya Samaj. At every stage in the conflict the party had known what issues were at stake, and what penalties and rewards attached to different courses of action. After a suitable interval, it was able to come to terms with its old rival, the Akali Dal, and, having redefined its goals in Punjabi politics, was less likely to be committed to campaigns of high principle in defence of Hindu nationalism. This pattern and this outcome stand in sharp contrast to that which formed around the campaign for the abolition of cow-slaughter at the end of 1966, when the Jana Sangh was once again called upon to honour a commitment to one of the oldest and most emotional causes of Hindu politics. However, on this occasion it found itself working with a range of relatively unknown and politically inexperienced pressure groups, groups capable of stimulating an agitational movement which could sweep the Jana Sangh into an outright and damaging confrontation with organized authority.

In legal terms, the call for the abolition of cow-slaughter had been reduced to the demand that the central government should give effect to Article 48 of the Constitution of India, which stated that the state should, amongst other things, take steps for 'prohibiting the slaughter, of cows and calves and other milch and draught cattle'. Although this Article belonged to the Directive Principles, and was therefore intended only to provide guidance to the states in the making of laws, there had been several attempts to persuade the central government to prohibit cow-slaughter through an Act of Parliament. However, Nehru had set himself firmly against such a course and in 1955 a committee of experts had decided that such a ban would not be in the best interests of the country.

When acts enforcing bans at the state level were adopted by the legislatures of Uttar Pradesh, Bihar, Madhya Pradesh and Rajasthan they were challenged in the Supreme Court, which ruled in 1958 that, although a total ban was justified on the slaughter of cows, the calves of cows, and the calves of buffaloes, it was unreasonable to ban the slaughter of female buffaloes, breeding bulls and working bullocks after they were no longer useful.[151]

The Jana Sangh consistently referred to the need for a ban on cow-slaughter in its manifestos, implying that it would serve both economic and religious ends; for example, the 1954 manifesto stated:

Cow is our point of honour, and the eternal symbol of our culture. Since immemorial times it has been protected and worshipped. Our economy too, is based on the cow. Cow protection, therefore, is not only a pious duty but an indispensable need. It is impossible to protect and improve cattle so long as its slaughter continues. The only way to stay the rapid decline of cattle is to ban its slaughter forthwith. Jana Sangh will impose complete ban on cow slaughter and with the cooperation of public and administration improve its quality.[152]

When the 1958 judgement of the Supreme Court was announced, the Jana Sangh's Central Working Committee claimed that it had made 'the values and objectives which prompted the States to ban cow-slaughter ineffective in practice' and it therefore called for an amendment of Article 48 of the Constitution and demanded that those states which had not instituted bans should do so 'at the earliest'.[153]

However, in spite of its rhetoric, the Jana Sangh left it to various other non-party groups to organize lobbying campaigns and demonstrations. In the mid-sixties, the initiative for a new national campaign came from the Bharat Gosevak Samaj (India Cow-Servant Society), which organized a two-day session of the All-India Goraksha Sammelan (Cow-Protection Conference) at Vrindavan, in the Mathura district of Uttar Pradesh, in August 1964. The Sammelan decided to ask the central government to pass legislation to ban cow-slaughter completely by Gopashtami (a day in the Hindu-calendar month of Kartik, which usually falls in October or November) in 1965, and to send a deputation to meet the President, the Prime Minister and other ministers and to

[151] This paragraph is based on Smith, *India as a Secular State*, pp. 483–9.

[152] 1954 Manifesto, *BJS Documents*, I, p. 68. See also Bharatiya Jana Sangh, *Manifesto* (1951), p. 5; 1958 Manifesto, *BJS Documents*, I, p. 119; Bharatiya Jana Sangh, *Election Manifesto 1957*, pp. 21–2; *Election Manifesto 1962*, pp. 16–17; *Principles and Policy* [New Delhi, 1965], p. 35.

[153] Central Working Committee, Bombay, 19 July 1958, *BJS Documents*, II, p. 59. The text in this source has the committee calling for an amendment of Article 46, but Article 48 was obviously the one intended.

place the demand before them. The session was blessed by Prabhu Datt Brahmachari, known as the Sant of Jhusi, who suggested that if the central government had not imposed a ban by a given date a peaceful and nation-wide agitation should begin. The organizers of this session had canvassed the support of as many interests as possible, and the list of people who sent their good wishes included the Jagatguru Shankara-charyas (the heads of the four principal monasteries of Hinduism), three state governors and three central ministers. Golwalkar, the RSS leader, had inaugurated the Sammelan, and Upadhyaya of the Jana Sangh had been one of the speakers, but the extent of their commitment to this venture was not clear.[154] In the following month the Jagatguru Shankaracharya of Goverdhan monastery, located at Puri in Orissa, presided over a convention at Amritsar, which also demanded a ban on cow-slaughter by parliamentary legislation.[155]

Although Parliament did not accede to these requests the fact remained that many of the state legislatures had already adopted appropriate measures by 1966; a total ban on cow-slaughter, as interpreted by the Supreme Court, had been imposed by this date in all the northern states and in Gujarat, the Vidarbha region of Maharashtra, Bihar, Orissa and parts of Mysore, and a partial ban, on the slaughter of young and useful cows only, had been imposed in several other states and regions, including Assam, West Bengal and Madras. Only Kerala and the coastal regions of Andhra Pradesh had not imposed any ban. However, the Government of India decided that more progress was required and on 23 August 1966 the Union Food Minister, Subramaniam, stated that the centre would once again draw the attention of the states to Article 48 of the Constitution.[156] Meanwhile, the cow-protection groups were mobilizing their resources for another attempt to bring about a total and comprehensive ban, and on 5 September they held a large demonstration outside Parliament House in New Delhi to make clear their views. A deputation led by Govind Das, a Congress MP, submitted a memorandum to the Home Minister, Gulzarilal Nanda, asking for central legislation to provide a ban,[157] while inside the chamber of the Lok Sabha, Swami Rameshwaranand, a Jana Sangh member, raised a commotion by trying to draw attention to the demonstration outside and was eventually suspended from the house for the remainder of the session.[158] Later in the month an organization

[154] *Organiser*, 31 August 1964, p. 8.
[155] *Statesman* (Delhi), 8 September 1964, p. 5.
[156] *P.D., L.S.* (Third Series), LIX, 23 August 1966, cc. 6455–6.
[157] *National Herald*, 6 September 1966, p. 5.
[158] *P.D., L.S.* (Third Series), LIX, 5 September 1966, cc. 9217–19.

known as the *Sarvadaliya Goraksha Maha-Abhiyan Samiti* (SGMS, literally, the All-Party Cow-Protection Great-Campaign Committee) was established under the presidency of Prabhu Datt Brahmachari, who announced that if no agreement for banning cow-slaughter had been reached by 20 November a 'mass *satyagraha*' would be launched in which about 100,000 persons would court arrest. He warned that he and others would begin fasts unto death on that day and that one-day hunger strikes would be held at district and tahsil levels.[159]

Indirectly the SGMS represented a wide range of Hindu religious institutions and Hindu nationalist associations, but as its campaign gathered momentum the responsibility for its decisions fell increasingly on a small group of leaders, which included Swami Karpatriji Maharaj (a prominent Ram Rajya Parishad figure), Swami Gurucharan Dassji Maharaj (President of the Bharat Sadhu Samaj), Muni Sushil Kumar (a leader of the Jain community) and Golwalkar of the RSS. The formal and spiritual leadership was provided by Prabhu Datt Brahmachari and by the Jagatguru Shankaracharya of Puri.

The central government was still endeavouring to influence the policies of those few state governments which had not yet imposed a total ban on cow-slaughter. Following Subramaniam's announcement on 23 August, the central Ministry of Food and Agriculture had communicated with state governments about the subject and on 8 October the Union Home Minister had written to the Chief Ministers of states in which only partial bans were in force, and to the governments of union territories, to remind them of Article 48 and of the 'widespread sentiments' in favour of a ban. He also pointed out that the central government was considering the formation of a committee on cow protection.[160] On 29 October, acting on a directive from the central cabinet, he sent out another set of letters to the Chief Ministers concerned and requested them

to consider this question further with a view to preparing legislations on the subject of cow slaughter for introduction in your state legislatures. I propose to announce that I have addressed the states concerned in this matter and that it is my expectation that they would consider this matter urgently.[161]

Then, on 2 November, the Congress Working Committee advised the central government to impose a ban on cow-slaughter in centrally

---

[159] *Hindustan Times*, 28 September 1966, p. 8; *Organiser*, 25 September 1966, p. 7.
[160] *National Herald*, 9 October 1966, p. 1. See also statement by the Union Home Minister, *P.D.*, *L.S.* (Third Series), LX, 4 November 1966, cc. 1360–2.
[161] *National Herald*, 30 October 1966, p. 4.

administered areas and union territories and to ask states where this had not been done 'to take similar action as soon as possible'.[162]

It was thus quite clear that the central government and the Congress leaders were working together to place pressure on the states to adopt further measures against cow-slaughter and, had the SGMS been more politically aware, it would have realized that there was less to be gained from agitational methods than from negotiations with the central ministers concerned. However, its programme of demonstrations had already become a series of individual and group actions which were intended to culminate in a large procession through the streets of Delhi on 7 November. At its meeting at Nagpur early in that month the Jana Sangh's Central General Council noted what was being done and assured the SGMS 'of complete co-operation'. It warned the central government that what it saw as its apathy was 'increasing public resentment':

The people have very deep feelings on the matter of the cow. If on any occasion this widespread public resentment goes out of control, the consequences would be serious and their responsibility will be completely on the Government. Hence the General Council strongly urges the Government to think seriously of the matter and ban cow-slaughter by amending the Constitution in the present session of Parliament.[163]

On 6 November the central executive of the Bharat Sadhu Samaj also warned that unless the government took such a decision before the 20th the movement would be continued with 'full strength'.[164]

The demonstration in Delhi on 7 November was organized by a number of associations, including the Hindu Mahasabha, the Jana Sangh, the Arya Samaj and the Sanatana Dharma Sabha. Groups of demonstrators assembled in different parts of the city in the morning and then went in procession to Parliament Street, where the leading members of the SGMS and some parliamentarians, including Vajpayee, were seated on a large improvised platform. There were women and children in the crowd, many saffron robes were in evidence, and flags bearing the cow emblem were held aloft. The leaders on the platform rose in turn to make speeches and the affair looked as though it would take a peaceful course until about 1.30 p.m. when, according to a later statement by the Home Minister, Swami Rameshwaranand stood up

[162] *Congress Bulletin*, November–December 1966, pp. 339–40.
[163] *BJS Documents*, II, pp. 78–9, quotation from p. 79. This resolution is attributed to the Central Working Committee, Nagpur, 2 November 1966, but the text shows that it was a resolution of the Central General Council which met at Nagpur between the 3rd and the 6th of November 1966.
[164] *National Herald*, 7 November 1966, p. 2.

and, evidently referring to his suspension at the time of the previous demonstration in September, asked those around him:

why are you sitting here? I am driven out of this Parliament? Why don't you go and force this Parliament to close down? Why are you merely sitting here? Better go and surround this Parliament and see that Members and Ministers do not come out of the Parliament House.[165]

From this point onwards the crowd became disorderly. In his account of what happened, Vajpayee said that Seth Govind Das and Prakash Vir Shastri spoke after Swami Rameshwaranand but that when he, Vajpayee, started to address the crowd a sadhu had snatched the microphone away from him.[166]

Now the violent incidents began. Groups in the crowd pushed forward and tried to break through the police cordons protecting Parliament House. Sadhus armed with spears and tridents were in the vanguard. The police tried lathi charges, and then tear-gas, but the rioting had spread well out of control. Some people rampaged through government buildings, others overturned vehicles and set fire to them; the house of the Congress Party's President, Kamaraj, was attacked; and buildings and property were damaged in adjacent localities, including Connaught Place. The police were forced to open fire and eight people (including one constable) were killed. A thick layer of smoke lay over the scene. Troops were brought into the city to assist in keeping order and a curfew was imposed.[167] By the 9th the police had arrested more than 1,450 people belonging to organizations connected with the SGMS, and Balraj Madhok, the national President of the Jana Sangh, was among them.[168]

Aware that their party's reputation for moderation was now at stake, the Jana Sangh's spokesmen tried to argue that the violence had been instigated by trouble-makers who had succeeded in infiltrating an otherwise peaceful demonstration and that the authorities were at fault for not having dealt more firmly with the disturbances. Speaking in the

---

[165] Cited in a statement by the Home Minister, Y.B. Chavan, in *P.D., R.S.*, LVIII, 17 November 1966, c. 1774.

[166] *Ibid.*, 16 November 1966, cc. 1454–5. In his account of what happened at this point, the political correspondent of the *Organiser* claimed that Swami Rameshwaranand withdrew his call to encircle Parliament House at the request of Prabhu Datt Brahmachari and that, while Prakash Vir Shastri was speaking, a few sadhus broke through the police cordon, whereupon an official decided to disperse the rally. It was then, according to this correspondent, that tear-gas shells began to fall on the platform and that the wires to the microphone were cut (*Organiser*, 20 November 1966, p. 2).

[167] The above two paragraphs are based on the account given in *National Herald*, 8 November 1966, pp. 1 and 6.

[168] *Ibid.*, 10 November 1966, p. 1. He was released on the 18th on an order of the Chief Justice of the Delhi High Court (*ibid.*, 19 November 1966, p. 5).

Lok Sabha immediately after the demonstration, U.M. Trivedi claimed that from the very beginning 'it was noticeable that some unruly elements had got in and it was the Government's duty to see...'. At this point he was interrupted but he insisted that

It was the duty of the Government to see that the situation would not go out of hand. Proper precautions ought to have been taken.[169]

However, there was no denying the party's close association with the SGMS. In an editorial the *National Herald* commented:

Swami Rameshwaranand, who is known to have incited a mob of unhinged minds with an inflammatory speech, has achieved temporary notoriety. In Parliament, Mr. Trivedi, leader of the Jan Sangh Party, had shown courage and decency in repudiating an unreasonably defiant swami. The more prominent of the Jan Sangh leaders, who were also parties to the demonstration, may have intended it to be peaceful, but they should not have associated themselves with others whom they must have known they could not manage.[170]

Then came the news that it had been Kedar Nath Sahni, the General Secretary of the Delhi State Jana Sangh unit, who had applied to the Delhi administration for permission to hold the procession on the 7th.[171]

The most detailed and considered defence of the Jana Sangh's position was offered by Vajpayee to the Rajya Sabha on the 16th. He insisted that the procession on the 7th had been organized by the SGMS and that the Jana Sangh was not included in that body. In his vivid description of the events of the afternoon he implied that groups of *provocateurs*, including a number of sadhus, had been planted in the crowd to stir up trouble and he demanded a full investigation of the incidents by a judge of either the Supreme Court or a High Court. Protesting against the number of arrests which had been made, he warned that the Jana Sangh would resist any attempt to use the incidents to attack the party:

why are these people being arrested? Again, why are those opposed to the Jana Sangh defaming us? Is it because the leaders of the Congress are disturbed by the increasing popularity of the Jana Sangh?[172]

Y. B. Chavan, who had succeeded Gulzarilal Nanda as Home Minister on the 13th, had this to say about the issue of responsibility

---

[169] *P.D., L.S.* (Third Series), LX, 7 November 1966, c. 1674. See also Upadhyaya's statement at Lucknow on the 8th (*National Herald*, 9 November 1966, p. 2).

[170] 'Democracy at bay', *National Herald*, 9 November 1966, p. 5.

[171] According to Jaisukhlal Hathi, the Minister of State for Home Affairs (*P.D., R.S.*, LVIII, 10 November 1966, c. 817).

[172] *Ibid.*, 16 November 1966, cc. 1449–59, quotation from c. 1457 (translation mine).

when the incidents were discussed in the Rajya Sabha on the 17th:

It was such a big demonstration; it cannot be undertaken by one person. There must have been many persons, organisations, their goodwill, their strength and their aid and it is their entire collective effort that really speaking can undertake a very huge demonstration of this type. Then out of the parties mentioned here, Jana Sangh was certainly one of the major participants in this.[173]

Highlighting the effects of Swami Rameshwaranand's remarks to the demonstrators just before the violence, he said:

it cannot be denied that he is a representative of the Jana Sangh in Parliament. I am only referring to the minimum facts. That was the beginning of the whole trouble.

Vajpayee interrupted to say that Rameshwaranand 'did not speak as a representative of the Jana Sangh'[174] but the Home Minister insisted on his point:

Now, naturally when such a thing happens, people will try to hold responsible those who led the movement, who participated in it, who organised it, who gave all support, moral, material and manpower support. Can the Jan Sangh deny that they did not do that?

Interrupting once more, Vajpayee replied: 'We only deny that we did not indulge in violence'.[175]

In spite of all the arrests, the campaign to ban cow-slaughter carried on; the Jagatguru Shankaracharya of Puri and Prabhu Datt Brahma-chari, who began fasting on the 20th, were taken into custody[176] but they continued to fast and by January 1967 their health was causing serious concern. Then, on 2 January the Working Committee and the General Council of the SGMS met together at Vrindavan and resolved to continue the movement; they requested the Jagatguru Shankaracharya of Jyotirmath to postpone a fast he had decided to undertake and appointed him, alongside Swami Karpatriji Maharaj and Swami Gurucharan Dassji Maharaj, to see to the conduct of the agitation.[177] In an effort to find a solution, the Union Home Minister offered to establish a committee representing central and state author-ities, the SGMS and expert opinion to examine the subject of cow-protection, but the representatives of the SGMS insisted that as a precondition the central government should agree to a ban on the

[173] *Ibid.*, 17 November 1966, c. 1773.
[174] *Ibid.*, c. 1774.
[175] *Ibid.*, c. 1775.
[176] *National Herald*, 21 November 1966, p. 1; 23 November 1966, p. 3.
[177] *Organiser*, 8 January 1967, p. 1.

slaughter of 'all progeny of the cow'.[178] Realizing that the campaign had now become a liability, however, the Jana Sangh's leaders began appealing for the fasts to be given up.[179] 'The Jana Sangh's posture is understandable', wrote the special representative of the *Statesman*:

Even if the fast is withdrawn now it does not stand to lose anything politically, because a ban on cow slaughter has been part of its election manifesto in the last three General Elections. On the other hand, it cannot be blamed if it wants to absolve itself of any responsibility for anything happening to those on fast.[180]

However, it was not until the very end of January that the agitation was scaled down. Prabhu Datt Brahmachari ended his fast on the 30th and the Jagatguru Shankaracharya of Puri ended his on the following day. The central government issued a statement, the result of a long period of informal negotiations, to the effect that within three months it would 'initiate vigorous steps' to persuade all states to comply with Article 48 of the Constitution; moreover, a committee was to be appointed to consider the matter of cow-protection and 'the suggestion that the Constitution should be amended to bring about a total ban on the slaughter of the cow and its progeny'. The statement concluded with the cautious sentence that 'The Government will give due weight to the recommendations of the Committee'.[181] Although the SGMS executive at first expressed dissatisfaction with the government's statement,[182] by the end of June 1967 the Union Food Ministry was able to announce that, on a twelve-member committee which was being set up to recommend steps to protect the cow and its progeny, the SGMS would be represented by Golwalkar, the Shankaracharya of Puri and Rama Prasad Mukherji,[183] and there the matter rested.

When it came to take stock of the campaign as a whole, the Jana Sangh must have realized that it had gained little from it: although its long-standing support for the principle of cow-protection had won it the approval of orthodox Hindus in the small country towns and the rural areas, its association with the day of violence in Delhi had reminded the urban middle class of the irrational and unpredictable aspects of Hindu nationalism and had damaged the reputation for moderation which the party had been trying so hard to earn.

---

[178] See *Statesman* (Delhi), 5 January 1967, p. 1; 6 January 1967, p. 1.
[179] See reports of statements by Vajpayee (*ibid.*, 7 January 1967, p. 1) and Upadhyaya (*ibid.*, 9 January 1967, p. 1).
[180] *Ibid.*, 10 January 1967, p. 1.
[181] *Ibid.*, 1 February 1967, pp. 1 and 12.
[182] *Ibid.*, 6 February 1967, p. 1.
[183] *Ibid.*, 30 June 1967, p. 1.

Conclusion

In this chapter we have seen the Jana Sangh wrestling with the paradox that the Hindu nationalism which it professed on behalf of all Indians was regarded outside the north as a particular variant of Hindi imperialism, an attempt to impose upon the rest of Indian society a peculiarly northern interpretation of its antecedents and its history. As it became aware of this difference of perspective, the party adopted a less rigid position, but as it did so in a piecemeal fashion its manifestos and policy statements retained many of their original integrationist and unitarian themes.

Within the northern region, the party stood for the policy of strengthening the unity of the Hindi heartland and of ensuring that the recognition of minority rights did not exceed certain very narrow limits; hence its stand against the granting of a separate territory within the Punjab region to the Sikhs on the grounds that they were essentially a sect within the Hindu community and not a self-sufficient religious group, and hence its determination to counter the efforts of Uttar Pradesh Muslims to extend the use of Urdu in the educational, administrative and legal institutions of the state.

Yet even in northern India, in what was really its base region, the Jana Sangh was unable to produce that rally of Hindu nationalist support which it had expected one day to sweep the Congress aside; the Congress units in the north had proved to be more resourceful and less liberal than the new party had assumed. Although Nehru and other members of his high command in New Delhi were genuinely enlightened and tolerant in their approach to questions of minority rights, many Congress politicians in the northern states were concerned to avoid any concessions which would weaken the position of Hindi or which, conversely, would provide room within which minority groups could achieve some degree of cultural autonomy. This was certainly the case in Uttar Pradesh so far as the Muslims were concerned: here the state Congress government kept rigidly to its Hindi-only policy and resisted very considerable pressure from the central government to recognize the rights of Urdu-speakers more fully. Consequently the Jana Sangh had little scope for attracting voters away from Congress on that issue. In the Punjab, Kairon succeeded in containing the territorial ambitions of the Akali Dal throughout his chief ministership (1956–64) and it was only after his departure that the Congress decided to accept the partition of the state in circumstances which gave the Jana Sangh no option other than to acquiesce in the outcome.

The Jana Sangh's increasing reluctance to use the methods of public protest to challenge the state governments probably reflected an awareness that the authorities had the resources and the strength to curb all but the most determined of agitational movements. When in fact the party was drawn towards agitation it was usually because it had allowed itself to become tied to less restrained groups, such as the Hindi Raksha Samiti in the Punjab in 1957 or the SGMS in the campaign against cow-slaughter in 1966. It was also a mark of the Jana Sangh's caution that it tended to direct its hostility not so much towards social groups (such as the Sikhs in the Punjab or the Muslims in Uttar Pradesh) as towards the state and central governments which it claimed were favouring these minorities; in other words, it behaved as though the state were the arbiter of relations between groups.

By the 1960s it was quite clear to the party that it had overestimated the potential support for Hindu nationalism in the north. Despite the enthusiasm of the Hindu élites for the task of restoring the Hindi heartland to its former pre-eminence, the great mass of ordinary Hindus were not easily moved by appeals to advance the cause of Hindi or to revive the ancient traditions of the region. As we have seen, in spite of the strenuous efforts made in the 1950s to speed up the introduction of Hindi for official purposes at the state level, when 1965 arrived there was nothing resembling a popular movement in the north to press the case for Hindi as the official language of the Indian Union. It was only in the south that strong feelings – against such an outcome – were expressed. Similarly, when the scheme to partition the Punjab was announced in March 1966, the only popular demonstrations against the idea of a Punjabi-speaking state occurred in the cities and towns in the western Punjab, where the Hindu minorities were located; the Hindus of Haryana accepted the scheme with little show of concern and it passed almost without notice in neighbouring Rajasthan and Uttar Pradesh. Yet this partition was an event of great significance in terms of linguistic politics because it redefined the boundaries of the western limit of the Hindi heartland well short of the international boundary with Pakistan. Nothing here resembled the energy and aggression with which German-speaking groups in the former Austro-Hungarian empire or Russian-speaking groups in the pre-1917 Russian empire had extended their social and political power at the expense of other linguistic groups. The Jana Sangh, in its support for Hindi as a national language and, in the Punjab, as a regional language, was speaking for an interest which had not yet found its voice.

6

The Jana Sangh and interest-group politics

Having considered the Hindu nationalist aspect of the Jana Sangh, we must now look at it in quite a different light, as one of a number of non-Congress parties endeavouring to attract various social groups whose material interests were being adversely affected by the policies of Congress governments, both central and state. The Jana Sangh's manifestos reveal that the party had firm views about which sections of society would sympathize with its general approach to questions of social and community relations. At the centre of its focus was a cluster of urban groups, chiefly small industrialists, traders and people on the lower rungs of the professional and administrative hierarchies, but it also saw itself as a party which could represent those sections of the working class employed in small enterprises and in the service industries. Within rural society, besides speaking for small traders, it was prepared to take the side of the peasants against landlords and big farmers.

We have two related tasks in this chapter. One is to describe how the party sought to establish special ties with these groups, and the second is to analyse the framework of ideas which the party used to justify and explain this aspect of its activity.

The Jana Sangh as the party of small industry and commerce

The Jana Sangh's rhetoric was directed neither to the closed world of the village nor to the open world of India's modern cities but to the middle world between these two extremes, that of the rural towns, the provincial professions, small industry, and country trading and banking. The party made much of the precariousness of this middle world, which it characterized as being threatened from two directions: from above, by the competitive individualism and the secular values of capitalism and from below by the first expressions of urban and rural populism, the growing power of caste associations, and the increased militancy of the Communist-led trade unions.

To provide a way forward for those placed in the middle world, the

Jana Sangh offered a social ethic which stressed the principles of corporatism and of family solidarity. At a general level it depicted an organic society in which social groups, though differentiated by their economic functions, were at the same time integrated within the whole community by relations of reciprocity and mutual support instead of being divided by conflict and competition. In specific terms it suggested that the institution of the joint family could serve a a model for the organization of firms, with managers and workers treating each other as kin rather than as parties to a contract. D.B. Thengadi, the party's trade union leader, made this point in an interview published in April 1965:

According to Bharatiya tradition, every industrial establishment is an industrial family with all those working within it as its industrial coparceners. Workers, including technicians and managers, are the coparceners of their respective industries.[1]

The same theme was taken up by Upadhyaya in an address to a seminar in Calcutta in March 1966:

Let us give a new form to this concept of family. Every corporate organisation or concern should develop into a family. The labour and management should work as members of one family. To inculcate this feeling, the concern should take upon itself all the responsibilities that the old joint family took of its members. Instead of Corporations and Joint Stock Companies let us develop coparcenaries. These coparcenaries can be combined into associations as modern versions of caste.[2]

Here was a social ethic which abstracted one aspect of caste, the joint-family system, and fused it with some of the positive aspects of capitalism such as enterprise, profit-making and advancement. It provided something of a half-way house between the economic and social restrictiveness of caste and the unrestrained individualism of modern urban life.

Convinced that this ethic was more likely to flourish in modest rather than large firms, the party argued that the organizational principles of small industries were in harmony with Indian social tradition and that they were the best means of providing employment and producing consumer goods. It therefore called upon the government to break up excessive concentrations of private industry and to ensure that small firms were given reserved sectors of the domestic markets and were not placed at a disadvantage in the competition for services, raw materials and licences. Although it supported the nationalization of industries

---

[1] *Organiser* (Delhi), 13 April 1965, p. 19.
[2] *Ibid.*, 10 April 1966, p. 10. See also an article by Upadhyaya, 'The rationale of Jana Sangh', *ibid.*, 25 January 1960, p. 5.

related to essential defence needs, it believed that the state could foster a private-enterprise economy provided that it was prepared to intervene occasionally to protect the weak against the strong. Very soon after the Jana Sangh was formed, Mookerjee had described this mixture of aims in the following terms:

While it is in favour of nationalization of key industries, it will fully encourage private enterprise subject to two conditions, namely, prevention of undue profiteering and of formation of groups or cartels wielding large-scale economic power. Only through a rational process of adjustments and by controlling the means of exploitation can class warfare be avoided. It believes in decentraliz-ation of industries and creation of conditions which will lead to village self-sufficiency. It will advocate the adoption of practical schemes under State auspices for the development of small and medium industries, by which means alone unemployment, specially among middle-class people, can be checked.[3]

In the same vein, the party's 1951 election manifesto had advocated steps 'to put a check on profiteering and concentration of economic power in the hands of the big few through cartels and combines', the 'progressive rationalisation and decentralisation of industry', and self-sufficiency in consumer goods 'through the widespread development of small-scale and cottage-industries on the model of Japan'.[4] On the latter point, the 1957 election manifesto was even more explicit:

To provide work for all and to free the society of the evils of concentration of labour and capital, Jana Sangha would take steps to decentralise economic power. Net-work of cottage and small scale industries will be established. To put an end to the competition between the small scale and large scale sectors, their spheres of production will be clearly demarcated.

Small industries will be the basis of all industrial planning, so the large industries will have to adjust according to them.[5]

In such phrasing, the Jana Sangh indicated its preference for an industrial system in which the government would ensure that small industry had enough public aid and sufficient security to develop into one of the major parts of the economy. In a book on the First and Second Five-Year Plans, Upadhyaya stated this argument in the following terms:

[3] Syama Prasad Mookerjee, 'The Bharatiya Jana Sangh', *Statesman* (Delhi), 21 December 1951, p. 4.
[4] *Manifesto of All India Bharatiya Jana Sangh* [New Delhi, 1951], p. 6.
[5] Bharatiya Jana Sangh, *Election Manifesto 1957*, p. 11. Cf. 1954 Manifesto, *Bharatiya Jana Sangh, Party Documents* (New Delhi, 1973), I, pp. 64–5; and 1958 Manifesto, *ibid.*, p. 108 (hereafter referred to as *BJS Documents*).

The Small Scale Sector had not promised much and the Plan had provided little for it but its achievements proved promising. It ventured in new lines of production and developed new techniques. It has established itself and can hardly be dislodged unless the Government places its political machinery and financial resources at the free disposal of the large-scale enterprise. On the other hand if the State comes to their help and the evolutionary process is speeded up, this Sector has a potential power of providing a solution to problems of economic stagnation and western industrialism.[6]

He made a related point regarding the Planning Commission's provision for heavy industries:

By taking up programmes of heavy industries the Commission intended to bring about a structural change in our society. Their aim is to build an industrial in place of an agricultural society. But we cannot build a pyramid from the top downwards. The base, *i.e.* the decentralized consumer goods industries, should have been laid first. Broader the base, bigger and higher the pyramid can be.[7]

The Jana Sangh's early policy resolutions had given the impression that its support for small industries involved support for village and cottage industries as well, but Upadhyaya now began to question the value of government assistance to the latter. With regard to the provisions of the Second Plan, he noted that

So far as small scale industries particularly handloom and khadi are concerned Government had decided to subsidise them, and that may be justified. But what technique the Plan proposes to adopt to see that this subsidy does not perpetuate some degree of disguised unemployment or under-employment in these industries is not known.[8]

He complained that the Second Plan allocations for village and small industries included only Rs 55 crores out of a total outlay of Rs 200 crores for 'the small scale industrial projects' whereas Rs 59.5 crores had been allocated to handloom weaving, Rs 16.7 crores to khadi (home-spun cloth), and Rs 38.8 crores to various village industries. He also claimed that an additional Rs 80 crores had been allocated for schemes involving *ambar charkha* (an improved hand-operated spinning unit).[9] Having advocated in his conclusion that decentralized small-scale industry 'should also be given first priority in the scheme of industrialisation', he went on to exclaim:

---

[6] Deendayal Upadhyaya, *The Two Plans: Promises, Performance, Prospects* (Lucknow, 1958), p. 157.

[7] *Ibid.*, p. 258.

[8] *Ibid.*, p. 201.

[9] *Ibid.*, pp. 258–60. The table on p. 259 includes data which are also presented in the table, 'Distribution of outlay for village and small industries', in Government of India, Planning Commission, *Second Five Year Plan* (New Delhi, 1956), p. 441.

Let the Commission get rid of fads for Ambar Charka and Palm-gur as also for Khadi and Neera.[10]

The party's 1962 election manifesto introduced the idea of 'rationalization' and thus sharpened the distinction which Upadhyaya had made:

To increase the productivity of small-scale industries and to make them stand on their own feet, they will be rationalized. In spite of heavy subventions the Khadi industry has not yet become economic. The Jana Sangh will set a time limit within which the industry will be required to become self-reliant. Handlooms will be converted into power-looms. Care will however be taken to ensure that no weaver is thrown out of work.[11]

The *Principles and Policy* document of 1965 went even further and proclaimed that

Most of the traditional village and cottage industries have ceased to be economic. By use of power and machine they should be rationalised and brought into the category of small industry. Unless their productivity is raised they can not survive. Protection is useful and necessary in the early stages, but it should not become a permanent feature.

It went on to note that artisans

have an important place in the village economy. With the advance of modernisation most of them are being displaced. Arrangements should be made to rehabilitate them.[12]

The 1967 manifesto did not even pretend that the party's championship of small industries was also a defence of the handloom, khadi, village and cottage industries; it simply stated that

Decentralisation, Swadeshi and labour intensity should be the criteria for our industrial development. It will reduce unemployment, inequalities and the foreign exchange shortage and in physical terms our achievement will be greater. Jana Sangh will evolve a pattern suited to the needs and conditions of our country and integrate it with the existing industries. Bharatiya Jana Sangh considers small scale decentralised industries to be most suitable for country's industrialisation. It will, therefore, give priority to small scale mechanised industries and provide them all facilities.[13]

[10] Upadhyaya, *The Two Plans*, p. 268. Palm-gur is a juice from which sugar is extracted and neera is a beverage; both are obtained from palm trees by tapping.
[11] Bharatiya Jana Sangh, *Election Manifesto 1962*, p. 19.
[12] Bharatiya Jana Sangh, *Principles and Policy* [New Delhi, 1965], pp. 37–8.
[13] Bharatiya Jana Sangh, *Election Manifesto 1967*, pp. 22–3.

As this quotation makes clear, by small industries the Jana Sangh
meant small factory units. According to one estimate, there were in 1960
approximately 36,460 small factories (i.e. those registered under the
Factories Act and having a fixed capital of less than Rs 500,000) in India,
employing about 1,338,000 people, or 38 per cent of registered factory
employment. They held 17.5 per cent of the fixed capital of all registered
factories, and contributed about 33 per cent of their gross output,
representing about 25 per cent of their net output.[14] However, at first,
large numbers of small enterprises remained unregistered and the actual
size of the sector became clearer only as records improved; thus, the
number of small-scale units registered with the Directorates of Industries
in the states grew from about 37,000 at the beginning of 1962 to nearly
100,000 by end of 1965,[15] and even the latter figure may have been well
short of the real total. Their relative importance within the industrial
structure varied a great deal from state to state. A survey of Uttar
Pradesh in 1960 found that small-scale units numbered 1,845 of the 2,483
factory units in the state, and that they employed 40,798 (or 14.58 per
cent) of the total of factory workers.[16] However, this sector was much
stronger in the Punjab, where in 1967 there were reported to be 14,589
small-scale units, employing 126,000 workers (or 76.36 per cent of the
total), with an investment of Rs 360 million and an annual production of
Rs 1,087 million, and only 114 medium-scale and 50 large-scale units.[17]
These figures relate to the smaller Punjab formed after the partition of
1966 but the size of the small-factory sector in the undivided Punjab had
been just as noticeable. This was explained by a survey organization in
the early 1960s in the following terms:

The factors that have contributed to the overall smallness of the industrial units
are the deficiency of natural resources (mineral and forest resources) for large
scale industry, lack of capital in large blocks backed by the requisite calibre of
entrepreneurial capacity and the fact that historically, industry in Punjab is still
very young.

---

[14] Government of India, Ministry of Industry, *Development of Small Scale Industries in
India: Prospects, Problems and Policies: Report of the International Perspective
Planning Team Sponsored by the Ford Foundation* (Delhi, 1963), p. 16 and Table 1
(Employment, capital and output in small registered factories by industry group,
1960), pp. 17–18.

[15] Government of India, Planning Commission, *Fourth Five Year Plan: A Draft Outline*
(New Delhi, 1966), p. 238.

[16] National Council of Applied Economic Research, *Techno-Economic Survey of Uttar
Pradesh* (New Delhi, 1965), pp. 136 and 264 (Table 41).

[17] *Hindustan Times* (Delhi), 25 July 1967, p. 5.

It also noted that

An industrial pattern dominated by small scale industry suffers from certain handicaps. Organizationally, it is weak and is unable to compete with large scale units in other than the local markets. Technically, it is either inferior or it tends to minimize the importance of quality, if a seller's market is prevailing, as in Punjab. Financially, it lacks the ability to build up sufficient reserves to introduce technological changes either to bring down cost or improve quality.[18]

However, although it was possible for the Jana Sangh to generalize about the weaknesses of small industries as a class, it failed to recognize that different categories of small industry faced quite different problems in their relationships with other economic sectors. There were, in fact, three clearly distinguishable categories: firstly, those small factories specializing in various branches of engineering, in chemicals and in scientific instruments, for example, which produced goods for large manufacturing industries and were not in competition with cottage and village industries; secondly, those factories which represented some degree of concentration and rationalization in what were mainly specialized handicraft industries, such as the manufacture of brass utensils and ornaments, carpets, lace, carved wood, bangles and pottery, where the skill of the individual artisan was the most valued asset and where factory methods did not threaten the predominantly cottage basis of production to any significant extent; and thirdly, those small units involved in the processing of agricultural, pastoral and forest products in such fields as wheat and rice milling, *dal* manufacture, oil crushing, cotton ginning, leather working and cloth making, in which factories were in direct competition with cottage and village industries for raw materials and primary products, local markets, and local supplies of specialized labour.

When the Jana Sangh went beyond its defence of small industries in general to make an appeal to specific sections, it tended to ignore the second category, the handicraft industries, and to appeal in quite different terms to the first and the third. In addressing the third category, the small agro-industries, it used the language of economic liberalism and, as we have seen, spoke of the need to rationalize village and cottage industries by ending their protected status and making them 'economic' and 'self-reliant'. However, in representing itself as the champion of 'modern' small industries, the first category, it adopted the language of planning and of state-regulated capitalism, arguing that the government had an obligation to help small manufacturing industries in the issue of licences, the allocation of raw materials, the reservation of markets, and

---

[18] National Council of Applied Economic Research, *Techno-Economic Survey of Punjab* (New Delhi, 1962), p. 78.

the provision of technical and other services. Congress was identified as the villain, too closely bound to big business to respond to the needs of small industries. 'Propaganda apart', claimed Upadhyaya in 1961

the small scale industry is not being given a chance to come to its own. Just think of it, the third plan allots about Rs. 4,000 crores for large-scale industry and only about a tenth of it for small-scale industry. Permits and licences are given to Congressmen and other favourites, who have no other use than to sell the same in the black market. But *bona fide* small manufacturers find it difficult to get either raw materials or power or even a telephone connection. I would even go so far as to say that the whole state apparatus favour [sic] the large-scale producer. The banks give him cheaper credit and greater accommodation. Where big units can get whole trains, small unit can's [sic] get even a wagon easily.[19]

In fact, however, both the central and the state governments were paying increasing attention to the needs of small industries, especially during the period of the Second and Third Five-Year Plans (1956–66). Although the Plans tended to place small-factory industries with village, cottage and handicraft industries as if they together constituted a single 'decentralized' sector of the economy, they did identify their general requirements, balancing proposals intended to increase their efficiency and competitiveness with the recommendation that they should be preserved and protected.[20] According to the distribution of legislative powers in the Indian Constitution, the development of small industries is a matter for the states, and state governments early established a number of agencies, such as the State Directorates of Industries, the State Small Industries Corporations, State Financial Corporations, and State Directorates of Economics and Industrial Statistics to assist them. At the centre, the Union government formed the Central Small Industries Organization to produce policies and programmes for the improvement of small industries, and the All-India Khadi and Village Industries Board (later Commission) and other agencies to offer assistance to the village and cottage industries. There also existed the Small Scale Industries Board, the National Small Industries Corporation, the Small Industries Service Institutes and an Industrial Extension Service.[21]

[19] *Organiser*, 15 August 1961, p. 9.
[20] See Government of India, Planning Commission, *The First Five Year Plan* (New Delhi, 1953), pp. 315–33; *Second Five Year Plan*, pp. 429–58; *Third Five Year Plan* (New Delhi, 1961), pp. 426–51; *Fourth Five Year Plan: A Draft Outline*, pp. 238–48. For a detailed survey of the Plans' proposals in this field, see A.H. Hanson, *The Process of Planning: A Study of India's Five Year Plans 1950–1964* (London, 1966), pp. 496–514. See also Government of India, Planning Commission, *Report of the Village and Small Scale Industries (Second Five Year Plan) Committee* (Delhi, 1955).
[21] On the services provided by central and state agencies see Ministry of Industry, *Development of Small Scale Industries in India*, pp. 62–83, and P.N. Dhar and H.F. Lydall, *The Role of Small Enterprises in Indian Economic Development* (Bombay, 1961), pp. 63–83.

Together these agencies provided small industry with a great deal of assistance in obtaining raw materials, in marketing, in finance and in the purchase of machinery. A scheme of industrial estates was begun during the Second Plan period so that where possible small industries could be grouped together to simplify the task of providing them with electricity, roads, stores and other facilities.[22] One journal noted in 1962 that the small-scale industries sector

> has always been a preferred – one is almost tempted to say pampered – sector, mainly because of the emotional appeal that 'smallness' appears to have to a State attached to welfare ideals. It has been frequently said that small industries have a 'special role' or a 'strategic position' in the nation's economy. Their significance, it is pointed out, rests on the fact that they are important ancillaries to large industries and on the theoretical assumptions that their capital requirements are low and employment potential high and that their growth leads to a desirable dispersal of industrial establishments. These assumptions are really of questionable validity but the conviction that small industries should receive all possible aid remains firm.[23]

This conviction showed no signs of weakening in the mid-1960s. For example, when the Lokanathan Committee on scarce raw materials proposed in 1965 that these should be allocated according to the priorities assigned to the goods industries were producing, regardless of whether the industries were small, medium or large in scale, the government accepted most of its recommendations,[24] an important concession as far as small-scale industries were concerned. A further sign of official approval was that the draft Fourth Plan proposed a total outlay of Rs 370 crores on village and small industries (compared with an estimated expenditure of Rs 219.56 crores for the Third Plan period), and that this sum included specific allocations to small-scale industries and to industrial estates of Rs 120 crores and Rs 25 crores respectively, compared with estimated Third Plan expenditures of Rs 62.67 crores and Rs 23.35 crores respectively.[25]

The fine network of specialized governmental agencies established around small industries served to draw them into a corporate relationship with the state and reduced the chances of their being attracted to party politics as a means of influencing public policies. Instead of dealing

---

[22] Dhar and Lydall, *Small Enterprises in Indian Economic Development*, pp. 35–62.

[23] From 'How large is "small"?', in 'Weekly notes', *The Economic Weekly* (Bombay), XIV, 24 (16 June 1962), p. 938.

[24] Government of India, Ministry of Industry and Supply, *Report of the Committee on Scarce Raw Materials, May 1965* (Delhi, 1966); *Statesman* (Delhi), 29 July 1965, p. 7; Planning Commission, *Fourth Five Year Plan: A Draft Outline*, p. 243.

[25] Planning Commission, *Fourth Five Year Plan: A Draft Outline*, p. 242 (table).

with broad issues of principle, the interest groups in the small-industries field tended to keep to specific issues which could be taken up in direct negotiations either with government departments or with public agencies, and to avoid making demands which could not form the subject of negotiation. Many of the small-scale industries may not have belonged to any organizations at all, but press reports indicate that there were a number of associations, such as the Small-Scale Woollen Factories' Association and the Federation of Industry and Commerce in the Punjab and the Sugar Mills' Association and the Oil Millers' Association in Uttar Pradesh, which claimed to represent them at the state level. These lay at the base of organizational hierarchies capped by the Federation of Indian Chambers of Commerce and Industry, the All-India Manufacturers' Organisation and the All-India Organisation of Industrial Employers. Such bodies, and their equivalents at the state level, relied more upon representation on consultative bodies and informal communications with specialist committees and government officials in their efforts to influence public policy than upon lobbying and open campaigning.[26] Small industries could raise general matters through such associations, but they had special difficulties related to size and eventually established their own national organization, the Federation of Associations of Small Industries of India (FASII), which began its series of annual meetings in December 1961, and concentrated on such matters as shortages of raw materials, inadequate allocations of foreign exchange, and difficulties with government departments.[27] Thus, while the Jana Sangh's advocacy of the cause of small industries undoubtedly earned it the goodwill and support of individual firms, in general neither small businessmen nor their interest groups were tied closely to the party.

The Jana Sangh was also interested in the possibility of establishing a base in the country and market towns among the wholesale and retail traders who bought produce from cultivators and supplied them and the urban population with consumer goods. Traders were better organized than small industrialists and occupied a secure position within the economic structure, but they were threatened by the government's willingness to increase indirect taxation at their expense and by the growing demand that the foodgrains market should be brought under control. They were prepared to face both challenges through their own

[26] For a general survey, see the chapter on 'Organized business' in Myron Weiner, *The Politics of Scarcity: Public Pressure and Political Response in India* (Chicago, 1962), pp. 97–129.

[27] For reports of annual meetings of the FASII see *Hindustan Times*, 16 December 1961, p. 3; *Statesman* (Delhi), 17 December 1963, p. 5.

town-based and regional associations, which were well established and resilient, but they had an obvious interest in searching out allies amongst the non-Congress parties.

In the early 1950s a further series of increases in indirect taxation was the most immediate source of anxiety to traders. State governments relied on several sources of taxation income, including land revenue, but they soon found that the most elastic of these was the general tax on the sale of commodities, levied either at a single point of sale or at several points in a chain of distribution, at percentage rates which varied between different classes of goods. Sales taxes were first introduced in Madras Province in 1939–40 and were instituted in most other provinces during the 1940s,[28] but after independence they were increased rapidly and in the tax-year 1959–60 they provided 30.53 per cent of the total tax revenue in all states.[29] In its early years the Jana Sangh was prepared to attack this system without quarter and its first national session in Kanpur in December 1952 adopted a resolution criticizing the taxation policy of the state governments:

Among the new taxes, the sales-tax that has been imposed in many states on necessities of life and at multiple points is extremely reactionary. As a result, agitations against it have been launched at many places. The Jana Sangh supports these agitations and condemns the way in which they have been suppressed.[30]

The third national session at Jodhpur in January 1955 proposed that the system should be modified in several respects; the Central Working Committee subsequently declared its sympathy for the Rajasthan anti-sales tax agitation of April 1955; and in April 1956 the party's fourth national session at Jaipur proposed that the tax should be abolished altogether.[31] Its 1957 election manifesto promised 'revolutionary reforms in the system of taxation': pledging that the party would try to abolish sales tax altogether, it said that it would first remove the tax from 'the necessaries of life' and from the products of cottage and small-scale industries; it also proposed uniform rates between states, reduction of

[28] The Times of India, *The Indian and Pakistan Year Book and Who's Who, 1951* (Bombay, 1951), p. 193.
[29] National Council of Applied Economic Research, *Techno-Economic Survey of Uttar Pradesh*, pp. 324–6 (Table 105).
[30] First National Session, Kanpur, 31 December 1952, *BJS Documents*, II, p. 122.
[31] Resolutions of Third National Session, Jodhpur, 2 January 1955; Central Working Committee, Gokak, 15 April 1955; and Fourth National Session, Jaipur, 21 April 1956, *ibid.*, pp. 122–4. On sales-tax policy in Rajasthan and on the hartal there see 'Rajasthan Newsletter', *Statesman* (Delhi), 22 September 1954, p. 4; 14 April 1955, p. 7.

the system to a single-point tax, collection at the production stage, and the abolition of inter-state sales taxes.[32]

However, in the 1960s the party's pronouncements on sales taxation were considerably toned down. Its 1962 manifesto simply stated that the necessities of life 'shall be exempt from indirect taxes'[33] and the 1967 manifesto, while calling for a taxation inquiry commission, restricted itself to supporting the abolition of sales taxes and other taxes on food articles.[34] This change of emphasis must have been forced on it by expediency: as a party with a reasonable prospect of taking power as a coalition partner in one or two states, it was obliged to discuss issues of general finance in responsible and realistic terms. By the 1960s it would have been quite impossible for an aspiring party of government to propose the ending of sales taxation without at the same time recommending an increase in either land revenue or state excise rates or both and arousing considerable opposition in the process. Thus constrained, all that the Jana Sangh could offer the traders was the promise of some reform of sales-tax procedures and the abolition of indirect taxes on food and other essential items.

For somewhat different reasons, the Jana Sangh did not form a direct and functional relationship with organized interests in the field of small industry and country trading. The small industrialists' associations, such as the FASII, had no need of a party to mediate between them and the state because they had no difficulty in attaching themselves to the framework of public agencies in the small industries field. As for the traders, they were usually well represented by hardy and resilient associations, often called Beopar (or Vyapar, meaning 'trade' or 'business') Mandals, which were capable of exerting considerable pressure on state ministries and departments without assistance from any political party. What links there were between the party and these two groups were based on their shared outlook; however, the party was not expected to represent their specific material interests beyond certain clearly understood limits.

The Jana Sangh as a party of the working classes

The Jana Sangh also claimed to speak for two important components of Indian urban society, white-collar workers and industrial employees,

[32] Bharatiya Jana Sangh, *Election Manifesto 1957*, p. 14. The same promises were made in the 1958 manifesto (see *BJS Documents*, I, pp. 111–12).

[33] Bharatiya Jana Sangh, *Election Manifesto 1962*, p. 21.

[34] Bharatiya Jana Sangh, *Election Manifesto 1967*, pp. 18 and 25–6.

but only in terms which were compatible with its essentially corporatist view of social organization. In one sense, the party kept faith with its clientèle in small business by refusing to use the rhetoric of class conflict in its appeals to employees. It began as and remained a party of class conciliation and co-operation.

At first glance, the Jana Sangh's manifestos and policy statements give the impression that the party was prepared to accept industrial relations based on contract. It readily acknowledged the rights of workers to form trade unions, to strike and to use collective bargaining, it supported the establishment of a permanent wage board and a specified national minimum wage, acknowledged the right of labour to share 'in the management and profits of industry', and recommended the use of conciliation and arbitration in the settlement of industrial disputes.[35] At the same time, however, it warned that workers should avoid serving the purposes of the Communists by taking part in strikes or joining trade unions which were against the national interest. A resolution on industrial relations adopted by the party's Central Working Committee in December 1958 put the matter as follows:

Our workers will do well to remember that their interests are perfectly identified with those of the entire nation and that any effort on their part to over-emphasise their sectional interests at the cost of the nation will only result in their isolation from the rest of the people. The interests of the workers as well as of the nation can be best served only if the former are freed completely from the evil influence of the anti-national elements and organised properly into a national federation of all the patriotic trade unions.[36]

The party's first move to establish a trade union which was both professional and patriotic was made in January 1955, when its third national session proposed the formation of a 'national labour organisation' which would 'rise above the argument of class-struggle, think from the point of view of national integrity and keep aloof from the un-Indian tendencies of Capitalism and Communism'.[37] In the following July a conference sponsored by the party's labour department decided to form a trade union association known as the Bharatiya Mazdoor Sangh (BMS), and an *ad hoc* committee was established for that purpose.[38] In

---

[35] See 1954 Manifesto, *BJS Documents* I, pp. 63–5; 1958 Manifesto, *ibid.*, pp. 107–11; *Election Manifesto 1957*, pp. 10–13; *Election Manifesto 1962*, pp. 22–3; *Principles and Policy*, pp. 40–1; *Election Manifesto 1967*, pp. 26–7.

[36] See the text given in S.L. Poplai (ed.), *1962 General Elections in India* (New Delhi, 1962), pp. 342–4, quotation from pp. 343–4.

[37] Third National Session, Jodhpur, 1 January 1955, *BJS Documents*, II, pp. 105–6.

[38] *Organiser*, 1 August 1955, p. 13.

August 1959 the General Council of this organization finally adopted a formal constitution.[39]

At this time trade union affairs were dominated by four large national federations, the Communist-controlled All-India Trade Union Congress (AITUC), the Indian National Trade Union Congress (INTUC), the Socialists' Hind Mazdoor Sabha, and the United Trades Union Congress.[40] However, although AITUC and INTUC in particular had drawn a number of individual unions into their fold, there were also many unions which were not affiliated with any one of the four established federations and, in any case, the proportion of industrial workers belonging to trade unions was still relatively low.[41] It was possible for a new federation such as the BMS to build up its strength without having to attract members and unions away from the rival organizations.

The first General Secretary of the BMS, D.B. Thengadi, had served as an RSS organizer in the 1940s, had been organizing secretary for INTUC in Madhya Pradesh (1950–51) and had then worked for the Jana Sangh unit in the same state (1952–54).[42] He rejected class conflict and placed a high value on organizational strength, national loyalty and the solidarity of the community. Writing in 1955, he maintained that

Like a family, the community had its life based upon mutual love and confidence, and consequently, its horizontal division could not even be dreamt of. It was further realised that the various communities are but different limbs of the same organism, i.e. the Bharatiya Nation. The Bharatiya social order thus implied the industry-wise arrangement, and not 'class'-wise division of the Society.[43]

As was clear from the context, Thengadi was using the term 'horizontal division' as a synonym for 'class division'. He contrasted his own position with that of other leaders:

They feel that they can subscribe to the theory of class-conflict and still continue as nationalists. They fail to perceive the incompatibility between class-conflict

---

[39] *Ibid.*, 10 August 1959, p. 3. For a detailed account of the development of the BMS, see Walter K. Andersen and Shridhar D. Damle, *The Brotherhood in Saffron: The Rashtriya Swayamsevak Sangh and Hindu Revivalism* (Boulder and London, 1987), pp. 129–33.

[40] See V.B. Karnik, *Indian Trade Unions: A Survey* (Bombay, 1966, second edition), pp. 141–72; Myron Weiner, *Party Politics in India: The Development of a Multi-Party System* (Princeton, N.J., 1957), pp. 152–4.

[41] See Planning Commission, *Fourth Five Year Plan: A Draft Outline*, p. 390.

[42] Government of India, Rajya Sabha Secretariat, *Parliament of India: Rajya Sabha: Who's Who 1970* (New Delhi, 1970), p. 316.

[43] 'The philosophy of Bharatiya Mazdoor Sangh', *Organiser*, 24 October 1955, pp. 6 and 12. See also his 'Philosophical background of the Bharatiya Mazdoor Sangh', *ibid.*, 12 December 1955, pp. 6 and 12; 16 January 1956, pp. 7 and 8.

and nationalism. Class-conflict partitions the nation horizontally. No patriot can tolerate such partitions – vertical or horizontal.[44]

In practice, the units of the BMS pressed claims within the law, drawing attention to firms which failed to implement wage awards,[45] assisting groups of workers in industrial litigation[46] and, in some cases, supporting strikes and agitations for improved rates of pay and working conditions.[47] However, in keeping with Thengadi's approach, the organization tried to avoid becoming involved in general demonstrations, especially those sponsored by the Communists or by AITUC; in 1966, for example, its Uttar Pradesh unit made a virtue of not participating in the UP *bandh* of 12 July.[48] Its recruitment policy was moderately successful; by August 1967, when its first national conference was held in New Delhi, it claimed to represent 495 trade unions with a total membership of 246,000, and to have built up nine state units and four national industrial federations–in sugar manufacturing, engineering, textiles and railways.[49]

The Jana Sangh's chief aim in the industrial relations field was to gain the allegiance of white-collar workers. In the private sector, the most important group was that of the bank employees, whose principal associations were the All-India Bank Employees' Federation (AIBEF), connected with INTUC, and the All-India Bank Employees' Association

---

[44] 'Beware of this, our enemy number two', *ibid.*, 15 August 1962, p. 15.

[45] For example, the General Council of the Uttar Pradesh unit of the BMS in May 1962 requested the state government to deal with the non-implementation of the Textile Wage Board Award by firms in some towns (*ibid.*, 21 May 1962, p. 7).

[46] The Kanpur unit of the BMS co-operated with an Industrial Employees Union in petitioning the Allahabad High Court on behalf of a group of unskilled workers whose claim for the payment of annual increments had not been granted by an Adjudicator. On 3 April 1962 the judge allowed the petition and decided to quash the Adjudicator's award, but he noted that the state government could refer the dispute back to the Adjudicator (*Statesman* (Delhi), 5 April 1962, p. 14).

[47] The 1962 report of the General Secretary of the Delhi State unit of the BMS recorded successful agitations in the Delhi Cloth Mills, in the Birla mills, and in D.C.M. cloth shops (*Organiser*, 23 July 1962, pp. 12 and 14).

At the end of 1963 the Punjab unit of the BMS supported a Karamchari Union in a dispute with the Shree Gopal Paper Mills at Yamunanagar. A Jana Sangh MP (Hukum Chand Kachhawaiya) went on a hunger strike at the mill gates in support of the union's demands and was arrested on 2 January 1964 (*Hindustan Times*, 2 January 1964, p. 5; *Statesman* (Delhi), 4 January 1964, p. 7). Another Jana Sangh MP, Swami Rameshwaranand, then undertook a *dharna* outside the Prime Minister's residence (*Hindustan Times*, 12 January 1964, p. 8). On the sequel see *Statesman* (Delhi), 14 January 1964, p. 7; 25 January 1964, p. 7; 5 February 1964, p. 12; *Times of India* (Delhi), 12 February 1964, p. 5; *Organiser*, 10 February 1964, p. 16.

[48] See report of resolution of the state executive committee, *National Herald* (Lucknow), 17 June 1966, p. 3.

[49] *Organiser*, 27 August 1967, p. 7.

(AIBEA), which was allegedly pro-Communist.[50] As a 'third force' between them, the Jana Sangh in 1964 established the National Organisation of Bank Workers (NOBW),[51] which scored an immediate success by winning over the All-India Punjab National Bank Employees' Association, previously affiliated to the AIBEF.[52] In the negotiations with the banks, which led to a wage agreement in 1966, only the AIBEF and the AIBEA represented the employees but the central government subsequently gave places to the NOBW on a tripartite industrial committee on the banking industry, to the annoyance of the AIBEA.[53]

The Jana Sangh and other political parties found difficulty in organizing support amongst government employees because of various conduct rules which governed the latter's conditions of service. For example, the Central Civil Service (Conduct) Rules of 1955 provided that no government servant

shall be a member of, or be otherwise associated with, any political party or any organisation which takes part in politics nor shall he take part in, subscribe in aid of, or assist in any other manner, any political movement or activity.

Other rules provided that no government servant should 'canvass or otherwise interfere or use his influence in connection with, or take part in, an election to any Legislature or local authority'; participate in any demonstration or strike regarding his condition of service; or join any service association of government servants which was not recognized by the government.[54] The Railway Services (Conduct) Rules of 1956 also contained a rule against railway servants joining a political party or taking part in a political movement or activity, and a prohibition on their joining any union or association unless its rules conformed strictly to those for the recognition of a service association of railway servants.[55] The Government Servants' Conduct Rules prevented trade unions of government employees from affiliating with any general federation, a category which included unions of private employees.[56] Exceptions were made for certain categories of government employees in industry, such

---

[50] On the background to the AIBEA, see Karnik, *Indian Trade Unions*, pp. 234–6.
[51] The NOBW was founded at a Kanpur convention of 25–26 April 1964. For Thengadi's inaugural address, see *Organiser*, 18 May 1964, p. 7.
[52] *Ibid.*, 5 October 1964, p. 8.
[53] *Statesman* (Delhi), 16 February 1968, p. 5.
[54] Rules 4(1), 4(4), 4-A and 4-B of the Central Civil Services (Conduct) Rules, 1955, in Durga Das Basu, *Commentary on the Constitution of India* (fifth edition), VII (Calcutta, 1967), pp. 932–6.
[55] Rules 4(1) and 19 of the Railway Services (Conduct) Rules, 1956, in *ibid.*, pp. 764–71.
[56] Karnik, *Indian Trade Unions*, pp. 225–6.

as railway servants and civilian employees of the Defence Department, but otherwise organizations such as the National Federation of Posts and Telegraphs Employees and the Confederation of Central Government Employees were independent of INTUC, AITUC and the other national federations.

Although it was not the only party to support the demands of government employees, the Jana Sangh was always prepared to argue their case in detail. Its first concern was to defend their right to form associations and to have their demands considered within an adequate machinery of negotiation and arbitration. It therefore became involved in the aftermath of a serious strike of central government employees in July 1960, as a result of which the government withdrew recognition from several of their unions and government departments began legal proceedings against some of their employees.[57] In the following month the Jana Sangh's Central General Council called not only for the reinstatement of the dismissed employees and for the restoration of recognition to those unions which had been penalized, but also pressed for the government 'to evolve and work out an effective mechanism for the redressal of grievances, which would make the right to strike a mere superfluity'.[58] Recognition was restored to most unions in September 1961 and in November the Jana Sangh's Central General Council demanded that it should be extended to the remainder and again pleaded for the reinstatement of all strikers to their former posts.[59] The central government had considered the possibility of banning strikes of this kind by law but eventually, in October 1963, it announced a non-statutory scheme of joint consultation and compulsory arbitration on the understanding that the scheme would apply only to those associations of government employees which abjured resort to strike action.[60]

The Jana Sangh's second concern was to endorse the demands of government employees for an alteration in the terms of their salary payments. The party's 1962 and 1967 election manifestos declared in favour of uniform pay-scales for central, provincial and local government employees and proposed improvements in the methods of awarding increments to take account of price increases (the system of dearness allowances). The 1962 manifesto recommended linking the

---

[57] *Ibid.*, pp. 255–67 and 271–2.

[58] Central General Council, Hyderabad, 28 August 1960, *BJS Documents*, IV, pp. 148–9. See also Ninth National Session, Lucknow, 1 January 1961, *ibid.*, pp. 149–50.

[59] Central General Council, Varanasi, 12 November 1961, *ibid.*, pp. 151–2. See also *Link: Indian Newsmagazine* (New Delhi), 24 September 1961, p. 12; and a statement by the Home Minister (Lal Bahadur Shastri) in *P.D.*, *L.S.* (Second Series), LVIII, 8 September 1961, cc. 8085–6.

[60] *The Indian Recorder and Digest* (New Delhi), November 1963, pp. 19–21.

dearness allowance to an index of prices and the 1967 manifesto stated that the party recognized 'the principles of cent percent neutralisation of dearness', that is, the method under which increments would compensate in full for the depreciation of salaries under inflation. This contrasted with the provision made in 1964 for compensation graded according to salary level, with the lowest paid receiving the highest proportion of compensation at a rate of 90 per cent.[61]

Thirdly, the party was concerned to deal with charges of inefficiency and corruption in government departments. It suggested that the chief fault lay not with the lower ranks but with senior officials, and with the hierarchical nature of the profession. The 1962 manifesto took up the latter point and said that

The Jana Sangh will remove the present feeling of inequality in the services, which creates a sense of inferiority in the lower grades and that of vanity in the officers. It will try to inculcate into them spirit of service to the people and a feeling of partnership in the great task of reconstruction of the country.[62]

The 1967 manifesto was more direct, stating that

Corruption, like water, flows from the higher to lower level. Besides, conditions of shortage and bureaucratic control breed corruption. It is, therefore, necessary that the top be reformed, shortage removed, delays eliminated and controls relaxed.

It went on to recommend the appointment of a commission 'to enquire into cases of corruption even at the highest level'.[63]

In general, the Jana Sangh cast its appeals to urban working-class groups within the framework of a corporate ideal of the state, rather than within that of a pluralist or a class-based ideal. It represented politics as a process whereby social groups constitute themselves as corporate entities and enter into co-operative and mutually supportive relations with each other. This approach was at least consistent with its general social philosophy and was presumably acceptable to the party's backers in industry and commerce; it also had some appeal for civil servants, whose employer was the state and who saw in the Jana Sangh an opposition party prepared to press their claims for a less restrictive right of association and for better material rewards. However, such an approach limited the party's ability to appeal to industrial workers who

---

[61] Bharatiya Jana Sangh, *Election Manifesto 1962*, p. 8; *Election Manifesto 1967*, p. 8. On the dearness allowance increments given to central employees in 1964, see Karnik, *Indian Trade Unions*, pp. 286–8.
[62] Bharatiya Jana Sangh, *Election Manifesto 1962*, p. 7.
[63] Bharatiya Jana Sangh, *Election Manifesto 1967*, p. 8.

were looking for a rapid and substantial improvement in their income and living conditions, even if this entailed open conflict with their employers and managers. On balance, then, the Jana Sangh was not in a good position to build up a substantial following as a workers' party.

The Jana Sangh and refugee interests

Another group in whose welfare the Jana Sangh claimed to have a special interest was that of the refugees who had emigrated from the areas which had become Pakistan to the towns and cities of northern India. There had been in fact two migrations, that of the 4.7 million people who came in 1947–48 to north-western India from the west and that of the 4.1 million who emigrated in waves from eastern Bengal between 1946, the year of the Noakhali riots, and 1956, when the inflow was reduced by a system of immigration certificates. Provision for the refugees was the responsibility of the Union Ministry of Rehabilitation. In dealing with the western migration, it had the advantage of the fact that Muslim families who had gone to Pakistan at the time of partition had left behind them a considerable amount of property, consisting, in the eastern Punjab and Rajasthan alone, of six million acres of agricultural land, 300,000 houses and shops in urban areas, and 700,000 houses in rural areas. Within the general framework of a compensation scheme worked out between India and Pakistan, the property left behind by refugees could be taken into account in arranging compensation for them in their new places of residence. In the north-western states about 570,000 families were settled on land left behind by Muslim refugees and there were about 300,000 vacant houses and shops in urban areas to assist in the rehabilitation of urban refugees. Additional compensation was provided by the central and state governments in the form of special housing schemes, loans and grants. The eastern migration presented different problems. In the first place, the refugees consisted chiefly of poor Hindu peasant families and, in the second, the government had very little evacuee property in West Bengal, Assam and other eastern territories to provide a firm economic base for compensation policies. Of the estimated 4.1 million immigrants from East Pakistan, about three million stayed in West Bengal, 487,000 went to Assam and 374,000 went to Tripura. The government helped another 122,000 to settle in other states and in 1958 formed the Dandakaranya Development Authority to establish refugee settlements in the Bastar district of Madhya Pradesh and the adjoining districts of Orissa.[64]

[64] The above paragraph is based upon an article by a special representative in New Delhi, dated 28 January 1962, in *Statesman* (Calcutta), 29 January 1962, pp. 8–9.

The Jana Sangh's general policy that India should take a hard line in dealing with Pakistan gained it some sympathy in refugee circles but the government's schemes for rehabilitating and compensating refugees were so comprehensive that the party had little opportunity for acting as a benevolent mediator between refugees and the state. All that it could do was to draw attention to alleged deficiencies in procedures and policies by demanding, for example, better terms of compensation for those with property left behind in Pakistan, more generosity in the allotment and sale of houses to refugees, and more assistance to refugees who were taking up new occupations. It also opposed restrictions on the entry of further immigrants from East Pakistan and criticized the implementation of the Dandakaranya scheme.[65] It is difficult to estimate the extent to which refugees identified themselves with the Jana Sangh as a result of such advocacy. In general, their support for the party was strongest amongst the western immigrants who settled in the towns and cities of north-western India and were drawn towards occupations in small industry, trading and government service. In Delhi, for example, the Jana Sangh was exceptionally popular in such areas as Karol Bagh and Patel Nagar, where large numbers of Hindu and Sikh refugees from the Punjab had established themselves in colonies.[66]

The Jana Sangh and the politics of land

In the years immediately following independence the central issues in rural politics were not those concerning marketing or credit or production but rather those relating to the tenure and use of land, and it was the Congress Party's land policies which set the standard against which agrarian radicalism and agrarian conservatism were measured. The Congress argued that landlordism should be abolished, that individual peasant proprietorship was the ideal form of land tenure, that land-users should pay land tax (or revenue) direct to the government rather than through intermediaries, and that village panchayats should be fostered in the interests of local democracy. To these ends

---

[65] See especially the resolution on the 'Rehabilitation of displaced persons', Sixth National Session, Ambala, 5 April 1958, *BJS Documents*, V, pp. 94–6. See also First National Session, Kanpur, 31 December 1952, *ibid.*, pp. 88–9; Second National Session, Bombay, 25 January 1954, *ibid.*, pp. 90–2; Third National Session, Jodhpur, 1 January 1955, *ibid.*, pp. 92–4; Central Working Committee, Hyderabad, 24 November 1957, *ibid.*, III, pp. 51–2; and also Bharatiya Jana Sangh, *Manifesto* [1951], p. 10; *Election Manifesto 1957*, pp. 18–19; *Election Manifesto 1962*, p. 9; *Election Manifesto 1967*, p. 13.

[66] For an analysis of the Delhi State Jana Sangh's concern for refugee interests in the capital, see Geeta Puri, *Bharatiya Jana Sangh, Organisation and Ideology, Delhi: a Case Study* (New Delhi, 1980), pp. 62–4.

it proposed that tenants should be given the right to acquire permanent land rights, provided that landlords were duly compensated and allowed to retain some land for personal cultivation, that ceilings should be imposed on the size of landholdings and the surplus redistributed, that scattered holdings should be consolidated into single units, and that co-operative farming should be encouraged for the benefit of poor cultivators. However, the problem of translating these policies into a concrete programme was a formidable one, given that land systems varied so much from region to region and that, under the Constitution of India, land and agriculture, along with taxes on land and agricultural income, had been placed under the legislative competence of the state governments. The task of implementation was therefore effectively delegated to Congress governments at the state level, and these varied considerably in their willingness to proceed with reforms.

The Jana Sangh was formed just at the time when some of these Congress ministries, most notably those in Uttar Pradesh and Bihar, were trying to carry the first wave of legislation into effect and when the landlords were still trying to protect their rights in the courts. In its first election manifesto of 1951, the new party endorsed the principle of individual proprietorship and set out a land policy which came very close to that favoured by moderate Congressmen. The relevant passage stated that

In the interest of increase in production and the betterment of the lot of the actual cultivator the party would take all steps to introduce land reforms so as to make the cultivator 'Kshetrapala', i.e., virtual owner of land. In the interest of the economy of the country the party would abolish Jagirdari and Zamindari as with compensation and distribute the land to tillers. Enough land, however, would be left with such Zamindars and Jagirdars as would settle down as cultivating farmers.[67]

This stand reflected the peculiar rural romanticism of the party's early workers and supporters, who looked on the villages and the country areas generally as places which had kept alive social and religious traditions which had been smothered in the cities and towns of northern India during centuries of Mughal and later British rule. They idealized the simple peasant and, while extending some sympathy to resident Hindu landlords, were generally hostile to the class of absentee landlords, whether Hindu or Muslim, who lived in the towns and sustained an Indo-Persian culture.

The Jana Sangh's position on land reform was first tested in Rajasthan, where the Congress government, having set out to abolish

[67] Bharatiya Jana Sangh, *Manifesto* [1951], p. 5.

jagirdari and zamindari tenures in the state, then made efforts to win over the landlords. As far as the jagirdari system was concerned, the Rajasthan Land Reforms and Resumption of Jagirs Act of 1952 had provided for the abolition of jagirs producing annual incomes of Rs. 5,000 or above, with compensation. The main group affected by this measure were the Rajput jagirdars, whose caste association, the Kshatriya Mahasabha, was the principal supporter of the non-Congress bloc, the Samyukta Dal, in the Rajasthan Legislative Assembly. However, in 1953 the Kshatriya Mahasabha held talks with the state government about the Land Reforms Act and the outstanding issues were then discussed with G.B. Pant, the Chief Minister of Uttar Pradesh. His findings were set down in the Pant Award of 1953, which recommended that jagirs below the Rs 5,000 mark in annual income should not be abolished, that tenants should not be evicted to provide *khudkasht* (home farm) for jagirdars, and that the terms of compensation should be improved.[68] Although acceptance of this settlement entailed something of a retreat for the Kshatriya Mahasabha and the jagirdars, the Pant Award was a clear indication that the Congress was prepared to come to terms with a social class which had hitherto been its most powerful opponent in state politics.

Such a development placed the Jana Sangh in a difficult position in Rajasthan. In the 1952 general elections for the state assembly its candidates had been amongst those whom the Kshatriya Mahasabha had endorsed, and seven of the eight Jana Sangh MLAs returned to the new house were jagirdars from constituencies in the southern region of Mewar while the eighth, Bhairon Singh, came from the northern area of Shekhawati. They were surprised to learn that their party's national manifesto had advocated jagirdari abolition[69] and must presumably have been ill prepared for the controversy which built up around the land question in the years which followed. The Jana Sangh made clear its lack of sympathy with the jagirdars shortly after the announcement of the Pant Award: Mauli Chandra Sharma, who was

---

[68] See Lloyd I. and Susanne Hoeber Rudolph, 'The political modernization of an Indian feudal order. An analysis of Rajput adaptation in Rajasthan', *Journal of Social Issues*, XXIV, 4 (1968), pp. 109–13, and also [Government of Rajasthan, Revenue Department], *Report on Rajasthan Jagirdari Abolition, by Pandit Govind Ballabh Pant, Chief Minister, Uttar Pradesh* (Jaipur, 1953). On the politics of Rajasthan in this period see: Lawrence L. Shrader, 'Rajasthan', in Myron Weiner (ed), *State Politics in India* (Princeton, N.J., 1968) pp. 319–96; Richard Sisson, *The Congress Party in Rajasthan: Political Integration and Institution-Building in an Indian State* (Berkeley, 1972); K.L. Kamal, *Spot Light on Rajasthan Politics (Traditional Challenge in an Indian State)* (Alwar-Jaipur, 1967); Kamal, 'Rajasthan: politics of declining feudal order', in Iqbal Narain (ed.), *State Politics in India* (Meerut, 1976), pp. 299–322.

[69] From interview with L.K. Advani, New Delhi, 15 May 1984.

then the Jana Sangh's national President, claimed at a press conference in Jaipur that the Congress government in the state had made a pact with a section of the jagirdars to dilute and delay jagirdari abolition,[70] and, on 20 September 1953, the working committee of the party's state unit directed its eight MLAs to break with the Samyukta Dal. It claimed that the Dal had been concentrating on preserving the interests of a particular class and community, presumably those of the Rajput jagirdars, and also criticized some Dal members for having tried to obtain enhanced compensation for resumed land.[71] Bhairon Singh and another MLA did in fact leave the Dal but the remaining six refused to do so and were expelled from the party.[72]

The irony of this stand on principle was that the Jana Sangh, having thus destroyed its links with the Rajput jagirdars, was left without any alternative base of support in the rural society of Rajasthan. It had little hope of winning over the substantial peasant community of Jats, for they remained firmly attached to the Congress Party, which offered them avenues for advancement and for influence on policy which were quite beyond the means of the Jana Sangh. Nor was the party able to forge an alliance with the group of petty Rajput landowners known as *bhumias*, who had also fallen out with the Kshatriya Mahasabha. In 1954 this group formed its own association, the Bhooswami Sangh, to further its demands for better terms of compensation and rehabilitation for small jagirdars.[73] Although the Jana Sangh's main spokesman, Bhairon Singh, was himself a *bhumia* and strongly defended the *bhumias'* cause in public,[74] the Bhooswami Sangh remained a self-sufficient organization, confident of its ability to press home agitational campaigns (like those which it waged in 1955 and 1956) and to bargain

---

[70] *Statesman* (Delhi), 14 September 1953, p. 4.

[71] *Ibid.*, 21 September 1953, p. 8. On the Rajasthan unit's opposition to compensation, see Bharatiya Jana Sangh, *Presidential Address: Shri L.K. Advani* (18th All India Session, Deendayal Nagar, Kanpur, February 9, 10 & 11, 1973), p. 27.

[72] See Kamal, *Spot Light on Rajasthan Politics*, pp. 68–9; and Kamal, *Party Politics in an Indian State (A Study of the Main Political Parties in Rajasthan)* (New Delhi, n.d.), p. 160.

[73] Rudolph, 'Political modernization of an Indian feudal order', pp. 113–20. On the general position of the *bhumias*, see *ibid.*, esp. pp. 106–7; 'Rajasthan Newsletter', *Statesman* (Delhi), 21 November 1952, p. 5; Government of Rajasthan, Revenue Department, *Report of the Rajasthan Khudkasht Enquiry Committee* (no publication details), pp. 5–6.

[74] At an annual conference of the Jana Sangh's state unit he asked the state government to appreciate the difficulties of the Bhooswamis and to deal with them sympathetically (*Statesman* (Delhi), 15 January 1956, p. 4). In April 1956 he moved a non-official resolution in the Legislative Assembly recommending that the government should call an all-party conference to consider the problem of rehabilitating the *bhumias*, but this was rejected (*ibid.*, 20 April 1956, p. 5).

directly with the authorities. Its main connection to party politics was through the Jana Sangh's rival, the Rama Rajya Parishad, and in the 1957 general elections the Bhooswamis' president, Thakur Madan Singh of Danta, was returned to the assembly as a candidate of the Parishad, as were two other leading Bhooswami figures, Thakur Keshri Singh of Pataudi and Tan Singh.

As the implementation of the land reforms proceeded in the late 1950s, the Bhooswami Sangh continued to negotiate with the state and central governments and in 1958 its representatives submitted a memorandum to Nehru, who was also asked by the Chief Minister of Rajasthan to arbitrate in certain matters regarding compensation.[75] The Prime Minister subsequently announced a further award in January 1959, after which the Rajasthan Land Reforms Act was again amended to provide for increased compensation and rehabilitation rates for small jagirdars.[76] All that the Jana Sangh could do by this stage was to be a spectator at what had virtually become a process of interest-group bargaining; its opportunity to establish a special relationship with the *bhumias* had passed.

The land politics of Uttar Pradesh proved equally unfruitful as far as the Jana Sangh was concerned. In that state the Congress government had gone steadily ahead with legislation to undermine the power of the former landlords and its Zamindari Abolition and Land Reforms Act 1950 had laid the basis for a system of peasant proprietors paying land revenue direct to the state rather than through intermediaries. However, this statute had not done away with the principle of hierarchy and had created a set of tenures differentiated from each other by ownership and tax rights. As a result, the various non-Congress parties were soon engaged in attempts to persuade the least privileged categories of tenure-holders to join with them in opposing the Congress.

The main distinction made in the UP Zamindari Abolition Act was that between *bhumidhars* and *sirdars*; whereas a *bhumidhar* was entitled to transfer his interest and to use his land for non-agricultural purposes, a *sirdar* was denied these rights; a *sirdar* paid as land revenue an amount equal to that which he had formerly paid as rent to a landlord, but a *bhumidhar* paid at a much lower rate; and, to obtain *bhumidhari* rights, a *sirdar* had to pay a lump sum equal to ten times his previous rental payment (this was subsequently changed to ten times his annual land

---

[75] See oral answers to questions, *P.D., L.S.* (Second Series), XVIII, 19 August 1958, cc. 1553–6.
[76] *Hindustan Times*, 17 January 1959, p. 9; 23 January 1959, p. 8; 16 April 1959, p. 6; 16 May 1959, p. 12. See also Government of Rajasthan, Revenue Department, *Report of the State Land Commission for Rajasthan: December, 1959* (Jaipur, [1959]), pp. 21–2.

revenue). These legal categories served to convert the previous regime of landlords and tenants into one of different types of independent proprietors; the former landlords became *bhumidhars*, having lost the lands they had rented to tenants but retained those which they had cultivated themselves (*sir*) and their home farms (*khudkasht*); and most of their former tenants became *sirdars*. In short, the UP Zamindari Abolition Act had changed one form of stratification into another, and had created a new pattern of issues and potential grievances in the process.[77]

The Congress, as the architect of zamindari abolition, had the support of the mass of ordinary peasants, or kisans, who owned as *sirdars* the land they had once worked as tenants, but it had less claim on the loyalties of the former landlords, who now constituted the largest proportion of the *bhumidhar* category, and the Jana Sangh may well have been tempted to take up their cause. The party was in sympathy with the views of those Hindu landlords who had been attracted to the Hindu Mahasabha in the British period and who favoured the advancement of Hindi and the preservation of Hindu traditions. The first President of the Uttar Pradesh Jana Sangh, Rao Krishna Pal Singh of Awagarh, was just such a landlord; a former army major, he had been a member of the United Provinces Legislative Council between 1926 and 1936, a president of the provincial Hindu Sabha and also President of the All-India Kshatriya Mahasabha.[78] However, in the end the UP Jana Sangh decided to aim its appeals at the upper levels of the *sirdars*, claiming that they had been unfairly treated. In a pamphlet issued at the time of its state conference in December 1955, the party expressed its approval of zamindari abolition while criticizing those of the Act's provisions which denied the kisan full ownership rights of his land and obliged him to pay to the state what he had previously paid to the zamindar as rent. It asked the government to enable peasants to obtain *bhumidhari* rights without having to pay ten times their annual land revenue payment; to return such payments as had already been made; to exempt kisans with

---

[77] On this Act, see P.D. Reeves, 'Agrarian legislation and rural society in U.P., India' (Unpublished M.A. thesis, University of Tasmania, Hobart, 1959), pp. 12–183; Walter C. Neale, *Economic Change in Rural India: Land Tenure and Reform in Uttar Pradesh 1800–1955* (New Haven, 1962), esp. pp. 211–58; Neale, 'Land reform in Uttar Pradesh', *The Economic Weekly*, VIII (28 July 1956), pp. 888–92; Baljit Singh and Shridhar Misra, *A Study of Land Reforms in Uttar Pradesh* (Honolulu, 1965), esp. pp. 67–85; Michael H. Johnson, 'The relation between land settlement and party politics in Uttar Pradesh, India, 1950–69: with special reference to the formation of the Bharatiya Kranti Dal' (Unpublished D. Phil. thesis, University of Sussex, 1975), pp. 94–8.

[78] *Organiser*, 10 September 1951, pp. 4 and 14; 22 October 1951, p. 1.

uneconomic holdings from payment of land revenue; to abolish the gram panchayat tax and to allocate a proportion of the land revenue income for villages; to reduce the irrigation tax; to tie the prices of farm commodities to those of all other commodities; and to halve land-revenue payments without delay.[79] To advance this assumed sectional interest the party established a peasant association known as the Bharatiya Kisan Sangh and set in motion local demonstrations in favour of its central demand for the halving of land-revenue payments.[80]

However, in this instance too the Jana Sangh's attempt to create a sectional base in rural politics produced no significant response. Its basic strategy, that of appealing to wealthy *sirdars* on the assumption that they greatly resented their exclusion from *bhumidhari* status, presupposed an extensive knowledge on their part of the legal and financial issues and a consequent ability to calculate the relative advantages of the two forms of tenure. This approach was unrealistic and it also attached too little importance to the point that the major factor affecting the economic status of ordinary cultivators was the selling price of foodgrains in local and regional markets, alluded to only by the proposal that the price of farm commodities should be linked with general commodity prices in some way. The party's main call, for halving the land revenue, was of a different order, but, although intelligible, it would have attracted support only at a time of famine or recession, because the land-revenue rates then in force were not generally regarded as a burden, except by cultivators with very small holdings. In any case, it was difficult for the Jana Sangh to attract widespread support so long as the grievances resulting from social and economic inequalities were being contained and diffused by the state's complex structures of caste and local communities. Had rural society in Uttar Pradesh broken down into a system of social classes, with farmers, rich peasants, poor peasants and agricultural labourers separated out as antagonistic groups, the Jana Sangh might well have established itself in some regions of the state as the party of the rich peasant, but rural politics did not take this form in the 1950s.

The Rajasthan and Uttar Pradesh cases illustrate how difficult it was for the Jana Sangh to develop a distinctive land policy which was both anti-landlord and anti-Congress so long as the Congress Party held to its

[79] Bharatiya Jana Sangh, Uttar Pradesh unit, *Manav ka Annadata: Kisan ki Mang: Lagan Adha Ho!* (Lucknow, [1955]), p. 12. This pamphlet was reviewed in *Organiser*, 5 March 1956, p. 12.

[80] See *Organiser*, 21 May 1956, pp. 3 and 16; 13 August 1956 (Special Issue), p. 35; 15 October 1956, p. 3. See also the General Secretary's report to the sixth national session of the party (*ibid.*, 14 April 1958, p. 9).

early position that individual peasant proprietorship was the most desirable and effective basis of land reform. However, in the late 1950s the Congress leadership was being forced to consider the possibility of more radical measures. By this time, information about the land system had become much more reliable and detailed, confirming earlier estimates that huge numbers of the agricultural population were dependent on holdings which were not large enough to ensure an adequate standard of living. According to the National Sample Survey, in 1953–54 fully 30,790,000 households (representing 46.9 per cent of the national total of 65,659,000 households) either owned no land at all or possessed holdings of less than one acre in size, the cumulative percentages showing that 74.4 per cent of the households owned less than 5 acres each and that 87.3 per cent owned less than 10 acres each.[81] The fact that the average size of a holding was only 4.7 acres, or about 6 acres if landless households were not included,[82] emphasized that a land-reform programme aimed exclusively or even mainly at a redistribution of holdings would be unrealistic, and proposals for some form of co-operative farming gained increasing acceptance.

Both the First and the Second Five-Year Plan documents recognized that the economic precariousness of small cultivators constituted a problem and proposed that, as a possible solution, the state might provide them with opportunities to form voluntary co-operative associations for credit purposes and for processing, marketing and farming activities, while strengthening village communities on a democratic basis.[83] These proposals amongst others were critically reviewed by an Agricultural Production Sub-Committee appointed by the All-India Congress Committee at a meeting in Hyderabad in October 1958, and its main recommendations were endorsed by the plenary session of Congress at Nagpur in January 1959. The resolution on 'Agrarian Organisational Pattern' adopted by that session made a number of proposals, including one that

---

[81] These figures are derived from Table 1.0, 'Estimated number of households and area owned by size-level of household ownership holding', in Government of India, Cabinet Secretariat, *The National Sample Survey: Eighth Round: July 1954–March 1955: Number 10. First Report on Land Holdings, Rural Sector* (Delhi, 1958), p. 47. The term 'household ownership holding' covers all agricultural and non-agricultural land owned by the usual members of the household as a socio-economic unit, excluding domestic servants, relations in temporary residence, paying guests, etc. (*ibid.*, p. iii). This early report was prepared on the basis of two sub-samples of the Central Sample (*ibid.*, pp. iii–iv) and was presented in first draft to the Government of India in September 1955, in revised draft in February 1956, and in final draft in January 1958 (*ibid.*, p. 1 n).

[82] *Ibid.*, p.v.

[83] See Planning Commission, *Second Five Year Plan*, pp. 201–8 and pp. 221–34.

The future agrarian pattern should be that of co-operative joint farming, in which the land will be pooled for joint cultivation, the farmers continuing to retain their property rights, and getting a share from the net produce in proportion to their land.[84]

Nehru made clear his own commitment to this proposal,[85] despite the lack of enthusiasm for it on the part of the state Congress leaders, and the opposition parties were therefore able to represent the Nagpur resolution as the sign of a major shift in the land policies of the ruling party. The Central Working Committee of the Jana Sangh claimed that the reference to farmers' retaining property rights after the pooling of land was 'futile and misleading', and argued that

such entry of property rights in the books of the farm is farce, since the owners are prevented from operating on their lands as masters with the full rights of disposal and management on their own responsibility and in accordance with their own plan of life.

In actual effect, co-operative farms are not radically different from the next state of collectives after the Russian and Chinese patterns (before the Communes).[86]

The party's Central General Council later decided to stage a campaign in October 1959 against the scheme[87] and its Central Working Committee envisaged this taking the form of conferences aimed at 'awakening the peasantry against inherent dangers of co-operative farming and prepare them for future struggle'.[88]

Both the Jana Sangh and the Swatantra Party were able to exploit for several years the propaganda opening provided by the Nagpur resolution: even as late as the 1962 election campaign Nehru was still referring to the ideal of co-operative farming in his local speeches[89] and the Jana Sangh was continuing to claim that the proposal was 'detrimental to democracy and unsuited to the needs of increasing production per acre of land'.[90] By this stage, however, it was already

[84] Poplai (ed.), *1962 General Elections in India*, p. 183.
[85] See his remarks at a press conference on 7 February (*Hindustan Times*, 8 February 1959, p. 6) and in Parliament (*P.D., L.S.* (Second Series), XXV, 19 February 1959, cc. 1935–48). See also Sarvepalli Gopal, *Jawaharlal Nehru: A Biography: Volume Three: 1956–1964* (London, 1984), pp. 113–18.
[86] Central Working Committee, Delhi, 15 March 1959, *BJS Documents*, II, pp. 64–6, quotation from p. 65.
[87] Central General Council, Poona, 8 July 1959, *ibid.*, pp. 68–9.
[88] *Hindustan Times*, 23 September 1959, p. 10. See also the statement by Nanaji Deshmukh, then secretary for the Eastern Zone, at Lucknow on 29 August (*ibid.*, 31 August 1959, p. 5).
[89] See his speeches at Gorakhpur on 14 January 1962 (*Leader* (Allahabad, Dak edition), 16 January 1962, p. 5) and at Shamli on 28 January 1962 (*ibid.*, 30 January 1962, p. 1).

becoming clear that the Congress Party as a whole was not pressing for major changes in the system of land tenure, and that future reforms would be restricted to the enforcement of ceilings legislation, the consolidation of holdings, and the improvement of tenancy conditions; when it was mentioned, co-operative farming was characterized as a voluntary arrangement, dependent on consent.

By 1963, indeed, the central question in land politics was whether the state Congress governments could continue to surmount the legal obstacles which were being raised against the implementation of the early reforms. Thus, in the judgement on the case *Karimbil Kunhikoman v. State of Kerala*, the Supreme Court had declared on 5 December 1961 that the Kerala Agrarian Relations Act of 1961 was unconstitutional to the extent that it applied to *ryotwari* lands in two taluks which had been transferred to Kerala from Madras in 1956, at the time of states reorganization. The court held that Article 31A of the Constitution of India, which protected various land reform laws from being challenged in the courts under certain of the Fundamental Rights, did not apply to the Kerala statute and that the *ryotwari* holdings in question were not 'estates' as defined by Article 31A.[91] To solve this problem, the Government of India decided to propose the amendment of Article 31A to avoid restrictive interpretations of the term 'estates' .

The result was the Constitution (Seventeenth Amendment) Bill, which was first considered by Parliament in 1963 and which proposed to amend Article 31A (2) so that 'estate' would include any land held under *ryotwari* settlement and indeed any land held or let for agricultural purposes. In December 1963 the Jana Sangh's national session at Ahmedabad declared that this proposal indicated that the Union government was 'seeking powers to seize land from the tiller of the soil under any kind of tenure for any purpose'.

Besides, in view of the Government's objective of collectivisation of agriculture under the guise of co-operative farming, this step cannot be looked at with equanimity. It creates apprehension that this power is being sought by amending the Constitution to put an end to peasant proprietorship and family farming.

The resolution declared the Jana Sangh to be totally opposed to this particular provision and directed all its units 'to organise a mass movement in support of the rights of the tiller to his land and labours'.[92]

[90] Bharatiya Jana Sangh, *Election Manifesto 1962*, p. 16.
[91] H.C.L. Merilltat, *Land and the Constitution in India* (New York, 1970), pp. 139–40 and 185–8.

However, neither the Jana Sangh's opposition nor that of the Swatantra Party proved a serious obstacle to the passage of the bill and, having been considered by a joint select committee of the two houses of Parliament, it was finally adopted at a special session of Parliament in June 1964.[93]

As its position on this legislation revealed, the Jana Sangh had by this stage settled for the policy of defending the tenure rights of those peasant proprietors who had been the principal beneficiaries of the land reforms of the 1950s. By keeping open the possibility of a further redistribution of land, however modest, the Congress showed that it was still a reforming party and thus enabled the Jana Sangh and the Swatantra Party to claim that they alone understood the need to strengthen and consolidate the principle of individual proprietorship embodied in the early legislation. The Jana Sangh dressed up this conservative message in radical language, as in the following paragraph in its manifesto for the 1967 general elections:

The objective of the land reforms is to assure the farmer about his cadastral rights so that he may be encouraged to invest in land and develop it. Land reforms enacted under Congress rule have failed to achieve this objective. Laws conferring various rights to the peasant have generally remained unimplemented. Then, there has been unending train of amendments. Further, slogans about cooperative farming and governmental farming have created in the farmers a sense of uncertainty about the future. Bharatiya Jana Sangh holds that land belongs to the tiller. Land reforms will be implemented to ensure this. An assurance will be given not to effect changes in laws which curtail the peasant's rights. Ejectments will be stopped.

Irregularities that are usually indulged in during land consolidation will be stopped. Land consolidation expenses will not be borne by the peasant.[94]

The party which had once recommended the abolition of zamindari and jagirdari without compensation was now prepared to envisage the approval of a different form of 'landlordism', that of the peasant proprietor:

[92] Bharatiya Jana Sangh, *Resolutions of the Eleventh Annual Session, Ahmedabad, Dec. 28, 29 and 30, 1963, and Working Committee, New Delhi, March, 1–2, 1964* (Delhi, [1964]), pp. 1–2. See also U.M. Trivedi, 'The seventeenth amendment is a colourable legislation', *Organiser*, 15 November 1963, pp. 51–2, and a speech by Trivedi, *P.D., L.S.* (Third Series), XXXII, 1 June 1964, cc. 383–8.

[93] When the bill came before Parliament in April 1964 it failed to obtain the required majority in the Lok Sabha (a majority of the total membership of the house and not less than two-thirds of those present and voting). It was finally approved by both houses at the special session of June 1964 (see Merillat, *Land and the Constitution in India*, pp. 190–3; *Indian Recorder and Digest*, July 1964, p. 2).

[94] Bharatiya Jana Sangh, *Election Manifesto 1967*, p. 19.

There are many farms which remain untilled because of restrictions on subletting. This has affected capital investment also towards the development of land. Bharatiya Jana Sangh will get records corrected and then allow subletting to tenants with uneconomic holdings and to landless farmers.[95]

The Jana Sangh and the politics of agricultural marketing

The Jana Sangh at first tended to be more responsive to the interests of traders in foodgrains, moneylenders and small industrialists in the food-processing sector than to the interests of the agricultural producers themselves. In the 1950s it, like the Congress, tended to reduce rural politics to a single issue, that of land ownership, and to argue that the chief aim of the state should be to provide land to the tiller, as if this action alone would create the conditions for increased production and higher returns for the peasant cultivator.

However, it was quite impossible for any political party to ignore the importance of peasant agriculture, which formed the life of the great majority of the Indian people. According to the 1961 Census, 82 per cent of the country's total population of 439.2 millions were to be found in rural areas, and the great proportion of these made their living directly or indirectly by growing food and cash crops. In the three years from 1956–57 to 1958–59 the average area under crops amounted to 326 million acres, of which 217 million acres were under cereals and 58 million were under pulses.[96] The proportion of the agricultural output which found its way into large markets was relatively small; according to the All-India Rural Credit Survey, on the basis of information collected in 1951–52, only about 35 per cent of total production was offered for sale by cultivators[97] and of that amount fully 65 per cent was sold in the villages.[98] Small cultivators were in a weak position in the grain markets; with little surplus produce for sale, they dealt mainly with local traders and moneylenders, to whom they also turned for high-interest loans, sometimes for economic purposes and sometimes to meet social obligations, such as weddings.

The Jana Sangh's early manifestos envisaged the state intervening to foster and protect a traditional scheme of peasant agriculture rather than

---

[95] *Ibid.*, pp. 19–20.
[96] National Council of Applied Economic Research, *Techno-Economic Survey of Uttar Pradesh*, p. 241 (Table 10).
[97] The Reserve Bank of India, *All-India Rural Credit Survey: Report of the Committee of Direction. Volume II: The General Report* (Bombay, 1954: third impression, 1956), p. 23.
[98] *Ibid.*, pp. 100–1.

to produce a system of modern farming capable of reducing the power of the moneylenders and the grain traders at the level of the village economy. Thus although the party's 1957 election manifesto, for example, spoke of establishing cottage and village industries, co-operative banks, and schemes of insurance for the villagers and for their crops and cattle, it dealt with the central problem – of increasing yields and profits for peasants – as if it were basically one of motivation. It mentioned steps to supply better seeds and manure but declared that the use of chemical fertilizers would be discouraged, as would the use of tractors for 'normal ploughing purposes'. The manifesto said that the party would try to establish parity between the prices of agricultural and industrial products, but did not mention the possibility of price incentives for farmers or of marketing reforms. The task of increasing productivity was assigned to 'country-wide campaigns' by means of which peasants would be 'encouraged and enthused to work harder for increased yield'.[99] By comparison, the corresponding passages in the Jana Sangh's manifestos for the 1962 and 1967 elections had become bland, technical and 'modern' in their style and prescriptions; they no longer declared against chemical fertilizers and tractors, and even proposed advance-price arrangements for the government purchase of farm produce.[100] However, the party's unredeemed preference for the ideal of the simple cultivator was revealed once more in the *Principles and Policy* document of 1965, which states that

The Indian farmer has evolved methods of farming most suitable to his circumstances. These age-long systems should not be abandoned suddenly in favour of methods which have not been fully tested, particularly in conditions similar to those existing in India. The Indian farmer has been practising rotation of crops, using manures and night soil after curing. He knows the value of bunding and plantation for checking soil-erosion. He has maintained the fertility of the soil for ages. Of course, for some time past, it has not been possible for him to put his knowledge to full use. His capital resources need to be augmented and fixity of tenure assured.[101]

Thus, in formulating its agrarian policy, the Jana Sangh faced a dilemma: on the one hand it wanted to demonstrate that it was a modern party, capable of making rational and constructive proposals for the improvement of the conditions surrounding peasant agriculture, but on

---

[99] Bharatiya Jana Sangh, *Election Manifesto 1957*, pp. 15–16. Cf. Bharatiya Jana Sangh, *Manifesto* [1951], pp. 3–5; 1954 Manifesto (*BJS Documents*, I, pp. 67–8); 1958 Manifesto (*ibid.*, pp. 112–13).

[100] Bharatiya Jana Sangh, *Election Manifesto 1962*, pp. 13–16; *Election Manifesto 1967*, pp. 17–21.

[101] Bharatiya Jana Sangh, *Principles and Policy*, pp. 31–2.

the other it was anxious to demonstrate its faith in traditional practices and arrangements. As a result it seldom took a clear stand on an issue but was inclined to balance mild prescriptions for increased public control with arguments that the peasant should be left to work out his destiny without interference. Postponement of choice was possible only so long as the Congress Party was similarly cautious in its agrarian policies, but once Congress began to edge towards more radical measures the Jana Sangh was forced to reveal its conservatism. This pattern can be illustrated most clearly in the politics of agricultural marketing in the 1950s and 1960s.

After the severe food crisis of 1943, the British authorities subjected the trade in foodgrains to a system of controls which included powers of procurement whereby supplies of grain could be assembled in surplus areas for distribution in deficit areas, powers of rationing scarce commodities and selling them at reasonable prices, procedures for preventing the rise of grain prices above specified ceilings, and powers to regulate inter-provincial trade. Controls were suspended in 1947 but they were reimposed in 1948 and remained in force until 1954.[102] Given its sympathy for traders, the Jana Sangh might have been expected to oppose the regulation of the grain trade, but in fact it was prepared to acknowledge that the government might have to intervene to deal with particular problems. The party's Central Working Committee declared its support in June 1952 for the distribution of foodgrains in areas where prices had risen, for decontrol 'after ensuring that sufficient reserve stocks are in the hands of Government and prompt and effective steps are taken against hoarders, profiteers and black-marketeers', and for the ending of restrictions on the movement of foodgrains 'after ensuring that big industrial areas continue to remain cordoned at the first stage and, if necessary, are served by special supplies from the Centre'.[103] The ambivalence was quite evident; although the party was prepared to accept that the rights of traders to make a profit on their transactions had to be curtailed at times of shortage in order to protect both

[102] On this period of controls see R.I. Duncan, 'Levels, the communication of pro-grammes, and sectional strategies in Indian politics, with reference to the Bharatiya Kranti Dal and the Republican Party of India in Uttar Pradesh State and Aligarh District (U.P.)' (Unpublished D. Phil. thesis, University of Sussex, 1979), pp. 109–16. See also Planning Commission, *The First Five Year Plan*, pp. 173–83; and Government of India, Ministry of Food and Agriculture, Department of Food, *Report of the Foodgrains Enquiry Committee 1957* (Delhi, 1957), pp. 17–35. For a general review of the history of policies affecting the pricing and marketing of foodgrains, see Uma J. Lele, *Food Grain Marketing in India: Private Performance and Public Policy* (Ithaca, N.Y., 1971), Appendix I, pp. 225–37.

[103] Central Working Committee, Delhi, 14 June 1952, *BJS Documents*, II, pp. 45–6.

producers and consumers, it was reluctant to accept the state as a trader in its own right and was therefore bound to resist any move to establish a public agency empowered to compete in or monopolize the wholesale trade in grain.

The Jana Sangh did not react strongly to the gradual reintroduction of controls in the period 1955–57, but it did oppose the decision of the National Development Council in November 1958 to recommend that the states should take over all wholesale trading in foodgrains.[104] The party's national session at Bangalore in December 1958 claimed that the proposed scheme would displace 30,000 wholesale and about 3,000,000 retail dealers and that it would lead to compulsory procurement and rationing. The resolution in question made clear that the party was prepared to accept the accumulation of buffer stocks, the establishment of fair-price shops in deficit areas, zoning, and ceilings and floors for prices,[105] but it was equally clear that it considered 'state trading' beyond such limits to be unreasonable.

In practice, the various controls used by the state governments differed considerably from region to region and did not, on the whole, represent a radical departure from previous policies. In any case, the willingness of the central government to insist upon further measures was also in doubt; although A.P. Jain spoke of the need for a more effective framework of controls when he resigned as Minister for Food and Agriculture in August 1959,[106] his successor, S.K. Patil, took the view that 'state trading' should be used only as an exceptional arrangement.[107] Controls were reduced during his period of office, between August 1959 and August 1963, and the Jana Sangh was therefore able to revert to its former role, of warning the central and state governments of the need to strike the right balance. In January 1960 its national session at Nagpur decided that

State trading in foodgrains should not be resorted to as Government monopoly. The Government should, however, enter the market for purchasing at the time of falling prices and for setting up fair price shops in times and areas of scarcity.[108]

---

[104] *Statesman* (Delhi), 10 November 1958, p. 1. On the detailed policy changes between 1954 and 1958, see Duncan, 'Levels, the communication of programmes, and sectional strategies in Indian politics', pp. 116–18.

[105] Seventh National Session, Bangalore, 28 December 1958, *BJS Documents*, II, pp. 61–2. See also Central Working Committee, Hyderabad, 24 November 1957, *ibid.*, pp. 57–8; and Central Working Committee, Delhi, 12 October 1958, *ibid.*, pp. 60–1.

[106] *P.D., L.S.* (Second Series), XXXIII, 22 August 1959, cc. 3926–8. His resignation was accepted on the 23rd.

[107] *Ibid., R.S.*, XXVI, 31 August 1959, cc. 2361–2. He took over the Food and Agriculture portfolio on the 24th.

[108] Eighth National Session, Nagpur, 25 January 1960, *BJS Documents*, II, p. 134.

As this shows, the party was now prepared to agree that the government's responsibility to control prices should be exercised as much for the benefit of the producer as for that of the consumer, and that the state should therefore offer to support selling-price in advance of the growing season; it even promised in its manifesto for the 1962 general elections that

Arrangements will be made by government to purchase agricultural commodities at a minimum price announced in advance of the sowing season. While fixing the minimum price, a certain amount of profit to the farmer, in addition to his cost, will also be included.[109]

Agricultural marketing became a serious issue again in 1964, when rising food prices forced the central government into action. In March it announced a decision to divide the country into nine wheat zones and at the end of the year it took steps to establish two major agencies, the Food Corporation of India and the Agricultural Prices Commission. The Food Corporation was authorized to purchase, store and distribute foodgrains while purchasing prices and quantities were to be set by the Ministry of Food and Agriculture, with the prior agreement of the states and in the light of advice given by the Agricultural Prices Commission.[110] The establishment of the Food Corporation gave the controls of 1965 and 1966, when statutory rationing and fair-price shops in the larger towns and cities were widely used, the appearance of a permanent and integrated system. The private trading interests and other opponents of the new arrangements concentrated their attacks upon the food zones, which effectively prevented free trading across state boundaries, and demanded their abolition. They found some support within the ruling party and the Minister for Food and Agriculture, C. Subramaniam, was forced at a meeting of the Congress organization's Subjects Committee, held on 11 February 1966 before a session of the All-India Congress Committee, to agree that the zonal system should be reviewed.[111] The Government of India accordingly appointed a Food-grains Policy Committee but its report, submitted in September 1966, far from criticizing the Food Corporation, recommended that it should be strengthened and that measures should be taken to make the existing marketing arrangements more effective. However, it also acknowledged that an important role remained for the private trade 'both in its own

---

[109] Bharatiya Jana Sangh, *Election Manifesto 1962*, p. 16.
[110] See Dilip Mukerjee, 'Policy on food', II, *Statesman* (Delhi), 20 July 1965, p. 6; Government of India, Ministry of Food, Agriculture, Community Development and Co-operation, Department of Food, *Report of the Foodgrains Policy Committee 1966* (Delhi, 1966), p. 13.
[111] *Congress Bulletin* (New Delhi), January–March 1966, pp. 65–75.

right and, very often, as one of the agents of Government within each State'.[112]

Although the Jana Sangh tolerated many features of the control system of the mid-1960s, including the establishment of the Food Corporation, it did press for the abolition of food zones and argued that various schemes of levy and procurement administered by the state governments should be ended.[113] At the same time, it insisted that it was not willing to move any further along the path to complete public control of the trade, for reasons which Upadhyaya stated as follows:

The doctrinaire extremes of a total nationalisation of the food grain trade or complete free trade must be avoided. The government should come as a partial trader to build buffer-stocks and also to regulate prices. Monopoly by the government will lead to corruption, and increase the cost of distribution. The government's present policy of entering the market as a big trader is correct. But they should not talk about complete nationalisation even as a concession to slogan-mongering Communists and their fellow travellers in the ruling party. It disturbs normal business and trade.[114]

In effect, the Jana Sangh had adopted a policy which defended the position of the private trader without denying that some measure of control was needed to protect the consumer and the farmer. It was trying to appeal to consumer interests by maintaining that its proposals for abolishing food zones were intended to restore business confidence, to enable the trade to work efficiently once more, and to bring about a lowering of prices and an ending of shortages. At the same time, it was trying to appeal to the private traders and the large farmers by opposing the system of levy and compulsory procurement, by recommending an end to zoning, and by advocating a limited role for the Food Corporation. Finally, it was reminding the small producer that it had accepted the basic principles of the minimum-price support system. Thus, while acknowledging that the Food Corporation would normally purchase grain at prevailing market prices, it was conceding that the corporation could, 'at the time of falling prices,... purchase all the grain

---

[112] Ministry of Food, Agriculture, Community Development and Co-operation, *Report of the Foodgrains Policy Committee 1966*, p. 42. For a detailed analysis of the reasons for the policy changes between 1964 and 1966, see Duncan, 'Levels, the communication of programmes, and sectional strategies in Indian politics', pp. 122–30.

[113] See Bharatiya Jana Sangh, *Election Manifesto 1967*, pp. 17–18, and the following policy resolutions: Central General Council, Gwalior, 10 August 1964, *BJS Documents*, II, pp. 148–50; Central Working Committee, Jabalpur, 10 July 1965, *ibid.*, pp. 71–3; Central General Council, Delhi, 17 August 1965, *ibid.*, pp. 73–4; Central Working Committee, Kanpur, 15 January 1966, *ibid.*, pp. 75–6; Thirteenth National Session, Jullundur, 1 May 1966, *ibid.*, pp. 76–8.

[114] Deendayal Upadhyaya, *Food Problem* (Bharatiya Jana Sangh, Delhi, 1964), p. 8.

offered at the previously declared support price' and that it could also enter into forward contracts with the producers 'and advance them money'.[115]

Conclusion

The nature of the Jana Sangh's sectional appeals throws some interesting light on its assumptions about the function of the state in regulating social and economic life. Claiming that producer- and consumer-groups could achieve a harmonious relationship within a corporate framework of society, it treated each group as if it were, potentially, an integral part of an organic whole; that is to say, it assumed that each group had its own function to perform within a social system in which the relations between groups were reciprocal and mutually beneficial. The party saw small industry not as a residual category within the industrial structure but as a coherent economic sector which drew upon the talents and skills of local entrepreneurs and met important consumer demands; it treated peasant proprietors not as petty producers but as small farmers who were perfectly capable of supplying sufficient foodgrains for the country's needs, provided that the government offered them the appropriate assistance and incentives; and it depicted the grain trade as an established business profession capable of making foodgrain markets work for the benefit of the community. Of course, the Jana Sangh acknowledged that certain conflicts of interest would have to be resolved to establish a fully functional relationship between the various groups within society; it took account of those conflicts which separated small industry from large industry, peasants from landlords, and traders from producers and consumers but regarded the state as a mechanism within which they would be minimized and controlled.

None the less, the party's corporatism was partial; it tended to offer the extension of the state's protective and regulatory framework specifically to those activities which it valued most highly within the economic structure – small industries, country trading and small-scale peasant agriculture – and to ignore social groups on the margins. To take some examples: the party's proposal that the state should help small industries in various ways was accompanied (in the 1962 election manifesto and in the 1965 *Principles and Policy* document in particular) by suggestions that village and cottage industries should be 'rationalised'; the party had very little to say about the provision of economic security for poor peasants and agricultural labourers beyond expressing its support for ceilings legislation; and its strong opposition to the joint co-operative

[115] Bharatiya Jana Sangh, *Election Manifesto 1967*, p. 17.

farming proposal of 1959 showed that it had no wish to see the state go further towards incorporating the rural poor within the organized economy.

The Jana Sangh's appeals to groups of workers were more complex, but held to the same pattern. In this case, the need for corporate solidarity was attributed not to the workers as a group but to industry as a form of social organization; the party assumed that workers and employers should be bound together by a reciprocal, family-like relationship and that, as an organic unit, they would develop functional ties with other groups in society. The formation of the Bharatiya Mazdoor Sangh as a trade union associated with the party was justified on the grounds that it would serve to regulate and settle industrial disputes within an ordered framework of common values and thus prevent the growth of class conflict.

The deficiencies of the Jana Sangh's social strategy go a long way towards explaining its comparative lack of electoral success in the 1950s and 1960s. In the first place, its preferred interest base was an extremely narrow one and could not have produced electoral majorities except in a limited category of constituencies; a party which was directing its appeals mainly to small industrialists and traders, and, more generally, to the lower-middle classes of the northern towns and cities was concentrating on a potential clientèle which was relatively small and comparatively isolated. When the party turned to address other more substantial social groups, such as the peasants and the workers, its statements of interest were inevitably coloured by its sensitivity to the values of its essential reference groups. In the second place, it was over-cautious in formulating its economic policies and was reluctant to strike out on its own. Although it stood up to the Congress on some issues, such as the 1959 proposal for joint co-operative farming and the demand for the complete nationalization of the foodgrains trade, it generally conformed to the government's line on economic policy. It could, for example, have formulated radical taxation policies instead of accepting the notion that land revenue and sales- and excise-taxes were the most reliable sources of public revenue at state level; or, anticipating the position taken later by the Swatantra Party, it could have come out much more strongly in the mid-1950s for a thorough-going liberalization of the domestic economy. Even the party's corporatism was presented in a hesitant and partial way, rather than as a systematic and convincing philosophy. For all its criticism of the ruling party, the Jana Sangh was very much a prisoner of the Congress Raj, accepting many of its economic and social values and unwilling to explore the possibility of a direct and radical attack on its basic assumptions about how the economy should be managed.

7

The Jana Sangh in electoral politics, 1951 to 1967

We have now considered the main factors which worked against the Jana Sangh's attempt to become a major party in Indian politics. It was seriously handicapped in electoral competition by the limitations of its organization and leadership, by its inability to gather support through appeals to Hindu nationalist sentiment, and by its failure to establish a broad base of social and economic interests. In this chapter we shall study how the party became aware of its weaknesses through its experience of constitutional politics and how it tried to compensate for them. The first section examines the party's initial strategy, based on the mistaken assumption that the Congress was about to disintegrate under the opposite pulls of Hindu nationalism and communism, and the second shows how a more realistic analysis of the political prospects in the mid-1960s enabled the party's leaders to consider seriously the possibilities of co-operation with other opposition parties. Finally, in the third section, we look more closely at the Jana Sangh's record in elections and compare the extent of its achievements in western Madhya Pradesh, in the Punjab and in Uttar Pradesh.

The general strategy, 1951 to 1962

At the outset, the founders of the Jana Sangh were strongly influenced by the theory that the Congress Party, which they regarded as materialistic and lacking in genuine principles, was about to disintegrate. They saw politics in independent India as developing into a system of two opposing forces, one, representing nationalism and democracy, centred on the Jana Sangh, and the other, representing totalitarian socialism, based on the Communist Party of India (CPI). Grounded on an idealistic notion that the essential values in Indian life were metaphysical ones, this theory presupposed that, as soon as the Indian people realized that their basic choice lay between parties which drew upon Hindu traditions for their inspiration and those which depended upon the rival and extraneous creed of communism, the Congress Party would be swept aside. The central idea was that of *nation*, not in the Congress sense of an existing community of diverse religious confessions and social groups but in the sense of an immanent community which had been created and sustained by the social and cultural traditions of Hinduism.

Such a way of thinking had been encouraged in the British period by the books of Savarkar and Golwalkar, but the problem which faced Hindu nationalist writers in the early 1950s was to predict the factors which would precipitate the transformation of party politics, given that the Muslim League had by then virtually disappeared in India. They claimed that Congress, held responsible by the nation for the partition of the subcontinent, would inevitably collapse and that before it withered away 'a new party must come up and take its place and thus prevent a political vacuum from developing into political anarchy'.[1] This was the outcome foreseen by K.R. Malkani, the editor of the *Organiser*, in the period immediately preceding the formation of the Jana Sangh: he wrote of the 'good government of Bharat' depending 'directly and fully on the formation of a nation-wide party which will be as much revivalist of ancient values as it will be futurist in its targets'.[2] At the level of ideas, he saw an essential conflict between *hindutva* and communism:

I am of the definite opinion that the remedy for our current ills lies in Hindutva and that Communism can be combated and conquered in Hindusthan by the Hindus through Hindutva. If we do not fortify the Hindu foundations of Bharat we stand in danger of losing one part after another even as we have already lost Sind, Frontier, one-third Kashmir, one-half Punjab and two-third Bengal.

The new party – if it is to serve and save the Nation – must be Hindu in purpose, plan and policy.[3]

The Jana Sangh's Hindu nationalism, and its idea of its own future status, was strongly influenced by such notions. However, it had been founded only a few months before the onset of the campaign for the first general elections of 1951–52 and its efforts to take part in these contests were necessarily improvised. In the Lok Sabha competition, the party nominated candidates in 94 of the 489 elective seats, polled 3.06 per cent of the valid votes, and returned three members (two from West Bengal and one from Rajasthan). In elections to the Legislative Assemblies it nominated a total of 727 candidates for 3,283 seats, secured 2.77 per cent of the valid votes, and returned 35 members (including 9 in West Bengal and 8 in Rajasthan). It nevertheless amassed more votes than its chief

---

[1] K.R. Malkani, *Principles for a New Political Party* (Delhi, [1951]), p. 2. See also Malkani, *The Rise and Fall of the Congress* (Delhi, [1951]).

[2] Malkani, *Principles for a New Political Party*, p. 3.

[3] *Ibid.*, p. 5.

Hindu nationalist rivals, the Hindu Mahasabha and the Ram Rajya Parishad, and its degree of support placed it within range of the other national non-Congress parties, whose shares of the votes in the Lok Sabha elections were Socialist Party 10.6 per cent, the CPI 3.3 per cent and the Kisan Mazdoor Praja Party (KMPP) 5.8 per cent, compared with the Congress Party's level of 45.0 per cent.[4]

Although the Jana Sangh established a degree of central control for this, its first campaign, there can be no doubt that the effectiveness of its regional campaigns varied considerably. The most vigorous and best-supported organizations were in the northern areas: in Uttar Pradesh, the state working committee appointed a parliamentary board early in October 1951 and issued detailed instructions on how district units should select candidates, recruit members and organize constituencies;[5] and the party's Punjab election board, which was in charge of the Himachal Pradesh, PEPSU and Delhi areas as well as the Punjab proper, had built up a formidable organization for the campaign, including 4,500 full-time and 13,000 part-time workers.[6] The consequence was a clear regional bias; the party contested higher proportions of seats and gained greater shares of the votes in the northern states than in other regions, with the exception of West Bengal and Madhya Pradesh, where the levels of support were comparable with those in the north.

Five years later the preparations for the second general elections were affected by the major reorganization of state boundaries carried out in 1956, but even before the changes had been made Deendayal Upadhyaya, as General Secretary of the Jana Sangh, was explaining the party's strategy within the new geography. He announced in June 1956 that the party would concentrate on Uttar Pradesh, the Punjab, Rajasthan and Madhya Pradesh, which it considered to be its strongholds, and that it would contest only a few seats in West Bengal and in the Maharashtra region and none in Assam, Orissa or the southern states.[7] Later, on the eve of the campaign itself, he revealed that this general approach was linked to a policy of ensuring sound organization at the local level; to this

---

[4]　The sources for these and other election statistics cited in this chapter are the *Reports* of the 1951–52, 1957, 1962, 1967 and some later general elections published by the Election Commission of India. The figures for the 1951–52, 1957, 1962 and 1967 elections relating to the Jana Sangh have been recalculated from the constituency returns published in these *Reports* and are set out below in Appendix I (for Legislative Assembly elections) and in Appendix II (for Lok Sabha elections). Some of the statistical data for Uttar Pradesh elections are derived from the UP Election Project, funded in part by the Nuffield Foundation, at the University of Sussex.

[5]　*Pioneer* (Lucknow), 16 October 1951, p. 3.

[6]　*Tribune* (Ambala), 1 November 1951, p. 5.

[7]　*Statesman* (Delhi), 30 June 1956, p. 1.

end, the party had decided to set up candidates mainly in those constituencies where it had carried out some work during the preceding five years, where it had established committees in at least one-third of the polling centres, and where primary members of the party constituted at least one per cent of the voters.[8] In the event, the party nominated 130 candidates in parliamentary contests and only 582 in assembly contests in the 1957 elections, but it achieved better results than in the earlier poll. For the Lok Sabha, it returned four members and obtained 5.97 per cent of the valid votes, compared with 47.78 per cent polled by Congress, 8.92 per cent by the CPI and 10.41 per cent by the Praja Socialist Party. In the Legislative Assembly elections, it returned 46 members (including 17 in Uttar Pradesh, 10 in Madhya Pradesh, 9 in the Punjab and 6 in Rajasthan) and polled 3.87 per cent of the valid votes in the country as a whole, with rates of 9.84 per cent in Uttar Pradesh, 9.88 in Madhya Pradesh, 8.61 in the Punjab and 5.41 in Rajasthan. The main weakening of its strength had occurred in West Bengal, where the absence of Mookerjee's personal influence had evidently counted against it.

In his analysis of the results, Upadhyaya revealed that the principle of nominating candidates only where the organizational requirements had been satisfied had not been fully applied and that, in general terms, it had been difficult to find suitable candidates. He complained that the state parliamentary boards had not forwarded the names of prospective candidates to the Central Parliamentary Board as requested and that consequently the choice of candidates had been made mostly at the state level. He also remarked that the delimitation of constituencies carried out in 1956 had 'disturbed some of the areas in which we had been working in a planned way for the last five years' and that this had also 'affected the number of candidates and our chances of success'.[9] Balraj Madhok pointed out later that the party had been handicapped by the lack of a leader of Mookerjee's calibre and by the shortage of election funds, which had obliged state and local units as well as candidates 'to fend for themselves as best they could on the strength of local support'. He also drew attention to the effects of propaganda which made out the Jana Sangh to be a communal organization,[10] and stressed the extent to which a popular rally had been formed around Nehru:

---

[8] Upadhyaya, press conference, Nagpur, 13 January 1957, in *Organiser* (New Delhi), 21 January 1957, p. 3.

[9] *Ibid.*, 14 April 1958, p. 8.

[10] Balraj Madhok, *Political Trends in India* (Delhi, 1959), pp. 119–20. Madhok argued that organized labour had been beyond the influence of the party and that this had been a handicap in industrial cities such as Bombay and Indore. He also discussed the 'diffidence' shown by the party's workers, apparently at the outset of the campaign (*ibid.*, pp. 120–1).

The one man who has been keeping this faction ridden organisation together is Pt. Jawaharlal Nehru. His personal prestige, hold over the masses and grip over the organisation had made him the one dispenser of favours in the Congress.[11]

Speculation about how and when the Congress would break up or divide was given fresh impetus by the formation of a Communist government in the state of Kerala after the 1957 elections, and the Jana Sangh's Central Working Committee warned in July 1958 that it was the only party 'which has the potentiality and equipment of meeting the Communist challenge and fill in the political vacuum which the disintegration of the Congress is sure to create'.[12] One possibility was that the Congress socialists might create divisions by pressing for radical policies, using as justification the resolution of the 1955 Avadi session of the party that 'planning should take place with a view to the establishment of a socialistic pattern of society'[13] and the scheme to expand industries in the public sector of the economy in the course of the Second Five-Year Plan (1956–61). Jana Sangh commentators therefore attached considerable importance to the resolutions adopted at the Nagpur session of the Congress in January 1959 favouring further measures of land reform, including co-operative joint farming, the completion of ceilings legislation by the end of that year, and the introduction of state trading in foodgrains.[14] Madhok claimed that the 'opposition to this policy from within the Congress, though demoralised and leaderless, is not insignificant' and that the left-wing leadership of the Congress was afraid of an alignment between the Congress right and the 'more organised and determined opposition coming from the Bharatiya Jana Sangh'.[15] He saw the CPI as standing ready to exploit this division:

The Indian communists and their Russian mentors are now fully aware of the strength and weakness of the Congress. They realise that in Pt. Nehru they have their best friend in the Congress. They are also conscious of the fact that right wing in the Congress is still pretty strong. So they aim at ingratiating themselves with Pt. Nehru and his socialist supporters to drive the wedge between them and the so called rightists and reactionaries in the Congress deeper and deeper.[16]

Madhok found the Praja Socialist Party to be indistinguishable

[11] *Ibid.*, p. 126.
[12] Central Working Committee, Bombay, 19 July 1958, *Bharatiya Jana Sangh, Party Documents* (New Delhi, 1973), IV, pp. 166–8, quotation from pp. 167–8 (hereafter referred to as *BJS Documents*). Cf. resolution of 7th national session, Bangalore, 28 December 1958, *ibid.*, pp. 169–71.
[13] *Congress Bulletin* (New Delhi), January 1955, No. 1, p. 3.
[14] S.L. Poplai (ed.), *1962 General Elections in India* (New Delhi, 1962), pp. 182–4.
[15] Madhok, *Political Trends in India*, pp. 128–9.
[16] *Ibid.*, p. 130.

ideologically from the Congress, and he concluded that the 'steady radicalisation of the Congress programme and policies which has brought it quite near to P.S.P. and the C.P.I.' had drawn to the Jana Sangh the attention of 'all those who do not want India to be engulfed by communism and totalitarianism'.[17]

Shortly after Madhok offered this analysis, the CPI was subjected to severe public criticism for its refusal to condemn China's policy in Tibet. The Dalai Lama fled to India on 31 March 1959, and the CPI came under attack for its reluctance to back the Government of India squarely in its dispute with China over the northern border. By September 1959 the Jana Sangh's Central Working Committee was asking 'all patriotic sections of the people' to isolate the CPI and

destroy its capacity for treason by educating the masses in respect of its treacherous role and thus accelerate the process of its elimination from India's politics.[18]

In more general terms, communism was still identified as the antithesis of Hindu nationalism so far as political ideals were concerned. Commenting on an article which had praised the principle of 'unity in diversity' for Indian society, Malkani argued that the Jana Sangh, the Hindu Mahasabha and the RSS

do not divide the country on the basis of race or religion or culture. They seek to unite it on the one granite foundation of national life. i.e. Bharatiya Sanskriti. The only other possible foundation is the hunger of men i.e. communism. The real battle in India thus is between Hinduism and communism. Congress is only an *ad hoc* phenomenon – a left-over of the British connection.[19]

The theme that a fundamental moral dichotomy lay beneath the surface detail of Indian politics also occurs in the writings of Deendayal Upadhyaya at this time, as in the following extract from an article which he wrote on the eve of the 1962 elections:

There may be a need of polarisation and reduction in the number of parties. But polarisation requires a nucleus. So far no party can claim to occupy that position. On an ideological basis the Jana Sangh and the Communists provide the nucleus round which the nationalists and the extra-territorialists have to gather.[20]

[17] *Ibid.*, p. 139.
[18] Central Working Committee, Delhi, 20 September 1959, *BJS Documents*, IV, pp. 173–4.
[19] 'Kamal' [K.R. Malkani], 'National revolution betrayed', *Organiser*, 6 June 1960, p. 5. Malkani was referring to Humayun Kabir, 'Congress ideology: a statement', *India Quarterly*, XVI, 1 (January–March 1960), pp. 3–23.
[20] From 'Your vote (3): changers and no-changers', 11 December 1961, in Deendayal Upadhyaya, *Political Diary* (Bombay, 1968), p. 129.

Jana Sangh writers were sceptical of the idea that the philosophies on which European parties had been based – conservatism, liberalism, democratic socialism and communism, for example – could have any real meaning for an Indian electorate, and they therefore attributed the relative success of the Swatantra Party, formed in 1959, to its ability to attract the unprincipled support of disaffected groups rather than to its endorsement of the precepts of economic liberalism. Upadhyaya considered that it had been born in reaction to the 'totalitarian trends' of Congress policy:

Jana Sangh is also opposed to these trends and therefore, to some extent, our path is common. But we get inspiration from different sources. Instead of basing our policies on momentary reactions to the Congress programme, Jana Sangh is the outcome of the creative instinct of the nation, and positive and constructive aspects of Bharatiya culture and life.

In their anxiety to establish their branches in all parts of the country the leaders of the Swatantra Party have committed a blunder by admitting into their fold opportunist and discredited elements. These elements have taken advantage of the party's policy of freedom in all except some economic matter, to create or support separatist demands.[21]

By this stage the Jana Sangh's leaders were looking ahead to the third general elections, which were expected to take place early in 1962. The ideas we have noted were more in the nature of reflections than statements of doctrinal principle but they evidently informed the thinking behind the party's general strategy, which was to keep relatively clear of electoral alliances with other parties, to preserve its separate identity and to plan ahead on the assumption that, sooner or later, the Congress Party would disappear in the course of the battle between Hindu nationalism and materialistic communism. In more concrete terms, the party was anxious to preserve the advantage which it had gained from having been recognized by the Election Commission of India as a national party and given its own electoral symbol, the *dipak* (lamp). It was therefore alarmed when the Election Commission decided to alter the conditions for the use of electoral symbols: instead of classifying some parties as national parties and some as state parties as for the elections of 1951–52 and 1957, the commission proposed recognition on a state-by-state basis, determined in each state by whether a party's share of the valid vote had exceeded 3 per cent in both parliamentary and assembly contests in the preceding general election.[22] The Jana Sangh objected to the scheme when it was circulated in draft and even after its publication Vajpayee moved an adjournment motion

---

[21] *Organiser*, 1 February 1960, p. 12.
[22] On the introduction of the new system, see Election Commission of India, *Report on the Third General Elections in India, 1962*, I, General (New Delhi, 1966), pp. 26–34.

in the Lok Sabha to complain about its provisions.[23] The party's main fear was that it would lose its former monopoly of the *dipak* symbol in those states where it lacked sufficient support to gain at least 3 per cent of the votes but where it still hoped to establish itself, and this fear proved to be justified; although the Election Commission gave the Jana Sangh full recognition in its northern base areas (Madhya Pradesh, the Punjab, Rajasthan, Uttar Pradesh and Delhi) and in Maharashtra, it achieved only semi-recognition in seven other states (Andhra Pradesh, Assam, Bihar, Gujarat, Madras, Mysore and West Bengal); in these the *dipak* was to be placed on the list of free symbols and to be available for use by other candidates where no Jana Sangh candidates were nominated. Moreover, in Kerala, Orissa, Himachal Pradesh, Manipur and Tripura and the party was given no form of recognition at all.[24]

In geographical terms, the Jana Sangh's strategy in the 1962 elections was still to concentrate on the north. Writing in December 1961, Upadhyaya explained that the party had decided 'to fight the elections in a big way' in Uttar Pradesh, the Punjab, Rajasthan, Madhya Pradesh and Delhi, and that in those areas it would try to contest all seats either with its own candidates or 'by lending support to candidates according to local arrangements'; in Madras and Assam only a few selected constituencies would be contested and in other states 30 to 50 per cent of the seats 'according to the strength of the party'.[25] He said that candidates would be nominated

only in areas where the party has sufficiently wide-spread organisation or in constituencies where a Jana Sangh candidate is required due to simultaneous elections to the Lok Sabha and the Vidhan Sabhas.[26]

Referring to the choice of candidates, he said that preference had been given to party workers and to those candidates who had stood for the Jana Sangh previously. People who had applied for Congress nominations and had been refused were

not encouraged by the Sangh to enter the elections on its ticket. The Jana Sangh also does not believe in importing candidates from outside [a constituency] and as a rule home constituencies have been allotted to them.[27]

---

[23] *P.D., L.S.* (Second Series), LIX, 20 November 1961, c. 129. This provoked a written statement from the Law Minister, A.K. Sen, referred to the discussions between the Election Commission and the representatives of political parties in August 1961 (*ibid.*, cc. 135–7).

[24] Notification of the Election Commission of India, No. S.O. 2316, 19 September 1961, *The Gazette of India Extraordinary*, Part II, Section 3 (ii), 21 September 1961, pp. 1571–4.

[25] Deendayal Upadhyaya, 'Jana Sangh and the general elections', in Poplai (ed.), *1962 General Elections*, p. 51.

[26] *Ibid.*, p. 52.

[27] *Ibid.*, pp. 52–3.

In spite of the considerable effort made by the Jana Sangh to increase the number and spread of its candidates in the Lok Sabha elections, the results were disappointing: although the party's total number of candidates rose from 130 in 1957 to 196 in 1962, and although it returned 14 members in 1962 compared with only 4 in 1957, its share of the valid vote increased only slightly, from 5.97 to 6.44 per cent. The Congress again dominated the election, returning 361 members with 44.72 per cent of the votes, and the most successful non-Congress parties proved to be the CPI, which returned 29 members and secured 9.94 per cent of the votes, and the Swatantra Party, which returned 18 members with 7.89 per cent of the votes. The Jana Sangh was on a par with the Praja Socialist Party (12 members and 6.81 per cent of the votes) but had done better than the Socialist Party, which returned 6 members and gained 2.69 per cent of the votes.

In 1962 there were Legislative Assembly elections in all the states except Orissa and Kerala, where mid-term polls had already been held. In these contests, Jana Sangh candidates were nominated for 1,140 of the 2,855 seats and 116 of them were elected. The party's share of the national vote in assembly elections was 6.07 per cent and it achieved its highest levels in the northern states of Madhya Pradesh (16.66 per cent), Uttar Pradesh (16.46 per cent), the Punjab (9.72 per cent) and Rajasthan (9.15 per cent), and it was also in these states that the bulk of its assembly members were returned (41 in Madhya Pradesh, 49 in Uttar Pradesh, 8 in the Punjab and 15 in Rajasthan). Elsewhere the results did not match expectations, and the party was also disappointed by its showing in the Delhi Municipal Corporation elections of February 1962 in which it won only 9 of the 80 seats compared with the 24 it had taken in the previous poll in 1958.[28]

In his analysis of the results, Upadhyaya suggested that what he described as 'ideological appeal' had played 'a very insignificant part' so far as the decision of the voter was concerned, and that the Congress 'claimed votes because no other party was big enough and because they alone had a leader of Pandit Nehru's calibre'. He nevertheless considered that Congress was vulnerable:

If the Congress wins it is not because the people like it but only because other political parties have failed organisationally and technically.

With experience and greater understanding and proficiency in the technique of electioneering, we can definitely look forward to a period not in the distant future when the Congress shall be dislodged.[29]

---

[28] The figures for the Delhi Municipal Corporation elections are from *Times of India* (Delhi), 8 March 1962, p. 3. See also Geeta Puri, *Bharatiya Jana Sangh: Organisation and Ideology: Delhi: a Case Study* (New Delhi, 1980), pp. 154–60.

[29] *Organiser*, 28 May 1962, pp. 2–4, 14 and 16, quotations from pp. 3 and 14.

Every minor party trying to make its way forward against the established mass and inertia of a major party, especially one with the apparent solidity of the Congress Party, is bound to reassure itself about the inevitability of a crisis which will transform the terms of party competition, rewarding those who are weak and humbling those who are strong. The danger with such wishful thinking is that it prevents the leaders of minor parties from seeing their major rivals for what they are, and analysing their strengths and weaknesses realistically. This was the case with the Jana Sangh. Its leaders and intellectuals placed too much weight on the notion that the party system in the 1950s expressed philosophical and cultural norms, and therefore that the Congress Party in some sense depended upon the respect given to pluralist and western ideas about society and the polity; it followed from this that Congress dominance would be undermined by the development of the basic conflict between Hindu nationalism, grounded upon Indian traditions, and communism, with its stress on collectivism and control as a means of achieving a new order.

Why did the Congress Party win elections so easily in this period? One factor, which both Madhok and Upadhyaya had acknowledged, was Nehru's attraction as a leader. There is a sense in which the three great victories of the Congress, in 1951–52, 1957 and 1962, were rallies of the people around his political personality and therefore, in very general terms, for the liberal, humanitarian and secular ideals in which he believed. However, although there were many Congressmen who shared those ideals, it would be wrong to assume that the party, in the sense of the mass of its local candidates and leaders, was an expression of them; the Congress was then the largest avenue to political advancement and influence and, without a great deal of discrimination, it absorbed a wide variety of ambitious people into its ranks; Nehru and his colleagues were obviously intent on ensuring that all Congressmen respected certain principles but the party's sudden shift into mass politics in the 1950s forced it to rely, for its election candidates and workers, on the diversity of groups which had built up around its local leaders during the nationalist movement.

A second factor was the Congress Party's ability to gather and distribute campaigning resources which were quite beyond the means of the opposition parties. It operated like a huge electoral machine, supporting its candidates with a seemingly unlimited supply of funds, workers and campaign literature. It showed no real interest in building up the local standing of its sitting members or in establishing particular zones of 'safe' seats; in any one general election it expected to lose large numbers of seats and to compensate for these losses by capturing equally large numbers of constituencies previously held by Independents or by the opposition parties. The effect of this approach was a massive turnover of seats and, certainly in the northern states, the obliteration of the underlying electoral geography.

As we have noted, Upadhyaya had tried to ensure that Jana Sangh candidatures were based on previously established networks of branches and party work, but one has the impression that the geographical focus of the campaign effort was far too diffuse. The party settled upon the northern states because these were the ones which contained its strongest units and, presumably, its most obvious initial support, but it appears to have underestimated the difficulty of making any serious headway against the highly organized Congress campaigns in this region. With hindsight, we can suggest that the party might have been better advised to concentrate on particular areas and to build up bases from which later expansion could have been attempted. Yet, as we shall see, in Uttar Pradesh and Madhya Pradesh it tried to equal the coverage of the Congress Party, and, no match for its immensely powerful rival, it inevitably dispersed its resources in the process.

We saw in Chapter 4 that the result of the leadership-succession crisis of 1954 was to place Upadhyaya, as General Secretary, in virtual command of the party and to determine that the party would adopt a relatively exclusive position, relying on the future potential of a young leadership group rather than on the older middle-class leadership that Mookerjee had personified. It is not surprising to find, therefore, that Upadhyaya and the younger leaders had a strong sense of the party's separate identity and of the need for it to stand alone, as the potential rallying point for any Hindu nationalist revival. The party's exclusiveness in the 1957 and 1962 elections was reinforced from without by attacks upon its links with the RSS, and its alleged communalism. Even when the Swatantra Party was formed in 1959, with views similar to those of the Jana Sangh on economic questions (if not on the role of English), Upadhyaya treated it with caution and not as a potential ally.

The general strategy, 1962 to 1967

In the 1950s the Jana Sangh's groups in the central parliament and the state legislatures were relatively small and ineffective, although individual personalities, such as Mookerjee and Vajpayee, had been respected for their debating skills. However, after the 1962 poll the party found itself with groups in Parliament and the northern legislatures which were large enough to figure significantly in negotiations and bargaining between the opposition parties; as a result, the party became more aware of the possibility of making alliances for limited purposes

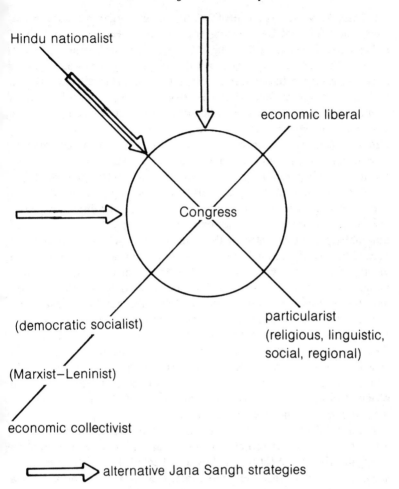

Hindu nationalist

economic liberal

Congress

(democratic socialist)

particularist
(religious, linguistic,
social, regional)

(Marxist–Leninist)

economic collectivist

alternative Jana Sangh strategies

Figure 1. Sectors of opposition to Congress in northern Legislative Assemblies, 1952–67

and, eventually, of joining electoral fronts. We can see this process at work if we look at the party's position in the Legislative Assemblies of the northern states and in the Lok Sabha in the years immediately following the 1962 elections.

In the assemblies of the four states of Uttar Pradesh, Madhya Pradesh, Rajasthan and the Punjab, the alternative approaches open to Jana Sangh groups may be considered with reference to Figure 1. This illustrates how the opposition to Congress was organized around two axes, one produced by differing approaches to economic and social policies and the other by differing ideas of how the state should relate to society. On the socio-economic axis, the Swatantra Party was attacking the Congress from the position of economic liberalism while the CPI and the socialist parties were doing so from the opposite pole, that of economic collectivism; and on the state–society axis, the pressure on Congress from Hindu nationalists in favour of a unitary state expressing Hindu values was balanced by the pressure of parties claiming to represent the interests of regional, social and religious minorities (the Akali Dal in the case of the Sikhs, for example, and the Republican Party of India on behalf of the agricultural labourers and the neo-Buddhist community). By 1962 it was evident that the spread of politics along both axes was developing the framework for a multi-party system, but one dominated from the centre by the Congress Party. It was still open to each of the principal non-Congress parties to hope for a transformation of the system which would leave it the dominant grouping. The Jana Sangh still aspired to become the core of an all-embracing Hindu nationalist rally, but it was now forced to realize that the system would change only by degrees and that the non-Congress parties had therefore to calculate their prospects in terms of alliances and combinations. For the Jana Sangh, the choice was either to join with the Swatantra Party in an exclusive alliance dedicated to the cause of economic liberalism or to aim for a broader grouping with a social-democratic orientation in which it might consider working with some of the socialist parties, though obviously not with the CPI.

Variants of this basic choice faced the Jana Sangh in each of the northern Legislative Assemblies, whose composition by sectors immediately after the 1962 elections is shown in Table 3. In the Uttar Pradesh assembly the Jana Sangh members constituted the largest non-Congress party and their leader, Yadavendra Datt Dube, the Raja of Jaunpur, became Leader of the Opposition, but the existence of several other well-established groups underlined the point that the most likely outcome of further Congress losses would be a coalition government and that the Jana Sangh had to see itself as part of a potential alliance rather than as an independent unit with a good chance of taking power in its own right. This was also the case in the Madhya Pradesh assembly, in which Virendra Kumar Saklecha of the Jana Sangh became Leader of the Opposition, but here the relative weakness of the Swatantra and CPI groups had produced a simpler pattern of alignments. Rather different conditions obtained in the Rajasthan assembly, where the Swatantra group, with 36 members, was the main unit in the opposition rather than

Table 3. *Affiliations of candidates returned in the 1962 general elections to the Legislative Assemblies of the northern states*

	Legislative Assemblies of			
Parties	UP	MP	Rajasthan	Punjab
A. *Congress*	249	142	88	90
B. *Opposition parties by sectors*				
(i) economic liberal				
Swatantra Party	15	2	36	3
(ii) Hindu nationalist				
Jana Sangh	49	41	15	8
Hindu Mahasabha	2	6	0	0
Rama Rajya Parishad	0	10	3	0
(iii) democratic socialist				
Praja Socialist Party	38	33	2	0
Socialist Party (Lohia)	24	14	5	4
(iv) Marxist–Leninist				
Communist Party of India	14	1	5	9
(v) particularist				
Republican Party of India	7	0	—	0
Akali Dal	—	—	—	19
Haryana Lok Samiti	—	—	—	3
C. *Independents*	32	39	22	18
Totals	430	288	176	154

Source: Legislative Assembly, Table 3, Candidates According to Parties, in Government of India, Election Commission of India, *Report on the Third General Elections in India 1962*, II (New Delhi, 1963), pp. 80–1, amended to include results in uncontested seats.

The Republican Party and Independent totals for Uttar Pradesh given in this source are 8 and 31 respectively, an error arising from an incorrect classification of an independent as a Republican Party MLA.

the Jana Sangh, with 15 members, and there was the additional complication that the Congress Party's grip on power was insecure; with 88 MLAs in a house of 176 members it was forced to recruit an Independent member to reinforce its majority and enable the retiring Chief Minister, Mohanlal Sukhadia, to form another government. In this situation, the Jana Sangh had to co-operate with the Swatantra Party so that any weakness on the Congress side could be exploited and a coalition government formed at short notice if the opportunity arose.

The party's position in the Punjab Legislative Assembly was equally complicated. In this state the 1962 elections gave the Congress a good majority, with 90 of the 154 seats, and further strengthened the Chief Minister, Pratap Singh Kairon, whose policies had aroused intense criticism from various quarters. However, the opposition groups which faced him in the assembly were divided amongst themselves, and there was little common ground between the two largest groups, the Akali Dal, with 19 members, and the Progressive Independent Party, credited with an initial membership of 22 members and led by Chaudhari Devi Lal, a former Congress leader from the Haryana region.[30] Devi Lal wanted to form a united front of opposition parties to harass the Kairon ministry but the Jana Sangh group of eight members responded cautiously.[31] In the case of the Punjab, indeed, the Jana Sangh was initially very reluctant to accept that its chances of sharing in government depended on alliances with other non-Congress groups and it was especially wary of agreeing to any course of action which would give an advantage to the Akali Dal, to whose demands for the advancement of the Punjabi language it was strongly opposed.

In the central parliament Congress remained in a strong position after the 1962 elections; it won 361 of the 494 elective seats in the Lok Sabha, and Jawaharlal Nehru was able to form another government without any difficulty. Among the opposition groups within the Lok Sabha were the Jana Sangh with 14 members, Swatantra with 18 and the CPI with 29. Although the Jana Sangh's Central Working Committee had decided that the party should not enter into alliances with other political parties in either the state legislatures or the Lok Sabha,[32] it was obvious that its parliamentary group would have to consider co-operation with the Swatantra members and possibly with other groups as well if it was to present any serious challenge to the Congress government. The opportunity to do so came much sooner than anyone had expected, for the Nehru ministry's prestige was damaged by the Chinese invasion of India's northern border at the end of 1962, and in May 1963 Congress lost three in a group of four parliamentary by-elections, in each case to a well-known and vocal opposition leader. Ram Manohar Lohia (Socialist) was returned in Farrukhabad (UP), J.B. Kripalani (Independent) in Amroha (UP) and M.R. Masani in Rajkot (Gujarat); only in Jaunpur (UP) was the Congress candidate returned, defeating the Jana Sangh's General Secretary, Deendayal Upadhyaya. Some observers saw in these losses the beginning of the long-awaited collapse of the Congress Party, and serious consideration was given to the possibility of building an opposition alliance to hasten the process. A proposal to amalgamate the Praja Socialist Party and the Socialist Party was under discussion at this time and on 1 June 1963 J.B. Kripalani raised the broader issue of

---

[30] *Statesman* (Delhi), 16 March 1962, p. 1; *Hindustan Times* (Delhi), 15 March 1962, p. 12.

[31] See special correspondent, Chandigarh, 'Punjab's new face', II, *Hindustan Times*, 6 April 1962, p. 7.

[32] The decision was taken at a meeting on 3–4 March (staff reporter, *Times of India* (Delhi), 5 March 1962, p. 8).

opposition unity in the course of a speech which he gave at an All-India Socialist Unity Conference at Lucknow. Having expressed the hope that a fusion of the socialist parties would prepare the way for the united action of all democratic parties opposed to Congress, he advocated an electoral alliance of these parties and adherence to a limited common programme.[33] His intention was evidently to exclude the CPI from the proposed combination, to build on the principle that the combined parties should nominate only one candidate between them in each constituency at the next elections, and to add items to the programme

from time to time with common consent to bring the parties progressively nearer each other till they coalesce, or at least a powerful coalition that can take over the reins of the Government becomes possible.

He also hoped that there would be discussion of his proposed programme and that it would be adopted at a meeting of the leaders of the 'democratic opposition parties'.[34]

The first reaction to Kripalani's scheme was unfavourable. On 10 June the delegates at the Praja Socialist Party's national conference at Bhopal adopted a resolution on the political situation which proposed that the PSP should challenge the Congress government independently on the basis of a radical ten-point programme and suggested that the 'deepening of the crisis' was 'likely to help the forces of reaction like the Swatantra Party and Jana Singh [sic] that stand opposed to planned economic development and creation of an egalitarian society'.[35] By contrast, the Jana Sangh's Central Working Committee expressed its willingness to work for common action and regretted that 'at this hour of national crisis, the PSP should have thought it fit, by its Bhopal resolution, to mar this spirit of cooperation'.[36] Two months later, during the monsoon session of the Lok Sabha, Kripalani moved a motion expressing want of confidence in the Council of Ministers and, although the motion was defeated by 346 votes to 61,[37] opposition spokesmen were able to represent the debate as the first step in a concerted move

---

[33] *National Herald* (Lucknow), 2 June 1963, pp. 1 and 8. See also Kripalani, 'The minimum programme', *Swarajya* (Madras), VIII, 1 (6 July 1963), p. 3; 2 (13 July 1963), p. 3; 3 (20 July 1963), p. 2; and 'Unity of the democratic opposition', *Organiser*, 15 August 1963, p. 7.

[34] 'The minimum programme', *Swarajya*, VIII, 3 (20 July 1963), p. 2.

[35] *Janata* (Bombay), XVIII, 21 (16 June 1963), p. 9. See also *Statesman* (Delhi), 10 June 1963, p. 7; 11 June 1963, p. 7.

[36] Central Working Committee, Allahabad, 13 June 1963, *BJS Documents*, IV, p. 182.

[37] *P.D., L.S.* (Third Series), XIX, 22 August 1963, cc. 2235–40. The chief Jana Sangh spokesman, U.M. Trivedi, is listed amongst those who voted against the motion, but he supported it strongly in his contribution to the debate (*ibid.*, 20 August 1963, cc. 1546–60).

against the government. Upadhyaya not only approved of the common
action but wrote as though he expected the informal alliance to lead at
some stage to a governmental alliance:

The Opposition had an easy time during the debate, but it will be on trial now
after the debate. Will they come nearer or drift farther apart? The leaders in the
opposition can definitely fulfil the part that they are destined to, if they take up
the challenge of the changing times.

It is a practical question and needs a commonsense answer. Let us hope that
informal get-together of these different opposition parties, that has so long
served, will, in the future also, evolve some formula for a joint working and forge
an alternative to the present Government.[38]

In the months which followed, various efforts were made to give
substance to the alliance. There were discussions between the parties in
the central parliament and Vajpayee, now a member of the Rajya Sabha
and the leader of the Jana Sangh's parliamentary group, told a news
conference on 10 November 1963 that further efforts would be made to
form a united parliamentary group of the non-Communist opposition
parties on the basis of a common programme.[39] An amalgamation of
some of the parties was also seriously considered; according to one
account, a proposal for the merger of the Jana Sangh and the Swatantra
Party had actually been accepted at a meeting of representatives of both
parties in New Delhi in September 1963, only to be shelved by a meeting
of the Jana Sangh's Central Working Committee in December.[40] In
January 1964, however, a scheme for a national democratic front
consisting of the Swatantra Party, the Jana Sangh, the Praja Socialist
Party and the Lohia Socialists was being canvassed and Balraj Madhok
took the view that, as far as Swatantra and the Jana Sangh were
concerned, a merger would be advisable:

If parties remain separate, strains and stresses are bound to be there. So in the
long run complete merger and setting up of a national democratic party is the
only solution which can provide an alternative pole to the people. This cannot be
done on the basis of joint actions on specific issues.[41]

Various schemes, including ones for co-operation and merger, were then
put to the state units of the Swatantra Party and the Jana Sangh; the

---

[38] 'This is the beginning of the end of this govt.', *Organiser*, 26 August 1963, p. 1.
[39] At Madras, 10 November (*Statesman* (Delhi), 13 November 1963, p. 5). Cf. his
statement of 17 November (*ibid.*, 18 November 1963, p. 7).
[40] Manga Ram Varshney, *Jana Sangh–R.S.S. and Balraj Madhok* (Aligarh, n.d.), pp. 22–
3. The Central Working Committee meeting was held on 25–27 December 1963, prior
to the 11th national session at Ahmedabad, on 28–30 December 1963.
[41] *Pioneer*, 14 January 1964, p. 5.

Punjab units of both parties supported the idea of a merger[42] but the Swatantra leaders were so discouraged by the general lack of response that they decided to concentrate instead on the much more limited objective of negotiating electoral understandings with the other parties as well, a policy approved by the national Swatantra convention at Bangalore at the beginning of February 1964.[43] The Jana Sangh followed this lead, and on 7 February Vajpayee explained that the Swatantra, Jana Sangh and Socialist Parties had agreed in principle to have electoral adjustments in future polls in order to avoid multi-cornered contests and to work together on specific issues inside and outside the legislatures.[44]

Later in the year the Jana Sangh and the Swatantra Party disagreed about what policies the Union government should pursue in its dealings with Pakistan over the Kashmir issue. In April 1964, M.R. Masani, the Swatantra General Secretary, spoke in favour of fresh elections to the Kashmir assembly as a prelude to talks between a new Kashmir government and the Government of India about the future of the state; he also claimed that a reunification of Kashmir would improve relations between India and Pakistan,[45] an approach with little appeal for the Jana Sangh. In July Masani said that his party would have no truck with the Jana Sangh unless it changed its policies regarding Pakistan and Kashmir[46] and Upadhyaya's reply made it clear that the disagreement was a serious one.[47] The prospects for even an electoral alliance between the two parties now appeared to be very remote.

At about this time, the Jana Sangh in the Punjab was drawn into a united front directed against the Chief Minister, Pratap Singh Kairon. The leader of the front was Devi Lal, and the charges which he and his colleagues had made against Kairon had been investigated by a commission of inquiry, which finally reported to the Prime Minister on

---

[42] *Statesman* (Delhi), 23 January 1964, p. 7; *Hindustan Times*, 23 January 1964, p. 5.

[43] See reports of statements by Masani in *Statesman* (Delhi), 24 January 1964, p. 7, and *Hindustan Times*, 31 January 1964, p. 6. For the text of the Bangalore convention resolution ('Electoral understandings') see *Swarajya*, VIII, 33 (15 February 1964), p. 18. See also a letter to the editor from Masani (dated 8 February, from Bombay) in *Times of India* (Delhi), 11 February 1964, p. 6.

[44] *Organiser*, 17 February 1964, pp. 3 and 15; *Statesman* (Delhi), 8 February 1964, p. 1. See also *Patriot* (Delhi), 9 February 1964, p. 4.

[45] Statement on 13 April in New Delhi (*Statesman* (Delhi), 14 April 1964, p. 4).

[46] *Ibid.*, 9 July 1964, p. 7.

[47] *Organiser*, 20 July 1964, p. 2. For a reply by Masani see *ibid.*, 3 August 1964, p. 12, and for a note by Upadhyaya see *ibid.*, 10 August 1964, p. 4. For a detailed analysis of the relations between the Jana Sangh and the Swatantra Party in 1963–64, see H.T. Davey, 'The transformation of an ideological movement into an aggregative party: a case study of the Bharatiya Jana Sangh' (Unpublished D.Phil. dissertation, University of California, Los Angeles, 1969), pp. 236–52.

11 June 1964. Kairon resigned office on the 15th amidst press speculation that he had been criticized by the commission, and he was replaced as Chief Minister by another Congressman, Ram Kishan. Devi Lal then tried to keep the united front in being and in July 1964 the opposition leaders agreed to fight the next elections with a common programme and a joint manifesto, a scheme which was further discussed in August at a convention.[48] The fragility of the understanding was revealed later when one of the principal non-Congress groups, the Akali Dal, revived its demand for a separate Sikh state, whereupon Devi Lal turned to support the idea of a Hindi-speaking state based on the Haryana region and the Jana Sangh took up the cause of keeping the Punjab united.[49]

Although the negotiations to form united fronts had broken down by the autumn of 1964 in both national and Punjab politics, the Jana Sangh had by this stage reluctantly accepted that its ambition to become a major party was unrealistic, at least in the short term, and that the best means of defeating the Congress lay in some form of co-operation with other parties. The issue for its intellectuals then became whether the Jana Sangh should at some stage remake its alliance with the Swatantra Party and form an exclusive national democratic front or party, or whether it should take part in forming a broad non-Congress bloc with a centre-left orientation. The latter possibility had been explored by Upadhyaya in an article published in November 1963, in which he distinguished three intersecting sets of Indian parties (democratic, nationalist and socialist) and sought to explain how their relationships were affected by these divisions. His central argument was that India under Congress rule was changing from democratic socialism to totalitarian socialism and that only a combination of democratic and nationalist forces could reverse this trend. In considering with which parties the Jana Sangh could reasonably co-operate, he judged the Praja Socialist Party and the Socialist Party to be democratic socialist rather than simply socialist in character but noted that they had taken nationalism for granted until very recently, while he regarded the Swatantra Party as lacking in nationalism and compared its economic and social doctrines unfavourably with those of the Jana Sangh:

The Swatantra Party is non-socialist to the extent of opposing all acts of the Government that seek to change the *status quo* in an effort to better the lot of the under-privileged. The Jana Sangh is non-socialist so far as it does not subscribe to the totalitarian concept of socialism but it definitely stands for social justice,

---

[48] *Statesman* (Delhi), 12 July 1964, p. 5; 21 July 1964; p. 4; 9 August 1964, p. 5.

[49] See *ibid.*, 4 October 1965, p. 12, on the Chandigarh convention convened by Devi Lal, who was Chairman of the Haryana Action Committee (*ibid.*, 10 October 1965, p. 1).

reduction of inequalities, changing of the *status quo* in most matters. By non-socialism it does not mean capitalism of *laissez faire* variety.

Having dismissed the Communist Party as 'wholly socialist and therefore neither democratic nor nationalist', he claimed that the nationalism of the Jana Sangh was more authentic than that of other parties because, whereas they considered that the Indian nation was still in the making, the Jana Sangh believed that Bharat had been a nation 'from times immemorial'.[50]

Upadhyaya had proposed a theory of the party system which took serious account of the philosophical dimensions of Indian politics. Instead of depicting the Congress Party as an amorphous centre he represented it as a replica of the regime which it had created, more socialist than democratic, and committed by its nature to extending further the bureaucratic and economic scope of the state. The Jana Sangh he saw as not only democratic and nationalist but as being significantly closer to the social democratic parties than it was to Swatantra as far as social and economic policies were concerned. Upadhyaya's general themes about the compatibility of democracy and material progress in India were carried further in the important party document, *Principles and Policy*, which he had helped to draft and which was adopted by the meeting of the party's Central General Council at Vijayawada in January 1965. He used the term 'integral humanism' to describe the ethical views which he ascribed to his party.[51] In his writings, the Jana Sangh was presented as a centre party open to ideas of reform and improvement as well as to those of nationalism and political liberalism.

The years immediately preceding the fourth general elections of 1967 saw significant changes in the major units of the party system and altered to some degree the pattern of relations which Upadhyaya had been considering. The Congress itself was shaken by two leadership-succession crises, the first following the death of Nehru on 27 May 1964 and the second that of his successor, Lal Bahadur Shastri, on 11 January 1966. The first crisis was resolved without any serious division in the party but the second, which was relatively unexpected, saw a brief rivalry between Morarji Desai, a senior Congressman, and Nehru's daughter, Mrs Indira Gandhi. She was eventually elected leader of the Congress

---

[50] 'National Democrats[,] Democratic Socialists & National Socialists', *Organiser*, 15 November 1963, pp. 21–2, quotations from p. 22. Some of the points in this article were made earlier by Upadhyaya in 'Your vote (3): changers and no-changers', 11 December 1961, in Upadhyaya, *Political Diary*, pp. 129–32.

[51] Bharatiya Jana Sangh, *Principles and Policy* [New Delhi, 1965]. See also Upadhyaya, *Integral Humanism* (New Delhi, n.d.), containing four lectures given by Upadhyaya in Poona in April 1965.

Parliamentary Party and then became Prime Minister, but it was by no means clear, immediately after these events, that she would inherit her father's considerable popular following. In addition, she faced policy problems of the first magnitude. It had become clear by 1966 that the rupee was seriously overvalued in relation to other major world currencies and that this was a restraint upon India's export industries, and in June the Government of India was obliged to devalue the exchange rate of the rupee. Finally, uncertainty about the availability of domestic and international resources for Indian development created further difficulties, and in November 1966 the Planning Commission announced that the preparation of the Fourth Five-Year Plan would be delayed. At the time of the 1962 elections, the Congress Party had shown complete confidence in its ability to stimulate and direct the country's economic development, but as it prepared for the 1967 contest it gave the impression of being confused and tentative about its basic policies. For the first time since independence, the ruling party was vulnerable to criticism and controlled opposition.

There were also changes on the left of the party spectrum. A group broke away from the CPI in 1964 to form a CPI (Marxist), which showed particular strength in West Bengal and a disposition to be more radical in its strategic thinking than the older party had been. In the same year an attempt had been made to effect a merger of the Praja Socialist Party and the Socialist Party but this ended in failure; the Praja Socialists resumed their independent existence and the former Socialists remained with the new Samyukta Socialist Party (SSP).

A number of non-Congress leaders, such as Ram Manohar Lohia of the SSP, tried to persuade the opposition parties to form electoral alliances without at the same time aiming for comprehensive policy agreements, but the Jana Sangh was still disposed to consider itself to be an independent force with its own identity. It was apparently satisfied with the Election Commission's decision to define it as a Multi-State Party, which meant that the *dipak* symbol was not only available to Jana Sangh candidates where the party was recognized, as in northern states, but also, on application, in states where its weak electoral performance in the past did not justify recognition, as in the south.[52] In geographical terms, it again concentrated its resources in the Hindi-speaking heartland and again gave permission to its local units 'to arrive at adjustments with other parties so that mutual contests may be avoided'. However, in endorsing this approach, the party's Central General Council excluded 'any sort of alliance with the Communist Parties' but

---

[52] See Election Commission of India, *Report on the Fourth General Elections in India 1967*, I, *General* (New Delhi, 1968), pp. 27–39.

approved general arrangements for sharing seats with the Swatantra Party in particular states.[53]

Polling took place in February 1967 and set in motion a complicated flow of events. The Congress won the Lok Sabha elections, returning 283 members to a house of 520, and Mrs Gandhi was then able to form another government at the centre, but in the parallel Legislative Assembly elections the Congress lost a great deal of ground to the opposition parties. The Jana Sangh improved considerably on the levels of support it had achieved in the 1962 elections. Its most striking advance occurred in Delhi, where it won 52 of the 100 seats in the Municipal Corporation and 33 of the 56 elective seats in the Metropolitan Council.[54] In the Lok Sabha elections it won 9.35 per cent of the votes and returned 35 members, and in the assembly elections it obtained 8.77 per cent of the votes and 268 seats, including good numbers in the northern states (98 in Uttar Pradesh, 78 in Madhya Pradesh, 26 in Bihar, 22 in Rajasthan, 12 in Haryana and 9 in the Punjab).

Once the elections were over, the Congress Party tried hard to hold on to power at the state level, while the opposition parties strove to form alliances sufficiently broad and stable to anchor coalition governments. The Jana Sangh's main interest was in the northern tier of states running from the Punjab and Rajasthan in the west to Bihar and West Bengal in the east. In Delhi, the secure Jana Sangh majorities on the corporation and the council enabled it to form an administration in its own right, but elsewhere its assembly groups were simply units in widely extended and uncoordinated non-Congress blocs and needed immediate advice on how to proceed in negotiations. The first guidance came from the party's Central Parliamentary Board, which directed the units in Bihar, Uttar Pradesh, the Punjab and Rajasthan to assist in the formation of non-Congress governments[55] but left unresolved the difficult question of whether they should work with members of the two Communist parties to this end. Before the elections, the Central General Council had spoken of extending 'the hands of cooperation to other national democratic opposition parties in those states where they may strive to form

[53] *BJS Documents*, IV, pp. 192–3. In this source the resolution is attributed to the Central Working Committee, Nagpur, 2 November 1966, but the authority cited in the text is the Central General Council, which met at Nagpur from 3 to 6 November 1966. In his subsequent report on the 1967 elections, Upadhyaya stated that arrangements were made with the Swatantra Party in Gujarat, Orissa, Rajasthan and Haryana but that attempts made in Bihar and Uttar Pradesh were unsuccessful (*Organiser*, 23 April 1967, p. 8).

[54] *Statesman* (Delhi), 25 February 1967, p. 4; *Hindustan Times*, 23 February 1967, p. 3. See also Puri, *Bharatiya Jana Sangh*, pp. 160–9.

[55] *Hindustan Times*, 1 March 1967, p. 1.

Government',[56] which clearly implied the exclusion of the Communists from any such endeavour. However, the party's Central Working Committee decided in mid-March that its units in Bihar and West Bengal should be exempted from the restrictions against joining coalitions containing Communists[57] and from this point onwards the bar was practically ignored.

In the weeks immediately following the 1967 elections, the Jana Sangh either joined or supported several of the northern non-Congress governments which were formed. In Bihar, the coalition government set up by Mahamaya Prasad Sinha included two ministers and one minister of state from the party and in the Punjab the initial United Front cabinet under Gurnam Singh contained the Jana Sangh leader, Baldev Prakash, and also a member of the CPI. Then, in quick succession, defections cost Congress its control of government in Haryana and Uttar Pradesh, and in these states also broad non-Congress coalitions were formed. In Haryana, the Jana Sangh did not accept representation in the ministry but offered its support in the legislature; in Uttar Pradesh it contributed five ministers and three deputy ministers to the administration formed by Charan Singh, who had broken with the Congress to establish a new party, the Jana Congress. The Uttar Pradesh coalition also contained two CPI representatives, one a minister and the other a deputy minister.

Almost of necessity, therefore, the Jana Sangh found itself going well beyond its earlier consideration of a national-democratic alliance which excluded the Communists and accepting what was in effect a united-front alliance of all the non-Congress parties. This participation in the various northern governments came under criticism at a meeting of the party's Central General Council in April 1967. Some delegates argued that the party should have kept clear of coalitions altogether and continued to aim at a majority of its own in the legislatures; others that it should at least have avoided joining coalitions which contained Communists. A reference to the party's conditional-support strategy in Haryana prompted Vajpayee to reveal that this approach had been considered in both Uttar Pradesh and Bihar as well:

Even though the Jana Sangh was the largest single group in the Opposition in U.P., it had suggested to Shri Charan Singh that he might form his Government *without* the Jana Sangh. The Jana Sangh had assured him full support from outside. Shri Charan Singh point-blank refused to accept the suggestion and said that he could not contemplate a non-Congress Government in U.P. without the Jana Sangh. A similar situation developed in Bihar too.[58]

---

[56] *BJS Documents*, IV, pp. 192–3, quotation from p. 192. On the dating and attribution of this resolution see n. 53 above.

[57] *Hindustan Times*, 16 March 1967, p. 16.

[58] *Organiser*, 30 April 1967, pp. 4 and 15. See also *Times of India* (Delhi), 23 April 1967, pp. 1 and 9; *Hindustan Times*, 23 April 1967, p. 7.

Both Vajpayee and Krishan Lal, secretary of the Punjab unit, emphasized that the political situation had been greatly changed by the election results and that the party had to adapt itself to new circumstances, even if this meant participation in coalitions and co-operation with Communists. The council then adopted a resolution which justified the formation of coalition governments by non-Congress parties where no single party had been able to obtain a clear majority:

The formation of these governments has been in deference to the popular sentiment, and fully in conformity with democratic traditions. Despite its ideological and policy differences with the other opposition parties, the Jana Sangh has agreed to join the governments with them on the basis of a minimum common programme. [59]

However, there were disagreements behind the scenes and Madhok revealed some years later that he had opposed the policy of joining coalitions which contained Communists.[60]

The period from 1962 to 1967, therefore, had shown the first signs that the Jana Sangh's young leaders who had taken control of the party in 1955 were beginning to weigh up the relative advantages of different strategies. As early as 1963, Upadhyaya had shown an interest in the possibility of taking the party more towards the centre of party alignments, from where it could have formed conditional ties with the Socialist parties, but others were equally interested in having the party keep well to the right and eventually link up with Swatantra in what was described as a National Democratic front. However, such considerations of strategy appear to have had little practical effect on the arrangements which the party's state units made for the fourth general elections. As a result, more because of inertia than because of deliberate choice, the Jana Sangh entered this contest with dispositions very much like those it had made for the 1957 and 1962 elections; once more it tried to cover all regions in Uttar Pradesh and Madhya Pradesh, instead of concentrating its resources in areas where they would have had most effect and making use of the opportunities for electoral alliances which had opened up so dramatically in the late 1960s. It is true that these elections yielded bigger

---

[59] Central General Council, Delhi, 21 April 1967, *BJS Documents*, IV, pp. 196–7, quotation from p. 196.

[60] See letter from Madhok to S.S. Bhandari, 23 November 1972, from New Delhi, in Varshney, *Jana Sangh – R.S.S. and Balraj Madhok*, p. 106; letter from Madhok to L.K. Advani, 7 March 1973, in *ibid.*, p. 138; a summary of a letter from Madhok circulated to Jana Sangh workers in March 1973 in *Times of India* (Delhi), 30 March 1973; and Madhok, *Murder of Democracy* (New Delhi, 1973), pp. 76–7. See also Madhok, *Stormy Decade (Indian Politics) 1970–1980* (Delhi, second edition, 1982), pp. 203–4; *R.S.S. and Politics* (New Delhi, 1986), pp. 60–1. For an extended account of these coalition arrangements, see Davey, 'A case study of the Bharatiya Jana Sangh', pp. 274–93.

gains in both seats and votes than the party had achieved in 1962 but only in Delhi were the groups of representatives big enough to give the party a commanding position in the formation of administrations; elsewhere, as in Uttar Pradesh and Madhya Pradesh, it was forced to tolerate what were effectively united-front alliances, involving degrees of accommodation and compromise in policy which it had not contemplated before the elections.

The electoral position of the Jana Sangh in the northern states

We must now look in more detail at the extent and solidity of the Jana Sangh's electoral performance in the northern area over the course of the first four general elections of 1951–52, 1957, 1962 and 1967. First, we shall examine the distribution of the party's candidatures and support by regions within the north in order to identify general patterns and trends, and then we shall discuss particular features of the party's electoral strategies in three places of particular interest, namely, the western part of Madhya Pradesh, the Punjab and Uttar Pradesh.

To facilitate comparisons of results over time, the area composed of the modern states of the Punjab, Haryana, Uttar Pradesh, Rajasthan and Madhya Pradesh has been divided into a set of 19 political regions (see Map 1), excluding the Union Territories of Delhi and Chandigarh. The returns for Legislative Assembly contests have been aggregated within these regions for all four elections and have been used to prepare two series of maps; the first of these shows the percentage of seats contested by the Jana Sangh within each region and the second the percentage of the valid votes obtained by the party in those constituencies which it contested in each region (rather than the percentage of all the valid votes cast in each region). The actual figures are given in Appendices III and IV.

The maps for the first elections of 1951–52 are interesting chiefly for what they reveal about the party's pattern of origin. The coverage map shows that, despite the fact that the party's state units had had very little time to prepare for the poll, they managed to find candidates for over 40 per cent of the seats in a surprising number of regions including the Punjab, all the valley regions of Uttar Pradesh, Kotah in Rajasthan, Rewa (corresponding, except for one district, with the then state of Vindhya Pradesh) and Malwa (the southern part of the then state of Madhya Bharat). The vote-share map shows the highest percentages in the regions of Udaipur (37.15 per cent) and Jaipur (24.82 per cent), but it should be remembered that on this occasion the Jana Sangh unit in Rajasthan belonged to an alliance headed by the Kshatriya Mahasabha and these levels should not be taken as indicators of the party's special

Map 1. Northern India: political regions

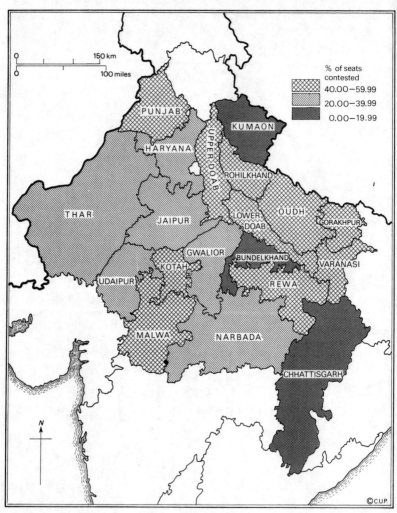

Map 2. Northern India: Jana Sangh percentages of seats contested, by regions, 1951–52

support. Elsewhere the peak of strength in Malwa (23.72 per cent) is supported by levels of between 10 and 20 per cent in several other regions.

The coverage maps for 1957, 1962 and 1967 illustrate the stages in the implementation of the policy of contesting as many seats as possible in both Uttar Pradesh and Madhya Pradesh. The build-up in Uttar Pradesh was the most rapid: already in 1957 the Jana Sangh was contesting over 60 per cent of the seats in the Upper Doab, Lower Doab

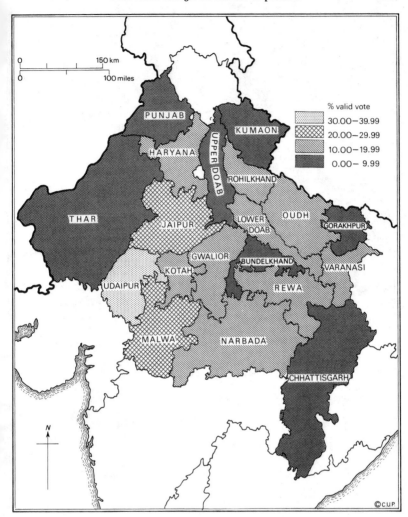

Map 3. Northern India: Jana Sangh vote shares in contested constituencies, 1951–52

and Varanasi regions: in 1962 it was contesting over 80 per cent of the seats in all regions; and in 1967 it sustained this level of activity and achieved complete coverage in the Lower Doab and Varanasi regions. The pace in Madhya Pradesh was slower but by 1967 the 80 per cent level had been exceeded in all regions except Gwalior. This policy of attempting to blanket the two states must have absorbed considerable resources, given the large number of candidates which had to be supported, and we are thus brought back to an earlier question: would

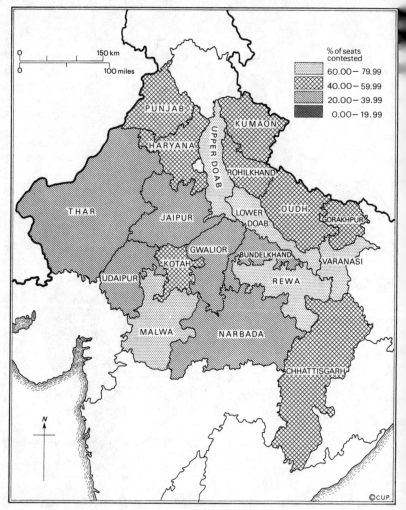

Map 4. Northern India: Jana Sangh percentages of seats contested, by regions, 1957

better results have been obtained (in terms of seats won) had the party concentrated its efforts on those regions where its early shares of the vote had been most encouraging? With this point in mind, let us turn to the vote-share maps and, for the moment, concentrate on the regional pattern within these two states. Given that Indian elections are conducted under the simple-majority method (in both single- and double-member constituencies for the first two general elections and in single-member constituencies from the 1962 elections onwards), and that

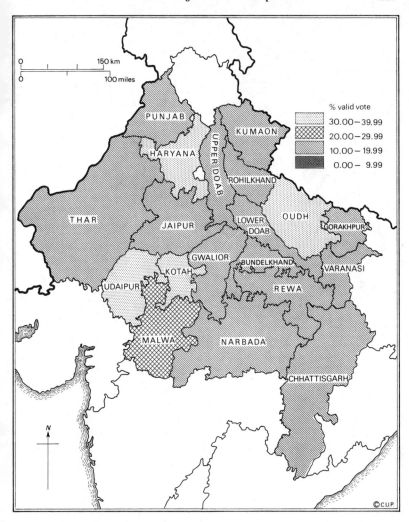

Map 5. Northern India: Jana Sangh vote shares in contested constituencies, 1957

a high proportion of the seats were contested by more than two candidates, it was possible for candidates to win seats with constituency votes of under 50 per cent – and in practice this was often the case. Where parties were concerned, the yield of seats became significant once candidates' vote-shares had risen above the level of 20 per cent and increased rapidly as those vote-shares moved closer to the 50 per cent mark. In interpreting these maps, therefore, we need to pay particular attention to the Jana Sangh's ability to register more than 20 per cent of

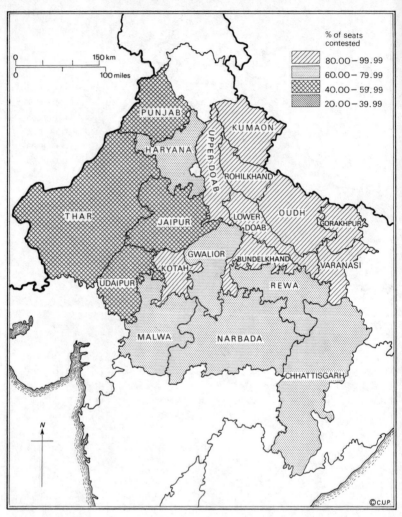

Map 6. Northern India: Jana Sangh percentages of seats contested, by regions, 1962

the votes in contested constituencies and thus to enter the range of support where harvests of seats became a real possibility. In 1957 this level was exceeded only in Malwa and Oudh in the Uttar Pradesh–Madhya Pradesh sector but by 1962 five regions belonged to this category: in the south Malwa had been joined by Narbada and in the north Oudh had been joined by Rohilkhand and Varanasi. It is at least arguable that the Jana Sangh would have achieved better results in 1967

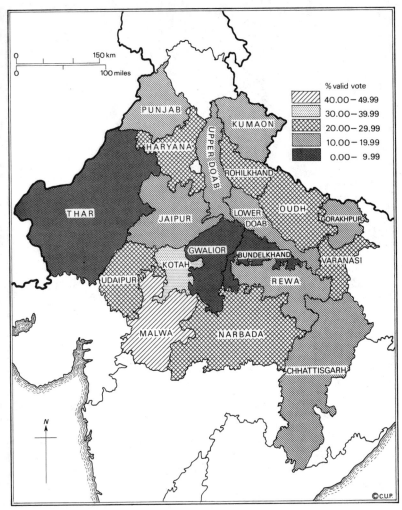

Map 7. Northern India: Jana Sangh vote shares in contested constituencies, 1962

by concentrating on these regions instead of aiming at complete coverage and majority-party status.

In Rajasthan the Jana Sangh's readiness to enter into alliances produced variable and relatively unpredictable patterns. Except in the Kotah region, its rates of coverage were generally low, mainly because it was prepared to participate in attempts to divide up the constituencies between the major non-Congress groups and thus to avoid splitting the

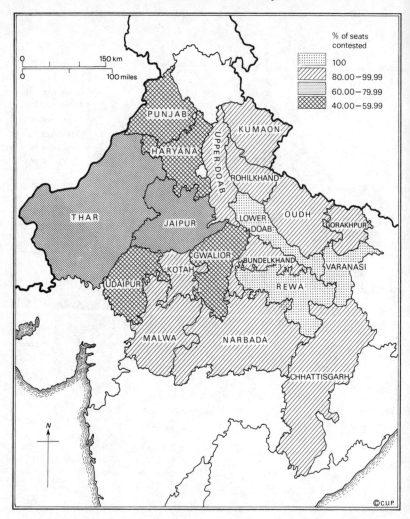

Map 8. Northern India: Jana Sangh percentages of seats contested, by regions, 1967

opposition vote. These agreements to avoid 'multiple contests' became
more efficient and comprehensive as election followed election, and the
relatively systematic apportionment of constituencies between the Jana
Sangh and the Swatantra Party for the 1967 poll explains why the Jana
Sangh's coverage fell so sharply between 1962 and 1967 from 54.79
per cent to 27.03 per cent in the Jaipur region and from 49.06 to 24.14
per cent in the Thar region. The relatively high levels of votes achieved by

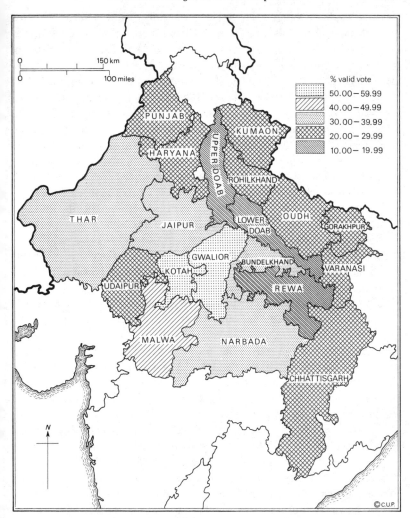

Map 9. Northern India: Jana Sangh vote shares in contested constituencies, 1967

the party in these two regions in 1967 were thus partly due to the Jana Sangh's candidates' receiving votes from Swatantra supporters as well as their own, whereas in the Kotah region they were partly a function of the party's association with the Maharaja of Jhalawar.[61]

The data for the two north-western regions are difficult to interpret

---

[61] Maharaja Harish Chandra of Jhalawar resigned from the Congress Party at the end of 1966 and joined an opposition group known as the Janta Party. Using the Jana

because the Jana Sangh was subject to so many diverse pressures in this area. Firstly, it was associated with the principle of a united Punjab, and therefore found itself pitted against the Akali Dal in the Punjab region and lacking support in Haryana, where regional loyalty has always been strong. Secondly, its roots were strongest amongst the Hindu population of the cities in the Punjab region and it always encountered difficulty in establishing itself in the predominantly rural Haryana area. Similarly, in the Punjab region itself its close association with urban Hindu interests restricted its ability to win support in the rural areas and it is not surprising to find that its coverage rate here remained below the 50 per cent mark; on the other hand, it was able to increase its largely urban support within these limits and its vote-share in contested seats rose from 7.10 to 21.19 per cent between the first and the fourth elections. In Haryana the coverage rate reached a peak of 62.96 per cent in 1962 and then fell back slightly to 59.26 per cent in 1967, well below the rates achieved in the neighbouring regions of Uttar Pradesh; on the other hand, its vote-shares were generally comparable to those obtained by the party in Rohilkhand and Oudh.

Electoral geography tends to raise more questions than it provides answers, and these regional surveys are no exception. To press our enquiry further, therefore, I have selected three cases which should enable us to examine particular issues; firstly, the distribution of the party's voting strength in the regions of Malwa and Gwalior in western Madhya Pradesh; secondly, the electoral problems which the party faced in the Punjab and Haryana regions; and, thirdly, the choice between coverage and concentration as presented in Uttar Pradesh.

Taken together, the Malwa and Gwalior regions generally correspond to the territory of the former state of Madhya Bharat, which was founded on 16 June 1948 after a merger of 25 princely states of the Central India Agency. Although the Congress Party was able to form the first government in the state, its position was by no means secure; it soon divided into factions and was unable to prevent the Hindu Mahasabha and the Jana Sangh from establishing themselves in particular areas. The relative advantage of Congress and its rival parties differed significantly between those territories which had once formed part of the provinces of British India, such as the Punjab and the United Provinces, and those which had been governed by princely states. In the British provinces, Congress had seasoned and experienced organizational units and, in

Sangh's *dipak* symbol, he contested and won the assembly seat of Khanpur but died soon afterwards, on 17 March 1967. The subsequent by-election was won by Maharani Shivkumari of Kotah, who stood as a candidate of the Jana Sangh (see *Statesman* (Delhi), 19 March 1967, p. 11; 30 June 1967, p. 6; 5 July 1967, p. 1).

the rural areas and country towns, had established widespread connections with professional groups, especially lawyers, and with peasant leaders; these it often placed in positions of power and influence, first in district and municipal authorities and later in the provincial legislatures. In the princely areas, however, Congress had had only a limited contact before independence with nationalist groups, mainly through the activities of the States' Peoples' Congress. Consequently, in the early 1950s its organizational units in states such as Madhya Bharat were raw and inexperienced, its connections with local notables were tenuous and untried, and it had not yet built up secure positions for its local leaders in district and municipal bodies. As a result, parties such as the Hindu Mahasabha and the Jana Sangh found it much easier to make headway in the former princely states than in the former British provincial areas. The Madhya Bharat unit of the Jana Sangh was particularly active; it had an energetic and resourceful General Secretary in Kushabhau Thakre and by 1956 he had recruited a membership of more than 10,000 distributed over 203 local committees.[62]

When the Jana Sangh's percentage votes are plotted across constituencies in the Malwa region it becomes clear that the party's support was unevenly distributed and that the areas of high support were usually those where its candidates were well-connected local leaders. One such area coincides generally with the southern districts of West Nimar (Khargone) and Dhar, where the valley of the Narbada River forms a narrow passage between the Satpura Range to the south and the Vindhya Range to the north. In both ranges there are large tracts of forest interspersed with open ground where communities of Bhils and Bhilalas are located. These two groups are classified as Scheduled Tribes and their numbers have justified the reservation of a succession of assembly and parliamentary constituencies in the area for Scheduled Tribe representation. Their demands were taken up at an early stage by Ram Chandra Bade, an advocate from Indore who was elected as a Jana Sangh candidate to the Madhya Bharat Legislative Assembly in 1952 from the double-member seat of Sendhwa, in West Nimar district. In 1953 he was reported to be organizing a delegation on behalf of the tribal people of the area [63] and in 1957 a reporter was impressed by his local standing:

My talks with the local men could not but give the impression that he is widely respected. The story goes round Nimar that he declined in the beginning to stand

---

[62] *Organiser*, August 1956 (special issue), p. 38.
[63] *Statesman* (Delhi), 23 August 1953, p. 4. For a biography of Bade, see Government of India, Lok Sabha Secretariat, *Parliament of India: Fifth Lok Sabha: Who's Who 1971* (New Delhi, 1971), p. 29.

on the plea that he did not have enough funds whereupon his supporters asked him not to worry on that account.[64]

The incorporation of Madhya Bharat within the new state of Madhya Pradesh in 1956 exposed the tribal groups to further administrative pressure. The Forests Department of the new state sought to protect the woodland areas by enforcing regulations intended to prevent local people from taking firewood and timber from existing stands and from occupying without permission lands required for reafforestation. These regulations caused resentment among the tribal groups and the Madhya Pradesh Jana Sangh took up their cause.[65] On 16 July 1962 Bade, claiming that about 200,000 cultivators had been threatened with eviction from lands which they had occupied for the previous ten years, led a demonstration outside the Chief Minister's house in the state capital, Bhopal.[66] The following day the Chief Minister, B.A. Mandloi, and his Minister of Forests announced that a special committee would be appointed to examine the encroachment on forest lands in the West Nimar district and gave an undertaking that persons in possession of such land would not be evicted before the committee had submitted its report.[67] Mandloi was succeeded as Chief Minister by D.P. Mishra, whose government decided in 1964 that a Governor's ordinance should be promulgated to authorize the removal of those who had taken illegal possession of forest lands. In practice, the government chose to keep in force the orders preventing interference with those who had occupied forest lands before July 1962 but to evict all those who had encroached on such lands after the date.[68] The result was a further clash between the authorities and the tribal cultivators; the *Organiser* claimed that in September 1964 the Forests Department and the police had evicted hundreds of families from the forest lands and that when Bade toured the area in October those who associated with him were victimized.[69]

Bade's championship of the tribal people of this area brought him a good measure of support in his bid to gain a place in the Lok Sabha.

---

[64] Staff correspondent, Indore, 'Madhya Pradesh election scene', *Hindustan Times*, 21 February 1957, p. 9.

[65] In November 1960 Upadhyaya commented upon the attention which the President of the Madhya Pradesh Jana Sangh had given in his address to the annual conference of his unit to the grievances of the *Vanavasis* (literally, forest-dwellers) and noted that about 20 per cent of the delegates to that conference were *Vanavasis* ('Madhya Pradesh tribals', 21 November 1960, in Upadhyaya, *Political Diary*, pp. 149–51).

[66] *Times of India* (Delhi), 16 July 1962; *Hindustan Times*, 17 July 1962, p. 5. See also *ibid.*, 11 July 1962, p. 5, and an excellent background piece in 'Madhya Pradesh newsletter', in *Times of India* (Delhi), 2 July 1962.

[67] *Organiser*, 14 December 1964, p. 15.

[68] *Link* (New Delhi), 1 November 1964, p. 15.

[69] *Organiser*, 14 December 1964, p. 15.

Although he lost the Nimar parliamentary contest in 1957, when he polled 40.56 per cent of the votes, he was returned for Khargone in 1962 with 53.15 per cent of the votes. He lost it in 1967, when his share of the votes fell to 43.83 per cent, but regained it against the tide in 1971, with 55.31 per cent of the votes. His reputation must also have helped the party to gather support in the associated and neighbouring assembly constituencies, and the Jana Sangh's share of the votes in those seats which it contested in the two districts rose from 35.60 per cent in 1957 to 54.37 per cent in 1962 before falling to 43.16 per cent in 1967. The party contested 12 of the 14 seats in the two districts in 1957, 11 of the 14 in 1962 and all 15 in 1967; one of its candidates was returned in 1957, all 11 in 1962, and 5 in 1967.

The second area of Jana Sangh concentration within the Malwa region lay immediately to the north of the city of Ujjain in the districts of Mandsaur and Shajapur, situated in the wheat- and cotton-growing part of the state. In Mandsaur the party won 6 of the 7 assembly seats in both the 1962 and 1967 elections and in Shajapur it won 4 of the 5 assembly seats in 1962 and all 5 in 1967. In addition, the parliamentary contests for the Mandsaur seat were won for the Jana Sangh by Umashankar Trivedi in 1962 and by Swatantra Singh Kothari in 1967. In Mandsaur district, the party was undoubtedly fortunate in attracting a number of prominent local people. Besides Trivedi, who had been President of the Nimach Bar Association and a member of the Working Committee of the Madhya Bharat Lawyers' Conference,[70] the party recruited Virendra Kumar Saklecha and Vimalkumar Mannalalji Chordia, both of whom proved to be very successful politicians at the district and state levels.[71] The party's links with particular rural interests may also have been important; the region contained many Rajput (or Thakur) notables who had been affected by the Zamindari Abolition Act and the Abolition of Jagirs Act passed by the Madhya Bharat legislature in 1951. A reporter noted in 1964, referring to Madhya Bharat as a whole, that the Jana Sangh 'has been able to find a social base in the dispossessed thakores [Thakurs]... who are cut off from the main stream of democratic life'.[72]

By contrast with the Malwa region, where it made early gains, the Jana Sangh at first made little headway in the Gwalior region against the strongly entrenched local units of the Hindu Mahasabha and the

[70] Biographical details from Trilochan Singh (ed.), *Indian Parliament (1952–57)* (New Delhi, n.d.), p. 296.

[71] For a biography of Chordia see Government of India, Rajya Sabha Secretariat, *Parliament of India: Rajya Sabha: Who's Who 1966* (New Delhi, 1966), pp. 65–6.

[72] Sunanda K. Datta-Ray, 'Madhya Pradesh' I, *Statesman* (Delhi), 11 May 1964, p. 6.

considerable influence of the former Maharani of Gwalior, Smt. Vijaya Raje Scindia, who was elected as a Congress member to the Lok Sabha in both 1957 and 1962. In the mid-1960s, however, the Jana Sangh's position improved considerably. First came defections from the Hindu Mahasabha: in October 1963 three of the senior Mahasabha leaders in the state announced that they were transferring their allegiance to the Jana Sangh and that several thousand of their followers were shortly to do likewise. One of these leaders was from Bhopal and the other two were from districts in the Gwalior region; the latter were Vrindavan Prasad Tiwari of Guna district, the leader of the Mahasabha's group in the state Legislative Assembly, and Niranjan Varma of Vidisha district, an advocate who had also served as General Secretary and as Vice-President of the All-India Hindu Mahasabha.[73] The second major change to the Jana Sangh's advantage occurred immediately before the 1967 elections when Smt. Vijaya Raje Scindia, having broken with the Congress, made an agreement with the party under which a number of her followers stood as Jana Sangh candidates, while she herself was nominated as a Swatantra candidate for the Lok Sabha and as a Jana Sangh candidate for the state Legislative Assembly. It was later reported that 25 members had been returned to the Legislative Assembly with her support, having stood either as Jana Sangh or Swatantra candidates or as Independents,[74] and a Jana Sangh spokesman admitted that 13 of his party's 75-member group in the new Legislative Assembly had been her candidates.[75] The combined effects of the Mahasabha defections and of the support of Smt. Vijaya Raje Scindia would help to explain why the Jana Sangh's percentage share of the votes in assembly seats which it contested in the region rose from 9.70 in 1962 to 51.58 in 1967.

This survey of the party's activities in the Malwa and Gwalior regions enables us to draw a number of conclusions about the reasons for its relative strength in this part of the north. As noted earlier, this was formerly an area of princely states and had therefore been much less open to the influence of the Congress during the British period than had regions in Uttar Pradesh. This probably explains, too, why local people of influence, such as Smt. Vijaya Raje Scindia in Gwalior and Virendra Kumar Saklecha in Mandsaur, had been much more able to retain their

---

[73] *Statesman* (Delhi), 26 October 1963, p. 7; 10 November 1963, p. 6; *Organiser*, 4 November 1963, p. 9. See also *ibid.*, 28 September 1964, p. 16, for a report of a meeting at Guna at which more than 100 Hindu Mahasabha members joined the Jana Sangh.

[74] *Hindustan Times*, 12 March 1967, p. 10. See also a report of a press conference given by Smt. Vijaya Raje Scindia at Delhi (*Statesman* (Delhi), 16 February 1967, p. 7).

[75] *Hindustan Times*, 18 March 1967, p. 6. Upadhyaya maintained in his report on the elections that four of the nominees of Smt. Vijaya Raje Scindia had won parliamentary contests using the Jana Sangh's symbol (*Organiser*, 23 April 1967, p. 8).

social and economic power than their counterparts in the former British provinces, and were therefore able to deal with political parties on equal terms. Faced with this kind of situation, a party might easily be tempted to accommodate itself to local power structures instead of building up its own relatively disinterested support by appeals to numerically important social groups. This was certainly not the case in West Nimar, where Bade appears to have built up a secure social base for the party, but it may well have been so in Mandsaur and Gwalior.

Recent events in these two regions underline this point. During the Janata period of 1977–80, the former Jana Sangh group was the major partner in the Janata Party in Madhya Pradesh and exercised considerable influence in the state government which took office in June 1977 with Kailash Chandra Joshi as Chief Minister. Joshi gave way to Virendra Kumar Saklecha in January 1978 but he in his turn was succeeded in January 1980 by Sunderlal Patwa, who was also a former Jana Sanghi and also from Mandsaur District. President's Rule was imposed on the state in February 1980 and Congress I (for Congress, Indira) won the subsequent assembly elections in May, but the rivalry between Saklecha and Patwa continued inside the Bharatiya Janata Party (BJP), which had been formed in April 1980 and was in many respects a continuation of the Jana Sangh. Relations between the two men and their supporters had deteriorated to such a point by the end of 1984 that Saklecha chose to leave the party[76] and, in the assembly elections of March 1985, stood as an Independent candidate in the contest for Jawad constituency. He was defeated by his Congress I opponent, but without his support the BJP was at a severe disadvantage. As a reporter remarked after the results were known:

Mr V.K. Saklecha lost the election but he saw to it that the BJP was wiped out in its citadel, the Mandsaur district. That Mr S.L. Patwa, the leader of the Opposition should have lost heavily from his hometown of Manasa, at the hands of a Congress green horn is an eloquent testimony to the damage that Mr Saklecha could cause.[77]

Another train of events had also reduced the importance of the BJP in the Gwalior region. Although Smt. Vijaya Raje Scindia remained as prominent a leader of the BJP as she had been of the Jana Sangh, her influence in Gwalior and its adjacent districts had been limited by that of her son, Madhav Rao Scindia. In December 1979 he became a member

[76] *Statesman* (Delhi), 29 November 1984, p. 4. See also Taroon Coomar Bhaduri, 'M.P. newsletter: shady deeds brought to light', *ibid.*, 14 November 1984, p. 6.
[77] Report by Taroon Coomar Bhaduri, *ibid.*, 9 March 1985, p. 7. Although defeated in Manasa, Patwa was returned to the assembly from Bhojpur seat in Raisen District.

of Congress I and won the parliamentary seat of Guna for that party in the Lok Sabha elections of 1980. Four years later, in the Lok Sabha elections which were held in December 1984 following the assassination of Mrs Gandhi, he was nominated as the Congress I candidate for the Gwalior seat, which had been represented by the BJP, and defeated Vajpayee, then President of the BJP, by more than 175,000 votes in one of the most notable reverses of that poll. In the subsequent state elections of March 1985 the BJP managed to win the constituency based on Gwalior city but it lost heavily in the region as a whole.

The coincidence of Saklecha's defection and of the party's loss of princely influence in Gwalior reduced in one election much of the advantage which the BJP had inherited from the Jana Sangh in these two regions. The high levels of support which the latter party had registered there at the 1967 elections must be considered, not as evidence of a successful and systematic bid for social support but as a by-product of alliances with powerful local leaders, alliances whose continuation depended upon a compatibility of interest between leader and party and on the ability of the leader to fend off challenges to his or her social and economic standing.

The second of our case studies takes us to the Punjab, where the local units of the Jana Sangh had to contend with an entrenched and seasoned Congress Party and also with the Akali Dal, which drew extensive support from the Sikh communities in the region, including those in the territories of PEPSU, composed of former princely states. Although it fought a vigorous campaign, the Jana Sangh failed to make any headway in the 1952 general elections in this part of India; it did not win a single seat in the assembly polls and attracted only 5.56 per cent of the votes in the Punjab state, while in PEPSU it gained only two seats and 3.23 per cent of the votes. A poor result had been predicted beforehand by a correspondent who wrote:

Paradoxically, its dependence on the RSS has proved a source of weakness rather than of strength.

Instead of allowing itself to be guided by the greater political wisdom of the Jana Sangh's Parliamentary Board, the RSS, which is supplying all the workers, has forced on the Board certain nominees whose only claim was their services as volunteers. [78]

Five years later, however, the Punjab Jana Sangh entered the second General Elections with more confidence: according to its General Secretary, Krishan Lal, it was concentrating its attention on 29 assembly seats and a few parliamentary seats in the reorganized state (which

[78] *Ibid.,* 21 December 1951, pp. 1 and 5.

incorporated the former PEPSU area) and it now had some popular heroes such as Yagya Datt Sharma, who in 1956 had fasted in protest against the proposal to divide the state into Hindi- and Punjabi-speaking regions. As Krishan Lal saw the situation:

We had no election experience before and now we have learnt election technique and cannot be outmanoeuvred by the Congress. We have developed leadership not only at provincial level but at district level too. We have many more Sangh members – 92,000 as against 19,000 in 1952.[79]

The results were encouraging: in the assembly elections the party won important urban seats in the western part of the state (Amritsar City East, Amritsar City West, Jullundur City North East and Ludhiana City) and secured the election of 9 candidates in all, despite the fact that its share of the valid votes in the state came to only 8.61 per cent.

In planning for the third general elections in 1962, the party changed its approach in certain important respects. One report mentioned that it was nominating candidates in Sikh and Muslim areas to pave the way for further efforts in future elections, sponsoring Scheduled Caste candidates in reserved constituencies and contesting more seats in the Haryana area and in the northern districts of Kangra, Hoshiarpur and Gurdaspur. The correspondent who made the report also noted that, whereas in 1957 the party had fought in almost equal numbers of urban and rural constituencies, on this occasion it would contest three rural seats to each urban seat. He continued:

in most of the rural constituencies, they will put up local candidates with rural background.

Therefore the party will appear before the electorate not as the urban, Hindu middle class party, which it was last time, but as a party with a much broader base, although the nature of its leadership remains practically unchanged.[80]

Such an attempt to broaden the campaign may have entailed dispersal of effort, because although the assembly results (9.72 per cent of the valid votes and 8 seats) are comparable to those of 1957, the party lost ground in urban areas; it managed to win two seats in Amritsar but was unsuccessful in Jullundur and Ludhiana. On the credit side, it won three parliamentary seats – Karnal, Rohtak and Mahendragarh.

At this stage the Jana Sangh's basic strategy was to build up support in the Hindi-speaking region of Haryana and in the Hindu-majority areas

---

[79] From a special correspondent in Amritsar, 'Punjab election scene', *Hindustan Times*, 12 February 1957, p. 9.
[80] Special representative, Amritsar, 25 December 1961, *Statesman* (Delhi), 26 December 1961, p. 8.

in the western districts, on the mistaken assumption that the Punjab would remain a single unit. The partition of the state in 1966 obliged the party to establish separate units in the two successor states, the Punjab and Haryana, and to work out new and appropriate strategies for each area. During the 1967 campaign, one observer noted that in Haryana the party had adopted the policy of recruiting candidates from the Jat, Ahir, Rajput and Gujar castes as a means of gaining support in rural areas, just as Congress had done in the British period, and he estimated that candidates from these castes constituted 75 per cent of the Jana Sangh's total of nominees and only 33 per cent of the Congress total.[81] In the Punjab, on the other hand, the party again concentrated its attention on Hindu areas in the main cities and worked out an electoral arrangement with the Swatantra Party.[82] The results reflect this difference of approach: in Haryana, where it polled 14.39 per cent of the votes in assembly elections, the Jana Sangh returned one parliamentary member and 12 assembly members from a mixture of urban and rural constituencies whereas in the Punjab, where its share of the assembly vote was 9.84 per cent, it won seven of its assembly seats in the major cities of ▲— ·   ), Ludhiana (2) and Jullundur (2) and also captured the .rliamentary constituency.

advantage of hindsight, we can see that the Jana Sangh was ,resented in the Punjab and Haryana regions with two quite different tasks. In the west, in the Punjab region, its target groups were the Hindus of the large cities of Amritsar, Ludhiana and Jullundur, and it was essentially on their behalf that it resisted the Akali Dal's campaign for a Punjabi Suba, and, in 1965 and 1966, opposed the partition which created the separate states of the Punjab and Haryana. By the 1967 election its identification with the Hindu sectors of these western cities was strong, and, again acting on their behalf, it began to explore the possibility of working with the Akali Dal within the new state. In the Haryana region, the social elements most likely to respond to an anti-Congress approach were the intermediate or backward castes, who constituted the bulk of the peasant farmers of the region, the Jats, Ahirs and Gujars, but the whole weight of the party's state unit was directed towards the campaign for preventing the partition of the state and defending the cause of Hindi, and it neglected to concentrate on direct and intensive appeals to the rural interests of the eastern districts until Haryana became a separate state. In the long run, it was a peasant-based party, the Lok Dal, which effectively captured this rural base in Haryana,

[81] D.P. Kumar, *ibid*, 15 February 1967, p. 7.
[82] On the arrangement with Swatantra, see special correspondent, Chandigarh, 28 January 1967, *Hindustan Times*, 29 January 1967, p. 7.

and used it to win the state elections of June 1987 while the BJP, as the successor to the Jana Sangh, played a relatively minor supporting role.

Whereas in the Punjab and Haryana regions the Jana Sangh pursued relatively limited electoral objectives, in Uttar Pradesh, the third and last of our case studies, the party considered from the outset that it could and would become a major party and it therefore contested as many seats as possible. Although it was aware of the need to build up a social base, the attempt to cover the state entailed what may be termed an 'organizational' approach, designed to construct a widespread net of local workers and managers and to employ that net to gather in a diffuse and heterogeneous anti-Congress vote. 'Election results', in Upadhyaya's words,

depend mainly on organisational strength. Public opinion against the Congress is strong and widespread. But it has got to be organised. It is like steam, which can rise and vanish in the sky or if siphoned properly can move a railway engine.

By 'organisational strength' he evidently meant the existence of committed workers at the base of the party:

We have national leaders enough. What we need are local leaders, the leaders of the street and the village – *'gali ka neta'* and *'gaon ka neta'*, as Shri Yagya Dutt Sharma put it. Our success will be directly proportional to the number and capacity of such leadership. Let us, therefore, not look up to New Delhi but feel our feet in the villages. Jana Sangh has to be in the vanguard of this organisational work.[83]

Before considering particular features of the Jana Sangh's electoral strategy in Uttar Pradesh, it is useful to take stock of the general trends in the party's performance in assembly elections in that state between 1952 and 1967, as set out in Table 4.

Table 4. *Uttar Pradesh: Jana Sangh candidates nominated and returned and percentage vote-shares in Legislative Assembly elections 1952 to 1967*

	General election years			
	1952	1957	1962	1967
Total of seats in state	430	430	430	425
Number of JS candidates	209	236	377	401
Number of JS candidates returned	2	17	49	98
JS percentage of valid vote:				
(a) in all constituencies	6.43	9.84	16.46	21.67
(b) in all constituencies contested by JS candidates	11.43	16.25	18.71	23.00

Source: UP Election Project, University of Sussex

Although the table shows a steadily rising trend of candidates nominated, seats won and votes gained, even by 1967 the levels achieved were well short of those expected of a major party, and since 1967 the Jana Sangh's support in the state has ebbed. Its representation in the Legislative Assembly fell to 49 members after the 1969 elections, rose slightly to 61 after the 1974 poll, and its successor, the Bharatiya Janata Party, won only 11 seats in 1980 and 16 in 1985, still in a house of 425 members. In retrospect, therefore, the Jana Sangh as an electoral force reached its apogee in 1967 and fell away thereafter; it is this first event, the bid for power that failed, that is our immediate concern.

Electoral politics in Uttar Pradesh were exceptionally fluid and unpredictable in the 1950s and 1960s. Both Congress and the non-Congress parties accepted high rates of candidate- and incumbent-turnover as the inevitable consequence of a political system in which attachments between parties and social groups were weak and sitting MPs and MLAs found it difficult to establish enduring local ties. In most parts of the state the abolition of zamindari in the early 1950s had shifted the centre of political gravity to village level, where the power of the landed castes was particularly important, and had thus created a highly segmented and localized pattern which made the linking up of loyalties and support across a constituency very difficult. Furthermore, the gathering of votes had come to resemble the operations of a market, with groups of voters deciding to pool their votes in a 'bank', and to use this capital in bargaining their support for candidates in return for concessions, often through intermediaries or 'brokers'. A candidate might succeed in gathering sufficient banks of votes to win a seat for the first time but, unless he were unusually successful in honouring his election promises, he was likely to be defeated by a more credit-worthy rival when he stood a second time.[84] Faced with such a system, the only general approach open to an ambitious opposition party such as the Jana Sangh was to establish a large number of localized electoral machines throughout the state in the hope that it could succeed in winning a scatter of seats, some of which it was bound to lose at the next polls. Such generalized efforts to cover the state could be expected to build up a widely distributed 'party vote', that is, support for the party

---

[84] On the market aspect of electoral politics, see F.G. Bailey, *Politics and Social Change: Orissa in 1959* (Berkeley, 1963), especially pp. 109–11 and 143–57; and 'Politics and society in contemporary Orissa', in C.H. Philips (ed.), *Politics and Society in India* (London, 1963), pp. 97–114. On the relationship between the high turnover of representatives and the 'negativism of political behaviour', see Surindar Suri, *1962 Elections: A Political Analysis* (New Delhi, 1962), pp. 49–70, especially pp. 50–1 and 64–5.

on principle, which could in time constitute a base sound enough for more controlled campaigns. Having accepted such an approach, which was implicit in its policy of trying to nominate candidates in as many constituencies as possible, the Jana Sangh was obliged to give priority to experimentation, dropping candidates who had failed to win their seats and searching out others deemed to have a chance of success, rather than standing by its tried campaigners in the hope that they would gradually accumulate support. The surprisingly high rate of turnover can be seen from the data in Table 5, which sets out the numbers of candidates and candidatures of the Jana Sangh in general elections in Uttar Pradesh to the Legislative Assembly and to the Lok Sabha between 1952 and 1967. Allowance should be made for the fact that the party was increasing its coverage during this period, and for losses to the pool of past candidates caused by death, illness, migration or changes of allegiance, but even so, the proportion of candidates in each cohort who were standing for the first time – 91 per cent in 1957, 81 per cent in 1962 and 70 per cent in 1967 – suggests that the party continued to place its faith in new blood and to discount experience throughout the period.

Table 5. *Numbers of Jana Sangh candidates and candidatures in assembly and parliamentary general elections in Uttar Pradesh 1952 to 1967*

Categories of candidates and candidatures	General election years			
	1952	1957	1962	1967
First candidature in 1952	248	27	23	14
First candidature in 1957		262	63	39
First candidature in 1962			358	89
First candidature in 1967				336
Total numbers of candidates	248	289	444	478
Additional candidatures	2	8	7	0
Total numbers of candidatures	250	297	451	478

Source: UP Election Project, University of Sussex

What social groups was the Jana Sangh trying to build upon in Uttar Pradesh and with what success? In the towns and cities of the state it was reported to have the backing of traders, small industrialists, some groups of civil servants, and refugees and lower-middle-class groups generally. The existence of this special support could explain why the party's share of the votes was higher in urban than in rural constituencies in the northern states as a whole from the first elections onwards,[85] but there remains the problem of why the proportion did not rise at a faster rate and reach a higher level by 1967.

According to the 1961 Census the urban population in Uttar Pradesh constituted only 15.90 per cent of the total population of the state. The five largest cities (the 'KAVAL towns') were Kanpur (971,000), Lucknow (656,000), Agra (509,000), Varanasi (490,000) and Allahabad (431,000) and ranked below them were another 12 centres with populations of over 100,000, 18 with populations between 50,000 and 100,000, 56 with between 20,000 and 50,000, 105 with between 10,000 and 20,000 and 388 with between 5,000 and 10,000.[86] Most of these towns and cities had developed as centres of trade, administration and small industry in an overwhelmingly agrarian economy and, despite their considerable differences, they represented variations on a basic combination of common units – foodgrain markets, old commercial centres, a modern business sector, the numerous residential *mohallas* of the middle classes, and the *bastis* housing industrial workers and the poor rural immigrants. The basic components of these general units were sets of households or streets associated with caste or communal groups, often self-contained to a marked degree. This was a society consisting of innumerable cells, and therefore not very responsive to general appeals; not only the Jana Sangh, but all political parties found great difficulty in penetrating it and establishing support without relying upon the mediation offered by caste, community or locality leaders.

One possible way for a party to have developed an urban base would have been to concentrate on gaining command of municipal administrations with the ultimate aim of controlling the essential services and sources of patronage and creating a political 'machine'. Elective municipal boards had been established in most towns in the British period and although certain of their powers were reserved for appointed officials to administer, the boards and their elected officers were responsible for important services, such as water supply, lighting, education and local public works. By 1953 there were Municipal Boards in the 120 largest centres, Town Area Committees in 265 smaller places and Notified Area Committees in 37 other towns. However, the establishment of political machines based on the extensive patronage of

---

[85] See Tables I:7 and I:8 in Myron Weiner and John Osgood Field, 'India's urban constituencies' in Weiner and Field (eds.), *Studies in Electoral Politics in the Indian States, III: The Impact of Modernization* (Delhi, 1977), pp. 28 and 29. In this study, Weiner and Field have aggregated the data for Legislative Assembly constituencies in cities containing 50,000 or more people at the time of the 1961 Census. In such urban constituencies in the northern group of states (Punjab, Haryana, Rajasthan, Uttar Pradesh, Madhya Pradesh and Bihar) the Jana Sangh's average vote rose from 10.9 per cent in 1952 to 29.6 per cent in 1967, while its average vote in rural constituencies in the same group rose at a lower level from 5.2 per cent in 1952 to 16.9 per cent in 1967 (see Table I:7, p. 28). Their data do not include the results for double-member constituencies in 1952 and 1957.

[86] National Council of Applied Economic Research, *Techno-Economic Survey of Uttar Pradesh* (New Delhi, 1965), pp. 237 and 238 (Tables 3 and 4).

either bosses or political parties was never a serious possibility. In the first place, the basic services in the towns were well established, reasonably efficient and usually staffed by professional administrators within the framework of the civil service and there was little scope for political groups either to subvert these services or to establish parallel ones. In the second place, it was the policy of the provincial government under the British and of the state government after independence to intervene at the first sign of inefficiency or corruption and, having suspended the municipal board concerned, to appoint professional administrators to assume authority until the affairs of the municipality had been restored to order. Such interventions sometimes uncovered financial disarray and degrees of petty corruption [87] but nothing to match the situation created by the city machines which existed in some American cities in the late nineteenth century.

Denied the means of achieving large-scale patronage and hindered by the cellular nature of urban society, the political parties were unable to establish themselves directly in municipal politics and were forced instead to make use of those urban leaders – successful advocates, merchants, contractors, money-lenders and caste and community heads – who had managed over the years to build up small parcels of support and influence. In local body elections, in which the constituencies were single- or double-member wards enclosing relatively small groups of localities, such urban leaders could often win seats as Independents. Even if they sometimes accepted party labels, their subsequent allegiance to the party group on the elected board would be limited and their tolerance of discipline small. As a result political alignments on the boards were extremely unstable and factionalism frequent. The importance of Independents in the 1953 municipal elections can be judged from Table 6, which summarizes the affiliations of persons elected as presidents and chairmen of municipal boards in the state after the election of ordinary members had been completed.

Thus, in these elections, Independent candidates had won 39 per cent of the chairmanships of the Municipal Boards, 52 per cent of the presidencies of Town Area Committees and 59 per cent of the chairmanships of Notified Area Committees. The Congress Party had won smaller shares despite the scale of its resources and despite its control of the state government. As for the Jana Sangh, its gains were few but it had at least demonstrated its ability to do better than every other non-Congress party except the Praja Socialist Party.

[87] See, for example, Government of the United Provinces, *Report of the Lucknow Municipal Board Inquiry Committee* (Allahabad, 1942).

Table 6. *UP municipal authority elections of 1953: affiliations of elected chairmen and presidents*

Affiliations	Chairmen of Municipal Boards	Presidents of Town Area Committees	Chairmen of Notified Area Committees
Congress	41	95	11
Praja Socialist Party	16	22	2
Jana Sangh	10	8	0
Communist Party	0	1	1
Revolutionary Socialist Party	1	1	0
Hindu Mahasabha	1	0	0
Independents	44	137	20
Totals	113	264	34

Source: Pioneer (Lucknow), 19 February 1954, p. 3. Elections were not held for seven Municipal Boards, one Town Area Committee and three Notified Area Committees.

On this occasion there were no elections in any of the five KAVAL towns, because the municipal administrations had been superseded in July 1953 pending the establishment of corporations. However, the opportunity for political parties to bid for control of these centres came in 1959, when the UP Nagar Mahapalika Adhiniyam (Municipal Corporation Act) was passed to provide for the formation of municipal corporations in the five cities. The first and crucial event in the setting up of the new bodies occurred on 25 October 1959, when the ordinary councillors were elected. The results were as shown in Table 7. Only in the industrial city of Kanpur did Congress come close to achieving an absolute majority but in the other four cities the large numbers of Independent councillors and the places obtained by the Jana

Table 7. *Numbers of councillors returned in the KAVAL Municipal Corporation elections of 25 October 1959*

Cities	Party affiliations of councillors						
	CON	JS	PSP	SOC	CPI	IND	Totals
Agra	16	7	1	0	0	30	54
Allahabad	18	5	10	2	0	19	54
Kanpur	33	4	3	3	3	26	72
Lucknow	13	26	6	0	2	16	63
Varanasi	17	14	0	0	6	17	54
Totals	97	56	20	5	11	108	297

Source: Pioneer (Lucknow), 28 October 1959, p. 1; 29 October 1959, p. 5. A repoll was held in the Katra Ward of Allahabad on 8 November 1959 and the results for this have been taken from the *Leader* (Allahabad), 10 November 1959, p. 1.

Sangh and the Praja Socialist Party showed that majorities in the new corporations would be difficult to form and to sustain. From the Jana Sangh's point of view the outcome was encouraging, especially in Lucknow, where, as we shall see, it seemed to stand a chance of gaining control of the administration.

The Municipal Corporation Act provided for a sequence of elections once the return of the councillors had been completed: first, the councillors were to elect a number of aldermen, and then both councillors and alderman were to elect the Mayor (whose term of office was one year) and the Deputy Mayor (whose term of office was five years). In Lucknow, on 25 November 1959, the 63 councillors elected seven aldermen – three Jana Sanghis, two Congressmen, one Praja Socialist and one Independent.[88] The Jana Sangh group on the corporation then came to an agreement with the Independents that the offices of Mayor and Deputy Mayor should be held by the members of each of the two groups in turn and that places on the Development and Executive Committees and on other committees of the corporation should be shared between them. This agreement led directly to the clear victory in the mayoral election of 19 December 1959 of Raj Kumar Shrivastava, the Jana Sangh's nominee, who secured 41 votes against the 13 obtained by his nearest rival.[89] However, the alliance went awry in the subsequent election for the important post of Deputy Mayor: when the Independents failed to agree on a common candidate, the Jana Sangh group put forward its leader, Ram Prakash Gupta. Thereupon the Congress, Praja Socialist and Communist members of the corporation combined with some Independents to secure the election of an Independent candidate, V.R. Mohan, by 36 votes to Gupta's 30 when the ballot was held on 6 February 1960.[90] For a period after this the Jana Sangh concentrated on winning over sufficient Independents and defectors from other parties to gain control of the corporation and of its most important committees. In the second mayoral election, on 23 January 1961, it secured the return of Girraj Dharan Rastogi, a millionaire money-lender, by 36 votes to 33[91] and the coalition based on the Jana Sangh secured the election of an Independent, Dr P.D. Kapur, to that office in both 1962 and 1963.[92] This pattern changed in 1964,

---

[88] *Pioneer*, 26 November 1959, p. 1.
[89] *Ibid.*, 20 December 1959, p. 1.
[90] *Ibid.*, 7 February 1960, p. 5. The votes cited are those registered at the end of the second round (the voting method was that of proportional representation using a single transferable vote). On the reasons for the breakdown of the alliance see statements by Ram Prakash Gupta and Rameshwar Agarwal on 7 February (*ibid.*, 8 February 1960, p. 5).
[91] *Ibid.*, 24 January 1961, pp. 1 and 5.
[92] *National Herald*, 17 April 1962, p. 1; 18 April 1962, p. 1; 22 April 1963, p. 3; 23 April 1963, p. 1.

when the Jana Sangh combined with Congress to secure the election of V.R. Mohan as Mayor[93] and shortly afterwards Ram Prakash Gupta was at last elected to the post of Deputy Mayor.[94]

Although the Jana Sangh failed to gain complete control of the Lucknow Municipal Corporation at any stage between 1960 and 1964, the party was nevertheless criticized for its management of municipal affairs. Matters came to a head on 3 July 1965 when the state government declared the municipal body to be an 'indebted corporation' under Section 152 of the Municipal Corporation Act.[95] Ram Prakash denied that the corporation was bankrupt and accused the government of conducting 'a political vendetta'.[96] Besides financial mismanagement, the ruling group on the corporation was accused of gifting away valuable and centrally located plots of lands to particular individuals and of delaying the consideration of cases of allegedly illegal encroachment on *nuzul* (escheated land) owned by the state government but administered by the corporation.[97] The term of the KAVAL corporations should have ended on 31 January 1965 but was extended for another year; however, on 26 January 1966 the state government issued an ordinance providing that, with effect from 1 February, the functions of the corporations would be taken over for two years by official administrators.[98] Fresh elections to four of the corporations were held on 31 July 1968 and in the Lucknow contest the Jana Sangh won only 7 seats out of 64, the remaining seats being won by Congress (33), Independents (20) and other parties (4).[99]

The Jana Sangh's failure in Lucknow illustrates how difficult it was for

---

[93] *Ibid.*, 29 April 1964, pp. 1 and 3.

[94] *Ibid.*, 7 June 1964, p. 3.

[95] *Ibid.*, 6 July 1965, p. 3.

[96] *Ibid.*, 8 July 1965, p. 3. See also his letter to the editor, *ibid.*, 14 July 1965, p. 5, and an article which he wrote on the financial affairs of the Corporation in *Organiser*, 8 August 1965, p. 15. For a contrary view, see letter from D.P. Joshi, an alderman of the Corporation, in *National Herald*, 29 July 1965, p. 5.

[97] These and other charges are set out in a series of articles in *National Herald*, 29 November 1965, p. 3; 1 December 1965, p. 3; 2 December 1965, p. 3; 4 December 1965, p. 3; 6 December 1965, p. 3; 13 December 1965, p. 3; 14 December 1965, p. 3; 16 December 1965, p. 3; 17 December 1965, p. 3.

For a letter from Ram Prakash Gupta replying to the charges of financial mal-administration, and a rejoinder from the reporter concerned, see *ibid.*, 20 December 1965, p. 3.

For other charges of favouritism see the report of the admission of a writ petition challenging the legal status of the Lucknow Municipal Corporation's Executive Committee before the Lucknow Bench of the Allahabad High Court in *ibid.*, 29 October 1964, p. 3.

[98] *Ibid.*, 26 January 1966, p. 1.

[99] Elections Directorate, Uttar Pradesh, *Results of Second General Elections to Nagar Mahapalikas – 1968: July 31, 1968* (Lucknow, 1969), p. 47.

this or for any other party to establish anything other than a temporary plurality on a municipal body in this state. The social groups from which the Jana Sangh drew its most consistent support were a substantial electoral force only in the middle-class residential areas and their associated commercial centres, and these were too small a base for a party intent on gaining a majority in municipal polls. The Jana Sangh had, therefore, whenever it established a group in a municipality, to take part in the frustrating and often fruitless business of trying to construct coalitions with Independents and other parties and, in doing so, was inevitably identified with the older tradition of municipal politics, in which the elected officials lacked a stable base in the plenary body.

Without a commanding position in the municipalities the Jana Sangh was at a disadvantage in its efforts to gain control of the assembly and parliamentary constituencies in the urban centres. As Table 8 shows, in Legislative Assembly elections it consistently polled a higher proportion of the votes in the seven largest cities than in the state as a whole, but even so its support was neither substantial nor sufficiently concentrated. It did not win a single assembly seat in these seven cities in either the 1952 or the 1957 elections and obtained only one (in Varanasi) in the 1962 elections. Its highest vote, in 1967, gave it 9 seats out of 23 but it won only four in the mid-term elections of 1969.

Table 8. *Uttar Pradesh: Jana Sangh percentage vote-shares in Legislative Assembly elections in seven cities 1952 to 1969*

	General election years				
Cities	1952 %	1957 %	1962 %	1967 %	1969 %
Agra	15.77	6.70	18.63	30.20	25.57
Allahabad	0.31	0.00	8.13	14.58	25.94
Bareilly	25.15	18.72	20.24	29.07	16.41
Kanpur	5.68	6.44	14.25	24.28	20.86
Lucknow	22.88	19.97	34.05	29.39	17.68
Meerut	11.27	11.33	20.82	28.87	27.52
Varanasi	22.34	17.45	33.92	34.50	34.86
Cities total	14.49	11.52	21.52	27.19	23.90
State total	6.43	9.84	16.46	21.67	17.93

Notes:
(1) Percentages are for Jana Sangh votes as a percentage of the total valid votes in all constituencies.
(2) The numbers of seats contested by the Jana Sangh were 13 out of 16 in 1952, 14 out of 21 in 1957 (no seats were contested by the party in Allahabad on this occasion), 19 out of 19 in 1962, 22 out of 23 in 1967 and 23 out of 23 in 1969.
(3) Some of the constituencies located in these cities also enclosed adjacent rural areas e.g. Kalyanpur (Kanpur) in 1967 and 1969.
Source: UP Election Project, University of Sussex

In the rural areas of the state, the Jana Sangh's 'natural' social base was even more restricted than in the cities. Its core groups of activists were typically located in the small towns within a district, from where they would work outwards to the villages. An election worker who supported Ram Manohar Lohia when he was contesting the by-election for the parliamentary seat of Farrukhabad in the summer of 1963 found that the Jana Sangh group consisted of 'shop-keepers and some lawyers and students', who resided mainly in the two largest towns of Farruk-habad and Fatehgarh:

Their strength in the smaller towns like Kannauj and Makrand Nagar was negligible, and in the villages practically nil. Above all they had no rank and file worth speaking of. Their assistance did not amount to much quantitatively, but to a certain extent it did qualitatively, for in an area where agriculture is the only prevailing economy (Farrukhabad has no industry of any sort) lawyers and traders take the place of the intelligentsia, and the local population give serious consideration to their views.[100]

Further to the east, in the district of Bara Banki, Dr Angela Burger, an American scholar, found a comparable group in the small town of Rudauli at the time of the 1962 election campaign. She identified ten Jana Sangh activists in the Rudauli assembly constituency and found that eight of them were resident in the town itself:

All are Banias who are shopkeepers and some are also moneylenders; all are members of the RSS. Their shops are located on the same street; all grew up together and have been long-time personal friends. Most are in their thirties. Only two rural activists were named – and these with difficulty; both are Thakurs, formerly small zamindars, and both have lived for some time outside the constituency in urban areas.[101]

The shops of these urban activists provided the core of what Dr Burger has described as a 'shopkeeper network', which the party employed to muster votes for its candidate.[102]

As we have noted earlier, the Jana Sangh combined its essentially organizational approach to electioneering with a series of appeals to particular interests and values, partly in the hope of arousing Hindu nationalist sentiment and partly in an effort to establish areas of sectional support around its economic proposals. It presented itself, for

[100] Suresh Vaidya, 'What Farrukhabad taught me', *Mainstream* (New Delhi), I, 42 (15 June 1963), p. 15.
[101] Angela Sutherland Burger, *Opposition in a Dominant-Party System: A Study of the Jan Sangh, the Praja Socialist Party, and the Socialist Party in Uttar Pradesh, India* (Berkeley, 1969), p. 145.
[102] *Ibid.*, pp. 146–7.

example, as being the only party capable of preventing the Congress from undermining Hinduism, and did so in a way which was often regarded by its opponents as being quite unscrupulous. Shortly after the 1962 elections, in which he had won the parliamentary seat of Basti in eastern Uttar Pradesh for Congress against a Jana Sangh opponent, Keshav Dev Malaviya complained that in the campaign the Jana Sangh had depicted the Congress as an irreligious party. Having found Jana Sangh flags in villages where no party had been before, he had asked one man who had given him the flag and was told:

Nobody. We who have watched the Congress spreading the anti-religious gospel, decided to go over to the Jana Sangh. I have prepared my own flag and put it on the house-top.

When asked why he believed that Congress was for the abolition of religion and against Hinduism, the villager replied:

I heard it in the town where the Jana Sangh leader was explaining how the Congress preached inter-caste marriages and abolition of the caste-system and was also advocating Hindu–Muslim unity on no-religion basis.

Malaviya also complained that the Jana Sangh had used a local incident to appeal to the emotions of upper-caste Hindus in the following terms:

The Hindu temple is a source of hatred for the Congressmen, the sanctity of the Ganga does not exist in the minds of the Congressmen, the Hindi language and script are bound to be destroyed by the Congressmen if they are allowed to remain in power. Jawaharlal is friendly to nations which want to grab India and is inimical to such countries as have helped us to rise from our slumber and have contributed to the coming of Swarajya.[103]

Besides offering itself as the champion of Hindu values, the Jana Sangh also tried to secure sectional support in the agrarian society of Uttar Pradesh. As we have seen, it sought unsuccessfully to rally those peasant proprietors who were defined as *sirdars* under the Zamindari Abolition Act of 1950 by proposing to halve their land-revenue payments and to make it easier for them to purchase the more advantageous *bhumidhari* status, and a few years later its strong opposition to the Congress Party's scheme for co-operative joint farming failed to arouse a significant response. Both these campaigns presupposed a greater awareness of economic issues than existed

---

[103] Keshav Deva Malaviya, 'Rise of the Jana Sangh: Congress must meet the challenge', *Indian Express* (Delhi), 30 March 1962, pp. 6 and 7. Versions of the same article were also published in *Link*, 1 April 1962, pp. 15–16 (as 'The challenge of casteism') and in *Socialist Congressman*, I, 24 (1 April 1962), pp. 4–6 and 17 (as 'An election review: dangers and lessons').

amongst the peasants at this time, and it may be that the party would have been better advised to have concentrated on social issues, especially those connected with caste status in rural society. Indeed, in the mid-1960s it may have come close to tapping one of the largest reservoirs of voting power in the state, the populous and widespread layer of the so-called 'backward castes' (Ahirs, Kurmis, Yadavas, Lodhis and Koeris) at odds both with the 'forward castes', such as the Rajputs or Thakurs, Brahmans, Kayasthas and Banias, and with the Scheduled Castes and their privileged educational and job reservations. By 1967, the Jana Sangh was aiming to base itself in central and eastern Uttar Pradesh on the Kurmis, Ahirs and Lodhas who had formerly supported the Lohia Socialists, but the formation of the Bharatiya Kranti Dal (BKD) seems to have prevented it from doing so.[104] This party, set up in May 1967 and led by Charan Singh, was grounded upon his extensive following amongst the Jats of western Uttar Pradesh and it rapidly attracted backward-caste support throughout the state, winning 98 seats and 21.29 per cent of the votes in the 1969 assembly elections. In contrast, in 1969 the Jana Sangh's total of seats in the assembly fell from 98 in 1967 to 49 and its share of the votes fell from 21.67 to 17.93 per cent, and a loss of backward-caste votes to the BKD may well help to account for this sudden fall in electoral strength.

In general, therefore, the Jana Sangh failed to establish a secure place for itself in the electoral politics of Uttar Pradesh in the 1950s and 1960s. Given its origins and its initial identification with middle-class and with trading and business interests, it might have been expected to grow first as an urban party, but, as we have seen, there were limits which it could not transcend; even in Lucknow, despite its relative advantage on the Municipal Corporation in the early 1960s, it was unable to establish itself as the ruling party. In the rural areas, its organizational resources were thinly spread, and its local successes were often related to special circumstances, such as the recruitment of an established social or caste leader. Yet through great stretches of the state there existed a potential base for an anti-Congress and pro-peasant party in the shape of the intermediate castes, such as the Kurmis, Lodhis and Yadavas. The Jana Sangh was at least aware of the importance of this layer as far as the central and eastern parts of Uttar Pradesh were concerned, but it was hardly in a position to win the race for their support, given its reputation for being a party closely tied to the social outlook of the upper castes, such as the Brahmans and Rajputs. Here, as in Haryana and Bihar, the party which eventually succeeded in enclosing and representing these

---

[104] From interview with Lal K. Advani, New Delhi, 15 May 1984.

groups was the Lok Dal, the linear descendant of Charan Singh's BKD of the late 1960s.

Would the party have been better advised to have concentrated on trying to create local strongholds for itself at subregional levels instead of trying to combat the Congress in every part of the state? The possibility should at least have been considered. The region most likely to have repaid intensive effort was Oudh, where the party's vote-share in contested constituencies in the 1957 election was 23.18 per cent (compared with 18.59 in Rohilkhand, 17.28 in Varanasi, 17.00 in Kumaon, 12.94 in the Lower Doab, 12.20 in the Upper Doab, 12.10 in Gorakhpur and 10.87 in Bundelkhand). Within Oudh, its candidates were achieving encouraging results in a scatter of constituencies in the three north-western districts of Kheri, Hardoi and Sitapur and in the large north-eastern district of Gonda, and it is at least conceivable that a policy of concentrating resources on the Oudh region within Uttar Pradesh, and on these two subregions within Oudh, might have produced secure fortress areas for the party from which more deliberate expansion would have been possible.

Conclusion

If we ignore the special circumstances which linked the early Jana Sangh to West Bengal as a result of Mookerjee's long association with Hindu nationalist politics in that state, we see a party whose particular origins and background tied it to the regions of the Hindi-speaking heartland. Within that broad area, it concentrated its attention largely on the huge states of Uttar Pradesh and post-1956 Madhya Pradesh and also on the Union Territory of Delhi; in these units it nominated candidates in as many constituencies as possible with the evident intention of emulating the Congress Party's machine-like, organizational style of election campaigning. While this method led to an outright victory in the municipal elections in Delhi in 1967, in Uttar Pradesh it resulted in a heavy turnover of candidates and incumbents and failed either to raise the party's state-wide vote to the level of about 30 per cent needed to return candidates in sufficient numbers to control the assembly or to establish one or two secure base areas. In Madhya Pradesh the outlook appeared to be more promising, given the relatively high levels of regional support obtained by the party's candidates in Malwa and (in 1967) in Gwalior, but, as noted above, the actual social support behind these levels was by no means as solid as it appeared to be in these early elections. Elsewhere, the party settled for a minority role: in Rajasthan it fell into a pattern of electoral alliances with the Swatantra Party, in

Punjab it aimed at a specialized Hindu constituency in the large cities, and in Haryana it delayed too long an attempt to come to terms with the intermediate castes of the rural areas.

By 1967 such electoral shortcomings were already making it difficult for the Jana Sangh to maintain its independence, and its distinctive philosophical position, within the party system. As election succeeded election and the Congress Party retained its grip on power, the Jana Sangh was compelled to abandon its hopes of becoming a major factor in Indian politics, the Hindu nationalist counter-force to insurgent communism, and to accept that it would have to work with other opposition parties in electoral, parliamentary and (eventually) governmental alliances. The first indication of a willingness to compromise came at the end of 1963, when the party was involved in discussions about a broad non-Congress front. Early in 1964 there were even talks about the possibility of merging the Jana Sangh with the Swatantra Party, but these came to nothing; the two parties drew apart because of differences of opinion about how the Kashmir problem should be solved. The Jana Sangh accepted the need for some limited arrangements about sharing seats with the Swatantra Party in particular for the 1967 general elections and after this poll the party's decision to help form a number of broadly based coalition governments effectively committed it to a policy of broad-based alliances.

Although this was by no means clear at the time, the Jana Sangh's reluctant agreement to work with other minor parties in order to challenge the Congress Party was an admission that its hopes of a major electoral breakthrough had been illusory. The results of the 1967 general elections gave it more seats and votes than it had ever had before but they also demonstrated that it lacked the level of support needed to establish itself as the major party in any of the large northern states.

8

Conclusion

Why did the Jana Sangh fail to become a major force in the politics of post-independence India, despite its claim to be the true representative of the national aspirations of the Hindus? The simple answer is that it failed to transcend the limitations of its origins. Its close initial ties with the Hindi-speaking heartland were, in the long run, a serious disadvantage; from the outset, the party was preoccupied with northern issues such as the promotion of Hindi, the defence of refugee interests, and energetic resistance to Pakistan. In addition, its interpretation of Hinduism was restrictive and exclusive; its doctrines were inspired by an activist version of Hindu nationalism and, indirectly, by the values of Brahmanism rather than the devotional and quietist values of popular Hinduism.

These problems were not insoluble and had Shyama Prasad Mookerjee, the party's first President, not died so unexpectedly in June 1953, he might well have persuaded his followers to be more expansive and flexible, and more pragmatic and adventurous in developing new policies; he undoubtedly sympathized with their Hindu nationalism and their distrust of Pakistan, but as a liberal constitutionalist and a Bengali he was naturally resistant to the authoritarian bent and the Hindi chauvinism of his northern colleagues. Had he lived longer, he would have been well equipped to exploit the opening in the party system created by Nehru's attempt to reorientate the Congress Party. Even during Mookerjee's lifetime, Nehru was insisting that the Congress should redefine and strengthen the boundary which separated it from Hindu traditionalism and that it should affirm its faith in secularism. From the mid-1950s onwards, he was also trying to convince it of the need to frame economic policies on socialist lines, to accept a larger role for the state in the planning and regulation of the economy, and to enlarge the public sector of industry. As the Congress slowly began to respond to his lead it moved leftwards and created a space on the right of the party system which could have been filled by a party or parties willing to speak for Hindu traditionalism, political and economic liberalism and a mild form of social conservatism. A politician of Mookerjee's ability could have taken up these themes and led the Jana Sangh away from its isolated starting point towards the territory which the Congress was leaving.

Such a change in position would have required an adjustment of the Jana Sangh's social strategy. Any party attempting to mount a major challenge to Nehru's Congress had to gain the attention and respect of India's influential middle classes and to demonstrate that it was an open and democratic organization, capable of responding positively to their ideas about the nature of parties and party politics. Mookerjee would therefore have had an interest in strengthening those aspects of the Jana Sangh's organization which resembled the pre-independence Congress Party, with its emphasis on collective leadership at the top and on the deliberative function of large plenary bodies devoted almost entirely to wide-ranging policy discussions. Thus reformed, the Jana Sangh could have provided the hinge for a broad-based alliance of national democratic parties and the party system itself would probably have developed towards a structure of two blocs, with such an alliance on one side and the Congress, the CPI and other left-wing groups on the other.

From this perspective, Mookerjee may be criticized for having allowed the Jana Sangh to become embroiled in the 1953 agitation over the constitutional status of Jammu and Kashmir, an issue which drew the party towards a confrontational style of politics and appeared to confirm its obsession with a peculiarly northern view of Hindu nationalism. However, it would still have been possible after that for Mookerjee to have returned to the course he had been charting in 1951 and 1952. His great assets were his own considerable personal standing and his skill and reputation as a parliamentarian, and, given time, he would almost certainly have strengthened his control of the party's organization and curbed the impulsiveness of the young workers whom he had recruited from the RSS.

The central issue during the leadership-succession crisis, which shook the party after Mookerjee's death, was whether executive authority would remain with men willing to continue his approach or would pass to a younger group of leaders who were convinced of the virtues of organizational discipline, close ties with the RSS, and an activist and militant expression of Hindu nationalism. In the event, victory went to the latter group and from 1955 onwards effective power rested with the party's central secretariat, headed by Deendayal Upadhyaya and supported by a hierarchy of young and zealous organizers. This group, by holding the party to an isolated position in the party system, effectively ignored the chance of appealing to the moderate sector of

Hindu traditionalist opinion and the equally important chance of representing those groups which were opposed to the Congress Party's economic policies on liberal grounds. It was only in the mid-1960s that fresh efforts were made to explore the possibility of a national-democratic alliance which would bring the party into closer touch with kindred groups.

The efforts of the Upadhyaya leadership to maintain the separate identity of the Jana Sangh would have been justified had Hindu nationalism become the great rallying philosophy of the 1960s, but this did not happen. There is little evidence that the intense convictions of the party's intellectuals were shared to any significant extent by even a substantial minority of Hindus. Indeed, on those occasions when the Jana Sangh's cautious endorsement of a Hindu nationalist cause led to its taking a political stand, it often found itself in an exposed position, lacking in public support; for example, having associated itself with the Arya Samaj in the defence of the ideal of a greater Punjab, with Hindi as the principal language, it found itself politically isolated in the regional conflicts of 1955–57 and 1965–66. In neither period did it arouse anything resembling a mass movement of Hindus to assert their territorial and linguistic claims. It was as though the community to which it was appealing existed to a large extent within the party's imagination.

It would be wrong to conclude from this that competing loyalties of caste, sect, dialect, locality and culture prevented Hindus from acting as a political community during this period. The fact is that many Hindus, and particularly those in the northern states, did indeed see themselves as a political community but they also saw the Congress Party rather than any one of the Hindu nationalist parties as their principal defender. This had undoubtedly been the case in the late 1930s and the 1940s, and especially so at the time of the 1946 provincial elections, when it was not the Hindu Sabhas but the northern Congress units which were seen as the shield of the Hindus in the vital contest with the Muslim League. When, during Nehru's Prime Ministership, the Congress High Command supported legislation reforming the laws governing marriage, divorce, succession and inheritance amongst Hindus while generally supporting the privileges of minority communities and acknowledging the right of Muslims to retain their own family law in the *shari'at*, the relationship between Hindus and the Congress did show considerable signs of strain. However, the essential bond continued to exist and remains as strong as ever; as one newspaper observed at the time of the Lok Sabha elections which were held after the assassination of Mrs Gandhi on 31 October 1984, 'every time the minorities become assertive,

Hindus tend to consolidate behind the Congress despite its professed commitment to secular values'.[1]

In northern areas the affinity between Hindus and the state units of the Congress has always been strong, despite the party's attachment to secularism at the central level. Throughout the 1950s and 1960s these northern Congress units were firm defenders of the status of Hindi as the official language in their states and showed respect for Hindu traditions. In Uttar Pradesh, for example, the Congress gave the Jana Sangh few opportunities to show itself the more zealous of the two in the cause of Hindi or the more determined to resist the claims of Urdu. It was also clear to the Jana Sangh that any attempt which it might make to outflank the northern Congress units by exaggerated appeals to Hindu sentiment could produce social responses which would be difficult to control; there was, for example, always an element of risk in the party's participation in the campaign against cow-slaughter, and the sudden and terrifying outburst of violence at the demonstration in New Delhi on 7 November 1966 showed how easily a crowd could cross the boundary between disciplined demonstration and anarchic rioting.

It is conceivable that, had it met with early success in the politics of interest-group representation, the Jana Sangh might have been persuaded to shift its weight more firmly towards the economic issues within its programme and to lessen its reliance on Hindu nationalist issues. However, the party's original reference groups (small industrialists and businessmen, traders, and employees in the lower ranks of the professions and the civil service) constituted an extremely limited and isolated clientèle. Furthermore, the party's social philosophy had a strong corporatist and preservatist bias, reflecting sympathy for the outlook of these reference groups, and this made it difficult for the party to appeal to the industrial workers and peasants, for whom social conflict and change were inescapable aspects of political life.

Having failed to produce any significant uprising of Hindu nationalist sentiment, and having adopted a relatively limited register of economic policies, the Jana Sangh lacked the means to establish a substantial social base for its organization in the regions of northern India. A more realistic party, willing to plan for success in the longer term, might have concentrated on establishing a limited number of strongholds at the subregional level, both to provide an electoral underpinning for stable groups of members in the central parliament and the provincial legislatures and to form a foundation for a deliberate expansion into marginal territory. Instead, in Uttar Pradesh, the party had en-

---

[1] 'Communities and choices' (editorial), *Statesman* (Delhi), 24 November 1984, p. 6.

eavoured to compete against the Congress in almost every part of the
tate and, as a result, it had become involved in the costly and wasteful
process of large turnovers of both candidates and incumbents. A similar
approach in the neighbouring state of Madhya Pradesh had yielded one
mportant advantage, the relatively high levels of support for the Jana
angh's candidates in the Malwa and Gwalior regions, but the setbacks
suffered by the BJP in these same areas in the state elections of March
1985 indicated that the party's early achievements had depended too
much on the local power of certain prominent individuals. Elsewhere in
the north the party's goals had been less ambitious: in Rajasthan it had
worked in alliance with the Swatantra Party in the 1962 and 1967
elections; in the Punjab it had become the party of the Hindu minorities
in the large cities; and in Haryana it had delayed until too late any
serious attempt to come to terms with the numerous intermediate castes
of that region.

All the above factors have to be considered in any explanation of why
the Jana Sangh's electoral expansion was so limited, but in each case we
are led back to the party's early decisions about general strategy and
their consequences. The triumph of the RSS group in the 1954
leadership-succession crisis had ensured that the strategy of building
strength in isolation would be given a long trial and this approach
undoubtedly gave the Jana Sangh internal cohesion and manoeuvra-
bility in the turbulent politics of the 1960s. However, the organizational
requirements of this strategy, with its emphasis on discipline and the
restriction of debate within the party, had made it unattractive to groups
which, while sympathizing with some of the party's aims, were accustomed to a more democratic and responsive style of operation. In Uttar
Pradesh, for example, the Jana Sangh was competing in the mid-1960s
with the Samyukta Socialist Party (SSP) to represent pro-Hindi
sentiment and with the Swatantra Party to represent economic liberalism, and it could have done so much more effectively had it not been so
widely suspected of communalism and of a dependent relationship with
the RSS.

Such limitations in appeal probably made the difference between
qualified success and decisive breakthrough for the party in the major
northern states in the 1967 general elections. In Uttar Pradesh, its vote-
share of 21.67 per cent yielded 23.06 per cent of the seats (98 out of 425)
whereas the Congress Party won 46.82 per cent of the seats (199) with
only 32.20 per cent of the votes; had the Jana Sangh's vote been in the
range 25–30 per cent, its gains in seats would probably have been much
higher proportionately, possibly in the range 120–150, and it would then
have been in a position to dominate the negotiations for a non-Congress

coalition which followed Charan Singh's defection from the ruling party within a few weeks of the poll. Constituency politics were less competitive in Madhya Pradesh, where the Jana Sangh's vote-share of 28.28 per cent produced a seat-share of 26.35 per cent (78 seats out of 296) and the Congress unit, stronger than its counterpart in Uttar Pradesh, won 167 seats (56.42 per cent) with 40.69 per cent of the votes, but the same conclusion can be drawn from this case; a marginally higher Jana Sangh vote would have produced a substantially higher share of the seats and thus placed the party in a commanding position in the bargaining which accompanied the formation of the non-Congress coalition in August 1967 following the collapse of the Congress administration. At this point, with virtual control of the two biggest states in northern India, the Jana Sangh would have been well placed to consolidate its gains and to strengthen its position in the national-democratic area of the party system.

That an opportunity had been lost was not at all obvious in the aftermath of the 1967 general elections, when Congress appeared to be on the retreat, but once the party lines hardened again, in 1968 and 1969, the opposition parties found that they had been successfully contained. It was they which were placed on the defensive following Mrs Gandhi's sweeping victories in the Lok Sabha elections of 1971 and the state elections of 1972, and the Jana Sangh in particular found itself with numbers in Parliament and the northern legislatures which fell well short of those achieved in 1967. Then came the Emergency period of 1975–77 and, in its wake, the virtual fusion of the main non-Congress groups, including the Jana Sangh, within the omnibus Janata Party. Following the collapse of Janata rule in 1979, a new period of multi-party politics began and the formation of the Bharatiya Janata Party in April 1980 offered a second chance for Hindu nationalists to bid for majority status in northern India. However, to date the BJP's electoral achievements have fallen well short of those registered by the Jana Sangh at the 1967 polls.

The intellectuals of each of India's minor parties look back to the 1950s and 1960s as a time of missed opportunities and though in most cases this is simply wishful thinking, those who were associated with the early Jana Sangh are justified in their regret. It is well within the bounds of possibility that a moderate, more open and more democratic Jana Sangh could have established itself as the governing party in one or two of the large states of northern India and become a significant force in national politics in the 1970s and 1980s.

Jana Sangh results in Legislative Assembly elections, 1951–52 to 1967

The figures below are calculated from constituency returns published by the Election Commission of India in the statistical sections of its election *Reports*, although those for Uttar Pradesh are also based on data collected for the UP Election Project at the University of Sussex.

The column headings for the tables below are as follows:

(1) Total number of Legislative Assembly seats
(2) Total number of Jana Sangh candidatures
(3) Total number of seats won by Jana Sangh candidates
(4) Jana Sangh vote to nearest thousand
(5) Jana Sangh vote as percentage of total valid vote in all contests
(6) Jana Sangh vote as percentage of total valid vote in all contests including Jana Sangh candidates.

Note: The total vote given at the foot of column (4) is the sum of the actual, rather than the rounded, figures.

1951–52 General elections

| | Jana Sangh performance in: | | | | | |
| | (A) Seats | | | and | (B) Votes | |
States	(1)	(2)	(3)	(4)	(5)	(6)
Part A						
Assam	108	3	0	7	0.29	6.80
Bihar	330	47	0	113	1.18	7.29
Bombay	315	2	0	5	0.04	4.03
Madhya Pradesh	232	76	0	251	3.59	9.01
Madras	375	2	0	8	0.04	8.92
Orissa	140	—	—	—	—	—
Punjab	126	62	0	278	5.56	10.55
Uttar Pradesh	430	209	2	1,077	6.43	11.43
West Bengal	238	85	9	415	5.58	12.57
Part B						
Hyderabad	175	2	0	2	0.04	5.99
Madhya Bharat	99	42	4	194	9.74	22.24
Mysore	99	23	0	62	2.26	8.88
PEPSU	60	23	2	44	3.23	7.09

Table (*Cont.*)

| | Jana Sangh performance in: | | | | | |
| | (A) Seats | | | and | (B) Votes | |
States	(1)	(2)	(3)	(4)	(5)	(6)
Rajasthan	160	50	8	194	5.93	18.84
Saurashtra	60	3	0	4	0.46	11.63
Travancore-Cochin	108	—	—	—	—	—
Part C						
Ajmer	30	15	3	28	11.95	21.74
Bhopal	30	9	0	11	4.92	11.61
Coorg	24	—	—	—	—	—
Delhi	48	31	5	114	21.89	29.04
Himachal Pradesh	36	10	0	6	3.35	9.36
Vindhya Pradesh	60	33	2	67	9.88	15.19
Totals	3,283	727	35	2,881	2.77	11.79

1957 General elections

| | Jana Sangh performance in: | | | | | |
| | (A) Seats | | | and | (B) Votes | |
States	(1)	(2)	(3)	(4)	(5)	(6)
Andhra Pradesh[1]	105	2	0	6	0.16	0.33
Assam	108	—	—	—	—	—
Bihar	318	30	0	130	1.23	13.32
Bombay	396	23	4	261	1.56	20.86
Kerala	126	—	—	—	—	—
Madhya Pradesh	288	127	10	732	9.88	20.33
Madras	205	—	—	—	—	—
Mysore	208	20	0	86	1.34	13.09
Orissa	140	—	—	—	—	—
Punjab	154	64	9	654	8.61	17.86
Rajasthan	176	47	6	257	5.41	16.31
Uttar Pradesh	430	236	17	2,158	9.84	16.25
West Bengal	252	33	0	102	0.98	6.89
Totals	2,906	582	46	4,386	3.87	16.52

[1] The total number of seats assigned to Andhra Pradesh was 301 but elections were confined to the Telangana region on this occasion, the remainder of the state having elected MLAs in a general election held in 1955. Two by-elections in constituencies in the original state were also held at same time as the 1957 general elections.

1962 General elections

| States | Jana Sangh performance in: | | | | | |
| | (A) Seats | | | and | (B) Votes | |
	(1)	(2)	(3)	(4)	(5)	(6)
Andhra Pradesh	300	70	0	122	1.04	4.19
Assam	105	4	0	11	0.45	9.00
Bihar	318	75	3	273	2.77	10.76
Gujarat	154	26	0	73	1.41	8.10
Madhya Pradesh	288	195	41	1,092	16.66	24.31
Madras	206	4	0	11	0.08	3.56
Maharashtra	264	127	0	548	5.00	10.08
Mysore	208	63	0	144	2.29	7.26
Punjab	154	80	8	655	9.72	18.40
Rajasthan	176	94	15	469	9.15	17.32
Uttar Pradesh	430	377	49	2,932	16.46	18.71
West Bengal	252	25	0	43	0.45	3.93
Totals	2,855	1,140	116	6,375	6.07	15.27

1967 General elections

| States | Jana Sangh performance in: | | | | | |
| | (A) Seats | | | and | (B) Votes | |
	(1)	(2)	(3)	(4)	(5)	(6)
Andhra Pradesh	287	80	3	292	2.11	7.90
Assam	126	20	0	57	1.84	11.49
Bihar[1]	318	271	26	1,411	10.42	12.43
Gujarat	168	16	1	120	1.88	21.70
Haryana	81	48	12	436	14.39	24.58
Jammu & Kashmir	75	29	3	132	16.45	28.49
Kerala	133	24	0	56	0.88	4.69
Madhya Pradesh	296	265	78	2,578	28.28	31.77
Madras	234	24	0	23	0.15	1.42
Maharashtra	270	165	4	1,094	8.18	13.15
Mysore	216	37	4	212	2.82	16.80
Orissa	140	19	0	22	0.54	4.07
Punjab	104	49	9	419	9.84	21.19
Rajasthan	184	63	22	790	11.69	34.84
Uttar Pradesh	425	401	98	4,652	21.67	23.00
West Bengal	280	58	1	168	1.33	6.33
Union Territories						
Goa, Daman & Diu	30	—	—	—	—	—
Himachal Pradesh	60	33	7	106	13.87	25.25
Manipur	30	—	—	—	—	—
Tripura	30	5	0	2	0.35	2.10
Totals	3,487	1,607	268	12,568	8.77	18.77

[1] In Bihar two Jana Sangh candidates were nominated for one constituency (no. 115) so that the number of seats contested in this state was actually 270 and the total number of seats contested was 1,606.

APPENDIX II

Jana Sangh results in Lok Sabha elections, 1951–52 to 1967

The figures below are calculated from constituency returns published by the Election Commission of India in the statistical sections of its election *Reports*, although those for Uttar Pradesh are also based on data collected for the UP Election Project at the University of Sussex.

The column headings for the tables below are as follows:

(1) Total number of Lok Sabha seats
(2) Total number of Jana Sangh candidatures
(3) Total number of seats won by Jana Sangh candidates
(4) Jana Sangh vote to nearest thousand
(5) Jana Sangh vote as percentage of total valid vote in all contests
(6) Jana Sangh vote as percentage of total valid vote in all contests including Jana Sangh candidates.

| | Jana Sangh performance in: | | | | | | |
| | (A) Seats | | | and | (B) Votes | | |
Election year	(1)	(2)	(3)		(4)	(5)	(6)
1951–52	489	94	3		3,246	3.06	13.38
1957	494	130	4		7,193	5.97	19.94
1962	494	196	14		7,415	6.44	16.73
1967	520	251	35		13,641	9.35	20.54

Legislative Assembly elections: percentages of seats contested by the Jana Sangh by political regions, 1951–52 to 1967

	Election Year			
Region	1951–52	1957	1962	1967
Punjab	46.36	40.70	47.67	47.12
Haryana	39.34	43.64	62.96	59.26
Kumaon	16.66	40.00	80.00	80.00
Upper Doab	58.82	60.29	83.82	86.76
Rohilkhand	50.98	56.00	94.00	93.88
Lower Doab	43.33	64.52	90.32	100.00
Bundelkhand	15.00	25.00	95.00	95.00
Oudh	55.34	53.33	90.48	95.10
Gorakhpur	46.03	50.85	81.36	96.49
Varanasi	53.19	60.87	84.78	100.00
Gwalior	21.95	31.43	65.71	57.14
Malwa	58.06	69.64	71.43	93.10
Rewa	54.39	64.86	75.68	100.00
Narbada	38.14	25.32	63.29	92.59
Chhattisgarh	17.07	40.74	66.67	92.86
Jaipur	29.35	20.55	54.79	27.03
Kotah	46.67	46.67	93.33	81.25
Udaipur	39.39	37.14	40.00	44.44
Thar	34.69	22.64	49.06	24.14

Source: Calculated from constituency returns published by the Election Commission of India

Notes

As can be seen from Map 1, on p. 221, these regions have been constructed within the boundaries of the states of Uttar Pradesh, Madhya Pradesh, Rajasthan, the Punjab and Haryana as of 1967 and do not include the state of Himachal Pradesh and the Union Territories of Chandigarh and Delhi. The Punjab and Haryana regions correspond to the states of those names as of 1967 and the regions in Uttar Pradesh, Madhya Pradesh and Rajasthan are composed of districts as of that year. Reorganizing the electoral data within these regions posed a number of problems, especially in dealing with the returns for the first general elections of 1951–52, and the following decisions should be noted:

1. The locality of Sironj in the northern part of Vidisha District in Madhya Pradesh belonged to Rajasthan before the states reorganization of 1956. The data for the Rajasthan constituency of Sironj in the 1952 elections have been included in the Gwalior regional data for that year.
2. Datia District, which was part of Vindhya Pradesh until states reorganization, has been included in the Gwalior region throughout the series.
3. The reorganization of territories which accompanied the partition of the Punjab in 1966 involved the incorporation in Himachal Pradesh of the hill districts and certain other small areas of the former Punjab, and returns from constituencies in these districts and areas have been excluded from the data for the Punjab and Haryana regions throughout the series.

Legislative Assembly elections: Jana Sangh vote-shares in contested constituencies: distribution by political regions, 1951–52 to 1967 (percentages)

	Election Year			
Region	1951–52	1957	1962	1967
Punjab	7.10	15.30	15.79	21.19
Haryana	16.19	22.95	21.74	24.58
Kumaon	9.90	17.00	12.39	20.30
Upper Doab	8.54	12.20	14.04	16.04
Rohilkhand	17.83	18.59	20.17	26.19
Lower Doab	11.20	12.94	13.06	18.38
Bundelkhand	8.69	10.87	9.21	34.10
Oudh	13.22	23.18	27.32	27.50
Gorakhpur	9.53	12.10	18.66	22.97
Varanasi	10.43	17.28	20.08	23.13
Gwalior	10.72	11.94	9.70	51.58
Malwa	23.72	31.17	42.98	41.89
Rewa	15.78	17.00	19.33	18.37
Narbada	10.37	18.54	22.50	30.09
Chhattisgarh	7.48	14.45	19.94	25.66
Jaipur	24.82	15.50	15.96	35.17
Kotah	13.36	23.46	32.27	50.84
Udaipur	37.15	20.15	28.59	26.19
Thar	6.68	11.52	7.97	31.19

Source: Calculated from constituency returns published by the Election Commission of India

SELECT BIBLIOGRAPHY ON THE BHARATIYA
JANA SANGH 1951–67

Primary sources

The most valuable source for material on the Jana Sangh in the 1951–67 period is the English weekly, the *Organiser* (New Delhi, but there is a good deal of information to be gained from the daily newspapers of northern India, especially the *Hindustan Times* (Delhi), the *National Herald* (Lucknow) and the Delhi editions of the *Statesman* and the *Times of India*.

Amongst party publications, the five-volume *Party Documents* (1973) is especially useful as a compendium of manifestos and policy resolutions, but its wording varies at times from that in separately published brochures of resolutions.

Manuscript

Oral History Transcript in Hindi of an interview with Mauli Chandra Sharma on 17 July 1974 by Hari Dev Sharma (Nehru Memorial Library, New Delhi, Accession No. 327).

Publications of the Bharatiya Jana Sangh (BJS)

(i) Policy resolutions of the Central Working Committee, the Central General Council and National Sessions of the party.

Party Documents, 5 vols. New Delhi, 1973.

Resolutions Passed by the Bharatiya Karya Samiti (All India Working Committee), at Patna on April, 22 & 23, 1961.

Resolutions of the Bharatiya Pratinidhi Sabha and the Working Committee, Varanasi, Nov. 12, 13, 14, & 15, 1961.

Resolutions of the Bharatiya Pratinidhi Sabha, Delhi, August, 11, 12, 1963.

Resolutions of the Eleventh Annual Session, Ahmedabad, Dec. 28, 29 and 30, 1963, and Working Committee, New Delhi, March, 1–2, 1964.

Resolutions passed by the Bharatiya Pratinidhi Sabha & the Working Committee, Gwalior, August, 11–15, 1964.

Resolutions Passed by the Bharatiya Karya Samiti and the Twelfth Session, Vijayawada (Andhra), Working Committee Jan. 21, 22, 1965, Session Jan. 23, 24, 1965, B.P.S. Session Jan. 25, 26, 1965.

266

Resolutions Passed by Bharatiya Karya Samiti on July, 10 & 11, 1965, Jabbalpur, Madhya Pradesh.
Resolutions Passed by Bharatiya Pratinidhi Sabha, August 17, 18, 1965, and Working Committee on August 15, 1965 & September 27, 28, 1965.
Resolutions Passed by the Bharatiya Karya Samiti (All India Working Committee) at its meeting at Kanpur on January 15, 16, 1966.
Resolutions Passed at the Thirteenth Annual Session and All India Working Committee, Jullundur, April 30, May 1 & 2, 1966.
Bharatiya Karya Samiti (All India Working Committee), Resolutions, Lucknow, July 12, 13, 1966.

(ii) Presidential addresses to National Sessions and meetings of the Central General Council

Eighth Annual Session, Presidential Address by Shri Pitamber Das, Raghuji Nagar, Nagpur. January 23, 24 and 25, 1960.
Ninth Annual Session, Presidential Address by Shri A. Ramarao, Lucknow, December 31, 1960.
Presidential Address by Shri A. Rama Rao at the Bharatiya Pratinidhi Sabha Session (General Council), Varanasi, Nov. 12, 13, 14 & 15, 1961.
Presidential Address by Prof. Dr. Raghu Vira, Tenth Session, Dec. 29, 30, 31, 1962, Bhopal (M. Pradesh).
Twelfth Plenary Session, Presidential Address of Shri Bachhraj Vyas, Vijayawada (Andhra), January 23 & 24, 1965.
Presidential Address by Prof. Balraj Madhok at the Thirteenth All India Session, Jullundur (Punjab), April 30, & May 1, & 2, 1966.
Presidential Address by Prof. Balraj Madhok at the Bharatiya Pratinidhi Sabha Session (General Councial[sic] Session), Nagpur, Nov. 3, 4, 5 & 6, 1966.

(iii) Constitutions and rules

Samvidhan evam Niyam [as amended by the party's seventh national session, Bangalore, December 1958]. Delhi, 1960 (Hindi).
Samvidhan evam Niyam [as amended by the party's eleventh national session, Ahmedabad, December 1963]. Delhi, n.d. (Hindi).

(iv) Election manifestos

Manifesto of All India Bharatiya Jana Sangh. Delhi, 1951.
Election Manifesto 1957. [Delhi, 1957].
Election Manifesto 1962. [Delhi, 1962].
Principles and Policy, Adopted by the Bharatiya Pratinidhi Sabha at Vijayawada, (Andhra) on January, 25 and 26, 1965. [Delhi, 1965].
Election Manifesto 1967. [Delhi, 1967].

(v) Pamphlets published by the BJS Central Office, Delhi

Integrate Kashmir: The Full Text of the Speech Delivered in the Parliament on the Kashmir Issue by Dr. Shyama Prasad Mukherji on 26 June, 1952. [1952].

Integrate Kashmir: Mookerjee–Nehru & Abdullah Correspondence. [1953].

Why Jammu Satyagraha? Dr. Mookerjee's last letter to Sheikh Abdullah & Report of Repression in Kashmir. [1953].

Kashmir Problem and Jammu Satyagraha: An Objective Study. [1953].

National Integration: Note Submitted by Sh. A.B. Vajpayee, Leader of the Jana Sangh Group in Parliament at the National Integration Conference Held at New Delhi, on Sept. 28, 29 & 30, 1961. [1961].

A Brief Outline of Policies. [1967].

The Jana Sangh Approach. 1968.

Recent Communal Riots: A Report. 1968.

Who Killed Upadhyaya? 1969.

Upadhyaya, Deendayal. *Food Problem.* 1964.

(iv) Pamphlets published by offices of state units of the BJS

Delhi Pradesh JS, *The Great Betrayal.* Delhi, 1965.

Punjab Pradesh JS, *The Case of Bharatiya Jana Sangh: Memorandum.* Jullundur, n.d.

Uttar Pradesh JS, *Manav ka Annadata: Kisan ki Mang, Lagan Adha Ho!* Lucknow, [1955]. (Hindi).

Books, pamphlets and articles written by leading BJS members

All Indian Languages Convention. *Address by Dr. Raghuvira, Sapru House, New Delhi, 11 & 12 August 1962.* No publication details.

Bhandari, S.S. (ed.), *Jana-Deep Souvenir: A Publication Brought out on the Occasion of the 14th Annual Session of Bharatiya Jana Sangh, Calicut, December 1967.* No publication details.

Jana Sangh Souvenir: A Publication Brought out on the Occasion of the 15th Annual Session of Bharatiya Jana Sangh, Bombay, April 25–27, 1969. No publication details.

Deshmukh, Nana, *RSS Victim of Slander: A Multi-dimensional Study of RSS, Jana Sangh, Janata Party and The Present Political Crisis.* New Delhi, 1979.

Madhok, Balraj, *Kashmir Divided.* Lucknow, [1950].

Kashmir Problem: A Story of Bungling. New Delhi, [1952 or 1953].

Dr. Syama Prasad Mookerjee: A Biography. New Delhi, [1954].

Hindu Rashtra: A Study in Indian Nationalism. Calcutta, 1955.

'Bharatiya Jana Sangh and the elections', in S.L. Poplai (ed.), *National Politics and 1957 Elections in India.* Delhi, 1957, pp. 61–4.

Political Trends in India. Delhi, 1959.

'Jana Sangh', *Seminar* (New Delhi), No. 34, *Election Analysis* (June 1962), pp. 36–7.

Kashmir: Centre of New Alignments. New Delhi [1963].

What Jana Sangh Stands For. [1966].

Why Jana Sangh? Bombay, [1967].

Portrait of a Martyr: Biography of Dr. Shyama Prasad Mookerji. Bombay, 1969.

Indianisation. Delhi, 1970.

Indianisation? (What, Why and How). New Delhi, [1970].

Murder of Democracy. New Delhi, 1973.

'Opposition in the Parliament and the state legislatures', in S.L. Shakdher (ed.), *The Constitution and the Parliament in India: The 25 Years of the Republic.* New Delhi, 1976, pp. 550–5.

Reflections of a Detenu. New Delhi, 1978.

Stormy Decade (Indian Politics) 1970–1980. Delhi, 1982 (2nd edition).

R.S.S. and Politics. New Delhi, 1986.

Mathur, Jagdish (ed.). *Jana-Deep Souvenir: A Publication Brought out on the Occasion of Mid-term Election, 1971.* Delhi, [1971].

Mookerjee, Shyam Prasad. *Awake Hindusthan.* Calcutta, [1944].

Upadhyaya, Deendayal, *The Two Plans: Promises, Performance, Prospects.* Lucknow, 1958.

'Jana Sangh', *Seminar* (New Delhi), No. 29, *Your Vote* (January 1962), pp. 20–3.

'Jana Sangh and the general elections', in S.L. Poplai (ed.), *1962 General Elections in India.* New Delhi, 1962, pp. 51–9.

Integral Humanism. New Delhi, [1965].

Political Diary. Bombay, 1968.

Oral interviews

Advani, Lal Kishinchand. New Delhi, 15 May 1984.

Deshmukh, Nana. New Delhi, 14 May 1984.

Madhok, Balraj.   (i) New Delhi, 20 December 1963.

               (ii) New Delhi, 12 May 1984.

              (iii) New Delhi, 15 May 1984.

Malkani, K.R. New Delhi, 9 May 1984.

Mathur, Jagdish Prasad. New Delhi, 10 May 1984.

Secondary sources

The most useful of the secondary sources listed below are Craig Baxter, *The Jana Sangh: A Biography of an Indian Political Party* (Philadelphia, 1969), which presents a detailed and informed narrative of the party from its origins to the end of 1967, and Motilal A. Jhangiani, *Jana Sangh and Swatantra: A Profile of the Rightist Parties in India* (Bombay, 1967), which systematically compared the Jana Sangh with the Swatantra Party.

Andersen, Walter K. 'The Rashtriya Swayamsevak Sangh', *Economic and Political Weekly* (Bombay), VII, 11 (11 March 1972), 589–97; 12 (18 March 1972), 633–40; 13 (25 March 1972), 673–82; 14 (1 April 1972), 724–7.

Andersen, Walter K. and Shridhar D. Damle. *The Brotherhood in Saffron: The Rashtriya Swayamsevak Sangh and Hindu Revivalism.* Boulder and London, 1987.

Baxter, Craig. 'The Jana Sangh: a brief history', in Donald Eugene Smith (ed.), *South Asian Politics and Religion.* Princeton, 1966, pp. 74–101.

The Jana Sangh: A Biography of an Indian Political Party. Philadelphia, 1969.

Burger, Angela Sutherland. *Opposition in a Dominant-Party System: A Study of the Jan Sangh, the Praja Socialist Party, and the Socialist Party in Uttar Pradesh, India.* Berkeley, 1969.

Curran, J.A. *Militant Hinduism in Indian Politics: A Study of the R.S.S.* New York, 1951.

Davey, H.T. 'The transformation of an ideological movement into an aggregative party: a case study of the Bharatiya Jana Sangh'. Ph.D. dissertation, University of California, Los Angeles, 1969.

Gould, Harold A. 'Traditionalism and modernism in U.P.: Faizabad constituency', in Myron Weiner and Rajni Kothari (eds.), *Indian Voting Behaviour: Studies of the 1962 General Elections.* Calcutta, 1965, pp. 162–76.

'Religion and politics in a U.P. constituency', in Donald Eugene Smith (ed.), *South Asian Politics and Religion.* Princeton, 1966, pp. 51–73.

Goyal, D.R. *Rashtriya Swayamsewak Sangh.* New Delhi, 1979.

Graham, B.D. 'Syama Prasad Mookerjee and the communalist alternative', in D.A. Low (ed.), *Soundings in Modern South Asian History.* London, 1968, pp. 330–74.

'The Jana Sangh and party alliances: 1967–70', *South Asian Review*, IV, 1 (October 1970), 9–26.

The Challenge of Hindu Nationalism: The Bharatiya Janata Party in Contemporary Indian Politics. Hull Papers in Politics, 1987.

'The Jana Sangh and bloc politics, 1967–80', *The Journal of Commonwealth and Comparative Politics*, XXV, 3 (November 1987), 248–66.

'The Congress and Hindu nationalism', in D.A. Low (ed.), *The Indian National Congress: Centenary Hindsights.* Delhi, 1988, pp. 170–87.

Heeger, Gerald A. 'Discipline versus mobilization: party building and the Punjab Jana Sangh', *Asian Survey*, XII, 10 (October 1972), 864–78.

Jhangiani, Motilal A. *Jana Sangh and Swatantra: A Profile of the Rightist Parties in India.* Bombay, 1967.

Johnson, E.W. 'Comparative approaches to the study of the Hindu communal political parties in contemporary India: some limitations in the applicability of (1) systems analysis and (2) political modernization and development theory'. Ph.D. dissertation, New York University, 1970.

Kamal, K.L. *Party Politics in an Indian State (A Study of the Main Political Parties in Rajasthan).* New Delhi, n.d.

Kapoor, Bishan. *The Dragon Unmasked (Role of the Jana Sangh in SVD Government in U.P.).* New Delhi, n.d.

Kelkar, D.V. 'The R.S.S.', *The Economic Weekly* (Bombay), II, 4 (4 February 1950), 132–8.

Kishore, M.A. 'The Jan Sangh: ideology and policy', *The Indian Journal of*

Politics, I, 2 and II, 1 (July–December 1967 and January–June 1968), 153–78.

Jana Sangh and India's Foreign Policy. New Delhi, 1969.

Lambert, Richard D. 'Hindu communal groups in Indian politics', in Richard L. Park and Irene Tinker (eds.), *Leadership and Political Institutions in India.* Princeton, 1959, pp. 211–24.

Malaviya, H.D. *The Danger of Right Reaction.* New Delhi, n.d.

Malkani, K.R. *Principles for a New Political Party.* Delhi [1951].

The Rise and Fall of the Congress. Delhi, [1951].

(ed.), *Organiser Silver Jubilee Souvenir 1973.* New Delhi, 1973.

The RSS Story. New Delhi, 1980.

Mookerjee, Umaprasad (ed.). *Syamaprasad Mookerjee: His Death in Detention: A Case for Enquiry.* Calcutta, July 1953 (1st edition) and September 1953 (2nd edition).

Pillai, K.R. 'Jan Sangh: a rightist opposition', *Political Scientist* (Ranchi, India), II, 1 (July–December 1966), 37–51.

Puri, Geeta. *Bharatiya Jana Sangh, Organisation and Ideology. Delhi: A Case Study.* New Delhi, 1980.

Purohit, B.R. 'Bhartiya Jana Sangh and the fourth general elections in Madhya Pradesh', *Journal of Constitutional and Parliamentary Studies*, II, 3 (July–September 1968), 47–63.

Raje, Sudhakar (ed.), *Pt. Deendayal Upadhyaya: A Profile.* New Delhi, 1972.

Destination: Nation's Tribute to Deendayal Upadhyaya. New Delhi, 1978.

Sahai, Govind. *A Critical Analysis of Rashtriya Swayamsevak Sangh.* Delhi, [1956].

Singh, V.B. 'Jan Sangh in Uttar Pradesh: fluctuating fortunes and uncertain future', *Economic and Political Weekly* (Bombay), VI, 3–5 (Annual Number, January 1971), 307–16.

Smith, Donald Eugene. *India as a Secular State.* Princeton, 1963.

(ed). *South Asian Politics and Religion.* Princeton, 1966.

Varshney, Manga Ram, *Jana Sangh – R.S.S. and Balraj Madhok.* Aligarh, n.d.

Weiner, Myron. *Party Politics in India: The Development of a Multi-Party System.* Princeton, 1957.

(ed). *State Politics in India.* Princeton, 1968.

INDEX

All page references in italics are to maps figures or tables.

Abdullah, Sheikh Mohamad, Prime Minister of Jammu and Kashmir, 36–7, 40

Agra (see also KAVAL towns), 111, 242, *247*

agricultural marketing, Jana Sangh policy *re*, 188–94

Agricultural Prices Commission, 192

Akali Dal, 34, 156, 236; agitation for Sikh state in the Punjab, 100–11 *passim*, 139–40, 142, 145, 147, 230; campaign for recognition of Punjabi in Gurumukhi script, 102, 122; joins United Front coalition in the Punjab, 146, 238

Alagesan, O.V., 134

Aligarh city, 123–4

Aligarh Muslim University, 111, 122–8

Allahabad (*see also* KAVAL towns), 242, *247*

All-India Bank Employees' Association (AIBEA), 172–3

All-India Bank Employees' Federation (AIBEF), 172–3

All-India Goraksha Sammelan, 148

All-India Khadi and Village Industries Board, 165

All-India Organisation of Industrial Employees, 167

All-India Rural Credit Survey, 188

All-India Trade Union Congress (AITUC), 171–2

Anjuman-i-Taraqqi-i-Urdu, 111, 116, 117, 119

Arya Samaj, 18, 95, 101; association with Jana Sangh, 77, 107; championship of Hindi in Punjab, 100, 106–9, 145; opposes partition of the Punjab, 104, 142–4; objects to designation of Chandigarh as Union Territory, 105;

and anti-cow-slaughter campaign, 151

Azad, Maulana Abul Kalam, 9

backward castes, Jana Sangh's appeal to, 238, 250

Bade, Ram Chandra, 231–3

Bhakra-Nangal hydro-electric and irrigation scheme, 146

Bhalla, Lala Balraj, President of Punjab Jana Sangh, 28, 29, 103

Bhandari, Sundar Singh, member of Rajya Sabha, central secretary of Jana Sangh, 59, 62, 74, 89–90, 91, 145

Bharat Gosevak Samaj, 148

Bharatiya Jana Sangh, brief history, 3–4; stages in formation, 26–8; first (provisional) Working Committee, 29; initial policies, 30–2; and Kashmir agitation of 1952–53, 32–41, 254; and Hindu nationalism, 41–2, 43–52, 94–100, 156–7, 197, 249, 253–8; succession crisis of 1954, 56–68, 206, 254, 257; central leadership, 1955–67, 68–71, 85–91, 219, 254–5, 257; and communal conflicts in the Punjab, 100–11, 138–47; and Muslim interests in Uttar Pradesh, 111–28; and the choice between Hindi and English, 128–38; and the demand for the abolition of cow-slaughter, 147–55, 256; and interest groups, 158–95, 256; and small industry and commerce, 158–69, 194–5, 256; and the working classes, 169–76, 195; and refugees, 176–7; and the politics of land, 177–88, 194–5, 240, 249–50; and the politics of agricultural marketing, 188–94, 195; electoral strategy, 196–220, 256–8; electoral position in northern states, 220–51, 256–8; proposed merger with

272

Dandakaranya Development Authority, 176–7

Das, Banarsi, 116

Das Commission (to inquire into allegations of discrimination in Punjab), 109n

Das, Pitamber, 78

Das, Seth Govind, 149, 152

Delhi Agreement (*re* Jammu and Kashmir, July 1952), 37

Delhi Pact (between India and Pakistan, April 1950), 23, 24

Delhi, Union Territory of, 111, 112, 119, 149, 151–3; Jana Sangh organization in, 27–9, 58, 60, 61, 64–6, 74–5, 80, 81, 90, 151–3, 198; Jana Sangh electoral fortunes in, 203–4, 217, 220, 251

Desai, Morarji Ranchhodji, 215

Deshmukh, Nana, central secretary of Jana Sangh, 62, 74, 75

Dev, Acharya Ram, President of Punjab Jana Sangh, 107

Devanagari script, 103, 110, 113–14, 129, 130, 131, 145

dipak symbol, 202–3, 216

Dogra community in Jammu and Kashmir, 36

Dogra, Prem Nath, President of Jammu and Kashmir Praja Parishad, 36, 38, 65; President of Jana Sangh, 78

Dravida Munnetra Kazhagam (DMK), 133, 135

Dravidian languages, 129

Dube, Yadavendra Datt, Raja of Jaunpur, 126–7

elections, general, 1951–52, 34, 179, 197–8, 231, 236, 239–41, 247–8, *259–60, 262*; 1957, 3, 70, 86, 106, 181, 198–200, 231–3, 234, 236–7, 239–41, 247–8, 251, *260, 262*; 1962, 71, 86, 185–6, 202–4, 206–10, 233, 234, 237, 239–41, 247–8, 249, *261, 262*; 1967, 3–4, 90, 146, 216–17, 233, 234, 236, 237–8, 239–41, 247–8, 250, 252, 257–8, *261, 262*; Lok Sabha, 1971, 233, 258; 1980, 235–6; 1984, 236, 255–6; state elections, 1969, 239, 247–8, 250; 1972, 258; 1974, 239; 1980, 235, 239; 1985, 235, 236, 239, 257; 1987, 238–9; Lok Sabha by-elections, 1961, 86; 1963, 86, 210, 248; performance of Jana Sangh in northern regions in assembly elections, 1951–52 to 1967, 220–30 (including maps), 251–2, 256–7, *263–5* (tables);

municipal elections in Uttar Pradesh, 242–7 (including tables)

English language, status of, 110, 113, 128–38

factory units, 163–4; number of small factories registered under Factories Act, 163

Federation of Associations of Small Industries in India (FASII), 167, 169

Federation of Indian Chambers of Commerce and Industry, 167

Federation of Industry and Commerce (Punjab), 167

foodgrains, acreage under, 188; government policy *re*, 190–3; Jana Sangh policy *re*, 188–9, 191–4; *see also* agricultural marketing

Foodgrains Corporation of India, 192–4

Ganatantra Parishad, 34

Gandhi, Indira, 88, 140, 142, 144, 215–16, 258

Gandhi, Mohandas Karamchand, 2, 10, 11, 18, 51, 95

Ghaffar, Kazi Abdul, 116

Ghosh, Aurobindo, 97

Ghosh, Deva Prasad, President of Jana Sangh, 78, 85

Goa *satyagraha* (1955), Jana Sangh's participation in, 69–70

Godse, Nathuram Vinayak, 11

Golwalkar, Madhav Sadashiv, head of RSS: biography, 7; arrested after Gandhi's assassination, demonstrates against ban on RSS, 14–15; tours India after lifting of ban, 17; discusses idea of forming new party with Mookerjee, 26; attitude towards agitation, 40–1; *We; or Our Nationhood Defined*, 45–8, 197; attitude to Muslims, 47; supports anti cow-slaughter campaign, 149, 150, 155

Government of India, Five-Year Plans, 160–1, 165, 166, 184, 200; and Hindu Code Bill, 19; and Official Languages Bill, 132

Gujarat, State of: Jana Sangh activity in, 82; Jana Sangh electoral performance in, *261*

Gujarati, 129

Gupta, Kunwar Lal, Secretary of Delhi Jana Sangh, 58

Gupta, Ram Prakash, 245, 246

CAMBRIDGE SOUTH ASIAN STUDIES

These monographs are published by the Syndics of Cambridge University Press in association with the Cambridge University Centre for South Asian Studies. The following books have been published in this series:

1 S. Gopal: *British Policy in India. 1858–1905*
2 J.A.B. Palmer: *The Mutiny Outbreak at Meerut in 1857*
3 A. Das Gupta: *Malabar in Asian Trade, 1740–1800*
4 G. Obeyesekere: *Land Tenure in Village Ceylon*
5 H.L. Erdman: *The Swatantra Party and Indian Conservatism*
6 S.N. Mukherjee: *Sir William Jones: A Study in Eighteenth-Century British Attitudes to India*
7 Abdul Majed Khan: *The Transition of Bengal. 1756–1775: A Study of Saiyid Muhammad Reza Khan*
8 Radhe Shyam Rungta: *The Rise of Business Corporations in India. 1851–1900*
9 Pamela Nightingale: *Trade and Empire in Western India, 1784–1806*
10 Amiya Kumar Bagchi: *Private Investment in India, 1900–1939*
11 Judith M. Brown: *Gandhi's Rise to Power: Indian Politics, 1915–1922*
12 Mary C. Carras: *The Dynamics of Indian Political Factions*
13 P. Hardy: *The Muslims of British India*
14 Gordon Johnson: *Provincial Politics and Indian Nationalism*
15 Marguerite S. Robinson: *Political Structure in a Changing Sinhalese Village*
16 Francis Robinson: *Separation among Indian Muslims: The Politics of the United Provinces' Muslims, 1860–1923*
17 Christopher John Baker: *The Politics of South India, 1920–1936*
18 David Washbrook: *The Emergence of Provincial Politics: The Madras Presidency, 1870–1920*
19 Deepak Nayyar: *India's Exports and Export Policies in the 1960s*
20 Mark Holmström: *South Indian Factory Workers: Their Life and Their World*
21 S. Ambirajan: *Classical Political Economy and British Policy in India*
22 M.M. Islam: *Bengal Agriculture 1920–1946: A Quantitative Study*
23 Eric Stokes: *The Peasant and the Raj: Studies in Agrarian Society and Peasant Rebellion in Colonial India*
24 Michael Roberts: *Caste Conflict and Elite Formation: The Rise of Karāva Elite in Sri Lanka, 1500–1931*

282